UNDERSTANDING 'RACE' AND ETHNICITY

Also available in the series

Understanding disability policy
Alan Roulstone and Simon Prideaux

"Disability policy has changed dramatically over the last fifty years and especially so since the turn of 21st century. Roulstone and Prideaux have produced a comprehensive and accessible analysis of these changes that will prove to be an invaluable text for students, researchers and policy analysts across a range of disciplines: highly recommended." Colin Barnes, University of Leeds

PB £21.99 (US$36.95) **ISBN** 978 1 84742 738 0 **HB** £65.00 (US$89.95) **ISBN** 978 1 84742 739 7
256 pages January 2012
INSPECTION COPY AVAILABLE

Understanding housing policy (Second edition)
Brian Lund

"An excellent historical and theoretical review of housing policy: thoughtful, well informed, critical and up to date." Chris Paris, Professor of Housing Studies, University of Ulster, Northern Ireland

PB £22.99 (US$34.95) **ISBN** 978 1 84742 631 4 **HB** £65.00 (US$85.00) **ISBN** 978 1 84742 632 1
352 pages April 2011
INSPECTION COPY AVAILABLE

Understanding the environment and social policy
Tony Fitzpatrick

"The intersection of social policy and environmental policy is strategically and morally vital yet has remained a strangely neglected area. No longer. This comprehensive book covers real world challenges, sustainable ethics, a host of applied policy issues, and some bigger questions about the possibility of a green welfare state." Ian Gough, Emeritus Professor, University of Bath

PB £21.99 (US$36.95) **ISBN** 978 1 84742 379 5 **HB** £65.00 (US$85.00) **ISBN** 978 1 84742 380 1
384 pages February 2011
INSPECTION COPY AVAILABLE

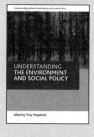

Understanding community
Politics, policy and practice
Peter Somerville

"In developing his conception of beloved community, Peter Somerville brings a fresh and radical perspective to communitarian theory and practice. This book will inspire and provoke readers in equal measure." Jonathan Davies, University of Warwick

PB £19.99 (US$34.95) **ISBN** 978 1 84742 392 4 **HB** £65.00 (US$85.00) **ISBN** 978 1 84742 393 1
304 pages February 2011
INSPECTION COPY AVAILABLE

For a full listing of all titles in the series visit www.policypress.co.uk

www.policypress.co.uk

INSPECTION COPIES AND ORDERS AVAILABLE FROM:
Marston Book Services • PO BOX 269 • Abingdon • Oxon OX14 4YN UK
INSPECTION COPIES
Tel: +44 (0) 1235 465500 • Fax: +44 (0) 1235 465556 • Email: inspections@marston.co.uk
ORDERS
Tel: +44 (0) 1235 465500 • Fax: +44 (0) 1235 465556 • Email: direct.orders@marston.co.uk

UNDERSTANDING 'RACE' AND ETHNICITY

Theory, history, policy, practice

Edited by Gary Craig, Karl Atkin,
Sangeeta Chattoo and Ronny Flynn

First published published in Great Britain in 2012 by
The Policy Press
University of Bristol
Fourth Floor, Beacon House
Queen's Road
Bristol BS8 1QU
UK

t: +44 (0)117 331 4054
f: +44 (0)117 331 4093
tpp-info@bristol.ac.uk
www.policypress.ci.uk

North American office:
The Policy Press
c/o The University of Chicago Press
1427 East 60th Street
Chicago, IL 60637, USA
t: +1 773 702 7700
f: +1 773-702-9756
e:sales@press.uchicago.edu
www.press.uchicago.edu

British Library Cataloguing in Publication Data
A catalogue record for this book is available from the British Library.

Library of Congress Cataloging-in-Publication Data
A catalog record for this book has been requested.

ISBN 978 1 84742 770 0 paperback
ISBN 978 1 84742 771 7 hardcover

Cover design by Qube Design Associates, Bristol
Front cover: photograph kindly supplied by Getty Images
Printed and bound in Great Britain by Hobbs, Southampton
The Policy Press uses environmentally responsible print partners

FSC
www.fsc.org
MIX
Paper from
responsible sources
FSC® C020438

Contents

Detailed contents

List of tables, figures, boxes and case studies

Tables

Figures

Boxes

Case studies

Acknowledgements

This book is dedicated to individuals and organisations engaged in the struggle against racism in all its forms, past and present. It is a struggle that has to continue; at a time when Europe's political leaders proclaim that multiculturalism is dead, they have little to say on the continuing racism that affects minority ethnic people in most aspects of their lives. We hope this book contributes to that fight.

The editors thank the authors, who delivered drafts on time and with good humour; we hope they will be pleased with the outcome. We are grateful also to staff at The Policy Press who supported the book through its stages with light, sensitive but persistent touches. Georgia Mortzou provided invaluable support and assistance in preparing the manuscript for publication; we are very grateful indeed to her.

A note on terminology

The word 'race' is used throughout in apostrophes, indicating that it is a social construct with particular historical connotations but no objective meaning. The editorial team were not completely agreed on whether the word ethnicity should be treated in the same way. The reader should assume this debate is still continuing! As an early chapter (Chapter 2) indicates, terminology in this territory is particularly sensitive and the issue of whether to refer to racialised minorities as black and ethnic minority groups, BME groups, BAME groups, minorities and so on also remains contested. For some people, including writers within the book, these acronyms remain interchangeable; we have chosen not to impose one single form of words or acronyms. Similarly, different words are used to define what are in fact similar processes: thus, some reports, for example, use the phrase 'ethnic penalty' in a way that suggests they are alluding to structural or institutional racism.

Notes on contributors

Karl Atkin holds a personal research chair in the Department of Health Sciences, University of York. He is a medical sociologist with a particular interest in qualitative research in multidisciplinary settings. Other interests include the experience of family carers; young people and identity; disability and chronic illness; and ethnicity and social disadvantage. He is executive editor of the journal *Ethnicity and Health*.

Laia Becares is Postdoctoral Research Fellow, Cathie Marsh Centre for Census and Survey Research, University of Manchester. Her work explores the association between racism and health, and the protective effects of ethnic density on the health of minority ethnic people.

Harris Beider is Professor in the Faculty of Business, Environment and Society at Coventry University, having been Professor in Community Cohesion at the Institute of Community Cohesion there and at the School of Public Policy at the University of Birmingham. Previously, he was Executive Director of the Federation of Black Housing Organisations.

Sangeeta Chattoo is a social anthropologist by background. She is currently a Research Fellow at the Department of Health Sciences, University of York and Associate Editor of the journal *Ethnicity and Health*. Her areas of research and writing include ethnicity and health; cancer, chronic illness and palliative care; kinship and caring; and biographical and comparative methods of social research.

Bankole Cole is Reader in Criminology at the University of Northumbria. His areas of expertise include criminal justice and security; and 'race', ethnicity and the criminal justice system. He is a member of the Ministry of Justice's advisory groups on statistics on 'race' and women. Recent publications include, with M. Mullard (eds), *Globalisation, Citizenship and the War on Terror* (Edward Elgar, 2007).

Gary Craig is Professor of Community Development and Social Justice at the University of Durham. He has worked in large-scale community development projects and four other UK universities. His research interests are in social justice, 'race' and ethnicity, local governance, and community development and he has published widely on the issue of 'race'. His most recent relevant book is *Child Slavery Now* (The Policy Press, 2010).

Ronny Flynn is an independent consultant recently returned from Solomon Islands, where she worked for UNICEF. From 2006 to 2010, she worked as Director of Health and Housing at the Race Equality Foundation in London, and was commissioning editor for their series of Better Health and Better Housing briefing papers. Prior to this, she worked at The Open University.

Saffron Karlsen is Senior Research Fellow, Department of Epidemiology and Public Health, University College London. Her work aims to enable a better understanding of the different ways in which 'ethnicity' has relevance in people's lives, both for developing awareness of potential group affiliations and as a driver of health and other inequalities, and engages particularly with the negative impact of forms of racist victimisation.

Frank Keating is a Senior Lecturer at Royal Holloway University of London where he is Programme Director for the MSc in Social Work. Frank's primary research interest is 'race' and mental health, particularly issues for African and Caribbean communities. Frank continues to advocate for racial equality and justice in mental health services.

Ian Law is Reader in Racism and Ethnicity Studies at the University of Leeds. His books include, with S. Swann, *Ethnicity and Education in England and Europe* (Ashgate, forthcoming), *Racism and Ethnicity: Global Debates, Dilemmas, Directions* (Pearson, 2010), and, with G. Huggan (eds), *Racism, Postcolonialism and Europe* (Liverpool University Press, 2009).

Patrice Lawrence led on equality in early childhood at the National Children's Bureau and coordinates a National Black Voices Network for practitioners in the children's sector. She has been an advisor on young people's engagement for the Neighbourhood Renewal Unit and on equality issues on various steering groups. She is also a published fiction writer.

Gina Netto is a Lecturer in the School of the Built Environment, Heriot Watt University. She has a long-standing interest in ethnicity and 'race', publishing widely, including in *Sociology, Housing Studies, Housing, Theory and Society, Public Policy and Administration, Social Policy and Administration, Public Health, Journal of Mental Health* and *Health Promotion International*.

Marilyn Roth is Research Associate, Department of Epidemiology and Public Health, University College London. Her work explores the relationships between immigration, culture and health, particularly as they relate to ethnic variations in health-related behaviours.

Ossie Stuart has written extensively on issues affecting disabled people from black and minority ethnic communities as an academic and independent researcher. He has been a member of the Joseph Rowntree Foundation's Independent Living Committee as well as being involved in the work of the Shaping Our Lives Network. He is now a freelance consultant working across all sectors.

Baljinder Virk has extensive experience in labour-market research and has worked in academic, third-sector and consultancy environments. She has a PhD in Policy Studies from Bristol University on *Labour Market Disadvantage among Ethnic Minority Groups*. She has been a Senior Analyst in a non-departmental public body, but writes here in a personal capacity.

Foreword

The British

Benjamin Zephaniah

Take some Picts, Celts and Silures
And let them settle,
Then overrun them with Roman conquerors.

Remove the Romans after approximately 400 years
Add lots of Norman French to some
Angles, Saxons, Jutes and Vikings, then stir vigorously.

Mix some hot Chileans, cool Jamaicans, Dominicans,
Trinidadians and Bajans with some Ethiopians, Chinese,
Vietnamese and Sudanese.

Then take a blend of Somalians, Sri Lankans, Nigerians
And Pakistanis,
Combine with some Guyanese
And turn up the heat.

Sprinkle some fresh Indians, Malaysians, Bosnians,
Iraqis and Bangladeshis together with some
Afghans, Spanish, Turkish, Kurdish, Japanese
And Palestinians
Then add to the melting pot.

Leave the ingredients to simmer.

As they mix and blend allow their languages to flourish
Binding them together with English.

Allow time to be cool.

Add some unity, understanding, and respect for the future,
Serve with justice
And enjoy.

Note: All the ingredients are equally important. Treating one
ingredient better than another will leave a bitter unpleasant taste.

Warning: An unequal spread of justice will damage the people and cause pain. Give justice and equality to all.

[With thanks to the author and publisher for permission to reproduce.]

PART I

Introduction

Introduction

Introduction

Gary Craig, Karl Atkin, Sangeeta Chattoo and Ronny Flynn

The book's aims

Discussion of ethnicity has remained peripheral to social policy's mainstream engagement with citizenship and welfare. Indeed, this book could be said to have started life in a keynote speech given by one of us to the 2006 annual conference of the Social Policy Association when he observed that:

> It is important to acknowledge that neglect of the issue of 'race' is not confined to social policy as *political practice*; it is shared by the *academic discipline* of social policy. It is still not uncommon for mainstream social policy texts to treat debates on 'race' and racism as marginal. This is striking considering that the social policy discipline is concerned centrally with issues of citizenship rights, welfare, equality, poverty alleviation and social engineering.... This failure of the social policy community also extends to social policy teaching and to the high-profile social policy journals.[1]

Five years on, little has changed, despite increasing media, political and policy interest in immigration, community cohesion and multiculturalism. The UK remains an ethnically and culturally diverse – some would say a 'super-diverse' – society, in which the core themes of social policy are played out. This, however, is not reflected in the literature. The Social Policy and Social Work subpanel of the 2013 Higher Education Funding Councils'

Research Excellence Framework, as originally constituted, comprised an entirely white group of academics, only one of whom regarded 'race' as central to their research interests.

This book, combining empirical insight with theoretical debate, offers an introduction to citizenship, equality and welfare, whilst highlighting dilemmas facing those attempting to accommodate these themes within the context of a multicultural society. These dilemmas are multifaceted, reflecting the complexity of current understandings and approaches. For example, lack of clarity in defining and using the notions of 'race' and ethnicity – and in conceptualising ethnic diversity and difference – contribute to confusion across different sectors of policy and between policy guidelines and practice. Policy and practice rarely acknowledge that everyone has an ethnicity. 'White' ethnicities are still silent, the taken-for-granted norm around which policy and practice discourses become organised; while minority ethnicities become somehow different, deviant, the 'other' and even exotic (see Chapter 2). Such wilful political neglect, in conjunction with more explicit racist formulations underpinning policy, reflects a dilemma of those Western, liberal democratic states struggling to provide accessible and appropriate welfare provision for culturally and linguistically diverse populations. These are long-standing, familiar problems. Our failure to engage with them contributes to flawed understandings, inappropriate responses and wasted resources. Offering a critical assessment of current understandings to improve outcomes for ethically marginalised populations is our core aim.

While most of the chapters reflect material and histories of particular policy areas specific to the UK, theoretical or historical connections can be made to other 'Western' countries. There is a depressing familiarity to many issues raised here. The well-understood processes of disadvantage and discrimination can sometimes delude some, familiar with the complexity of current debates, into thinking that there is little else to do. Further, too many individuals and organisations respond minimally to the requirements of legislation, failing to act on policy recommendations. It is worth reminding ourselves of the most significant critique of institutional racism by Macpherson, inquiring into the death of Stephen Lawrence. This is not only because it is a definition to which many authors in this collection return, but because it remains an area whose relevance many policymakers continually fail to comprehend or relate to their own organisation's practice and policies. Institutional racism is:

> The collective failure of an organisation to provide an appropriate and professional service to people because of their colour, culture and ethnic background. It can be seen or

> detected in processes, attitudes and behaviour which amount
> to discrimination through unwitting prejudice, ignorance,
> thoughtlessness and racist stereotyping which disadvantages
> minority ethnic people. (Macpherson, 1999, para 6.34)

Some – notably the Metropolitan Police – now reject the charge of institutional racism. Other organisations, such as the National Health Service (NHS), increasingly argue that greater understanding and better use of evidence means sufficient change has already taken place. Our experience – and that of all the authors here (most from minorities themselves) – is that despite a growing body of evidence, practice is slow to change, very slow in some policy and geographical areas. There remains much to be done.

The extensive range of legislation seeking to challenge racism and discrimination often reinforces political complacency, suggesting that issues of 'race' and racism have been dealt with. Chapter 4 reflects this and, by tracing the development of legislation, illustrates how each new Act points to its predecessors' failures. Similarly, our growing awareness has not always equated with more responsive welfare provisions, and emerging positive policy responses remain unevenly distributed across the UK. Indeed, our inability to act on evidence and replicate good practice remains a fundamental barrier in facilitating equality.

Broadly, the sensitivity and effectiveness of such responses correlate with the length of time that minorities have settled in particular parts of the UK. Recent migrants face similar prejudice and discrimination to that experienced by the newly arrived migrants of 40 years ago; so do minorities living in more rural areas. Outside major metropolitan areas, progress towards effective responses to diversity has been slow. Rural areas have a long way to go, particularly as their rate of growth of minority populations is now faster than in urban localities. Long-established minorities, however, face continued discrimination and disadvantage, while finding their experience reified and misunderstood. The direct racism 'they' experience competes with the more subtle, ever-changing, indirect and systemic discrimination, emphasising 'their' difference while maintaining 'their' metaphorical status as the 'other'.

Conceptualising the 'other'

There are many examples here highlighting the dangers and implications of racialising minority ethnic cultures, in turn reflecting a more general failure to transform understandings of citizenship, diversity and equality into effective policy and practice. Emphasising and learning from these examples is a key aim of this book, especially given the observation that many of the problems associated with inequitable outcomes are long-standing and frequently repeated. Most empirical social science research has long discredited essentialised stereotypes of minority ethnic families, who 'look after their own'. These ideas sadly, however, continue to surface in many practitioners' attitudes. Similarly, the stereotype of fatalism as a peculiar feature of South Asian cultures persists in the nursing and medical literature, and is often used to explain poor outcomes for chronic health conditions, such as diabetes and heart failure. There is little recognition that fatalistic attitudes (invoking God's will, or luck) do not preclude active engagement with a chronic condition or its treatment (and are certainly not unique to those cultures; see Chapter 6). Further, the association with culture implicitly associates the problem with the individual practices and behaviours of the 'other', rather than the failure of collective welfare provision to understand and engage with difference; a tension reflected in many chapters (eg Chapters 7 and 8).

Despite the emphasis of policymakers and funding bodies on multidisciplinary research, mainstream social policy, healthcare and welfare research seems happily unfamiliar or unwilling to engage with wider debates on the complex intersectionality between notions of 'race', ethnicity, culture, religion, gender, socio-economic position and citizenship (see Chapter 2). This book attempts to bridge this serious gap, reflecting our commitment to ensuring that critical engagements with issues of 'race', ethnicity and citizenship become central to debates within mainstream social policy, rather than a convenient 'add-on' further reinforcing the marginalisation of disadvantaged minority ethnic groups. As this book demonstrates, there is much to be said for seeing ethnicity as part of a broader engagement with inequality and citizenship.

Hence, one of our primary concerns here is not to offer neat, prescriptive cultural descriptions or solutions, purporting to explain and manage ethnicity. Rather, we aim to offer a more reflexive and self-critical discussion contextualising diversity and difference, without recourse to simplistic explanations and naive solutions that, paradoxically, can perpetuate disadvantage and discrimination. The production of a book such as this effectively represents a contradiction, one familiar to those working in this field. We are trying to address the marginalisation of 'race' and ethnicity in social policy, but find ourselves writing a book in which this process of marginalisation is highlighted rather than displaced. This is why we hope books such as ours will not be necessary in the near future. Ethnicity will be part of the mainstream, integrated fully into social policy debates. This is also a challenge.

We are aware of how much our ideas about ethnicity have changed over time, in response to both developing theoretical understandings and the changing nature of the ethnic composition of those living in the UK. There is now considerable diversity both within and between UK minority ethnic populations, although policy, practice and research have been painfully slow to engage with it. There are, for example, established minority ethnic populations, from South Asia and the Caribbean who settled in the UK during the 1940s, 1950s, 1960s and 1970s; 70% of them came as or are now British citizens, and span a range of up to three or four generations (Chapter 3). Further, more than half of all people of minority ethnic backgrounds now living in the UK were born there. The aspirations and expectations of the younger generation as citizens might be quite different from those of their parents or grandparents, while also showing continuities. This reflects the complexities associated with understanding identity. There are also more recently arrived, possibly short-term, migrants from Central and Eastern Europe, and refugees, largely from Africa, the Middle East and Afghanistan, who have come in substantial numbers since the mid-1990s. There remain neglected groups, such as Chinese populations (of which there are at least four main groups: mainland Chinese, Hong Kong Chinese, Taiwanese and Malay Chinese), and Gypsies, Travellers, Roma and other 'invisible' white minorities (those of Irish, Polish, Turkish and Greek backgrounds, for example, who have long histories of settlement in the UK). Finally, the UK is beginning to see an increase in people who regard themselves as mixed-heritage; such an increase could explain the relative decline in those who identify as African-Caribbean.

This book attempts to reflect this diversity, although the uneven availability of empirical material means that such reflection is sometimes necessarily theoretical, demonstrating gaps in our knowledge. Consequently, conceptual clarity, sensitive to context, is important when debating 'race' and ethnicity, as we come to understand when ethnicity makes a difference to people's experience, but also, just as importantly, when it does not (see Chapter 2). This is far from straightforward, but is a necessary precondition for ensuring 'race' and ethnicity become part of mainstream discursive practices. Such debates also help policy and service provision by making sense of such wide-ranging diversity within and across ethnic groups, while also ensuring coherent and thought-out responses in the face of potentially overwhelming difference.

In many ways, our book embodies these discussions. As the reader will see, chapters use different definitions of ethnicity. We have not, as noted, imposed consistent definitions, but attempted to reflect the complexity of current debates. We were also aware that imposing uniform definitions might undermine conceptual clarity, a problem often hindering understandings of 'race' and ethnicity. All this is perhaps not surprising, since ethnicity is a multifaceted concept. This, although reflecting how people live their lives, can lead to analytical imprecision, which frustrates policy and practice. Ethnicity is notoriously difficult to define and has come to embody a broad range of ideas, such as language, religion, faith, culture, nationality and shared heritage. Ethnicity has increasingly also been seen as a political symbol, defining not just exclusion by a powerful majority, but also, conversely, a source of pride and belonging – in other words, a mobilising resource, enabling minority ethnic populations to celebrate their difference *and* make legitimate demands as UK citizens. The reader will see all aspects of these definitions employed by the authors represented here.

Further, an individual's age, gender, faith, sexual orientation, disability and socio-economic position, as well as how others respond to these different dimensions of identity, mediate experience. In some circumstances and contexts, these aspects of identity may be more important than ethnicity in making sense of a person's situation. Current research and policy debates, however, struggle to engage with the relationship between ethnicity, socio-economic status, age and gender, the outcome of which can obscure fundamental similarities as well as differences among populations. Social or economic class position, for example, might sometimes explain more of the discrimination faced by minority ethnic populations than ethnicity per se. Establishing a theoretically-informed account of ethnicity, making sense of these debates for use in policy and practice, is another important theme here.

Understanding policy and practice

Finally, there is a more explicit policy dimension, a central analytical feature of individual chapters. As well as describing current policy debates about managing ethnic diversity in a variety of key welfare settings (defining welfare broadly to include, for example, labour market and criminal justice issues) and contexts (including poverty, disability and gender), we attempt to provide critical commentaries on the origins and implications of broader discursive practices, which tie these settings and contexts together.

The 'Janus-faced' nature of progress in social policy (and practice) provides an overarching theoretical link, offering continuity between chapters. Hence, legal responses to institutional racism and policy emphases on cultural competence and positive action represent proactive responses on the part of the state to tackle disadvantage and discrimination. Implementation, as noted, remains a long-standing problem – with many organisations still prepared to ignore the practical implications of policies they may have developed – and occurs alongside atavistic anxieties about the willingness and ability of minority ethnic populations to 'integrate' into mainstream British culture and adopt British values, whatever they are. Our ability to reconcile such potential contradictions will influence the development of social policy in this field.

UK governments have recently pursued policies of community cohesion (an agenda also driven by issues of national security), aiming to facilitate a national identity and a more inclusive society; where a shared sense of 'Britishness' is offered as a means of managing and, in some ways, superseding a multicultural society. Community cohesion tacitly recognises the importance of empowering communities and tackling inequalities, although there remains an unresolved tension, quite apart from how it is perceived by minorities (in particular, those of Muslim faith) as a means of increasing the surveillance of them. To what extent can a defined sense of 'Britishness' appropriately accommodate diversity and difference? Or will it be used to remind minorities of their 'otherness', in a way that pathologises their difference?

For some, a major criticism of UK multiculturalist policies (recognising and 'tolerating' cultural and religious differences) has been that minorities are free to retain key parts of 'their own' culture, undermining 'traditional' notions of Britishness and 'British' values. Some argue that the failure of minorities to integrate into 'British' culture weakens government policies of effective community relations and community cohesion, contributing to urban disturbances over the last 30 years, and culminating in the 2005 London bombings. However, research into these assertions, common in popular political and media discourse, suggests that minority ethnic groups do not hold significantly differing value systems from the white UK mainstream. There is then the issue of exclusion and in particular the extent to which individuals feel encouraged to be part of and participate in the activities associated with the identified (or imagined?) normative values and assumptions of the broader society. This, of course, is not simply about ethnic diversity, and the meaning of citizenship is likely to be an important theme in how social policy as an academic discipline develops. These debates will develop further in the wake of the British Prime Minister's assertion early in 2011, following that of the German Chancellor, that multiculturalism is effectively 'dead'. We do not agree with this assertion. We hope this book will explain why we feel that, and provide its readers with a clear framework for challenging that view (also see Part IV).

It should neither be forgotten that progress in discussion about diversity and difference occurs against the background of a long-standing repressive and restrictive approach to immigration, which implies that ethnic diversity is still perceived as being somehow harmful and a problem to the British state. One fundamental tension within the British state has been between the apparently liberal concern for good community relations on the one hand, and the need to secure this through harsh immigration policies on the other; a tension that has on occasion tied liberally inclined politicians in knots (see Chapter 4).

The UK is not alone in trying to come to terms with these tensions, and many of the themes outlined in this book will have a wider relevance to income-rich, Western industrialised societies, which have – generally for historical reasons connected with their imperialist pasts – populations characterised by diversity. The book, however, is less concerned with international social policy or, indeed, the relationship between income-rich nations, such as the UK, and other less wealthy nations. This is not to undermine the importance of such debates. Our focus was required to be on the UK, but we would argue that an edited volume, with a more international flavour, would make an equally important contribution to social policy and one which places the dilemmas facing the UK in a wider global context.

Recent discussion on the remit of devolved parliaments and broader debates about the relationship between the different parts of the Union offer another, more localised reminder of the importance of context. Is an idea of an all-encompassing 'British' identity sustainable in Scotland, Wales and Northern Ireland? And to what extent can the national identity of these countries embrace ethnic and cultural diversity? As a more practical expression of their growing autonomy, these nations may adapt different policies whose outcomes may have different consequences for the minority ethnic populations living within them. Personalisation, although not without meaning in other parts of the Union, is very much an 'English' policy (see Chapter 7). While acknowledging such changes and the need to understand them, we would argue that core ideas such as discrimination and racism, alongside the difficulties of defining and explaining ethnicity, assume relevance, irrespective of where they occur.

Outline of the book

We have been concerned to offer a thoughtful review of the literature and research, and to confront many of the mistaken assumptions about minorities informing research, policy and practice, while simultaneously trying to make sense of the struggles faced by the state and the broader society in accommodating diversity. There are few social policy or social welfare books that address the issue of 'race' and ethnicity within a wider coverage of a range of welfare issues (Law's [2003] *Race, Ethnicity and Social Policy* being an obvious exception), and apart from the three in-depth introductory contextual chapters, we have deliberately chosen to go for width rather than depth. There is a reasonably good 'race'-related literature in some specific areas of social welfare (such as health and housing – see the output of the Race Equality Foundation, for example, or the journals *Ethnicity and Health* or *Diversity in Health and Care*). In other areas, however, there is a paucity of good literature and we try, through the work of individual chapter authors, to signpost what exists.

Those readers wishing to look at specific areas in more depth can turn to these sources, listed in the extensive References. We have also attempted to help point readers to other less accessible sources both in the References and in the additional resources listed at the end of each chapter. Despite its length, given pressure on space, we have still had to make difficult choices about content. If the general literature is poor at engaging with broad issues of 'race', it is even worse at addressing recent changes in the demography of the UK. These include the overall growth in numbers of refugees and those seeking asylum, economic and other migrants from East and Central Europe, and other communities with a relatively short history of settlement in the UK – such as Somali and Afghani minorities. The book addresses the situation of these groups as far as possible, although there remains a lack of useful data for more recent groups (and, indeed, for some historically ignored groups such as Gypsies, Roma and Travellers); this ought to be redressed as a matter of extreme urgency both in quantitative and qualitative terms. We say relatively little about the situation of refugees as these are the subject of a parallel book in this series (Sales, 2007). There is still relatively little research into the experience of long-standing minority ethnic populations living in Scotland, Wales and Ireland, something continuing debates about devolution have brought into sharper focus (see, eg Yousaf, 2010). Some welfare sectors described here are devolved responsibilities, others (particularly social security) are not; we try to reflect sectors where experience differs and has been researched.

Leaving all this aside and following this general Introduction, Part II contains three extended chapters offering an introduction and core foundation on which to make sense of ethnicity and 'race'. Chapter 2, reflecting on concepts, theories and discourses, focuses on the theoretical limitations of 'ethnicity' and its use as a framework for conceptualising the needs and experiences of minority ethnic people. It argues that, given the historical roots and semantic underpinnings that see ethnicity as a euphemism for racism in general and cultural racism in particular, the field of ethnicity, health and social care has remained highly specialised and marginal to mainstream academic, policy and practice discourses. This, ironically, reinforced the marginalisation of minorities, who become peripheral to debates on politics and citizenship, despite wider shifts within policy and practice towards a more inclusive society. This, in contrast with the original use of ethnicity as a marker of boundaries between competing communities (ie the processes of inclusion and exclusion), has led to a conflation between the ascription of ethnicity as an essential defining characteristic of (only) immigrant communities – reconstituting these as *minority ethnic communities* – and inscribing the immutable stigmata of difference through a combination of the three terms. The chapter thus provides an overarching self-critique of the field, offering a conceptual link between the different parts and chapters of the book, and providing a reference point for subsequent chapters, especially those in Part III.

Chapter 3 reviews the history and pattern of settlement of minorities in the UK. Every local authority area in the UK now has a settled minority ethnic population. Some have had a recent substantial increase of migrant workers (often in areas that previously were largely mono-cultural). Others have received substantial numbers of refugees. Many regions of the UK, particularly within specific parts of urban areas, receiving migrants from hitherto unfamiliar parts of the world, are becoming 'super-diverse' with 50 or, in some cases, many more different languages commonly spoken. These patterns of settlement raise significant issues for policy development and service delivery for local government, health bodies and the third sector, although the responses of these agencies have been, at best, uneven. The chapter, laying out the historical origins of minority ethnic settlement in the UK, long before the UK became a 'United Kingdom', questions assumptions that suggest diversity is a recent phenomenon. It reviews historical, economic, social, political and cultural factors shaping current patterns of settlement, including internal migration of the UK's minority communities, pointing to a range of policy and service issues needing to be addressed as well as the impact that settlement has historically had on local policies and services.

The final chapter in this contextual section, Chapter 4, provides a historical review of the development of policy, politics and practice. Following on from Chapter 3, it acknowledges the contribution that immigrants – especially early cohorts soon after the Second World War – made to the development of public services such as the NHS and London Transport and key industries such as the textile, hosiery and footwear industries. This connects with the eight welfare-sector-specific chapters in Part 3. Chapter 4 also provides a political and policy context for those chapters by referring to central government policy. It documents how policy, particularly since the 1950s, existed in a state of tension. On the one hand, there has been increasing repressive and restrictive immigration policy supported by a vociferously xenophobic media and, initially at the margins, but more recently less so, increasingly fascist political parties. On the other hand, there has been a series of more 'liberal' domestic policies attempting to manage internal diversity from, initially, assimilation policies, through 'race' relations, community relations and multiculturalism, to, most recently, community cohesion. The last of these have legitimised – implicitly and explicitly – a return to the language of assimilation, arguing – falsely we would claim – that minority communities are turning inwards on themselves and, in the process, providing a refuge for those driven by extremist views. This chapter demonstrates how initial welfare policy and practice was at best colour-blind, but more usually openly racist in its approach to minorities. Early research showed how welfare gatekeepers operated on the basis of racist assumptions ('they look after their own'; 'they wouldn't want to live here'), excluding minorities from the full benefits of the welfare state. It was not until the 1980s, when black and Asian minorities began to organise politically and demand culturally sensitive welfare policies, that those making policy or delivering services were forced to begin to examine their own policies and practices. Chapter 4 ends by reflecting on how conceptualisations of the 'race problem' are changing, examining the practical meanings of concepts such as overt discrimination, multiculturalism, institutional racism and essentialism, and discussing how such terms arose and the different ways they have been used in policy, politics and practice.

Part III presents eight chapters, each focusing on one specific welfare sector and weaving theoretical insight into the presentation of empirical material. Themes outlined in the first part of the book, such as the meaning of ethnic diversity, the consequences of historical compromises and the implications of confused and contradictory policies, all find expression. The authors – chosen to reflect expertise in their respective areas, with a good gender and minority ethnic balance – worked to the general template provided by the publishers for the series as a whole in terms of style and presentation, providing lists of additional reading and key electronic resources, in addition to boxed examples of particular issues, key illustrative case studies and questions for discussion. Beyond this, we asked the authors for a historical review of the policy context and the state of current knowledge in their field in a way that incorporated a series of dimensions. These included: gender; disability; user involvement; a focus on diversity and difference; the implications for different minority groups, especially as between long-standing black and minority ethnic (BME) groups and more recently settled or arrived groups; social class; and the relationships between the public, private and third sectors. To support their analysis, the authors provide models of good practice and policy and challenge myths around 'race' and ethnicity.

Inevitably, the amount and scope of evidence available varies between sectors. The chapters in Part III are thus uneven in their coverage and the depth to which they are able to develop their analysis. This also reflects the nature of the sector, the level of theoretical insights developing in relation to it and the particular expertise and interests of the authors. Some areas are relatively well-researched with much material to draw on; in others, the extent of knowledge is still shamefully limited and a description of the territory has yet to be adequately theorised. Despite covering many welfare sectors – housing, health, social care, children's services and education, the labour market, income maintenance, mental health and criminal justice – there are other areas that we would like to have included. Old age, an increasing feature of the more established minority ethnic populations, although mentioned in several chapters, is worthy of more detailed discussion, particularly given the obvious implications for policy and practice. There is also no chapter on the role and experience of the third sector (or 'voluntary and community sector' as it is also known) where a recent review points to systematic underfunding and marginalisation even within what is a relatively marginal third sector as a whole (see Craig, 2011). The chapter on education largely covers the period of full-time schooling and does not deal in detail with higher education. This again is worthy of separate treatment, particularly given recent revelations about the failure of widening participation strategies to facilitate access for BME students to the self-styled 'best' universities. Nor were we able to address, in an era witnessing profound cuts in public expenditure and a corresponding increase in private welfare, the role of minorities in the private welfare sector. Such evidence as is available suggests that the private sector largely feels free to pay little attention to issues of 'race' and diversity;[2] this is hardly surprising since trades unions, now paying greater attention to issues of discrimination than was historically the case, are substantially under-represented within private-sector companies, where union density is 17%, compared with the public sector, where it is 60%. This discrepancy is particularly apparent in the most exploited parts of the private sector where most of the UK's estimated 600,000+ irregular workers are located (Wilkinson and Craig, 2011). Meanwhile, the government's association of the Equality Act with needless red tape, restricting the growth of enterprise, belies any commitment to hard-fought, social justice (see www.redtapechallenge.cabinetoffice.gov.uk/equalities/).

In terms of specific and changing contexts, long-standing chronic illness and disability is equally important and, although touched on in several of the chapters, is likely to feature significantly in future writing. To what extent does the experience of chronic and long-standing disabilities differ among diverse ethnic groups? How well will self-management work in multicultural contexts? Political participation and engagement with civil society equally reflect broader concerns worthy of further and more intensive investigation. Ethnic density, for example, is emerging of potential analytical value in explaining a whole range of experiences and behaviours, reflecting a creative tension combining resilience, participation and social exclusion. Related to this, we have not been able to draw together evidence on the experience of minorities in areas where ethnic density is very low, particularly in small towns and rural and remote areas, another key area for research.

We also wanted to avoid the danger, inherent in separate chapters on differing divisions of welfare, of overlooking the cumulative effect of different aspects of disadvantage. Cross-references between chapters have thus been made as frequently as possible. For example, a lack of access to health care and poverty means 'a child born to a mother born in the Caribbean is twice as likely to die before the age of five, than a child born to a UK-born mother' (Rutter, 2011, p 9).

The book has been a collaborative effort. Our intention is to stimulate debate in what is a contested area, with the hope that by making such debates accessible, social policy incorporates ethnicity and 'race' as part of its mainstream concerns, rather than relegating it to the margins, reflecting only specialist interests that are the concerns of others. This is why our book is broadly aimed not just at students, academics and researchers, but policymakers, those delivering and receiving services, and politicians, all of whom have an important role to play in improving the way we respond to diversity both now and in the future. The book is, thus, in every sense a contribution to the research enterprise, bringing together, as it does, a unique collection of material often located in relatively inaccessible sources. As with the minority experience, we thereby hope to make 'invisible' policy issues visible.

Notes

[1] The speech was later reproduced in an edited form as Craig (2007).

[2] Again this could be the subject of a separate book. For an analysis of how minorities are under-represented in the higher echelons of management, see Vasista (2010); for a statement on how the private sector ignores issues of diversity, see Craig et al (2009b).

Part II

Theoretical, historical and policy contexts

'Race', ethnicity and social policy: theoretical concepts and the limitations of current approaches to welfare

Sangeeta Chattoo and Karl Atkin

At the start of the '60s we invited the guest workers to Germany. We kidded ourselves for a while that they wouldn't stay, that one day they would go home. That isn't what happened. And of course the tendency was to say: let's be 'multikulti' and live next to each other and enjoy being together, [but] this concept has failed, failed utterly. (German Chancellor, Angela Merkel, cited in *The Guardian*, 18 October 2010)

Overview

This chapter provides a critical overview of the field of ethnicity and its close association with 'race' and nationality. By exploring key concepts and theories underpinning debates surrounding ethnicity, it highlights the limitations of current approaches informing policy and practice and suggests alternative ways of thinking about ethnicity in addressing challenges facing Britain as an increasingly diverse society. The chapter will:

- explore the links between the concepts of 'race', ethnicity and nationality;
- examine the limitations of current understandings of ethnicity when discussing health and social welfare;

- provide empirical examples to illustrate the implications of diversity when considering access to welfare provision;
- reiterate the need to think about dilemmas and contradictions underpinning health and welfare provision in a diverse society; and
- offer an alternative conceptual framework to address challenges posed by an increasingly diverse society.

Key concepts
citizenship, ethnicity, 'race', social policy, welfare

Introduction

This chapter will deconstruct the theoretical underpinnings of the concept of ethnicity and trace its relationship with 'race' and nationality. It will be argued that, given the historical roots of ethnicity as a euphemism for racism in general and cultural racism in particular (focusing on cultural and religious difference rather than racial characteristics per se), the field of ethnicity, health and social care has remained highly specialised and marginal to mainstream academic, policy and practice discourses. Hence, while highlighting policies and practices sustaining the disadvantage and discrimination suffered by people of 'minoritised' groups, which have slowly prompted a shift towards a more inclusive society, a focus on ethnicity has also ironically reinforced the marginalisation of people from minority ethnic communities, often making them (special and) peripheral to broader debates about politics and citizenship. The field is marked by continuities and discontinuities, prompting us to recognise various contradictions at different levels. The conceptual and pragmatic tensions within policies related to immigration and particular 'immigrant' groups will be explained in greater historical detail in Chapters 3 and 4; and through specific case studies of particular policy areas outlined in Part III. Here we examine these contradictions, using our analysis to provide an alternative conceptual framework better suited for understanding a multicultural society.

Contrary to its wider usage within the social sciences, the language of state-sanctioned policy and practice and state-sponsored research on health and social welfare treat 'ethnicity' as an essential defining characteristic of only immigrant, *minority ethnic communities*. A combination of these three seemingly inseparable terms often results in cumulative disadvantage in access to appropriate services and welfare support for certain groups. Hence, bureaucratic institutions representing the state, for both practical and ideological reasons, treat people of minority ethnic background as more or less undifferentiated collectives of (metaphorical and literal) 'immigrants' (Lo and Stacey, 2008). Consequently, minority communities are defined through stereotypes of culture, religion and tradition, rather than as citizens in their own right negotiating their multiple identities differently within specific social and political contexts (Bhabha, 1994; Baumann, 1997; Werbner, 1997). Such a focus on culture often deflects attention away from structural issues of socio-economic inequality and forms of institutional cultures and racisms that sustain various forms of disadvantage and discrimination (see Gunaratnam, 1997). Further, as highlighted by black and post-colonial feminist writers, it is important to understand the role of *intersectionality* between 'race', ethnicity, gender and class in shaping women's experiences of disadvantage and partial citizenship rights (Anthias and Yuval-Davis, 1992, pp 96–131; Mirza, 2009a; Phoenix, 2009; see also Chapter 4). These intersections are not cumulative or fixed, but contingent on different subject positions and histories of migration. As a result, we find heterogeneity in experiences of social disadvantage for women of black, white, South Asian or other minority ethnic groups (Yuval-Davis, 2006). A sole focus on structural disadvantage (class or gender) or a homogenised notion of a 'racialised community' can, therefore, underplay the significance of plural and creative modes of engaging with various aspects of 'race', ethnicity, culture, gender and citizenship at individual and collective levels (see Werbner and Modood, 1997).

Notwithstanding the intellectual debates, *dominant* discourses of self-identity within a group can, at strategic moments, also use simplified notions of culture, portraying an idealised, timeless vision of 'tradition' and a cohesive community, to set themselves apart from others (see Anderson, 1991). This meaning of culture, as a static, tangible set of shared normative values and rules passed on from one generation to the next, is thereby mobilised for political and economic purposes, enabling communities to assert solidarity of interests premised on shared values. Policy discourses often reinforce these perceptions and generalisations about other cultures in search of simple workable solutions to what are increasingly complex problems.

This approach contrasts with culture as an analytical concept used in the discipline of Sociology. Here the concept refers to a dynamic process of interpretation and negotiation of shared values, dissent and change marked by gender and generation as well as the material circumstances of individuals. As suggested by Baumann (1997, p 219), in conjunction with a *dominant* discourse projecting a cohesive community, we often find a *demotic* discourse that reflects communities and cultures within the community. Far from being a unity, the community is a dialogic site of constant moral debate and conflict between right and wrong ways of doing things. Bureaucratic norms underpinning welfare, however, often reflect the cultural values of a majority, glossing over internal differences related to ethnicity and gender as well as socio-economic position (see Atkin and Chattoo, 2007; Lo and Stacey, 2008).

This chapter reiterates the need for critical reflection on the popular use of the term 'ethnicity' in discourses related to health and social welfare. This is all the more important in view of recent estimates showing that nearly 50% of people of minority ethnic origin currently living in the UK have been born there. This has important implications for notions of citizenship and how we define and address ethnic diversity. Old ways of conceptualising ethnicity, closely related to colonial ideas of 'race' and nationality, have little relevance to how people of immigrant origin make sense of their plural identities within the context of citizenship and political participation. This chapter, therefore, provides an overarching self-critique of the field and a conceptual link across the different sections and chapters of the book. We are, however, aware of the dangers of trying to predefine these conceptual terms, which might have slightly different connotations within the specific contexts of following chapters. Given this, the present chapter provides a 'social landscape' and a conceptual backdrop for the themes and concepts used throughout the book. The aim is to provide the reader with critical tools to engage sceptically with the idea of 'ethnicity', whatever the context and location, and use this understanding to develop better-informed and more sophisticated social policies.

Linking ethnicity, 'race' and nationality

Ethnicity refers to a process of self-identity and form of social stratification and is: 'as much the product of internal arguments of identity and contestation as of external objectification' (Werbner, 1997, p 18). 'Ethnicity' is best defined as a field of enquiry helping us to locate the material and cultural context within which ethnic identities, premised on notions of shared descent, heritage and culture (encompassing religion and language), are constantly redefined and contested by different social groups. We do not have a unitary theory of ethnicity or a concept with a predefined content. As explained by Fenton:

> ethnicity refers to the *social construction* of descent and culture, the social mobilisation of descent and culture, and the meanings and implications of the classification systems built around them. People or peoples do not just possess cultures or share ancestry; *they elaborate these into the idea of a community founded upon these attributes.* (Fenton, 2003, p 3, original emphasis)

A particular social group might redefine itself (or be redefined by others) over time as a national, religious or racial group, using either an 'idiom of race' or an 'idiom of ethnicity' (see Banton, 2000). The claim by Albanians to Kosovo as an independent state in 2008, and counterclaims by Serbs about Kosovo being a part of Serbia, provides a good example of a historically persistent ethnic conflict translating into a dispute over a state's territorial boundaries. As Anthias (1992, p 25) observes, transformation of such claims is 'linked to political projects and may be the outcome of state and other discourses in interplay with economic and other cultural resources or aims of the group themselves or others'.

Hence, it is important to bear in mind that ethnicity, culture and community do not refer to fixed or essential characteristics that people 'have', but rather to dynamic processes of self-identity and differentiation involving the negotiation of boundaries of inclusion and exclusion between groups. These boundaries are fluid and shift according to the context of social interaction and struggles over power and resources over time (Hall, 1996). One major feature of this process of self-identification and differentiation is that a sense of shared culture (within a group) is reproduced in everyday interactions between members of different ethnic groups (Barth, 1969), often resulting in the codification of culture as coterminous with difference. Further, within the post-colonial context of the history of immigration patterns in the West and especially the UK, 'ethnicity' is used to designate immigrant, minority cultures/groups. Hence, it acts as a source of social stratification, perpetuating forms of disadvantage and discrimination through what is now perceived as 'cultural racism', rather than racism per se (see Modood, 1997, p 155; for a note on 'race' and other forms of racism, see later). This reminds us of the affinity between the concepts of 'ethnic group', 'race' and 'nation', which share an emphasis on a notion of common descent and culture.

The word ethnic has its root in the Greek word *ethnos*, broadly implying people living together; a tribe, nation, caste – and could be used to exclude groups, for example, non-Athenians and non-Jews. The word in its adjectival form *ethnikos* had two meanings denoting 'national' and 'foreign'. The earliest written English language citation implies 'heathen and foreign'. The meaning shifted towards a generalised notion of 'race' and common racial or cultural character during the 19th century, until 'race' was replaced by 'ethnic' during the 1930s to designate minority cultural groups or those who were not Christian or Jews (see Fenton, 2003, pp 14–16).

'Race', racism and cultural racism

The notion of biologically distinct 'races', invoking relatedness through common genealogy or blood, first deployed in the 19th century, was closely associated with a fascination in biology and anthropology for the non-European (African, Asian, Native American and Australasian) peoples, often seen as the 'savage other'. Interestingly, earlier 18th-century meanings of 'race', despite being Eurocentric, reflected a concern more with what made us similar rather than different (see Porter, 2001). Indeed, political thinkers, such as Jeremy Bentham and Adam Smith, questioned the morality of subjugating other nations by evoking John Locke's notion of toleration (and paving the way for the abolition of slavery). By the 19th century, however, anthropometric recordings of physical characteristics (such as height, skin and eye colour, or weight of skull as a parameter for intelligence) and cultural descriptions of 'natives' as the 'distant other' formed the core legitimising strategy. This sat alongside the need to exploit raw materials, labour and markets (Judd, 1996); and the Christian values of salvation used by missionaries to colonise indigenous peoples perceived as being intellectually, morally and culturally inferior to Europeans (see Said, 2003). Ironically, Wilberforce, despite his instrumental role in ending the British slave trade (see Chapter 3), advocated sending missionaries to India, declaring that Hindu deities were 'absolute monsters of lust, injustice, wickedness and cruelty' (cited in Keay, 2004, p 429).

Pseudo-scientific theories and methods of classifying racial types reached their logical conclusion in the mass extermination of the Jews, other so-called 'racial' minorities (such as Roma) and disabled people in Europe during the 1930s and 1940s. This belies their supposed respectable origins, which culminated in the growth of eugenics in the latter half of the 19th century (Mazower, 1998). As an ideology and a social movement, social Darwinism or eugenics (Greek for 'good birth') grew out of a simplistic and corrupt adaptation of Darwin's ideas of 'natural selection', inspired by the Malthusian theory of overpopulation (see Burleigh, 2005). One of the key proponents of this theory, Darwin's cousin and statistician, Francis Galton, propagated the idea of having a 'national breeding policy' for improving the 'national stock' during the 1860s (see Kuper, 2002, p 183). Deterministic views on 'race' underpinning the UK eugenics movement were intertwined with notions of class, gender and disability and wider concerns about social 'deviants' perceived as a threat to the moral or physical well-being of society. Hence, racial/immigrant groups (including white minorities such as the Irish, who have an ethnically ambivalent position in the United Kingdom), single mothers, the unemployed, as well as people with physical, mental or learning disabilities were deemed as socially and politically unfit to be granted full, substantial citizenship rights (Brendon, 2002). The horrors of the Holocaust have sometimes obscured the enthusiasm for and respectable popularity of eugenic thinking among social and political thinkers at both ends of the political spectrum, including the Webbs, Keynes, Beveridge and Barnardo (Williams, 1996). Consequently, for much of the late 19th and early 20th centuries, eugenics was a perfectly acceptable idea, popular across much of Europe and North America and full of good intent, and seen as a way of improving the lot of ordinary people by improving the racial health of the nation.

The controversial policy of the forced sterilisation of mentally disabled people across the UK and many countries of the world in the first half of the 20th century sought to prevent the reproduction of people considered to have 'faulty genes'; the theory, albeit with a more liberal emphasis on informed choice, laid the foundation for modern genetics (Kerr and Cunningham-Burley, 2000). The National Socialists' infamous Law for the Prevention of the Hereditarily Diseased Offspring came into force in Germany during 1933 (see Evans, 2005). The legislation covered not only people with physical, mental and learning disabilities, but also those with epilepsy or alcoholism and, by default rather than law, people of mixed racial origin or the so-called 'Rhineland bastards' (children whose fathers were 'colonial' French troops stationed there during the occupation of the 1920s/30s). The seeds of the policy were to be found in the 'social improvement' practices initiated during the liberal democratic Weimar Republic (Peukert, 1991); and in the first eugenic Sterilisation Act enacted in the US (Indiana) in 1907 (and followed by other states) resulting in 15,000 Americans being sterilised by 1930 (Porter, 1999, p 640). Sterilisation programmes reached a peak during Nixon's presidency in the 1970s. The federal government supported a Medicaid-funded sterilisation programme that, although seen to be 'voluntary', largely targeted poor and black, African-American people and Native American women who were provided with little information about the procedures involved (see www.ratical.org/ratville/sterilize.html [September 1998]). Even though forced sterilisation has since been defined as a violation of human rights in Europe and much of the Western world, Czechoslovakia followed a policy of sterilising Roma women in 1973, while the last forced sterilisation was performed in Oregon in 1981. The policy had wider reverberations for poor and disabled women in the US (see ***Box 2.1***).

Box 2.1: Sterilisation of the 'unfit' (see Martin, 2010)

Women incarcerated after having been convicted of drug use during pregnancy or child abuse were, in several states, given the option to take Norplant to avoid or reduce the length of incarceration. Norplant has also been suggested as a 'cure for poverty', coercing poor women to take this medication for substantial periods. The Illinois Appellate Court denied an attempt to have a mentally disabled woman sterilised against her will. This echoes the 1927 *Buck* v *Bell* decision that saw the US Supreme Court uphold a ruling that made it legal to sterilise those who were considered socially unfit; among the undesirables were numerous disabled women. In his decision then, Justice Holmes stated:

It is better ... if instead of waiting to execute degenerate offspring for crime, or let them starve for their imbecility, society can prevent those ... manifestly unfit from continuing their kind. Three generations of imbeciles is enough. (See http://www.guardian.co.uk/commentisfree/libertycentral/2010/may/04/forced-sterilisation-women-motherhood [4 May 2010])

Martin (2010) suggests that debating the right of the poor or women with neurological conditions to reproduce reflects a persistent, deep-seated social Darwinism in politics (see the Eugenics Archive Blog at: www.eugenicsarchive.org/eugenics [posted 24 September 2010]). These views are not restricted to politics and politicians alone; there are vocal proponents of the idea within established academia in the UK and elsewhere (see *Box 2.2*).

Box 2.2: Pro-forced sterilisation (eugenics) debates

Edward Stourton chairs a live BBC debate in which Professor David Marsland defends his view that the mentally and morally unfit should be sterilised. Marsland is Emeritus Scholar of Sociology and Health Sciences at Brunel University, London and Professorial Research Fellow in Sociology at the University of Buckingham. He argues that the only way to prevent the abuse and neglect of children whose parents are incapable of looking after them is to stop them from being born in the first place. It should be open to police and social workers to recommend that drug addicts, alcoholics and the mentally disabled should be irreversibly sterilised – and the courts should be able to enforce this. Challenging his views will be three expert witnesses including a senior social worker, a drugs charity lawyer and a moral philosopher (see http://info-wars.org/2010/08/26/pro-forced-sterilisation-eugenics-debate-on-bbc-radio/ [26 August 2010]).

The rise and persistence of social Darwinism since the Second World War has to be analysed alongside a severe critique of the theory and the concept of biologically distinct races. Especially within the British context, this has led to the substitution of 'race' by ethnicity which, nevertheless, continues to invoke features of 'race' in terms of 'essential' difference related to descent. Consequently, 'race' and ethnicity are often used interchangeably, leading to some confusion. 'Race' also continues to have a contested legal status in the UK (see Chapter 4), while some authors, taking their lead from the US, continue to use 'race' in parentheses to emphasise its political meaning. The term ethnicity, however, has tended to assume increasing significance in the UK policy literature.

How far are 'race' and ethnicity different concepts?

In the past and within the social sciences, 'race' and ethnicity were treated as different analytical concepts; 'race' implying nature or relatedness through genealogy or blood, while ethnicity suggested relatedness through common history and culture. This corresponded with notions of citizenship by *jus sanguinis* (by genealogical link) and *jus soli* (place of birth or soil). The two categories, of course, imply each other and cannot be treated as mutually exclusive. Just as ethnicity evokes a sense of common heritage, kinship and descent, 'race' and racism are not only descriptive terms for physical difference, but involve potent cultural metaphors and value judgements justifying negative/discriminatory attitudes (eg the term 'Paki' used for Asians in general). This is reflected in many modern states recognising both types of claims to citizenship (Wade, 2007), although the two notions of citizenship are still problematic to reconcile in countries such as France and Germany.

Further, the theory of distinct biological races that can be hierarchically arranged, and which predict intellectual, moral and social qualities, was extensively challenged during the 1940s/50s in the aftermath of the Holocaust. It is now well-recognised that there are huge variations in physical characteristics within as well as between racial groups, and that the boundaries of racial groups are fluid due to the constant movements and intermingling of peoples from different geographical parts of the world, earlier associated with particular racial 'types'. The idea of there being such distinct racial groups, therefore, has become unsustainable, even though racism remains a pervasive theme of our social and political domains, sometimes evoking racial categories, while, at other times, emphasising a form of cultural imperialism.

The term 'racism' has been part of the British lexicon since the 1930s. Its meaning and political significance have, however, shifted over time. For many decades, racism was associated with an *ideology* structuring power, privilege and economic opportunities in favour of the dominant/majority ethnic group/s. The overt political context has gradually been replaced by a new focus resulting in what has been termed as *cultural racism* or *racialisation of culture* in the UK (Banton, 1987). The latter has recourse to essentialised, immutable cultural and religious differences of immigrant, minority communities, which are seen to be in conflict with traditional 'British values' and a 'British way of life', threatening the idea of a British nation as a cohesive, self-defined homogeneous unity in the imaginary past (see the section discussing the rise of 'community cohesion' in Chapter 4). People of immigrant origin (however long ago that immigration may have been), who might be different in terms of their culture (language, religion, dress, diet, gender and kinship relationships), are perceived as a threat to national identity and dominant (white) cultural values, and pushed to the political periphery. The animated political debate on the practice of consanguineous marriage among Muslims of South Asian origin, who suffer a higher incidence of birth disorders and certain genetically inherited conditions, such as thalassaemia, reminds us how boundaries of liberal multiculturalism are defined by default/dominant white cultural values (see *Case Study 2.1* for a summary of the issues underpinning the debate; see also Ahmad and Bradby, 2007; Darr, 2009). Cultural amnesia about the practice of 'cousin marriage' in (white) Britain in the past, well-documented in literature (see Shaw, 2001; Kuper, 2002), serves to redefine such practices as alien and exotic. At the same time, a focus on culture and tradition deflects attention away from the disproportionate levels of poverty, unemployment, discrimination and lack of social capital faced by some people within these communities, resulting in poor communication and understanding about such health issues as well as a lack of access to appropriate health and social care services (see Bradford and District Infant Mortality Commission, 2006; see also Chapters 3 and 4). These social factors are more likely to contribute to childhood disability and chronic illness than marrying one's first cousin per se, which in any case usually only assumes importance when couples carry the same recessive genes.

Case Study 2.1: Cousin marriages

'First-cousin marriage' has come to dominate debates about genetic conditions in South Asian populations in a way not found in other ethnic groups, including the majority population. Over the years, several NHS Trusts (eg in Birmingham) have specifically established policies to discourage people from marrying their cousins as a way of reducing the incidence of thalassaemia. Indeed, evidence suggests that some parents believe that thalassaemia is 'caused' by marrying a cousin, which in itself can evoke feelings of guilt. The transmission of thalassaemia, however, is the same as in sickle-cell disorders or cystic fibrosis. When both partners carry a trait, there is a one in four risk in every pregnancy that their child could be born with the disorder. Consanguineous marriages, therefore, are only at risk of producing a child with thalassaemia if both parents carry the thalassaemia trait. Hence, information and genetic counselling related to thalassaemia needs to focus on mode and risk of transmission rather than stigmatising the practice of 'cousin marriage' as the cause.

Defining the cultural values or practices of minority communities as deviant and looking for 'acculturation' as the solution to their social and health care needs thus serves the same ideological purpose as policies of assimilation did in the past (see also Chapter 4). As is clear from the remarks of the German Chancellor on the 'failures' of multiculturalism, recent policies aiming at repatriation of the Roma in France, widespread stereotypes of Muslims as 'terrorists' and cultural racism in all its various guises remind us about the boundaries of the notion of a liberal, democratic state (see Kumar, 2008; Modood, 2008). Boundaries of inclusion and assumed categories of what is legitimate citizenship occur through a different and yet familiar discourse on ethnic/cultural/religious difference. Before turning to nation and nationality, we explore the analytical meaning of institutional racism and its implications for social policy.

Institutional racism

The term *institutional racism* was first discussed as an analytical category over 20 years ago (Glasgow, 1980); its political origins lie in the 1960s' Black Power movements in North America (Zuberi, 2001). In the UK, political credibility of the concept dates back to the MacPherson Report (1999), following the inquiry into Stephen Lawrence's murder (see Chapters 4 and 12). This eventually led in 2000 to a significant amendment to the Race Relations Act 1976, placing a statutory responsibility on public organisations to promote diversity and tackle institutional racism. The term has since been used widely to explain the inability of public services to respond to the needs of an ethnically diverse society (Karlsen, 2007a). The implications of this have been carried forward to the Single Equality Act 2010, which recognises that discrimination can be cultural and systemic (see Chapter 4).

At its simplest, institutional racism occurs when the overt or covert policies of an institution lead to discriminatory outcomes for people from minority ethnic communities, irrespective of the motives of the individual employees of that institution. To some extent, the term shifts the responsibility for discriminatory actions or attitudes from individuals to the organisation, meaning it is difficult to make individuals culpable for their own actions. On the positive side, the term recognises various forms of prejudice and discriminatory attitudes towards minority ethnic groups operating in the wider society and condoned within an institutional culture. The common forms of institutional racism engender either a lack of recognition or misinterpretation of the needs of minority ethnic people. While lack of access and adequate language support for non-English speakers remains an issue, professional assumptions about cultures other than their own often contribute more to poor communication and overtly discriminatory policies at an institutional level than language per se (Netto et al, 2001a), as the following two examples show (see *Case Study 2.2* and *Box 2.3*).

Case Study 2.2: Sickle-cell disorders

Sickle-cell disorders, more common among people of African and Caribbean origin, are associated with, among other things, severe pain commonly known as a 'painful crisis'. Evidence from both the UK and North America suggests that people in pain are denied effective pain relief as a consequence of two persistent racist myths (see Atkin and Anionwu, 2010). The attitudes of healthcare professionals, therefore, reveal deeper racialised perceptions of 'black' people (see Rouse, 2009). First, healthcare professionals believe 'black' patients have lower pain thresholds and therefore exaggerate their pain. Second, they believe that 'black' young men are more likely to get addicted to pain medication than other men. A young man of African-Caribbean origin, taking part in research said: 'They [nurses] are really quite nasty. They say stupid things, like "Oh be quiet. You are not really as bad as you say"' (quoted in Atkin and Ahmad, 2000, p 62). Another young man of African-Caribbean origin in his 20s remarked: 'I know what nurses think, they see a black man and they think "We are not giving him any drugs. He will only get addicted". I wish they would understand. They have no idea what it is like' (quoted in Anionwu and Atkin, 2001, p 90).

The recent recognition of discriminatory treatment received by African-Caribbean and African-American men in mental health services offers another reminder of a similar set of essentialist constructions of 'race' and ethnicity (see Bhui et al, 2004; see also Chapter 11), as does 'racial profiling', underpinning the stop-and-search policies of the police (see *Box 2.3* and Chapter 12).

Box 2.3: Racial profiling

'Black people are 26 times more likely than whites to face stop and search'

An international report says that police in England and Wales are more likely than others to use racial profiling when stopping people without evidence that they have committed a crime. Analysis by the London School of Economics and the Open Society Justice Initiative found that there are 41.6 Section 60 searches for every 1,000 black people compared with 1.6 for every 1,000 white people – making black people 26.6 times more likely to be stopped and searched. Asians were 6.3 times more likely to be stopped than whites, according to the analysis of Ministry of Justice figures for 2008–09. US civil rights activist, Jesse Jackson, arrived in London to campaign against stop-and-search discrimination based on racial profiling. (Data released in 2011 showed Asians were stopped 42 times more often than Whites.) (*The Observer*, 17 October 2010, p 22)

Ironically, one of the responses to addressing the needs of a multi-ethnic population in the UK has been the 'fact file' approach to culture. This involves introductory booklets or 'training packs' on religious/cultural practices of minority groups such as Hindus, Muslims, Jews, Chinese and so on, aimed at 'empowering' professionals to deal with issues of diversity and equity. This approach, often underpinning educational programmes for 'culturally competent practice', is likely to present static, idealised views of cultural norms and practices, creating an illusion of a solution to a complex situation (Lo and Stacey, 2008). This leaves us with the moot question: how do we create an understanding of cultures other than our own without essentialising difference, and how do we acknowledge the coexistence of diverse cultures (and religions) within a nation? The final section of this chapter unpicks this tension alongside exploring ideas of inclusion and exclusion. Before we come to that, a note on the semantic links between 'race', nation and nationality is in order, particularly since it contributes to our understanding of how ethnicity is used in discourses related to citizenship and welfare policies.

'Race', nation and nationality

The word 'nation' is said to have found its way into the English lexicon through French, and has retained its Latin root (*Natio/nasci*) associated with birth, tribe or common descent. Earlier definitions assumed the aggregate to be coterminous with a 'race'/ethnic group, sharing a common language, history and heritage, and usually occupying a state or political territory. More recent definitions, however, concede the idea that a nation can incorporate people of one or more cultures and descents, forming a single state (such as Australia); or an aggregate of people sharing a common descent, language and history, but not constituting a state (such as the French Canadian nation) (see Kymlicka, 2001). The idea of a deterritorialised nation and multiple nationalities seems to clash with constant struggles between ethnic groups over the redrawing of territorial boundaries of state- and nationhood along ethnic/religious lines, as we have seen across Russia and much of Eastern and South-Eastern Europe. Hence, the ideas of ethnic groups, 'race' and nation are socially constructed, intersecting in different ways within particular political contexts and changing over time. The declaration of the Republic of Kosovo as an independent state in 2008, recognised by some UN member states, is a good example of this (Beaumont, 2010).

Such debates have particular salience for the UK. As mentioned earlier, nearly 50% of people of minority ethnic origin living in the UK were born there and might be the second, third or fourth generation of families who moved and settled there in the past. This reminds us of the dilemmas of diasporic identities involving plural claims to ethnicity, nationality and citizenship within a global context (see eg Koshy, 2008). As outlined in other chapters, different minority ethnic groups have different histories of settlement, linked closely (especially for those of African, Caribbean or South Asian origins) with particular post-colonial histories and socio-economic profiles. We know that certain ethnic groups (eg of Bangladeshi, Pakistani, African and Caribbean origins) face higher levels of unemployment and socio-economic disadvantage than do the white majority and other minority ethnic groups (such as those of Indian and Chinese origins; see Chapters 9 and 10). It is this close conflation with socio-economic features that makes an analysis of the cumulative impact of ethnicity complex (as it tries to make sense of the impact of variables such as country of origin, religion, language and other aspects of culture, such as gendered patterns of education and employment). Recent migration and the presence of ethnic groups from the EU, Iraq, various African countries and Afghanistan seem to confirm this pattern (see Chapters 3 and 4).

These collective histories and profiles do not, however, necessarily pre-empt the negotiation of individual identity and significance of the notion of ethnicity in relation to 'race' (often defined as 'colour of my skin') or nationality or, indeed, socio-economic position. The following excerpt from research conducted with young people of Pakistani origin (between 2000 and 2003) in Northern England provides an example highlighting the complex interplay between these three terms and why we need to specify the context and meanings at play (Atkin and Chattoo, 2007).

Case Study 2.3: Dress as cultural identity

Yasmin (not her real name) was 15 years old. She was born and grew up in an inner-city neighbourhood in England, in a Muslim family originating from Pakistan. She went to a 'rough' comprehensive school. Her white schoolmates picked on girls like herself for wearing a hijab as it was seen to symbolise a lack of choice and freedom at home. Wearing a hijab was, however, central to Yasmin's religious and ethnic identity. At the same time, her resistance to the racist attitudes (to religious difference/immigrant origin) of white schoolmates translated her ethnic origin into the inalienable part of herself:

Yasmin: It's our decision really if you want to wear it [hijab] or not.... Yeah, I think it's important for us because that's like the, our, you know, we're known as Pakistanis, and that's like, you know ...

Interviewer: Where you came from?

Yasmin: Yeah, that's it ... even though, you know, you say you're British, you are British, but then again, you know, in some people's eyes, you're Asian British, not like *British* British [her emphasis].

Interviewer: But do you feel that that's where you came from although you were born here?

Yasmin: But then again, if you go back on the parents, you know, if the parents were not here, obviously you would be a Pakistani. Then again, you know, it's the way you feel. So I sometimes do say, 'Yeah, I am British', but then again, sometimes they can discriminate, you know, then you feel as if, 'Fine, okay, I'm not British, but at least I'm a *Pakistani*' [her emphasis]!

Yasmin recognised her Pakistani origin as being an essential feature of her identity through kinship links, culture as encompassing religion, dress, language, as well as the 'way she felt' or was perceived by others. In her voice, religious and cultural difference (symbolised in the hijab) is celebrated as a mode of resisting wider racist constructions of minority cultures. However, being of Pakistani origin did not have any salience for some young people of a similar background.

Yasmin's case study illustrates how ethnicity is a dynamic process involving the negotiation of self–identity in relation to significant others within a particular context, rather than a fixed attribute of groups per se. However, dominant voices within ethnic groups as a collective (such as self-styled 'community leaders' or those adhering to particular versions of religious doctrine) can project a cohesive image of their culture, religion or family/kin relationships. It is, therefore, essential that we differentiate between these idealised self-descriptions of community and our analytical framework for making sense of (operationalising) ethnicity and 'race', as suggested by Baumann (1997) and as discussed earlier. This is one of the ways in which we can proceed in dealing with the challenges of welfare provision in a multi-ethnic society and address the goal of providing 'culturally sensitive' health and welfare services, without recourse to broad generalisations and stereotypes.

Why focus on operationalising ethnicity?

One of the common features of research within the field of ethnicity, health and social welfare is a dichotomy between individualism and familism, corresponding to white majority (Western) and minority ethnic (Eastern/other) cultures, respectively. Hence, despite the fact that people from a majority (white) background also share an ethnic background, ethnicity is often treated as synonymous with an exotic feature of minority communities, designating their immigrant origins (see earlier). Explanations for the health and social care needs of people from the majority white community (also treated as a homogeneous whole) are premised on a notion of individuals making autonomous choices; while those of people from minority ethnic backgrounds are located within culture, tradition, religion and extended family values. For example, South Asian communities, despite internal diversity related to ethnic origin, religion, language and socio-economic position, are treated as a conglomerate of well-defined cultures. 'Asians' are perceived to be living in patriarchal, extended family structures where young people and women, in particular, have no choice and families 'take care of their own'.

In recent research on cancer (treatment-)related threats to fertility, the authors found old stereotypes of fatalism, gender and extended family structure persisting in the attitudes of some professionals working within the fields of cancer and reproductive medicine. This occurs despite decades of research evidence illustrating the complex patterns of diversity and difference within and similarities across ethnic groups (Chattoo et al, 2010; see also www.york.ac.uk/healthsciences/research-information/conference-cancer-survivorship/). *Case Study 2.4* provides an example of how similar responses of people from white and South Asian backgrounds to infertility and treatment were interpreted by professionals in different frameworks.

Case Study 2.4: Culture and fertility

'Asians' without qualification are believed to follow the tradition of 'arranged marriage', excluding notions of individual choice and romantic love. Following the same logic, any strain or breakdown of conjugal relationships due to infertility of a partner is attributed to a 'pro-natalist' culture and to men who, due to family pressures, are perceived as being less supportive of women having trouble in conceiving. However, examples of white partners breaking off relationships in a similar situation are attributed to interpersonal strain and choice. For example, one of the professionals mentioned the case of a white man whose fertility was affected by treatment related to cancer. He broke off a long-term relationship with his partner who was keen on having a child using donor insemination. Neither her desire to have a child nor his inability to 'get his head round' donor insemination were attributed to 'culture' or a wider set of shared values. In contrast, an 'Asian' man's refusal to let his wife use preserved embryos from a previous relationship was attributed to both personal and cultural reasons. Similarly, sharing information about fertility treatment selectively with family and friends, much respected as a matter of *privacy* in a white family, is construed as *secrecy* within South Asian families who, it is assumed, will not tell anyone about a child's donor conception. This attitude disregards evidence about 'secrecy' surrounding donor conception in the wider white culture.

Personal views of professionals about minority religious or cultural values and professional judgements about conjugal/gender or intergenerational relationships can have implications for the treatment options and quality of information and support offered to individuals. Equally importantly, in focusing on cultural difference, people of immigrant origin are treated as partial citizens, somehow 'less civilised', who need to be brought into the fold of (taught) core liberal values of the 'host society'. It is assumed (invoking colonial constructions of the 'distant other') that, with time, they will assimilate and integrate into the 'British way of life' (see Chapter 4).

Further, bureaucratic policies, procedures and language reinforce the status and feelings of partial citizenship experienced by the 'immigrant'. The British Home Office document to help people undertaking the Citizenship Test, introduced recently, is a good reflection of the tensions underpinning the process of inclusion and membership for new citizens. Apart from knowing an idealised version of British history and 'way of life', they also have to pledge allegiance to the Queen, an act not required of the white majority, to be recognised as full citizens (see www.lifeintheuktest. gov.uk/ and also Chapter 4). Further, cultural and historical differences between the English, Scottish, Welsh and Irish are easily overlooked within this construction of a British identity.

How can our discussion help create an 'evidence base' to inform policy and practice?

This brings us to a more central dilemma of providing welfare provision in any multi-ethnic state where welfare provision, by definition, involves contested, plural social values regarding the relationship between the individual, family and state. As Taylor (1994) observes, multiculturalism implies that Western social democracies need to move beyond the 'politics of recognition' focusing on different needs, to a 'politics of difference' committed to responding to these needs. The challenge remains in accepting difference with a political commitment to making sure that such difference does not become a basis of inequalities. Taylor's notion of 'politics of difference' poses a tension between the challenges in *representing difference* and *responding to diversity*. This is reflected in provision for health, social care, housing, education and employment, as well as broader legal provisions defining the democratic rights and duties of citizens in relation to those of the state (Law, 2003). Policies and practices related to health and social care involve moral judgements about social life and relationships – rather than reflecting *rational* choices in a value-neutral sense of the term (Eliaeson, 2002). Hence, in any multi-ethnic, multicultural society, there will be some tension between the use of default social and legal values, often representing a dominant majority, and the acceptance of such values by people of different ethnic groups (Bauman, 1992). Recognising and addressing difference, however, is not mutually exclusive with fundamental similarities in the human condition and responses to adversity, illness, deprivation and social exclusion. Recognising and respecting difference also falls within a wider ambit of a discussion on universal human rights, as embodied within the European Court of Human Rights, and this is likely to be an important theme in future discussions.

A comparative perspective is important in helping policymakers and health and social care professionals understand the similarities and differences in experiences and issues faced by people of different ethnic and religious groups. Such a perspective will help formulate policy and practice guidelines that are culturally sensitive, reflecting the complexity of people's lives, without relying on essentialised perceptions of particular cultural or religious groups. For example, people seeking infertility treatment, irrespective of ethnicity, have similar needs and ethical concerns related to the use of various reproductive technologies, especially those involving gamete donation from a third party (Culley and Hudson, 2009).

Yet an analytical focus on 'ethnicity' and 'ethnic monitoring', paradoxically, reinforces notions of cultural difference, positioning minority ethnic groups a priori as being 'racialised' and marginalised. This is not to deny differences located broadly in culture or religion, or that many people from minority ethnic communities suffer socio-economic disadvantage and discrimination and may not have access to appropriate services. However, the danger of such a framework is that it reproduces individual subjects as passive victims of their social positioning by virtue of their ethnic background, without analytical scope to suggest how individuals negotiate or resist such constructions or loci of power represented by state, medical and welfare organisations.

We therefore need to have more critical insights into how professionals make assumptions and judgements about the needs of people from minority ethnic groups and what implications these might have for the level of support offered to them in different contexts. For example, Muslim women may not be offered prenatal investigations/diagnoses since it is assumed that they will not be willing to terminate pregnancies (see Atkin and Anionwu, 2010). Termination is an emotionally and ethically difficult decision for all couples irrespective of religious/ethnic background. Muslim couples, like most other couples, make decisions about potential termination on various biographical, emotional and pragmatic factors. Religion can provide moral boundaries for choices related to prenatal diagnosis and an explanation for why a particular choice (to terminate or not) may be considered just or unjust, given the particular circumstances of a couple and/or their own faith (Atkin, 2009b). Nonetheless, religion as a collective body of beliefs and practices does not predefine individual negotiations of moral choices related to prenatal diagnosis (Shaw, 2000; Remennick, 2006). Often there are different interpretations of the use and acceptability of particular medical interventions across and within Muslim (and other religious) communities (see Inhorn, 2006).

Such theoretical complexities are closely linked to more practical methodological issues of how research findings and analyses are intrinsically related to sampling strategies (see Atkin and Chattoo, 2006). If a sample does not represent the complexity and diversity of a population, research findings or policy guidelines are bound to be skewed. For example, given its demography, a sample of people of Pakistani origin taken from the Manningham area of Bradford is bound to over-represent people from Mirpir, with high levels of unemployment among a cohort laid off during the recession of the 1970s. Similarly, the ethnic label 'white' refers broadly to a national 'majority' that is assumed to be a non-problematic, homogeneous category, without reference to minorities within majorities (such as, white people of Irish, Polish, Jewish origins and recent immigrants from Eastern Europe), and their culture or religion. In contrast, 'South Asian' is a heterogeneous category that denotes four countries of origin within the Indian subcontinent (with Sri Lanka often excluded), where regional, linguistic and religious affiliations as well as different histories of migration and settlement predominate (see earlier).

Any comparison between a sample of white and South Asian people, for example, is based on dissimilar units of analysis. Meaningful comparison must draw on analytical categories that are specific to the context of analysis and can be operationalised (in terms of content), so that we can explain similarities and differences across ethnic groups without taking recourse to an a priori positioning of the subject within a 'racialised'/ marginalised community, forever fighting the ghost of the post-colonial world (Ahmad and Bradby, 2007). This is not to contest the centrality and contribution of a focus on ethnicity as a framework for explaining racism, discrimination and processes of marginalisation made in the field so far. Rather, given the changing demography of Britain, we need critically to evaluate this framework to be able to address the needs of a culturally, religiously and linguistically diverse society. This involves two kinds of changes at a methodological level that can inform policy and practice, as described in *Box 2.4*.

Box 2.4: Making sense of diversity

1. Critically examine how we operationalise ethnicity (by outlining content or meaning), at both the macro-level of population and communities and the micro-level of individual subjects; and
2. develop comparative methods of analysis that destabilise the binary opposition between the immigrant and host, West and 'rest', particularly since for over 50% of people of immigrant origin born and brought up in the UK, the centre stage for the politics of citizenship has already shifted.

Conclusion

The current framework of ethnicity underpinning health and social welfare provision serves to reinforce perceptions of 'settlers' as partial citizens or 'permanent minorities' (Koshy, 2008). We need to destabilise the dualism between majority and minority, immigrant and host, and traditional and Western cultures and reiterate the view of culture as a dynamic process marked by social divisions of gender, generation and socio-economic position. This requires an anti-essentialist conceptual shift in recognising difference as part of the self rather than a defining feature of the other as exterior to the self. As suggested by Hall (1996), we need to disentangle ethnicity from its anti-racist paradigm and use it in a positive context of identities (and culture as language) that is both specific and responsive to dialogue and transformation (for an analytical review, see Papastergiadis, 1997). Such a move can help us challenge historically specific discrimination against men and women of minoritised cultures, focusing on the intersectionality between ethnicity, gender and socio-economic position, and grant equal citizenship rights to those who might, at different points of time in history, be considered settlers or immigrants. An absence of such a framework, we suggest, is the main reason why, despite a focus on multiculturalism and anti-racist legislation in the UK, we have made little progress in tackling racism and addressing prejudice and discrimination in health, employment and welfare provision (see also Chapter 4).

Finally, returning to our earlier point about cultural competence, as social scientists, we need to be critical about what constitutes 'evidence'; who is producing it; and how professionals are being certified as 'competent'. On the surface, the basic components of different models of cultural competency cover the three areas of *cultural sensitivity*, *cultural knowledge* and *cultural skills* (Kim-Godwin et al, 2001). It is assumed that a combination of such skills, knowledge and sensitivity will enable health and social care professionals to address issues of difference and diversity. However, each component assumes a static notion of culture as a set of shared systems of beliefs and values that can be described and 'known' in order to be incorporated into short training courses for health and social care professionals. Gunaratnam, following Giddens' notion of an 'abstract system' (that helps define boundaries and responses to the uncertain), suggests that such attempts at regulating practice and responses to caring can 'undermine equity and erode responsibility for emotional and moral thinking through their attempts to simplify and control the threat of the unfamiliar' (Gunaratnam, 2008b, p 25).

However, she also shows how individual healthcare professionals challenge such attempts at the codification of responses in their negotiation of emotional complexities in the lives of individuals they are caring for, highlighting uncertainties and dilemmas posed by caring within the context of old age and death. This serves as a reminder that collective values underpinning professional codes and practices are interpreted and negotiated differently in practice by different individuals. Further, any understanding and responses to diversity and pluralism have to be part of the larger process of living in, being educated in and feeling part of a plural or diverse society.

Questions for discussion

- Why do we need critically to evaluate the use of 'ethnicity' as a social construct and what does 'ethnicity' mean?
- What are the historical links between ethnic groups, 'race' and nation? How does a historical perspective help us understand and critique current ideas about ethnicity, 'race' and racism?
- What does the notion of intersectionality within black feminist writings help us understand?
- What conceptual and methodological shifts do we need in order to address difference and diversity in health, education, employment and welfare provision in a multi-ethnic society?
- Is it possible to address cultural, religious and ethnic difference in service provision without treating difference as the essential feature defining people of immigrant origin?

The history and pattern of settlement of the UK's black and minority ethnic[1] population

Gary Craig

"Go back to your own f*****g country!" (A group of Irishmen attacking a Caribbean man, London, 1954 [personal account by the author's grandfather])

Overview

This chapter traces the history of minority migration to, and settlement in, the UK. Initially based on invasion, at different times it has been driven by persecution of minorities in other countries, compulsion (as for slaves), economic migration for reconstruction or to meet the needs of the labour market, family reunion, or by migrants seeking better standards of living. In the past 50 years, patterns of settlement have been shaped by the natural growth and distribution of a settled minority presence. Now, over 50% of the UK's so-called ethnic minority population were born in the UK.

Certain themes recur throughout history, such as categorising immigrants as the 'other', which, underpinned by racist ideologies, have led to discrimination and difficulties for minorities in pursuing lives as equal citizens to the 'host' white British population. Historical debates find expression in how we understand ethnicity today.

The chapter suggests that notions of majority and minority shift over time. The present demographic mix in the UK is not simply the product of recent migrations, but of change over 2,000 years; virtually all the UK population has genes and cultures reflecting migration both from within the British Isles and outside them. This challenges ideas of a homogeneous British 'race' and identity and 'Britishness' reflecting a set of values relating solely to white UK-born residents.

Key concepts
demography, diversity, migration, settlement

A brief history of early minority settlement

Black and minority ethnic (BME) people have been living in the UK in observable numbers for at least 500 years, reflected in public records such as diaries, published accounts, portraits and official accounts (Porter, 1991). Originally, these people came from other countries, although, by 1505, minority ethnic people were being born in England. The earliest records of minority arrivals are those of Nubian (now probably termed Black Sudanese) soldiers/slaves arriving from 55BC,[2] accompanying the invading Roman armies. These conscripts and volunteers from Rome's vassal states accompanied what today would be called Italians. Some descendants of these early migrants were later seized by Vikings and transported elsewhere, including Ireland, illuminating early Irish minority settlement. Successive waves of invaders – Romans, Angles, Saxons, Danes, Vikings and Normans – themselves constituted minorities until assimilated into the 'British' nation. The present 'white British' majority population is thus constructed from successive migrant minorities, with diverse ethnic, cultural and linguistic backgrounds. Yet, over time, particular minorities have been objectified and constituted as the 'other', and subjected to different forms of exclusion and discrimination.

Jewish people, for example, came at various times, from countries including France, Belgium and Spain. Relatively large-scale Jewish immigration occurred during the 5th–15th centuries, seeking opportunities as moneylenders, but also resulting from their harassment and expulsion from other countries. This pattern continued through early 20th-century East European pogroms and the Nazi holocaust to the present day, creating the Jewish diaspora. Their financial resources proved useful for monarchs, militaries and land-owning supporters to finance military adventures at home and abroad, with English kings borrowing extensively from moneylenders from 1164 onwards. King Henry II (1133–89) had protected Jews, but despite the usefulness of their financial services, and substantial tax revenues, the stereotypical Jewish moneylenders became targets of persecution. This was generated by Crusaders arguing that Christians should deal with the killers of Christ in their midst before freeing Jerusalem from the hands of 'infidel' Mussulmen. Pogroms against Jewish people occurred at the end of the 12th century, notably at the coronation of Richard I, at Norwich and Lincoln in 1189/90. In York, the small Jewish community gathered within Clifford's Tower for protection and to celebrate the feast of Shabbat ha-Gadol. The Tower was torched by a mob, incited by a Christian monk. Many Jews took their own lives, others were burnt to death; those fleeing were massacred. Alongside similar attacks, severe taxation was imposed on Jewish moneylenders under pain of torture and death (Dobson, 1995).

Prejudice, discrimination, stereotyping and racialising the 'other' have, therefore, been long-standing features of the history of immigrant settlement, often legitimised by state policy. Later experiences of Jewish populations further demonstrate this. Jews were banished in the 13th century but readmitted by Cromwell in the 17th. Attempts by British governments to alter their status, such as the 1753 Act legalising their naturalisation, were rejected following anti-Semitic riots across England (Porter, 1991). One of the first modern Immigration Acts (1905) aimed to reduce Jewish refugee migration from Central and Eastern Europe (Williams, 1996; see also later).

The first few Muslims also came to Britain in the 12th century. Queen Elizabeth I later offered to form an alliance against Spain with an Islamic leader, presumably from North Africa (Ansari, 2004).

Invading Anglo-Saxons (from present-day Germany) and Vikings (from Denmark and Norway) had already added to the European ethnic mix. Descendants of Vikings remained within North-Eastern Britain long after original invaders had returned home. For example, a small settlement of what would now be called Danes lived in Thirsk, North Yorkshire in the 12th century (Bogg, 1926). The names of East Yorkshire villages such as Skirpenbeck and Fangfoss testify to the early settlement of Scandinavians. People from Wales, Scotland and Ireland also migrated to England – forming 'Celtic minorities' – for reasons including intermarriage between wealthy local families and families of similar status from other countries. Examples are those of Matilda from Boulogne, France, who married Henry I, later remarrying a wealthy baron from Anjou, and of Catherine of Aragon, Spain, Henry VIII's first wife. Ireland, itself populated by invading Celts from Wales since the 8th century BC, then subject to Norman and English invasions throughout the 500 years leading to Cromwell's conquest in the 17th century, was a British colony until the 20th century.

Over the past 200 years, millions of native Irish migrated to the UK and elsewhere as a result of poverty and famine and form one of the largest minorities within the UK. This is formally recognised in the 2001 census, which introduced the category of 'white Irish', estimated at 600,000. Gypsies were 'first recorded in the British Isles in the early part of the 15th century' (Cemlyn and Briskman, 2002); by 1530 there are 'official enactments recorded against them' (Hawes and Perez, 1995, preface). They were labelled 'Gypsies' due to their perceived resemblance to 'Egyptians' although it is now believed they originated in North-West India, as linguistic studies link the Roma language to Hindi and Sanskrit (Matras, no date).

The history of black settlement in the UK largely starts with the history of slavery. Most slaves captured in coastal African regions were trans-shipped directly to the American subcontinents (Quirk, 2009). Some were brought to the UK and confined to domestic labour, including as footmen and nursemaids, and were the object of curiosity. The British viewed black slaves, including the relatively few who lived in England in the 18th century, as British chattels rather than British citizens (Porter, 1991). Most lived in and around London and other ports such as Bristol and Liverpool (Eltis and Richardson, 2010), although a few – probably servants – lived in rural areas, attested to by occasional gravestones in village churchyards (see Dabydeen et al, 2010, introduction). Scotland's role in the slave trade – and its subsequent abolition – has been largely overlooked, but much sugar and tobacco passed through Glasgow and a black population developed there also (Mullen, 2005).

Box 3.1: Slaves as citizens or the 'other'?

Although the British and French were frequently at war, throughout much of the 16th to 18th centuries, their military leaders agreed on one thing: every 'negro', wherever s/he was, was a slave. Slaves captured in war were confiscated as merchandise rather than exchanged as prisoners. The first English slaver was John Hawkyns in 1563. Initially, Queen Elizabeth I claimed that carrying off Africans was detestable and would call down the wrath of the gods: soon afterwards, however, Hawkyns became the comptroller of the English navy and a freeman of Plymouth (Fryer, 1984). The state's stance towards slaves *within* Britain was contradictory. Although some were freed, becoming resident in England, thus technically English citizens, edicts continued to be issued against them. The Privy Council ordered that all 'negroes and blackamoors' should be deported in 1596, and, in 1601 (just before the Poor Law), declared that 'the Queen's own natural subjects were greatly distressed in these hard times of dearth', meaning that the settled English population resented others settling (Fryer, 1984, p 10; see also Walvin, 1984). Twenty-five years before the first slave settlement of Barbados, it is hard to find a clearer indication of the 'other' status of Africans in the eyes of the English and it is a precise precursor of the racist formulations of the 20th and 21st centuries, particularly at times of high unemployment. Witness, for example, then-Prime Minister Gordon Brown's infelicitous phrase claiming 'British jobs for British workers' as the UK recession deepened in 2009.

The status of black people was tested more fully through the law during the 18th century, especially through the Somerset case (Schama, 2005), where it was argued by Granville Sharp that a toleration of slavery was in fact a toleration of inhumanity. A famous – if reluctant – legal ruling was handed down that slaves could not lawfully be deported against their will and that all people in Britain were subject to its laws. This, in effect, meant that (black) slaves could not technically exist in Britain (a ruling later overturned).

The slave trade was driven by economic interests (claims that international trade could not happen without slave labour) but facilitated by racism, fed by myths about black people and underpinned by an ideology that they were subhuman (Judd, 1996). By 1713, slavery provided substantial income to Britain when Spain granted England the right to supply not only British but all Spanish American colonies with hundreds of thousands of African slaves. Consequently, by 1772, the UK black population increased rapidly. As Dabydeen et al (2010, p viii) note:

> since the later 16th century, black men and women have had a constant presence ... as servants of the rich ... members of the London poor ... campaigners, merchants, students, writers, musicians, soldiers, sailors, broadcasters, doctors, nurses, sporting personalities and members of every imaginable occupation.

Box 3.2: Migration and links to seafaring

Most early African immigrants came to Britain as slaves, some jumping ship when here (Walvin, 1984). A few came as free seafarers; others were freed by owners as reward for years of service. London, Liverpool and Bristol became slave-trading centres, in the last two instances largely founding their economic growth upon it. Cities with docks serving international trade became home to Britain's first concentrated minority populations, including many Muslims. In these and other cases (Cardiff, Glasgow and Tyneside), they later witnessed the arrival of, eventually, thousands of seafarers from countries with significant maritime histories that provided unskilled labour (notably, Chinese and Yemenis) to work below decks in mercantile shipping (Ansari, 2004). These minorities remain today, although the decline in the late 20th century of mercantile shipping led Yemenis to migrate to other industrial centres, such as Sheffield, to the steelmaking industry. The development of the slave trade was dependent on the maintenance of Britain's imperial power – in Africa, India, the West Indies and, until 1789, the USA – but also sustained that power by providing a seemingly endless source of cheap labour.

Some migrants arrived by strange routes. For example, 200 black slaves from Dutch plantations accompanied William of Orange when he arrived in 1688 to become King of England. By 1772, there were approximately 14,000 'minority' people in Britain, mostly black, some from Asia, out of a population of eight million, in other words, less than one quarter of one percent (Fryer, 1984). The Muslims among them were either ex-slaves or traders: 'by 1725 English society was "pretty well accustomed to them"' (Ansari, 2004, p 50). The migration of Muslims, particularly from South Asia, increased with Britain's imperial reach, reflecting wider movements of indentured labour from South Asia to Britain's 'possessions'.

After the slave trade

The liberal myth is that the British slave trade was abolished in 1807, largely because of the campaigning of Wilberforce and others. The parliamentary campaign was effective in raising consciousness of the horrors of slavery, and slavery withered away by the end of the 18th century, although not formally abolished until the 1833 Act of Parliament. Black resistance and self-organisation was significant in making slavery uneconomic: slaves increasingly challenged their owners' authority and left their households. Essentially, slavery became unprofitable (James, in Fryer 1984, p 207; Eltis 2000; Eltis and Richardson, 2010). Partly in response to the vagaries of the law and to help gather support for slaves, black organisations formed and campaigned, black prisoners being supported by the wider black community. Some freed black people worked as craftspeople and on the land, women as seamstresses and nurses. Freed slaves such as Equiano (2007 [1789]) who could read and write began to agitate about the conditions under which slaves existed in the Caribbean and the Americas.

Prejudice against black people remained embedded in society. William Cuffey, son of slaves, campaigned vigorously within the Chartist movement in the early19th century. He was convicted of treason and transported to Tasmania in 1843, where he continued to campaign for workers' rights. Racism took new forms (see eg Fryer, 1984), often led by government example. The treatment of black American slaves who fought for Britain in the American War of Independence illustrates the discriminatory way in which black people – whether technically citizens or not – were treated. Black slaves who fled at the end of the war to British Canada were resettled on poor farming land in Nova Scotia, then transported back to the disease-ridden, impoverished coast of Sierra Leone – where slavery was still active – under the lure of forming the first black colony (Schama, 2005). Those who came to the 'motherland' faced a life of poverty, an experience repeated in the 20th century. Black ex-slaves were also denied the levels of relief given to white ex-soldiers.

One continuing thread throughout the history of black and minority settlement in the UK has been how racism has legitimised discriminatory social and economic treatment of the 'other' within private and public domains. Historically, this has not solely been about white racism against those of different skin colour. As the United Kingdom was formed over hundreds of years, the Scots, Irish and Welsh were incorporated into a unitary nation. Even after the Act of Union, Scots, Irish and Welsh were minorities within a white Protestant English nation state, discriminated against and subject to racist violence based on their geography, culture and, in many Scottish and Irish instances, their religion (Porter, 1989). This relationship only began to reverse with partial devolution of Scotland, Wales and Northern Ireland (Nairn, 2003) with, ironically, reports of racist attacks against English people residing in Wales and Scotland. The picture is more complex at a micro-level. For example, by 1841, 5% of the Scottish population was of Irish descent and antagonisms between Scots and Irish were frequent occurrences: this tension continues to be played out around Glasgow's football stadia.

From the 16th century, Britain nevertheless developed a reputation as a refuge from political persecution. Some minority arrivals – such as Jewish people, protestant Huguenots in the 16th century onwards or Turkish refugees in the early 19th century – were seeking asylum from political or religious persecution. This is ironic since from the early 20th century, Britain became obsessed with controlling the flow of refugees, now having one of the world's harshest immigration regimes.

The rise of the 'other'

The construction of British identity begun in English society during the 18th century required a conception of the 'other'. We have seen this operate in relation to Jewish populations and black slaves, but it became associated with other minorities seen as not sharing white, Protestant Britishness (equated to Englishness). Violent anti-popery was commonplace; Methodists were treated as 'cockshires' and Scots- and Irish-baiting 'were national sports' (Porter, 1991). European neighbours, especially the French, were also targeted. As this sense of national identity became more confidently asserted, anyone who was different or perceived as threatening to newly asserted British ideals, ambitions and way of life found themselves classified as inferior and in some cases an enemy (Judd, 1996). Britain was not alone in this (Clark, 2007), but chauvinistic suspicion of the 'other' became ingrained in national discourse, the consequences of which are still felt today. In Scotland, similarly, notwithstanding strong Scottish presence in many British colonies, successive waves of migrants – from Ireland, Jewish people, Indians, Italians, Lithuanians and, most recently, English and Polish people – have all been characterised as the 'other' to be portrayed as an economic and social threat (Maan, 2004).

Box 3.3: Early justifications for racism

By the end of the 18th century, racism began to be justified intellectually on pseudo-scientific grounds (see also Chapter 2), the first major openly racist tract being produced by Long in his 1774 *History of Jamaica* (Fryer, 1984). The notion of black and blackness had long been associated with negative meanings: mourning, death, illness, evil, sin and danger. To this portrayal were added notions of sexual depravity, being monkey-like, ugly and abnormal. It was not far from being able to declare, drawing on 'scientific' myths, that people could be graded hierarchically in terms of the colour of their skin, with black at the bottom. The established Church attested to the fact that Noah's son Ham, cursed by God for killing his brother Shem, was himself black. Intermarriage was argued against as it would corrupt the 'purity of English character'. This pseudo-scientific racism developed strongly through the late 18th and early 19th centuries, seemingly supported by the writings of Linnaeus, who provided an apparently scientific set of national characteristics, shaped by racism. The British Irish population, growing to meet the constant demand for labour to drive the Industrial Revolution, experienced a similar process. Irish were popularly portrayed as violent, drunk, fecund and stupid; the additional barrier of religion was emphasised to underline obstacles to intermarriage. The Scots and Welsh had long been regarded as inferior to the English and hostility to Catholics was overlaid on this (James, 2005). Relative toleration of local customs, cultures and habits, characteristic of British commercial engagement in India during the late 18th and early 19th centuries, became replaced by growing political hostility and condescension. India became increasingly associated with filth and disease and was blamed for cholera outbreaks (Hamlin, 2009). This generated a long association between ethnicity and health, as minority ethnic populations became portrayed as carriers of disease. Present-day examples include the links between AIDS and Africa and more localised associations between TB and recent migrants to the UK, alongside the renewed call (a feature of 1960s' debates) for all migrants to be subject to health checks before being allowed to enter the UK (Porter, 1999; see also Chapters 4 and 6).

In Ireland and African countries, their attributed subhumanity was to be used as an argument against claims for self-government. Nineteenth-century racism was not, however, confined to a handful of cranks: most British scientists and intellectuals took it for granted that only people with white skin were capable of thinking and governing, a view prevalent well into the 20th century. As one MP put it during a parliamentary debate in the 1920s, 'inferior races were unfitted for advanced British institutions such as representative democracy' (cited in Fryer, 1984, p 163). This is a view that, while rarely expressed overtly, continues to be held by some politicians; witness Tory MP Alan Clark in a House of Commons debate in the 1990s talking about African governments in terms of 'Bongo Bongo land'.

Increasingly, social and economic class intersected with 'race' and difference. Although Britain's trade had often depended on negotiating with upper-class rulers, most British migrants until the late 19th century were of lower socio-economic classes. Reflecting a trend continuing to the present, migrants were portrayed as a threat to the indigenous working class, rather than as 'workers in common'; frequently, trades unions opposed immigration. Some Indian migrants came as servants; these tended to be Muslims, some later becoming destitute. However, there was also a trickle of upper- and middle-class Indians by the mid-19th century coming to Britain to study law and medicine: many went to Scottish universities from 1850 onwards (Ansari, 2004).

As the Labour movement became more organised throughout the 19th century in economic and political spheres, ruling-class attitudes towards 'labour agitators' – as troublemakers whom it was impossible to conceive of as able to govern – were also reflected in its stance towards 'natives', a further illustration of how 'race' and class were increasingly intertwined in political discourse.[3] Black and Irish people were regarded as impecunious, undercutting English working conditions, and there was often agitation against them. As in Africa, the problems of the Irish in Britain – of poverty, ill-health and poor housing – were created by conditions imposed in their native countries by Britain, the colonising power. The Irish made a very substantial contribution – only latterly recognised – to the Industrial Revolution, building urban and transport infrastructure. The contribution of other minorities was significant, though less prominent, in part because of their much smaller numbers.

Despite formal abolition of slavery, it continued in much of the British Empire. In India, millions of slaves were transformed in 1843 into bonded labourers. Within the Empire, colonial opposition to self-government continued with the bloody suppression of the Indian Revolt (1857) and the Jamaican Uprising (1865). The potato famine drove Irish people to

Britain in the mid-19th century: 300,000 adults migrated in a decade, 100,000 moving to London alone. Many died of cholera and dysentery in the labour camps of Northern England as they built canal and railway networks, contributing strongly to the growth of political and trades union movements (Holland et al, 2009).

Within Britain, minorities largely remained hidden, although in some cases a hostile focus was constructed by the state: 'Local surveillance and harassment of gypsies became one of the tasks of local authorities as they developed, while "philanthropic" attention was aimed at the eradication of their way of life' (Cemlyn and Briskman, 2002, p 54). Minorities were, however, by now organising more formally, attracted by the writings of radical thinkers. Black radicals were attracted to men like Thomas Paine and some were an easy target for repression and, in some cases, execution. Many were internationalists (Fryer, 1984), joining trades unions and the Chartist movement in the early 19th century. However, it was the activities of their white male counterparts that remained engrained in British history. For example, (black) Mary Seacole was as active in promoting the health and welfare of soldiers as was (white) Florence Nightingale in the Crimean war (1853–56), but remained in obscurity until recently; Mary Prince was the first black slave to have a biographical narrative, but it is far less well-known than that of Equiano. It was a similar story in culture: the music of (black) Samuel Coleridge-Taylor (1875–1912), 'the English Mahler', was briefly regarded as highly as that of his famous European contemporaries, such as Grieg (1843–1907), but then written out of history.

By the end of the 19th century, political activism amongst Britain's minorities had grown significantly, linked to growing demands for national liberation. The Indian Home Rule Society and Pan-African Association were connected to continuing political agitation in their 'home' countries by those working and living within the UK and those in colonies, with prominent leaders such as Gandhi spending time in London in this period. These movements were encouraged by the growth of the Independent Labour Party and by support from prominent left-wing politicians such as Hyndman and growing European revolutionary fervour. What Fryer (1984, p 278) calls 'challenges to empire' emerged strongly in this period.

Black political activism also took more formal turns. The first black person to hold local government office in Britain became a councillor in Battersea, South London in 1906; the first 'minority' MP was Dada Naroji, of Indian origin, elected in Finsbury in 1892. By the turn of the century, new groups had begun to migrate to the UK including Chinese people, who had been drawn into trading relationships but had also worked in the merchant navy. Many more Jewish people arrived at the end of the 19th century, fleeing pogroms in Russia and Poland, mostly to London but also to Gateshead, Leeds, Hull, Glasgow and Liverpool. Racism against them was acute, stirred up by the British Brothers League, the forerunner to the National Front, and their arrival led to the first UK legislation concerned with controlling immigration, the Aliens Act 1905 (Walvin, 1984). Probably 700,000 Jewish people came to Britain at this time, most travelling across Britain to the US. More than two million people from Scandinavia, Central Europe and Russia – 60% of those migrating to and through the UK at this time – passed through Hull in the 80 years to 1914, often being transported in highly insanitary conditions and subject to virulent abuse from the local population.

The early 20th century

Migration to the UK in the 20th century can also be seen as a direct consequence of British colonisation. In the early part of the century, most black people were not activists, nor were their exploits the subject of public record. They were poor labourers, not just as 'below–decks' seafarers, but also in other labouring jobs. White workers were at this time as racist as their ruling-class equivalents. This attitude continued into the First World War, where, despite a major contribution from black soldiers, white soldiers still regarded them as inferior. The Army hierarchy promoted a view expressed in 1886 by the Adjutant General that black people, as 'lazy cowards', would undermine the British Army's power (Walvin, 1984, p 38). He seems to have overlooked the astounding courage of the Ashanti and Zulu nations, who won military victories even when faced by technologically better-equipped Western armies. After the First World War, and during the Depression of the 1930s, white workers were encouraged by racist propaganda, again often with the connivance of right-wing trades unions and racist ideologues (Fryer, 1984), to regard black labourers as an economic threat. Tensions again grew and there were 'riots' in South Tyneside, Liverpool and Cardiff, all areas where long-standing sea-based workforces had settled. In reality, these 'riots' were often protests against poor housing and working conditions, then used as an excuse by white racists – who often suffered the same poor conditions – for acts of retaliation against the 'other'.

By the early 1920s, the Pan–African Congress campaigned openly for the liberation of African nations, not reflected, however, in domestic political organisation. The League of Coloured Peoples promoted the welfare of people 'in an alien land' (that is, the UK); this was not a radical campaigning organisation, but a social club, employment and welfare agency. Other organisations developed with equally modest aims, such as the Coloured Men's Institute. In 1938, a UK branch of the Indian Workers' Association was established in Coventry with a more political intent. At a broader level, black and Asian people resident in the UK during the 1930s gained the franchise. Many were politicised by African, Caribbean and Asian leaders such as Nkrumah, Nehru, Menon, Padmore, Makonnen, Kenyatta and Nyerere, all studying in the UK and agitating for national independence during the 1930s and 1940s. What emerged was a growing class of educated black and Asian leaders who challenged the right of Britain to rule their countries of origin.

The experience of the Second World War mirrored that of the First, with some differences. Although black soldiers became officers, it was only for the duration of the war, their contribution largely overlooked in official war histories. By then, however, the notion of 'black' as 'unable to govern' was under further challenge: Labour leader Attlee commented in the early part of the war that 'we fight this war for all peoples … I look for an ever-increasing measure of self-government in Africa' (cited in Fryer, 1984, p 333). Prior to and during the war, one quarter of a million refugees from Central and Eastern Europe arrived, Jewish, Polish and other people fleeing fascism. The Jews were more likely than their 20th-century predecessors to be middle class and economically independent, and had significant impact on the local economies of cities such as Leeds, Manchester and London. Many trades unionists continued to campaign against immigration, fearing for their jobs.

By 1955, the Trades Union Congress (TUC) was condemning all racial discrimination, though with little impact on the day-to-day activities of most trades unions (see Chapter 4). Racism remained prevalent. Only during the war was the 'colour bar' lowered within industry, to be replaced when it ended. Otherwise, it existed across all sectors of life, in hotels, the armed forces and housing and labour markets. In areas such as Liverpool, where black people had settled relatively peacefully after the First World War, racism again took violent forms. By 1948, there were 8,000 black residents in Liverpool and the National Union of Seamen organised to stop them getting work. Racist riots took place with the collusion of the police and led ironically to the development of formal and informal political responses among black communities. The Constantine case, a prominent West Indian cricketer successfully suing a hotel for refusing him accommodation, showed that the law could be used to protect Black Britons' citizenship rights if the plaintiff had enough support. Gilroy's (2007) photographic history of migrants after the Second World War reflects 'glimpses of the struggle and everyday practices of Black Britons throughout the country's difficult process of becoming post-colonial' (see also *The Guardian* special supplement *Lives on Film*, 15 October 2007). For most black and Asian people, however, trying to settle in Britain was oppressive, as captured by the infamous boarding house notice – 'no Irish, no dogs, no Blacks' (Beckett, 2009).

Other sectors of the economy such as textile mills, heavy engineering, public transport and the health service were seriously short of labour at the end of the war. The huge growth in post-war immigration, stimulated by recruitment by employers and political exhortation by unlikely figures such as Enoch Powell (Minister of Health in 1953), occasioned different responses. The media talked of 'willing hands', underlining their contribution to the labour market and economic reconstruction, as the Empire Windrush arrived in 1948 (Phillips and Phillips, 1998), increasing the numbers of minorities resident in the UK. Black Britons, South Asian Britons and East Europeans who had been active in the war effort also decided to remain in Britain. Polish people formed a sizeable settlement in Scunthorpe (where there are still two Polish clubs), working in the steelworks.

Box 3.4: The Empire Windrush, an iconic moment

The Empire Windrush was a German passenger cruiser later used as a troop ship and hospital ship. The British navy seized it in 1945, changed its name and converted it to a troop carrier. In 1948, en route from Australia, it docked in Jamaica. An advertisement in the main local paper that month offered cheap transport to anyone wanting to work in the UK. When it left Jamaica it had 300 passengers below deck and 192 above. Most travelling were ex-service personnel who had fought for the British and believed they had promises of jobs. Half found work straightaway for the NHS and London Transport, but most, despite their British passports, found Britain far from welcoming. Many were initially housed in a former deep shelter in South London. Their first port of call was the labour exchange in nearby Brixton, thus contributing to the growth of the African-Caribbean population there. The post-war experiences of Black Caribbeans and the continuing dominant stance of racism is captured poignantly in *Small Island* (Levy, 2007).

At the same time, post-war governments tried to encourage immigrants to return to their countries. These included about 150,000 Polish servicemen and dependents who fought from British bases, and East European political dissidents, most of them reluctant to return to hostile, even terminal, responses from Stalinist governments. Meanwhile, tens of thousands of other migrant workers were recruited from European labour camps to fill gaps in the UK labour market.

As a result of government and private-sector recruitment, the numbers of Black Caribbean and South Asian people grew steadily. By 1958, for example, 125,000 West Indians had arrived in Britain, representing up to a tenfold increase in their population. Four thousand were recruited by London Transport alone as drivers and conductors, and thousands of nurses and ancillary health workers were recruited into the emerging NHS. About 55,000 also came from the Indian subcontinent, particularly India and, to a lesser extent, Pakistan, by 1958. These migrants had British passports and were British citizens. As their numbers grew, calls increased to stop immigration virtually before it had started (see Chapter 4). The right to British citizenship for all members of the Empire was one of the first casualties of such debates.

We now turn to developing patterns of settlement and the post-war demography of Britain's minorities. A similar tale could be told regarding migration into other Western European countries, although the picture varied because of the impact of specific factors such as colonial history, the need for reconstruction, the nature of the labour market and immigration regimes.

Post-war settlement patterns

Patterns of contemporary minority settlement within the UK were shaped initially by historical factors (such as the slave trade and the history of empire). More recently, they were shaped by local economic and industrial profiles and, at a micro-level, by cultural needs, for example, for strong communities to support religious and cultural practices, and by the racism that continues to distort local housing and labour markets (see especially Chapters 4, 5 and 9). For example, strong Caribbean settlement within Brixton in South London resulted primarily from availability of large rooming houses, where significant numbers of migrants could be housed paying, collectively, super-exploitative rents.

Large-scale post-war immigration from the Caribbean, Africa and South Asia was stimulated most of all by the need for labour. In the past 30 years, more specific regional factors have impacted. These include forced exoduses from Vietnam, Hong Kong and Uganda, and recently a rapid growth in refugees seeking asylum and in economic migration from many countries including, since 2004, Central and Eastern European EU Accession states.

Post-war migration growth was initially rapid, but was then limited by alarmist political reaction, expressed through ever-tighter immigration legislation, a trend still continuing today (see Chapter 4). The picture of immigration throughout the 1960s/70s, following the 1962 Act, is one of panic surges in immigration ahead of further controls being imposed on immigration from certain parts of the world. A chart of numbers immigrating shows peaks, for example, in 1963 and 1973, as anxieties grew amongst would-be immigrants (from South Asia and East Africa in particular) about the UK government closing previously open doors.

The major instrument for monitoring minority populations has been the decennial census. The nature of questions asked has changed over the past century, so direct comparisons are not easy to make. The 1991 census was the first to ask direct questions about ethnicity. Figures prior to that date were informed estimates, confused by definitions such as 'those born in the New Commonwealth and Pakistan' (which had withdrawn from the Commonwealth), thus including many white people returning to the UK after colonial independence. The 2011 census figures will be available in 2013; meanwhile 2009 intercensal estimates are the best available, although not for small areas.

Table 3.1 shows approximate data on the numbers of individual minority ethnic groups in the UK in 1951 and 1961 drawn from census and Labour Force Survey data and immigration statistics. Other estimates put both total figures at about 30% higher and, in 1961, the number of total 'aliens' (ie including all people of non-British origin, regardless of being citizens or not) at 415,700.

Table 3.1: *Numbers of minorities in the UK in 1951 and 1961, respectively*

	1951	1961
Indians	30,800	81,400
Pakistanis	5,000	24,900
'West Indians'	15,300	171,800
'Far East'	12,000	29,600
West Africans	5,600	19,800
Total 'coloured'	74,500	336,600

Several points are worth noting. The largest single group was 'West Indian' (incorporating many of what were to become independent states), whose growth in this decade was over 1,000%. Those of Indian origin increased by just under 200%, whereas those of Pakistani origin (including those who later became Bangladeshis) increased by 400%. The categories of Far Eastern and West African origin grouped together several different countries, many of them independent by 1961. In 18 months around the 1961 census, the rate of immigration accelerated markedly because of impending restrictions. In some areas, there were a few people of what is now designated as 'mixed race' or 'mixed heritage' (including, in Cardiff, the singer Shirley Bassey), but this group (as with White Irish) was not separately categorised until 2001. The picture of nationality, settlement and ethnicity itself had become increasingly complex, and hidden behind this picture was another one of micro-change within groupings. For example, Britain's Chinese population was moving away from its connections with seafaring into, first, laundry work, and then, from the 1960s, food provision (Craig et al, 2009b).

Throughout the 1960s, black faces became more common in major conurbations, workplaces and in certain housing areas, where minorities continued to be 'ghettoised' because of racism in the housing market. Individual achievements were occasionally celebrated in the media as slightly exotic events, as happened with Norwell Gumbs, the first black police officer (1968) and the first black traffic wardens (1966). The arrival of black players in popular sports such as football did not prevent them being the subject of racist abuse (including within the Football Association itself, one official of which felt that it would be difficult for black players to establish themselves in the UK as 'they don't like to play in the cold and wet' [Turner, 2008, p 212]). South Africa's refusal to accept a 'mixed race' player, Basil D'Oliveira, in the 1968 English cricket touring party led to the tour's cancellation, more, it seems, because of hurt national pride than a principled anti-racist stance. Popular hostile or at best curious attitudes to immigrants were captured by contemporary accounts (Patterson, 1965).

By 1971, the total 'non-white' population (note again the racialised formulation) in Britain was 1.4 million, the largest single group being from the Caribbean. The size of the white New Commonwealth population was probably underestimated (white immigrants generally receiving light-touch bureaucratic treatment). This suggests the rate of growth of the BME population had been greater than officially noted. Minorities in Britain were already not the same thing as immigrants: more than one third of that 1.4 million had been born and grown up in Britain. That proportion increased to 40% by 1976, by which time the 'non-white' population was about 1.85 million, 3.4% of the UK population. Thus, while immigration, despite legislative attempts to control it, continued to grow numerically, a significant element of minority growth now resulted from natural growth in the settled population, with many people classified as 'ethnic minorities' being born in the UK and being British citizens. It is now appreciated, for example, that young people born and brought up in the UK have different experiences and expectations from their parents, who may still perceive themselves as 'immigrants' (Ali, 2003). This creates potential distinctions within ethnic groupings between those born in the UK and those not. Chapter 2 explores the general theoretical implications of this, while the following chapters look at its meaning for policy and practice.

The BME population continued to be concentrated within certain districts in a few urban centres. For example, the first Indian settlers only arrived in York, a medium-sized northern city, in the late 1970s (Craig et al, 2009b). This reflected a much longer-established pattern, whereby migration to places outside the major urban and seafaring centres as well as to Scotland, Northern Ireland and Wales lagged well behind that in major English cities (for Wales, see Llwyd, 2004; Williams, 2005; for Scotland, see Maan, 2004). For rural dwellers, 'immigrants' have largely remained an exotic, unwelcome phenomenon. One further education lecturer recalled settling in Lincoln in the 1960s where he suffered racist abuse: when visiting a local school to talk about India, he was asked 'Mister, India, is that in Africa?' (Henderson and Kaur, 1999).

The 1991 census

The 1991 census suggested that the minority population was about 3 million, 5.5% of the total UK population. During the 1980s/90s, the overall picture of minority settlement was shaped by various factors – continuing immigration, despite frequent legislation designed to slow or even halt it (see Chapter 4), but also natural growth and by specific events (such as the expulsion by Idi Amin of 31,000 'Ugandan Asians' mainly of Indian Gujarati descent). These place-specific phenomena continued into

Table 3.2: Population of Great Britain by ethnic group, 1981 and 1991

Ethnic group	1981 (N)	Mean for 1989–91 (N)	Percent change
White	51,000	51,808	1
Minority ethnic groups (all)	**2,092**	**2,677**	**28**
West Indian	528	455	−14
African	80	150	88
Indian	727	792	9
Pakistani	284	485	71
Bangladeshi	52	127	144
Chinese	92	137	49
Arab	53	67	26
Mixed	217	309	42
Other	60	154	157
Not stated	608	495	113

Source: Population Trends, 67:1 and Labour Force Surveys 1990 and 1991, Series LFS No 9 (London: HMSO), Table 6.29.

the 1990s with the Vietnamese boat people, Hong Kong residents opting to exit from what had become a Chinese province, and Bosnians and Kosovars fleeing genocide in Yugoslavia. These were, however, relatively small numbers in the context of overall refugee flows, which accelerated during the 1990s. The rate of growth of different minority groups was, however, markedly different. Those of Bangladeshi origin now appeared as a separate category following its independence, but the vague category of 'Arab' remained.

Notable trends included the continuing decline in the 'West Indian' population, which had been overtaken by those of Indian origin as the single largest non-white minority; the relatively rapid growth of Pakistani, Bangladeshi and African groupings; and the overall rapid growth of minority populations as a whole. Natural growth differed between distinct minorities, with Bangladeshis and Pakistanis having – despite higher infant mortality rates – substantially higher fertility rates than other groups. They also had substantially lower mortality rates, reflecting the younger age profile of later-arriving minorities (see Chapter 6; see also Ahmad, 1994). Mortality rates moved towards the norm, but although 'West Indian' rates doubled between 1981 and 1991, they were still barely one third of that of white populations by 1991. Fertility and mortality rates illustrate the changing age profile of differing minority populations. The ageing Caribbean population, some of whom were beginning to migrate back to the Caribbean saw its fertility rate drop from 36 to 21% between 1981 and 1991 (and its mortality rate increase from 2.1 to 4.1%). The fertility and mortality rates of the UK Chinese population remained roughly steady over this period at around 80% and 3%, respectively.

In the 1970s/80s, there was substantial out-migration, particularly of UK-born white residents; net migration was of those leaving the UK until 1984. From the 1950s/60s, as with the Yemenis, the UK Chinese population reinvented itself, moving into fast-food production, becoming the most dispersed minority within the UK, finally present in every local authority including in the most remote areas. Since 1991, despite reservations about the focus of the 'ethnic' question (changed again in 2001 and 2011), it has been possible to map differential patterns of settlement in a fairly precise way to show, for example, differing regional concentrations of minorities or the relationship between ethnicity and religion (eg Dorling, 1995). The 1991 census required people to identify themselves as belonging to one of the groups listed in *Table 3.3*.

The 10 categories were those most customarily used for policy purposes; but the longer list represents the various categories used by respondents, and grouped in census outputs. Both the 'West Indies' and 'Caribbean' terms were in use amongst the population and the 'Arab' population had

Table 3.3: *Ethnic categories, 1991*

Fourfold classification	Tenfold classification	full listing
White	White	White
		Irish
		Greek/Greek Cypriot
		Turkish/Turkish Cypriot
		Mixed White
Black	Black Caribbean	Black Caribbean
		Caribbean Island
		West Indies
		Guyana
	Black African	Black African
		Africa – South of Sahara
	Black Other	Black Other
		Black British
		Black – Mixed Black/Other
(South) Asian	Indian	Indian
	Pakistani	Pakistani
	Bangladeshi	Bangladeshi
Chinese and others	Chinese	Chinese
	Other Asian	East African Asian
		Indo-Caribbean
		Black – Indian Subcontinent
		North Africa/Arab/Iranian
		Mixed Asian/White
		British Ethnic Minority (Other)
		British (no indication)
		Other Mixed Black/White
		Other Mixed Asian/White
		Other Mixed – Other

been slightly disaggregated to identify those from Iran (early refugees). However, to take another ethnic category, Polish (to become extremely important by 2011), there was no obvious overarching category in which such people could be located. This and other issues were picked up in the 2001 census, which used the categories in ***Table 3.4***, allowing people to specify a particular ethnic origin in their own words. The 1991 census outputs in relation to ethnicity have been analysed in detail (CRER, 1992; ONS, 1993; Peach, 1996). Between the 1991 and 2001 censuses, the Fourth

Table 3.4: *Ethnic categories, 2001*

White	British
	Irish
	Any other white background (please write in)
Mixed	White and Black Caribbean
	White and Black African
	White and Asian
	Any other mixed background (please write in)
Asian or Asian British	Indian
	Pakistani
	Bangladeshi
	Any other Asian background (please write in)
Black or Black British	Caribbean
	African
	Any other black background (please write in)
Chinese or other ethnic group	Chinese
	Any other, please write in

National Survey of Ethnic Minorities (Modood et al, 1997) provided both quantitative and qualitative profiles of Britain's minority populations.

From 2001 to the present

The 2001 census outputs, although not directly comparable with those of 1991, enable us to observe important trends. The Black Caribbean population had reversed the previous decade's decline, growing slightly, but was being caught up by Black Africans; both were behind Pakistani and the largest minority, those of Indian origin. The Chinese population had almost doubled, in part because of large numbers of economic refugees leaving Hong Kong as well as political refugees from mainland China. The total White population was now 92% of the total UK population, this including White Irish and White Other, with White Irish, at 1.2% of the total population, revealed as one of the largest single minority populations. This group included a substantial number of Gypsies/Travellers, although some of these will have categorised themselves in other ways. Because of their nomadic life and continuing persecution, they remain an 'invisibilised' group even within the UK's minorities, as are the Roma, arriving since the early 1990s (Mayall, 1995; Clark, 2006). The 'pathologising of gypsies and denial or disregard of their minority ethnic and cultural status persist' (Cemlyn and Briskman, 2002, p 54). The 'Mixed' category had now grown to more than 1.2%, the fastest-growing category in the population, and this has important policy implications, possibly explaining part of the decline in those identified as of African-Caribbean origin. Overall, the minority ethnic population had grown by 53% between 1991 and 2001, a rise from 3 million to 4.6 million, while the UK population grew by 4% (about 2.2 million); 73% of this growth was due to BME groups. Kyambi (2005) has derived a visual mapping of patterns of settlement and origins of major minority groups and much of the census output has been available online in relation to key aspects of ethnic identity.

Figure 3.1 gives an overall picture of the growth of differing minority populations over the past 50 or so years.

Figure 3.1: *Growth of minority ethnic populations in Britain, 1951–2001*

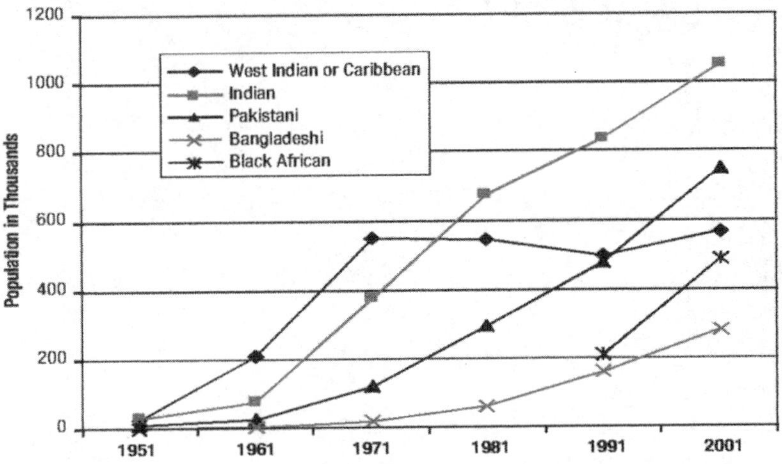

Source: Data for 1951–91 reproduced from Peach (1996); data for 2001 from 2001 Census Key Statistics Table 6.

Britain's minority population was still far from evenly distributed across the country. Approximately 45% of all minorities lived in London (representing 29% of the total London population), which therefore housed the largest concentrations of all major minority groups except for the Pakistani population, concentrated more highly in Bradford (where minorities comprised 22% of the population as a whole) and the North-West. Thus, 78% of all Black Africans and 61% of all Black Caribbeans lived in London. Roughly 13% of all minorities lived in the West Midlands, particularly in Birmingham (with a minority population of 39%) and the Black Country, with no other region having 10% of its population coming from minorities (White, 2002). In Scotland and Wales, minority populations were about 3% and 2%, respectively, with less than 1% in Northern Ireland. In these areas, virtually no minorities lived outside major conurbations. In Northern Ireland, indeed, there has been little policy concern with ethnic minorities until recently, a consequence of the focus on religious divides and sectarianism. There was net emigration from Northern Ireland until 2003 (much later than on the British mainland), but, as on the mainland, the arrival of refugees and migrant workers, and natural growth, has led to a relatively rapid increase in the BME population to, now, about 5% (McGarry et al, 2008).

Table 3.5: *Population of the UK by ethnic group, 2001*

Total population	Numbers	Percentage	Percent of non-white population
White	54,153,898	92.1	
Mixed	677,177	1.2	14.6
Indian	1,053,411	1.8	22.7
Pakistani	747,285	1.3	16.1
Bangladeshi	283,063	0.5	6.1
Other Asian	247,664	0.4	5.3
Black Caribbean	565,876	1.0	12.2
Black African	485,277	0.8	10.5
Black Other	97,585	0.2	2.1
Chinese	247,403	0.4	5.3
Other	230,615	0.4	5.0
All minority ethnic populations	4,635,296	7.9	100.0
All population	58,789,194	100.0	

Some large cities, such as Stoke-on-Trent and Hull, also had very small minority populations (because of the nature of the local labour market. but also an absence of chain migration) until fairly recently. Then, in the latter case, large-scale government dispersal of refugees, combined with substantial migration from Central and Eastern European countries joining the EU in 2004 to work in agricultural and related work close to the city, led to a rapid increase. In most rural areas, minority populations remained small (shire counties and smaller towns typically having minority populations of less than 2%). However, they grew more rapidly than the UK average, the largest single group usually being those of Chinese origin, spread more evenly across the whole of the UK than any other minority. An analysis of the pattern of settlement of Britain's minorities by *The Independent* newspaper in 2006 claimed that the least ethnically diverse community was Easington, in County Durham, where the chances of bumping into someone from a different ethnic group were computed to be just 2%. In rural Lincolnshire, not usually associated with ethnic diversity, one in four births at a district hospital was said to be to ethnic minority (Central and Eastern European) parents.

Contrasts between the settlement of longer-established minorities and more recent migrants are highlighted later. Notable is the complementary nature of settlement patterns (although whether settlement for migrant workers is permanent or temporary remains open). Migrant workers have largely gravitated – because of employment opportunities – to areas with historically small BME communities. This has shifted racist discourse – much of it previously located in an urban context – to more rural contexts (NYBSB, 2006; Athwal et al, 2010). Additionally, because recent migrants were working in rural or remote areas, levels of exploitation in the labour market appear to have increased substantially (Wilkinson et al, 2009).

There were also marked variations between urban populations. In London in 2001, the Boroughs of Brent and Newham had 'minority' populations of 55% and 61%, respectively, whereas the Boroughs of Havering and Bromley's minority shares were 5% and 8%. London boroughs tended frequently to be associated with particular ethnic minorities, with 'Bangladeshis' concentrated in Tower Hamlets, 'Indians' in Ealing, 'Turkish' in Haringey and 'Black Africans' in Lambeth and Southwark. The same differentiation occurring at micro-levels led the Chair of the Commission for Racial Equality to suggest that Britain was 'sleepwalking into segregation' (Phillips, 2005), a claim forensically challenged by statistical analyses (McCulloch, 2007; Finney and Simpson, 2009). As Smith (1989, p 37) had earlier observed, in any case, why should minorities pursue segregation 'in the more run-down segments of the housing stock, rather than in areas where they could secure the symbolic and economic benefits associated with suburban life'.

Analysis of migrant worker populations (Adamson et al, 2008) showed that the mix of national origins varied considerably between localities, even within regions, but it will be some time before we know whether this migrant worker population settles. Local advice workers have noted a shift in the nature of enquiries being made by migrant workers away from issues of workplace exploitation to questions about family benefits and tax. Finney and Simpson's analysis also reminds us that, where spatial segregation has occurred, it was often the consequence of racism in the labour and housing markets, limiting choices open to less well-off minority groups.

More than one third of all Pakistani and Bangladeshi owner-occupiers and renters were living in housing without one or more basic amenities (Nazroo, 1997a) with many South Asian people only able to access owner-occupation, even in the worst housing, through collective purchases. It also challenged myths about minorities – that Britain was becoming a country of ghettoes, that minorities wanted to live in segregated neighbourhoods, and that the growth of minority clusters is caused by 'white flight'.

While it is true that Britain's minorities continue in the 21st century to remain concentrated in the most deprived areas, this is not equivalent to suggesting that they are segregated and, in particular, self-segregated. Overall, as Owen (2006) observes, as well as being concentrated to some degree, Britain's minority population is youthful (with the proportion of Bangladeshis, Pakistanis and Black Africans under 16 each about twice that of the UK white population), remain largely economically disadvantaged (Platt, 2007b) and continue to grow relatively rapidly. One positive aspect of ethnic concentration is that it allows for the development of ethnically based resources, including faith-based organisations. This is clearly illustrated by the grouping of Jewish establishments in the (relatively affluent) northern wards of Leeds, and of Muslim organisations in its deprived southern wards.

The 2011 census results will not emerge until after this book is published; changes to questions about ethnicity and national identity will hopefully increase our understanding of diversity, focusing on issues of national identity, ethnic group, religion and place of birth. Different questions are being asked in different parts of the UK with questions probing national identity not asked in Northern Ireland. Recent discussions initiated by the Coalition government question whether the census needs to be so detailed or is needed at all, suggesting that data could be collected from other agencies. Given the problems faced by agencies in recording and collecting data on ethnic density (and the unwillingness of most private-sector agencies to do so), proposed changes could be a backward step in our understanding of diversity. They would make it more difficult to challenge continuing myths about migrants and Britain's settled BME population; for example, a 2002 MORI poll asked people what the proportion of 'immigrants' was. The general population believed the answer to be 23%; the real figure then was about 6%, including those born in Britain.

Current trends and patterns of migration during the early part of this century show increasing numbers of countries from which migrants have come. This is a result of increased levels of political asylum-seeking from countries with limited connection with Britain – such as Somalia, Afghanistan and the Congo – and economic migration from newly acceding countries of the European Union in 2004 and 2007. This leads many to assume that the size and diversity of minorities has increased substantially since 2001. In some areas, commentators now refer to super-diversity (Fanshawe and Sriskandarajah, 2010) or to the extraordinary mix of ethnic origins to be found even in areas with previously small minority populations. As a special report in *The Guardian* (18 October 2003) put it, reflecting on the lives of children from virtually every country in the world now resident in the UK, 'Born everywhere, raised in Britain'. A detailed study of York, not known for ethnic diversity, identified 92 different ethnic/national origins speaking at least 79 different languages (Craig et al, 2009b). ONS intercensal estimates showed the White British population in 2006 to be about 84.2% of the total population. Larger minority groups included Indian (2.0%), Pakistani (1.5%), Black African (1.3%) and Black Caribbean (1.1%), some now large enough for detailed accounts of their own history and pattern of settlement to be published (for Muslims, see Ansari, 2004; for the UK Chinese, see Chan et al, 2003). Fanshawe and Sriskandarajah (2010, p 5) suggested that 'Britain is not only more diverse than ever before but that diversity itself is growing more diverse. Today, identities are more complex and fluid than they used to be.' Data on BME groups do not reflect much of the migration linked to refugees seeking asylum (most of whom were refused and many of whom disappeared from official data), nor the 600,000–800,000 irregular workers currently residing in the UK. An 'experimental' release of data by the ONS suggests that the 'non-white' British population of England and Wales may be 9.1 million – or about 17% (*The Guardian*, 19 May 2011, p 8).

The maps in *Figures 3.2* and *3.3* indicate this diversity and its distribution across the UK. One insight that has emerged has been the extent to which 'new' migrants have used faith-based groups as an anchor as they negotiate new lives for themselves (see Chapter 2). This contrasts with the experience of immigrants of the 1950s and 1960s, who gravitated more towards trades unions (despite initial hostility from the unions) and the Labour Party (Wills et al, 2010). The relationship between ethnicity and religion is a complex one as was already clear from the 2001 census (*Table 3.6*), showing that we cannot simply read across from a person's ethnic group to make assumptions about their religious orientation, or vice versa. London alone hosts Muslims from over 50 ethnic backgrounds.

One issue remaining constant across the past 600 years has been the continuing persecution, discrimination and racism against the Gypsy/Roma/Traveller population, and their consequent high levels of deprivation, often obscured in official statistics, but now finally recognised in public accounts (Neale et al, 2009; Hills, 2010). Roma fled persecution in mainland Europe only to experience it in Britain (Craig, 2011).

Figure 3.2: *All ethnic minorities, 2001 census*

Figure 3.3: *Proportion of migrant workers per 1,000 of population*

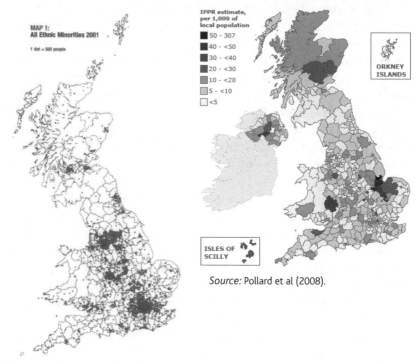

Source: Pollard et al (2008).

Source: Lupton and Power (2004).

Table 3.6: *Ethnic group by religion (extracts, %)*

	Christian	Hindu	Jewish	Muslim
White	76	0.02	0.53	0.38
Other White	63	0.09	2.39	8.61
Mixed	52	0.87	0.47	9.72
Other Mixed	48	1.22	1.09	14.10
Asian or Asian British	4	23.46	0.08	50.10
Indian	5	45.00	0.06	12.70
Black or Black British	71	0.26	0.08	9.33
Chinese or Other	27	0.69	0.54	12.80

Source: ONS (2001)

The history and patterns of UK minority settlement are, as this account shows, complex and changing and ones that, to some degree at least, are specific to the UK (although similar factors shaped migration to and from other European countries). Much took place in the context of overt or covert racism and hostility, well-captured in the title of Winder's (2004) detailed account, *Bloody Foreigners*.

Summary

The numbers, types and origins of migrants were determined by Britain's historical links and its international and national political and policy frameworks, but, increasingly, have been shaped by wider and more contemporary economic and political factors (IPPR, 2007). This has led to a constantly changing pattern of settlement in which categories of ethnic minority, majority, immigrant and settler have also been fluid, challenging our ideas about a unitary, coherent British identity.

• Differing factors were significant until the late 17th century, including invasion and war, political persecution, and economic migration. As immigration developed, it became associated with the concept of the 'other', generating prejudice, racism and discrimination.
• The main cause of BME immigration was the slave trade until the mid-19th century, by which time substantial immigration had occurred from Ireland.
• Largely temporary immigration from British colonial territories was an increasingly important factor from the late 19th century onwards and into the 20th century. Many of these migrants came for education and to learn political skills before returning home to lead political struggles for independence. Immigration also resulted from increasing trade with other countries.
• The most significant flow of migrants occurred after the Second World War, stimulated by the settlement of refugees and post-war reconstruction. This was almost immediately limited by increasingly legislative restrictions.
• In the late 20th century, immigration reflected both family reunion and also the impact of war and political upheaval, leading to substantial flows of refugees, many of them seeking asylum.
• Throughout the whole of the second half of the 20th century, an increasing driver for the growth of the UK minority population was natural growth among the settled BME population.

- In the early part of the 21st century, the most significant migrant flow to the UK was of economic migrants from new EU member states. Many of these migrants are unlikely to settle permanently.

Britain's population is now characterised as being 'super-diverse' with settled minorities living in every UK local authority area. This population varies from one area to another in terms of the mix of settled BME populations, asylum-seekers and refugees, migrant workers, and new migrant communities, with varying – but increasingly complex – implications for policy. Ideas of what ethnicity is and the meaning of diversity are changing, but these changes have yet to be grasped effectively by most public and private agencies. Previous ways of classifying and debating the issue are no longer relevant and require increasingly sophisticated responses (see Chapter 2).

Questions for discussion

- Name 10 prominent black or Asian figures from UK history prior to the 20th century.
- What were the key factors shaping migration to Britain in the 1950s and 1960s? Would the picture have been different in France and Germany and, if so, why?
- Why do some cities or areas have large minority ethnic populations, while others have relatively small ones (give some examples)?
- In what ways was the 2001 census better – or worse – than previous ones in helping us understand changes in the UK minority population? Does the 2011 census improve on this?

Electronic resources

- The main source of data for understanding the pattern of settlement of minorities across the UK is the website of the Office for National Statistics (www.statistics.gov.uk/hub/). The link to population provides data relating, for example, to population change, estimates, migration, fertility rates, regional populations or populations by individual local authorities.
- Most local authorities should have mapped their own minority populations as part of wider mappings of poverty and disadvantage. The hypothetical website for Anytown Council is available at: www.anytown.gov.uk
- Data about migrant workers can be obtained either from the Department for Work and Pensions' website (www.dwp.gov.uk/asd/statistics.asp – for National Insurance Numbers data, mapped by place of residence), or through individual local authorities, which had access to the Workers Registration Scheme data (which mapped migrant workers by place of work, type of work etc till 2010). The DWP website is quite difficult to navigate.

Notes

[1] In this chapter, we use black and minority ethnic (BME) groups as a generic term to describe those who are perceived as distinct from the majority white host population by virtue of being a numerical minority with a history of immigrant origin and/or different cultural, religious and linguistic heritages, although its relevance is questioned in present-day debates (see Chapters 2 and 4). 'Minority ethnic' and 'ethnic minority' are here regarded as interchangeable terms.

[2] We acknowledge that there is a debate about the use of BC and AD to denote temporal periods; unfortunately there is no universal agreement about an alternative.

[3] The relationship between 'race' and class, despite the work of the eponymous journal, remains under-researched and theorised (Fenton, 2003) and is perhaps key to understanding present-day ethnic diversity (see Chapter 2).

Policy, politics and practice: a historical review and its relevance to current debates

Ronny Flynn and Gary Craig

Overview

- This chapter links the theme of immigration to the specific contributions made by black and minority ethnic (BME) people to UK employment and economic growth.
- It highlights the tension between the search for migrant labour and the subsequent treatment of those recruited. The chapter provides a link with ideas on immigration and migration raised in Chapters 2 and 3.
- The chapter also examines domestic policies employed to 'manage' immigration and 'race' relations, and their underlying contradictions and effects. The contradictions between restrictive immigration legislation and legislation aimed at tackling disadvantage have been a feature of government policy since the 1950s.
- The move from an 'assimilation' policy through to multiculturalism and now back to a form of assimilation, in the guise of community cohesion, suggests that policy responses have come full circle, finding new expression in a different political and demographic context.

Key concepts

anti-racism, assimilation, community cohesion, immigration policy, multiculturalism

Introduction

Migrants have come to the UK since Roman times (see Chapter 3). Their numbers, however, were relatively small until the end of the Second World War. Since then, Britain has experienced increasing levels of immigration, driven by the need for economic reconstruction and rapidly expanding public services. Levels accelerated during the 1960s but were then reduced by restrictive immigration policy and a slowdown in economic growth. Migrants have become more diverse, coming initially from former British colonies, but increasingly from countries with little historical or political connection with the UK. By the beginning of the 21st century, a wide range of geographical, cultural, political and religious backgrounds was represented, with some cities hosting people from more than 100 ethnic or national origins. Diversity is now giving way to the concept of 'super-diversity' (Fanshawe and Sriskandarajah, 2010).

By the 1980s, a substantial proportion of the UK minority ethnic population was UK-born and, by the year 2010, it was over 50% (see Chapter 2). While political concern, fuelled by media panic and right-wing agitation, has led to restrictions on immigration, governments have also sought to manage multiculturalism through policy initiatives known as 'race' relations, community relations and, now, community cohesion. Consequently, restricted immigration practices exist alongside a stated policy (and legislative) commitment to tackle discrimination and racism.

Invited migrant labour and racism

During the first half of the 20th century, white Jewish, Polish and Irish immigrants and refugees were important sources of semi- and unskilled labour to the UK in times of shortage. These groups experienced racism, hostility and scapegoating: 'Jewish refugees were simultaneously accused of taking British workers' jobs and of living on welfare, in the same racist – and self-contradictory – mythology which opponents of immigration continue to employ against migrant workers today' (Brown, 1995).

The need for labour was soon followed by restrictions on immigration: a common trend in understanding immigration policies from the 20th century. The Aliens Acts of 1905 and 1919 restricted the employment of 'alien' workers in Britain, forming the basis of all immigration acts until 1971 (see Chapter 3). The 1905 Act established a new system of immigration control and enabled entry to be refused if people could not support themselves. If migrants became homeless, lived in overcrowded conditions or needed poverty relief within 12 months of entry, they were deported (Williams, 1996). The 1919 Act strengthened the provisions of previous legislation, being introduced in a climate of intense nationalist, anti-Semite and anti-German feeling created by the First World War. Trades unions and a cross-section of parliamentary opinion supported both Acts (Brown, 1995).

Before and during the Second World War, Irish people filled labour shortages. Afterwards, Britain looked towards their former colonies and Commonwealth members to boost the workforce. The emphasis was on rebuilding Britain and securing economic growth:

> In the early 1960s government ministers, as well as private employers, started to recruit directly in the West Indies. These included Enoch Powell, who actively encouraged the migration of medical staff from India and the West Indies during his time as Minister for Health. The London Transport executive made an agreement with the Barbadian Immigration Liaison Service. Other employers, such as the British Hotel and Restaurant Association, made similar agreements. (Brown, 1995)

Nurses, like other employees, were actively recruited to Britain; once here, they were soon made to feel inferior as familiar practices outlined in previous chapters re-emerged (Levy, 2007; Brown, 2006). They were, for example, encouraged to take the State Enrolled Nurse (SEN) qualification rather than the more prestigious State Registered Nurse (SRN) one, the latter a passport to increased pay and promotion (Doyal et al, 1981, quoted in Mama, 1984, p 27). Workers came from Pakistan to the jute mills of Dundee and were recruited from India to London and northern England to work in industries such as textiles and steel:

> Indian and Pakistani men worked the unpopular night shifts, while the predominately female (white) workforce worked during the day. The result was a racially segregated workforce. In many mills in West Yorkshire 50–80 per cent of workers were South Asian. (Moving Here, no date)

Not surprisingly, many migrants felt badly misled. They found qualifications not recognised by British employers or trades unions. Indeed, unions were seen to be in league with managers to restrict opportunities for migrants (Hero, 1991), who, by the late 1970s, were beginning to protest against their exclusion from better-paid and more comfortable jobs held by white workers, as demonstrated by the Grunwick dispute (Beckett, 2009). During much of the 1960s and 1970s, however, minority ethnic people worked for less pay than their white counterparts, often finding themselves in jobs for which they were overqualified (Blakemore, 1990).[1] Even the 'elite' professionals were not equal if they were from a minority group – doctors often had to work in poor conditions, practising less popular specialties (such as psychiatry), or in locations unpopular with other (white) doctors, such as inner-city or remote areas like the Welsh valleys (Pati, 2003). In 1958, the first 'modern' British 'race riots' occurred in Nottingham and Notting Hill, both initiated by white people, but blamed on black migrants. This blaming of BME people for the racism they experience has been a persistent response. Police generally did not intervene and evidence has emerged of the 'virulently racist attitudes of the police towards blacks' (Muir, 2005). Copycat riots occurred in and outside of London and these tensions were beginning to influence policy (Kynaston, 2008). The initial belief in assimilation came to seem naive and increasingly unsustainable (see later). Policy attention switched to the numbers of minority ethnic people living in the UK; the volume of migration was perceived to be the cause of tensions between the majority population and recently arrived migrants. Here lie the origins of the 'numbers game', which now dominates UK policy on 'race'.

Calls for immigration control grew throughout the 1950s and 1960s despite assertions that it was not a 'black' problem but a 'white' problem (Rex, 1969). Racism was seen by anti-racist campaigners to be institutionalised, legitimised and nationalised, sowing the seeds for later critiques challenging the state's engagement with ethnic diversity. Initially, the Labour Party adopted a more liberal view to diversity, but competed with the Conservative Party to 'be tough' on immigration once in government (Beckett, 2009). The Labour Party, however, remains the only party to introduce major legislation to tackle discrimination and disadvantage faced by minority ethnic populations (in a series of five Acts in 1965, 1968, 1976, 2001 and 2010). Nonetheless, immigration control also became a feature of successive government policy, as part of the struggle to manage a multicultural UK, interwoven with legislation to tackle racism and discrimination (Bhavnani et al, 2005). The first modern immigration Act appeared in 1962.

This far and no further: no longer welcome

> ... a centuries-old tradition of free entry to the UK ended in 1962. (Hansen, 1999, p 816)

The Commonwealth Immigrants Act (1962) was introduced by a Conservative government and:

was the first legislation to introduce state regulation of Commonwealth immigration and ... the first ever entry restrictions on British Commonwealth citizens, by making primary immigration dependent upon the possession of a work voucher. Given that the intended targets of the Act were all black or Asian ... the 1962 Act also marks the first of a series of racially discriminatory pieces of legislation which have combined to lay the basis for the notoriously racist immigration laws for which Britain is so famous today. The 1962 Act enshrined in law for the first time the ... notion that immigration equals black immigration, a notion upon which all successive immigration legislation has been built. (Brown, 1995)

Under the Act, employment vouchers were issued to Commonwealth immigrants in three categories: those who had jobs to come to (Category A); those who had skills and qualifications 'likely to be useful in this country' (Category B); and unskilled workers (Category C), a category that disappeared by 1964. A Commonwealth Immigrants Advisory Council (CIAC) was set up to advise the Home Secretary on immigrant welfare and integration, which Sivanandan writes was 'as if to compensate for the discrimination now institutionalised' (1982, p 108). The Labour Party, hostile to the Act while in opposition, not only kept, but also strengthened, it in government. The second category of 'useful' skills and qualifications was limited to doctors, dentists, nurses, teachers and graduates in science and technology, firmly linking Commonwealth immigration to the requirements of the British economy. The increase in skilled workers that followed effectively drained Commonwealth countries of skilled and professional personnel (Sivanandan, 1982), creating future problems. Many health professionals recruited in the 1960s have now retired from employment, prompting a panic about shortages in the NHS (Batty, 2003; Pati, 2003), particularly since they worked in areas of high deprivation such as the South Wales valleys.

Before the end of the 1960s, the 1962 Immigration Act was followed by several others. These Acts changed the nature of immigration and the relationship of BME people to employment, the state and other citizens. The 1968 Act specifically aimed to stop immigration of Asian people with British passports, driven out of Kenya by Africanisation policies. It was passed rapidly by a Labour government largely responding to public pressure, highlighting the racism, hypocrisy and U-turns that were common during the 1960s' and 1970s' political responses to 'race'. The 1968 Act meant that:

> A parliamentary Labour party that had claimed a profound commitment to the Commonwealth ideal of multi-racialism ... effectively stripped British citizens, whose entry was controversial only because of their skin colour, of one of citizenship's basic rights. A Labour party that had passed a series of liberal measures ... – on hanging, divorce and abortion, and homosexuality – passed legislation that even its supporters admitted to be illiberal and 'racialist'. (Hansen, 1999, p 833)

As a consequence, 'some 200,000 individuals holding only British citizenship were abandoned, effectively stateless, in Africa or India, and some of these individuals are still waiting to enter the United Kingdom today' (Hansen, 1999, p 810). It was only in 2002, after 30 years of campaigns, that the government amended the Immigration, Nationality and Asylum Bill to give East African Asians, stateless since 1968, the right to live in the UK.

Against the backdrop of restrictive immigration legislation, on 8 November 1965, the Labour government passed the first 'race' relations legislation. The 1965 Act forbade racial discrimination in public places such as shops and restaurants. Private boarding houses, employment and social housing were not covered and overt discrimination continued to operate, but it demonstrated recognition of the inherent and institutional racism in the UK. The Race Relations Act 1968 strengthened the 1965 Act by making it illegal to refuse housing, employment or public services to someone on the grounds of colour, 'race' or ethnic or national origins. It also created the Community Relations Commission, aiming to promote harmonious community relations (see later). Both pieces of legislation, however, made discrimination a civil rather than a criminal offence, and placed the burden of proof on the prosecution to demonstrate intent.

As already mentioned, the Race Relations Bill (1968) was on its journey through parliament at the same time as the Commonwealth Immigration Act. *Table 4.1* illustrates this pattern of developing 'race' and community relations policies in tandem with restrictive immigration legislation.

The tensions are evident, and the state response to the welfare needs of minority ethnic communities remained ambivalent throughout the 1960s and 1970s (Craig, 2007). There has been increasingly restrictive access to state welfare alongside specific funding to local authorities, for example, through section 11 of the Local Government Act 1966 and urban aid programmes, to assist 'integration' of minority communities. The 'twin-track' state response, aimed at improving integration while restricting immigration, had implications for BME populations (Solomos, 2003). Divided families were one consequence; men who had settled in the UK during the 1950s and 1960s found it increasingly difficult to bring family members over to join them (discussed later). Even formal citizens with a British passport and voting rights did not enjoy equality of substantive citizenship and access to the array of state-funded social welfare. Expectations were that minority ethnic communities should prove their deservingness, literally and symbolically (Ahmad and Husband, 1993).

Table 4.1: *Key immigration and 'race' relations legislation in the UK since 1962*

Immigration legislation	'Race' relations legislation
1962 – Commonwealth Immigrants Act was the first legislation to restrict the right of commonwealth citizens to reside in the UK	
	1965 – first Race Relations Act: racial incitement became a criminal offence, and some forms of direct racial discrimination a civil wrong; put the emphasis on settlement through local conciliation committees and the Race Relations Board. The Act was seen to have weak enforcement and needed to be extended
	1966 – Local Government Act made provisions for the education and welfare of 'immigrants' through specific funding
1968 – Commonwealth Immigrants Act, controlled the entry of Kenyan Asians with British passports	1968 – Race Relations Act extended the existing Act to cover public and private employment and housing
1971 – Immigration Act introduced recourse to public funds provisions. The notion of 'patriality', which favoured immigration from 'white' commonwealth countries as 'right of abode', was limited to those with prior links to the UK, for example, a parent or grandparent born here	
	1976 – Race Relations Act extended the previous Acts by identifying direct and indirect discrimination, providing for positive action in some circumstances and establishing the Commission for Racial Equality (CRE)

Immigration legislation	'Race' relations legislation
1981 – British Nationality Act reclassified UK citizenship into three categories, one consequence being that children of 'British Overseas Citizens' of Asian background born in the UK could not automatically have citizenship	
1993 – Asylum and Immigration (Appeals) Act introduced fingerprinting and removed rights to public-sector housing	
1996 – Asylum and Immigration Act penalised employers employing those without the appropriate documentation	
	1998 – Human Rights Act gives further legal effect in the UK to the fundamental rights and freedoms contained in the European Convention on Human Rights
1999 – Immigration and Asylum Act introduced vouchers for support, and devolved dispersal and accommodation to the National Asylum Support Service (NASS)	
	2000 – Race Relations (Amendment) Act introduced a statutory obligation on all public agencies to eliminate racial discrimination and promote good community relations
2002 – Nationality, Immigration and Asylum Act introduced new induction/accommodation/removal centres for asylum seekers and withdrew support for individuals who are 'late' or unsuccessful applicants	
	2003 – Race Relations (Amendment) Act introduced new definitions of indirect discrimination and harassment
2004 – Asylum and Immigration (Treatment of Claimants) Act withdrew support from families with children under 18 in selected areas of the country and limited rights of appeal	

Immigration legislation	'Race' relations legislation
2006 – Immigration, Asylum and Nationality Act introduced a new asylum model giving greater control over asylum seekers	2006 – Racial and Religious Hatred Act seeks to stop people from intentionally using threatening words or behaviour to stir up hatred against someone because of their beliefs
2007 – UK Borders Bill gives immigration officers further powers, decreases rights and imposes further penalties	
	2010 – Equality Act streamlines previous equalities legislation but is weakened by the incoming Coalition government

Source: Adapted from Law (2010), and Solomos (2003, pp 57, 59)

The Immigration Act 1968 was passed before Enoch Powell made his incendiary 'rivers of blood' speech resulting in his sacking from the shadow cabinet. Powell appeared to receive massive support from the majority of the British population polled at the time (Hansen, 1999), suggestive that the Wilson government's Act, steered through by Home Secretary James Callaghan, reflected the mood of large sections of society, including many trades union members such as dockworkers (Sivanandan, 1982). The effect was that those who had the right to live and work in the UK and were already here were made to feel even more unwelcome and reminded of their 'otherness'.

What is rarely mentioned is that the emigration of White Britons during the 1950s/1960s was considerable (Brown, 1995) and, until the mid-1990s, was regularly *more substantial* than the numbers of immigrants. This has also been the case in recent years. In 2008, emigration from the UK was 427,000 and immigration 590,000, leaving 163,000 net immigration (ONS, 2009b). The implications of this, however, have rarely informed debates on immigration.

Further restrictions

According to a BBC summary (2002a):

> Under political pressure, the government legislated three times in less than a decade to make immigration for non-white people harder and harder. By 1972, legislation meant that a British passport holder born overseas could only settle in Britain if they, firstly, had a work permit and, secondly, could prove that a parent or grandparent had been born in the UK. In practice,

this meant children born to white families in the remnants of Empire or the former colonies could enter Britain. Their black counterparts could not.

During the 1980s, further restriction on immigration was introduced following an increasing fear among the majority white population of what Margaret Thatcher, while in opposition, described as being 'swamped' by people with a different culture (see Beckett, 2009). Following this, the British Nationality Act 1981/82 introduced a tiered system of citizenship. It gave several million citizens with UK-born grandparents (almost all white) the same right of abode in the UK as British citizens. At the same time, other British citizens had no right of abode under the Act, the majority of them of Indian, Chinese, African Caribbean or other non-European descent (Skellington and Morris, 1996b).

From 1983, immigration legislation continued to centre on reducing the number of people who could come to the UK, especially through marriage. This 'primary purpose rule', introduced by the Conservative government, was used to exclude young men from Bangladesh, India and Pakistan who wished to marry British women, or women settled in the UK, often being of working age. In further years, it was tightened so that the burden of proof was on the applicant, and, by 1990, the refusal rate was 60% of applications (Parekh, 2000a). The rule was found to discriminate on sex grounds in only deterring men from applying for entry, so was extended to apply to women, ensuring the 'even-handed' nature of the British state. However, the rule was selectively applied to keep out women from the Philippines, but not from America or Australia (Parekh, 2000a). South Asian women were affected badly by these Immigration Acts, since the majority of their men had travelled to the UK alone. Families became further divided and men became isolated, as they were increasingly unable to bring families to the UK to be with them. This is also the era of the infamous 'virgin tests', administered by immigration officers who physically tested whether women claiming to immigrate in order to marry were virgins (see Ahmad, 1993). In 1997, the Labour government abolished this primary purpose rule, acknowledged to be discriminatory.

During the 1990s, the immigration debate moved from 'Commonwealth' immigration to refugees and asylum-seekers. The 1971 Act had allowed 'illegal' immigrants to be detained. Two further Acts reinforced this. The Asylum and Immigration Appeals Act 1993 supported detentions and the Immigration and Asylum Act 1996 drastically affected the rights of those seeking asylum, removing benefits. This was reinforced in the Immigration, Asylum and Nationality Act 1999, which removed rights of migrants to many public resources. Consequently, several London hospitals, briefly at least, insisted on seeing people's passports before beginning treatment. This legislation was regarded as brutal, victimising and exclusionary and the subject of a number of challenges in the courts and in the European Court of Human Rights (Sales, 2007). In Scotland, campaigns against dawn raids on 'failed' asylum-seekers in 2007 met with some success (BBC News, 2007).

As Britain became more integrated within Europe, the political issue of whether this would allow many immigrants in 'by the back door' became increasingly heated, finally coming to the boil early in the 21st century following the 2004 EU enlargement. The idea of 'British jobs for British people', for example, was exploited by the major UK political parties and immigration became an important feature of the 2010 general election for the first time since 1979 (see Beckett, 2009). The election of several members of the British National Party to the European Parliament further reflected growing resentment of immigration among certain sections of the British population, as does the Euroscepticism found among much of the Conservative and UK Independence parties. With the changing membership of the European Union, the 2000s saw workers from new member states coming to the UK. When entering the country, these migrants again worked in industries with labour shortages, made little demand on public resources and were useful to the economy. Research showed that EU migrants made a 'substantial net contribution to the UK fiscal system', paying 37% more in taxes than they received in welfare payments (Dustmann et al, 2009, p 18). Researchers found that, on average, migrants were younger and better educated than the native population, as well as being 60% less likely to claim benefits and 58% less likely to live in social housing. Scotland, however, which was slowly depopulating, has been noted for maintaining a more welcoming stance than other parts of the UK, being cited in research as the most welcoming place to live (Clifford, 2010), and has challenged the Coalition government clampdown on overseas student visas (*Herald Scotland*, 2010). Many of these migrant workers were badly exploited, however (Wilkinson et al, 2009).

Anyone now applying to become a UK citizen has by law to meet specific requirements. These include attending a ceremony and taking an oath of allegiance; meeting English language standards; and taking a 'Life in the United Kingdom' test. They answer questions that many UK citizens cannot answer, some of which are criticised for their inaccuracy (Glendenning, 2006). The point of such tests was to create a sense of 'Britishness', albeit one increasingly disputed. The 2010 Coalition government also announced plans to introduce English language tests for all those coming to the UK from non-European Union countries to marry or join a partner (Cole,

2010). It remains to be seen if racism will be further exacerbated by future change.

The Race Relations Act 1976 and subsequent amendments

Both the 1965 and 1968 Acts were repealed by the Race Relations Act 1976, which was broader in scope and covered discrimination on the grounds of 'race', colour, nationality and ethnic and national origin in the fields of employment, the provision of goods and services, education, and public functions. It made prosecutions easier too, by removing the idea of intent and by broadening what was seen as discriminatory behaviour. The 1976 Act also established the Commission for Racial Equality (CRE) to ensure the Act was implemented, and to allegedly address the failures of the Community Relations Commission. It had a wider remit, covering private discrimination and acts of indirect discrimination; however, procedures were lengthy and complicated, and very few successful cases went to completion. This continues to be a feature of much equality legislation and has important consequences as much of what is permissible is determined by case law. Therefore, despite its intention, the 1976 Act struggled to have an impact. There were few investigations and fewer prosecutions, as was also the case with previous legislation (Turner, 2008). This led Sivanandan, then Director of the Institute for Race Relations, to describe the Act thus: 'never mind teeth, it had no gums' (Beckett, 2009, p 444). The problems of enforcing legislation remained ongoing, affecting subsequent attempts.

In 2000, following the Macpherson Report into the death of Stephen Lawrence, the Labour government introduced amendments to the Race Relations Act 1976. A potentially powerful piece of legislation, it was premised on the idea that institutional racism was engrained in the fabric of British society. It charged all public organisations with a statutory responsibility to promote equality and tackle discrimination (Atkin, 2009a). Although welcomed in principle, it has been criticised for its exclusion of racisms based on gender, class and nation (Mirza, 2003), raising the question of whether examining and tackling the bureaucratic procedures associated with implementing the Act will also tackle the *causes* of racism (Bhavnani et al, 2005). We return to this Act later, in particular to its relationship with the Single Equality Act 2010.

'Managing' immigration and 'race'

We have reflected on the changing legislative context influencing state policies on ethnic diversity. We now explore the broader social context and the policy responses emerging. Social and legislative contexts occur in parallel and overlap with previous discussions. This will inform our subsequent engagement, along with an acknowledgement of how the language of 'managing' immigration and 'race' articulated itself more explicitly from the 1960s onwards, giving rise to the practices whose theoretical implications are outlined in Chapter 2. Here we explore their policy impact.

Table 4.2: The broad policy context for managing 'race' relations in the UK

Approach	Assimilation	Multiculturalism	Community cohesion
Era	1960s–late 1970s	Late 1970s , 1980s early 1990s	2000s
Policy issue	Labour migration	Managing diversity	Asylum and terror
Rationale	'race' riots	Co-opting protest	Security

Source: Adapted from Lewis and Craig (2010, p 11).

Initial government thinking on immigration did not plan for a multicultural society, assuming minority ethnic populations would assimilate into a 'British way of life' and cultural differences would disappear (Cashmore and Troyna, 1990; Gouldbourne, 1998). Migrants would thus be speaking English, dressing as the majority white population did and 'leaving their culture' at the school gates. To help facilitate this, for example, children from Asian families in Bradford and Southall were not allocated similar schools. To ensure that no one school became associated with a minority population, children were 'bussed' to distant schools (Brah, 1996; McLoughlin, 2009).

Assimilation policies were accompanied by ideas pathologising the experience of minority ethnic groups, 'blaming the victim', both implicitly and explicitly for 'deviant' cultural practices (Lawrence, 1982). Problems occurred, it was argued, because people did not speak English, married their first cousins, adopted unhealthy diets, had children without husbands and misunderstood the role of the welfare state (Atkin, 1996). Such ideas informed policy in the 1980s and early 1990s, having a strong influence on current understandings of ethnic diversity (Atkin and Chattoo, 2007; see also Chapter 2). The children of single, working mothers of Caribbean background were seen to be at risk of neglect and needing to be 'rescued'. Social work practice at the time internalised these assumptions. The over-representation of Caribbean children in public care was a direct expression of beliefs that black parenting was inferior and their children at risk of harm (ABSWAP, 1983; Pennie and Best, 1990).

In state education, African Caribbean children were labelled as 'educationally subnormal' and segregated into 'special schools' and classes (Kowalczewski, 1982). Theories concerning their supposed lower IQ helped clinch the argument. Asian children were also labelled as 'backward' through their need to learn English (Bryan et al, 1985; Williams, 1996). Later, Coard's (1971) work described how the system made West Indian children 'subnormal'. Health services worked with similar assumptions. During the 1970s, many Asian children were found to have rickets, explained by their inadequate diet. Government-sponsored health campaigns such as the Asian Mother and Baby Campaign and the Stop Rickets Campaign aimed to improve the health of Asian children, but were based on deficit models of parenting and culture. The majority population had also suffered from rickets in the early 20th century, but, since the 1930s, had benefited from vitamin D supplements and additions to flour and margarine. Consequently, rickets had been eradicated. However, for those of Asian background, poor diet was blamed rather than using preventive intervention strategies benefitting the majority population (BBC News, 1999; Bivins, 2007).

In a much-quoted speech of 1966, Roy Jenkins, Labour Home Secretary, spoke out against assimilation, in favour of integration: 'I define integration, therefore, not as a flattening process of assimilation but as equal opportunity, accompanied by cultural diversity, in an atmosphere of mutual tolerance. That is the goal' (quoted in Lester, 2009, p 4).

Brah (1996) has argued that such reasoning assumed that there was a level playing field of equal opportunity from which to build 'race' equality, which put the emphasis on human characteristics such as tolerance as the key to success, while ignoring social, economic and structural aspects contributing to inequality. Nonetheless, the seeds of multiculturalism, which flourished in the late 1970s and early 1980s, were sown. The failure to name and condemn racism has been a theme in a number of writings on this period (Carby, 1982; Kowalczewski, 1982; Troyna, 1984; Essed, 1994). Those advocating strategies based on an acknowledgement of structural disadvantage and racism would successfully challenge the 'weak' version of multiculturalism initially supported by governments, at least theoretically; their impact on policy and practice, however, was more limited.

In the meantime, multiculturalism came to replace assimilation, becoming the basis of formal policy, peaking in the early 1980s. This weak form of 'multiculturalism' called for a celebration of cultures and the valuing of difference, but also led to its own forms of racism. Addressing power inequalities and institutional racism were not prominent features of a multicultural approach; cultures were naively regarded as meeting on equal terms. The emphasis was on developing mutual understandings of each other's cultural norms and assumptions; once achieved, racism and discrimination would disappear (see Atkin, 2009a). The problem with this focus on culture, however, was that minority cultures became judged in relation to the majority white culture, leading to unfavourable comparisons (noted earlier).

Culture was not attributed to white people, just to black. In this way, minority ethnic family life was seen as 'other' and difference was emphasised at the expense of similarities and differences *between* and *within* ethnic groups. Elements of such assumptions persist today (see also Chapter 2).

One unintended consequence of multiculturalism was that cultural diversity was used against minority ethnic populations (Gilroy, 1992; Karlsen, 2007b). Healthcare problems of minority ethnic families became associated again with their supposed 'deviant' cultural practices and lifestyles (Ahmad and Bradby, 2007). Atkin and Chattoo (2007) note how, in the 1980s, health and social care agencies could explain away small numbers of ethnic minorities on their caseloads by saying 'they look after their own' (see also Craig et al, 2000). Despite being discredited, these views were commonly expressed by health and social care practitioners as late as 2005. Further, it remains common in training material to see one-page explanations of Muslim, Hindu and Sikh culture, to which patients' beliefs are expected to correspond. Such explanations present static views of cultural norms and values, devoid of context (Atkin and Chattoo, 2007), creating the illusion that they offer a solution to an extremely complex situation (Chattoo and Ahmad, 2004). During the 1980s, multiculturalism became increasingly challenged by anti-racism, which tended to see cultural explanations as surrogate forms of racism. According to anti-racist strategies, assimilation, integration or multiculturalism did not address power inequalities or the structures and systems that perpetuated racism. Racism needed to be named, acknowledged and dealt with. Black women were active as academics, theorists and practitioners, and black feminist theory was making a substantial contribution to 'race' equality (*Feminist Review*, 1984).

Anti-racism and 'the end of anti-racism': the rise of black struggle

By the beginning of the 1980s, a groundswell was taking place, building on the self-help-organised industrial movements of the 1960s described by Brah (1996), Sivanandan (1982, 1985), Parmar (1982) and others. Both women and men from minority ethnic groups were active in challenging unfair and racist practices in workplaces, and writing about them. The children of migrants coming to the UK in the 1950s/60s were educated in the UK and took their place in the workforce for granted. Many had joined public services and there were now more black academics, psychiatrists and teachers than in the 1960s. In addition, significant organisations had been set up locally and nationally such as the Southall Black Sisters, the Organisation of Women of African and Asian Descent (OWAAD), and the Association of Black Social Workers and Allied Professions (ABSWAP). These groups' messages were now that racism was inherent in the systems and structures of British society – the institutional racism that was finally named and shamed by the Macpherson Report in 1999 – and that without black inclusion, there could not be progress in addressing 'race' equality. There were also concerns expressed about police racism and brutality, much focused on the deaths of Blair Peach, a white teacher fatally assaulted by a police officer at an anti-racist demonstration in Southall, and of Cherry Groce and Cynthia Jarrett, two Caribbean women experiencing police brutality during the searching of their homes in Brixton and Tottenham. These events fuelled the disturbances of 1981 and 1985, which were seen as a sign that black people would not tolerate continued racism without fighting back.

During the 1980s, questions were asked about the meaning of the category 'race', with minorities centrally involved as academics and practitioners in these critiques and questions (see Chapter 2). Racism came to be named explicitly as a product of the systems and structures that excluded black people, and perpetuated it. This showed 'race' and 'ethnicity' to be socially constructed, that is, having no biological, scientific or fixed reality (except the reality of racism), and were concepts that could change according to the power relations at the time (Ahmad, 1993a). Plurality, multiple identities and intersectionality were highlighted and explored by Anthias and Yuval-Davis (1983), Hall (1992) and black feminists such as Bhavnani and Phoenix (1994) among others.

The 1980s led to a new multiculturalism, recognising cultural difference alongside structural disadvantage and institutional racism. As Ballard (1989) observed, culture was not a problem per se, it was more how cultural difference was perceived. A more reflexive approach became the basis of culturally capable practice (Dominelli, 2004; Papadopoulos et al, 2004) and informed this 'new' multiculturalism. Tensions, however, remain associated with the influences of previous debates. Essentialism, long discredited in academic circles, re-emerged as mainstream policy and practice responded to 'super-diversity' (Chattoo, 2008). The 'new' multiculturalism also attracted a different form of criticism associated with a concern to establish community cohesion.

The attack on the 'new' multiculturalism

A major criticism of current UK multiculturalist policies has been that minorities are free to retain parts of their own culture, tending to undermine 'British values' or, as Trevor Phillips has put it, 'a core of Britishness' (Cheong et al, 2007). Where these so-called 'British' values have been identified, such as freedom of speech and personal security, democracy, fairness, and justice, research has shown (Rutter et al, 2007) that these are as equally valued by new migrants and resident minorities in this country as by the majority population (Jayaweera and Choudhury, 2008). Some, however, argue that the failure of minorities to integrate into British culture has undermined government policies of community cohesion, contributing to urban disturbances over the last 30 years and culminating in the 2005 London bombings.

As Parekh (2000b) reminds us, whether people like it or not, multicultural societies are a fact of life and cannot be wished away – other than by the violence of ethnic cleansing. This fact, however, has yet to translate into truly multicultural policy frameworks. Those who now argue that multiculturalism has failed or is dangerous demonstrate little understanding of what a multiculturalist policy framework is trying to achieve. Prime Minister Cameron's 2011 statement asserting both the end of multiculturalism and, disgracefully, its supposed links with terrorism is an extreme example of such utterances. Currently, debates in the UK (and elsewhere) are increasingly winding the clock back to the assimilation policy mentioned earlier.

Those arguing in favour of multiculturalist policy maintain that it is possible to incorporate people from different backgrounds, respecting difference and diversity in most aspects of culture, provided it is done within an acceptance of human rights and anti-discrimination legislation and practice as, for example, laid out in the UN Charter of Human Rights (see Craig et al, 2009a). The failure thus lies with the British and other settled states and not with those minorities subject to its policies.

Anti-racism, equality and diversity, and community cohesion

The fourth national survey of minority ethnic groups (Modood et al, 1997) provided comprehensive evidence on inequality of experience between minority ethnic groups and the majority population. Instead of aggregating data from the different groups, this survey identified their experiences separately and highlighted patterns of inequality to do with ethnic origin, social class, gender and religion as well as in specific services such as mental health, employment, housing and education. Coupled with the Human Rights Act 1998 and the election of a Labour government, which seemed more amenable to promoting equality, the scene seemed set for progress. Devolution from 1999 also allowed the devolved nations to develop and implement their own policy frameworks, some of which benefited 'race' equality.

The Macpherson Report (discussed earlier) precipitated a major shift in 'race' equality policy. The murder of Stephen Lawrence, a young black man killed by four white men in London, and the subsequent inquiry, posed a huge challenge to public services, which remains today. Institutional racism could not be denied and was named in authoritative terms (Macpherson, 1999, Recommendation 12 and para 6.34; see also Chapter 1).

The definition facilitated changes to 'race' equality legislation in the UK. The Race Relations (Amendment) Act 2000 laid the emphasis and responsibility squarely on public institutions to promote 'race' equality, to monitor their services and report and publish the results. Any service in receipt of public money had a duty to develop a 'race' equality scheme (and action plan). The then Commission for Racial Equality had a watchdog brief.

Rather than focusing on the continuing racism in British society evoked by the Act, leading politicians continued to attack multiculturalism (Johnston, 2007). Disturbances in several Northern English towns during the late 1990s and local and national enquiries (Cantle, 2001; Ouseley, 2001) led to a national policy on community cohesion (Home Office, 2001a). The concerted attack on multiculturalism that followed from the Macpherson Report, the Northern 'disturbances' and the new deracialised focus on community cohesion can be interpreted as an attempt by the state to divert attention away from racism into a channel which (again) blamed minorities for social and economic ills affecting the UK population (Worley, 2005; Chouhan, 2009).

Services continued to struggle with the requirement to monitor ethnicity, publish their data and provide leaderships that reflect the communities served. In 2007, the then Healthcare Commission searched for evidence of Primary Care Trusts that had published 'race' equality schemes, finding a serious lack of compliance with the legislation (Healthcare Commission, 2009). To date, no prosecutions have followed and this, as we have seen, is often an undermining feature of legislation.

Community cohesion

Despite improvements proposed by the new 'race' equality legislation, the pace of change was slow; communities continued to face deprivation and disadvantage. The government had also begun to argue that a major difficulty facing Britain's minority ethnic communities was their failure to 'integrate' and their desire to lead increasingly separate lives, both geographically and culturally, at odds with the traditional values of white Britishness (discussed earlier). The fact that the meaning of 'Britishness' was not a consensual one even across the four UK countries, was overlooked (BBC Wales, no date).

The concept of community cohesion displaced 'race relations' as the basis for policymaking (Worley, 2005), creating a tension that remains unresolved. Both central and local government (LGA, 2002; Home Office, 2004) published detailed guidance on the meaning of community cohesion, each pointing to what they understood to be the meaning of Britishness. For example, the Home Office acknowledged the continuing presence of racism and discrimination, arguing that 'to be British means that we respect the laws, the democratic political structures, and give our allegiance to the State' (Home Office, 2004, p 6). Then it also contradictorily suggested that 'to be British does not mean assimilation into a common culture so that original identities are lost' (ibid). It concluded, also contradictorily, that respect for the law, fairness, tolerance and respect for difference were values shared by all Britons, of whatever ethnic origin (see also Forrest and Kearns, 2000). There is clearly confusion over what Britishness really is (Runnymede Trust, 2009).

The domestic 'Northern disturbances' were followed by the shocks of, first, the attacks on the World Trade Center and the ensuing 'war on terror', and then by bombings in Madrid, Bali and London, together with Western military intervention in Iraq and Afghanistan. These have been characterised in both populist and some serious discourse as a struggle between two civilisations: the West and Islam (Huntington, 1996). The far right has argued that some of Britain's minorities have no commitment to integrating and should therefore be 'encouraged' to return to their countries of origin, overlooking the fact that many are British-born and raised. Cultural tensions are also apparent in responses to government attempts to legislate against religious incitement (Jan-Khan, 2003).

Community cohesion now appears to be the acceptable 'race' policy shaping local responses. For example, because of differing income subsidies to local government, it has compelled local government to adopt the community cohesion theme. Public Service Agreement 9 requires it to 'bring about a measurable improvement in "race" and "community cohesion"' (www.nao.org.uk/psa/publications.aspx), and influence the direction of third-sector activity. Although the government published a community cohesion and 'race' equality strategy in 2004 (Home Office, 2004), later policy documents often dropped the notion of 'race' equality. In 2008, the CRE was abolished and its work incorporated into a single equalities organisation, the Equalities and Human Rights Commission (EHRC), which many argue has effectively downgraded the work on 'race' relations for which the CRE acted as a focus. Despite warnings of segregation geographically, the government-established Commission on Integration and Cohesion (CIC) also argued that 'the national picture is a positive one: perceptions of cohesion are good in most areas – on average 79% of people agreed that people of different backgrounds got on well in their local area' (CIC, 2007, p 8).

The strategy has been increasingly criticised by academic, policy and activist commentators alike. First, although community cohesion appears to have replaced 'race' as the organising factor for local work between communities, it is clear that 'race' – or a particular racial or ethnic identity (being Muslim) – is the prime concern of policymakers and the police. Worley (2005, p 483) argues that 'talking about communities enables language to become deracialized while at the same time the language of community cohesion draws upon earlier discourses of assimilation'. Secondly, the focus of the Prevent agenda has been criticised as narrowing down extremist behaviour to the acts of a few radical Muslims. It is then generalised frequently to Muslims as a whole rather than focusing equally, if not more strongly, on far-right political parties, which have generated racialised disturbances in many cities over the past 50 years (JUST, 2009). Thirdly, the assumption that the UK's minority populations are becoming increasingly separated from one another and from the mainstream UK white population, concentrated into areas in which extremists might ferment 'race' and religious hatred, has been challenged by demographic analyses. Finney and Simpson (2009), for example, demonstrate that the charge that the UK is becoming geographically segregated and claims that minorities want to live in segregated neighbourhoods are myths. Segregation, where it occurs, results from structural constraints and processes shaped by racism in housing and labour markets, by poverty and housing (un)affordability. These findings are supported by a Scottish study (Hopkins, 2004).

If Britain's minorities are leading 'parallel lives', the evidence suggests that this is because racism continues to affect every aspect of their lives (Platt, 2003b; Hopkins, 2004; Craig, 2007). Labour-market participation is seen as the key to integration (Rutter et al, 2008), but research demonstrates how structural and individual racism affects most minorities' access to decent work, placing women at a particular disadvantage (Mirza, 2003). Rutter et al's work also demonstrates that integration and, by implication, cohesion is a long process, not to be driven by short-term political agendas. This presents a direct challenge to the typology developed by the Institute of Community Cohesion (ICoCo, 2009) for example, since it is clear that Britain's minorities still do not have access to equal opportunities, equal outcomes or the rights enjoyed by the majority population for reasons located externally to minority communities themselves. The suggestion that social cohesion is undermined by increasing diversity has also been challenged by research. This shows that age, class and place – factors not solely shaped by ethnicity – were more important in affecting cohesion than ethnicity or religion, and that dealing with inequalities together with focusing on values such as supporting both unity and difference are critical in promoting good community relations (Hickman et al, 2008).

More recently, the Department for Communities and Local Government published *Tackling Race Inequality: A Statement on Race* (DCLG, 2010), summarising achievements since the Macpherson Report and outlining future plans for 'race' equality. Although emphasising the intersections of class and other inequalities, the policy sets out a commitment to continue tackling 'race' inequality. There were anxieties that 'race' could take less prominence if other equalities were highlighted, echoing concerns about the Equality Act 2010 discussed later, but John Denham the then Communities Secretary, denied that this was the case (Be-Utd, 2010; Travis, 2010). However, he simultaneously argued that it was time to 'move on' from 'race'. This policy was linked to a £6 million programme of funding for the voluntary and community sector to assist with implementation of government objectives. The Coalition government, however, announced its list of voluntary-sector strategic partners in early 2011: none were BME-led.

In parallel to community cohesion policies and initiatives, equalities legislation was being reviewed with a view to streamlining existing legislation such as the Sex Discrimination Act, Race Relations Acts and the Disability Discrimination Act. What emerged was an Equalities Bill (2010), which incorporated existing 'race', gender and disability legislation and added religion (and non-religious belief), sexual orientation and age to the list. The Act accepted the multifaceted and institutional nature of discrimination, which could be cultural and systemic. Some, however, criticised the timing of the legislation as premature, when there was still so much to be done to implement the Race Relations (Amendment) Act 2000. The fear of 'race' equality becoming less of a priority became a reality as some local authorities made their own interpretations of the CIC's recommendations on single group funding. They made decisions not to fund organisations that focused on just one of the equality strands, arguing that all equality strands need to be promoted in order to achieve cohesion. This led to Southall Black Sisters, a women-led 'race' equality organisation, losing its funding from Ealing Council. Subsequently, the organisation took the council to the High Court and won their case. In a landmark decision, Lord Justice Moses ruled that there was no contradiction between funding specialist services in order for cohesion to be achieved (Southall Black Sisters, 2008).

The Single Equality Act 2010 has been reviewed and significantly weakened by the new government prior to decisions on the timing of implementation (see www.equalities.gov.uk/equalitybill.aspx; also EHRC, nd), and some aspects – such as the requirement for public bodies to work to reduce inequalities based on class disadvantage – have been scrapped. The Home Secretary, Theresa May, has declared equality to be 'a dirty word'. Statutory agencies are still waiting for guidance on what their other specific public duties will be. These are to be available during 2011 and are likely, however, to have a legal duty to eliminate aspects of discrimination, harassment and victimisation and establish equality of opportunity (see www.equalityhumanrights.com/advice-and-guidance/new-equality-act-guidance/equality-act-starter-kit). More specific duties will include annual publication of data on how the organisation's activities have impacted on protected characteristics (eg sex, 'race', sexual orientation, disability, age, religion and belief). Evidence must also be used to set specific and measurable equality objectives, which need reviewing only every four years (previous legislation suggested that this should take place annually) (see Government Equalities Office, 2010).

Summary

'Race' policy and practice has moved from overt racism in the early part of the 20th century, through a series of Acts aimed at curbing racial discrimination and promoting 'race' equality, while parallel legislation has sought to curb black immigration, thereby undermining progress and questioning government commitment to and credibility in 'race' equality. More recently, institutional racism has been given more attention; services still struggle to redress inequalities and, within them, to share power and engage with minority ethnic communities. The increasing presence of minority ethnic leaders and senior managers in the workforce and greater visibility of minority ethnic academics and researchers continue to help services avoid complacency.

There is no consensus on how much has been achieved since the Macpherson Report and the Race Relations (Amendment) Act 2000 came into force. It can be argued that 'race' equality will be difficult to achieve while the overarching framework of ideology represented by current and past immigration legislation remains. The rise of community cohesion adds to the uncertainty. Moreover, at the time of writing, it seems unlikely that the 2010 Coalition government will continue to drive 'race' equality reforms, and may use spending cuts and budget deficits as an excuse to stifle progress. The early signs are not promising.

Questions for discussion

- Describe key aspects of 'race' thinking and how it evolved in the 20th century. Summarise the position now, giving examples of how this thinking manifests itself in policy and practice.
- Identify and describe three policy approaches to managing 'race' and 'race relations' since 1950, and give practical examples of these approaches in action in one or more public services.
- To what extent does legislation help tackle inequalities? And to what extent is policy and practice being informed by the struggles of BME communities?
- Does community cohesion undermine the idea of multiculturalism? What are the advantages and disadvantages of the new Equality Act combining all previous legislation on discrimination?

Further reading

Bhavnani, R., Mirza, H.S. and Meetoo, V. (2005) *Tackling the Roots of Racism, Lessons for Success*, Bristol: The Policy Press.

Brah, A. (1996) *Cartographies of Diaspora: Contesting Identities*, London: Routledge.

CCCS (Centre for Contemporary Cultural Studies) (1982) *The Empire Strikes Back: Race and Racism in 70s Britain*, London: Hutchinson, in association with the CCCS, University of Birmingham.

Sivanandan, A. (1982) *A Different Hunger: Writings on Black Resistance*. London: Pluto Press.

Solomos, J. (2003) *Race and Racism in Britain* (3rd edn), Basingstoke: Palgrave.

Electronic resources

- The BBC websites have historical news items on 'race' and immigration: http://news.bbc.co.uk/hi/english/static/in_depth/uk/2002/'race'/short_history_of_immigration.stm#1914
- The Joseph Rowntree Foundation funds research that includes immigration and inclusion, and has included a 'race' programme: http://www.jrf.org.uk
- The Institute of Race Relations has had a long-standing critical eye on current debates on 'race': www.irr.org.uk

- The Office for National Statistics (ONS) has up-to-date figures on immigration, employment, family structure, population growth and other aspects of minority and majority ethnic lives: www.ons.gov.uk
- Scotland Against Racism has a history of immigration, up-to-date policy and much more: www.scotlandagainstracism.com

Note

[1] This situation has continued to be the case with the more recent A8 and A2 migrants with, for example, Polish medical practitioners picking fruit in the UK.

Part III
'Race', ethnicity and welfare sectors

Minority ethnic communities and housing: access, experiences and participation

Harris Beider and Gina Netto

Overview

This chapter is concerned with black and minority ethnic (BME) communities' experience of housing, specifically, their access to housing, housing circumstances and participation in housing markets. It will:

- consider minority ethnic housing experiences within the context of immigration and settlement;
- introduce the concepts of direct and indirect racial discrimination;
- examine changes brought about by growing progress towards 'race' equality and increasing emphasis on community cohesion;
- pay particular attention to the role of the public sector, including black-led housing associations, given its role in accommodating those on low incomes; and
- consider the implications of research for improving the position of BME communities in housing strategies, policy and delivery.

Key concepts

access, community cohesion, homelessness, housing associations, owner-occupation, participation, renting

Introduction

The experiences of BME communities within the UK housing system can be understood in the context of post-colonial and other immigration and settlement histories: growing progress towards 'race' equality, and wider changes in providing housing for people on low incomes. Drawing on research conducted mainly in England and Scotland, this chapter considers some of the key issues affecting BME groups' access to housing and their experiences of the housing system, including lack of access to housing (homelessness). It then considers participation, discussing the rise and decline of English black-led housing associations. Specific attention is paid to the social rented sector and the role that black-led housing associations have played in developing provision for BME communities. In addition, the position of minority ethnic owner-occupiers – living in homes they own – is also considered, including those who have no choice but to buy homes due to the lack of suitable alternative accommodation. The role of the private rented sector in accommodating those who are not able to buy their homes or access the public rented sector – a trend likely to increase in the current financial climate – is also acknowledged. The chapter concludes by considering recent policy initiatives and their potential for overcoming the difficulties discussed.

In the UK, along with other European countries where social housing has been prioritised, responsibility for housing resides within central government, with local authorities and voluntary-sector agencies implementing centrally driven policies (Edgar, 2004). There are some local variations, partly because housing is a devolved responsibility within the UK. Compared to many other European countries, the UK has a relatively large social rented sector. However, this has shrunk considerably since the post-war period, changing the housing market from a predominantly rental one in the 1950s to nearly 80% owner-occupation now (Phillips and Harrison, 2010). This is due to various reasons, including the lack of investment in local authority housing, cuts in new-build and the Right-to-Buy scheme. This scheme involved the sale of council properties to tenants at heavily discounted prices, enabling them to benefit from capital gain. Other major changes in the housing environment since the 1950s are large-scale slum clearances, an increase in amenity levels and a decrease in overcrowding (Lakey, 1997).[1] There have also been major shifts in the governance of housing through (often large-scale) transfers of stock from local authorities to housing associations. This has led commentators to argue that housing interventions since 1979 have taken place within an increasingly neoliberal environment (Phillips and Harrison, 2010). However, it should be noted that a number of legal and policy initiatives have also been designed to address various forms of discrimination in public services, including housing. Recent cuts to social housing proposed by the Coalition government, including in rural areas, will result in the loss of many of the 'gains' achieved, including a rise in homelessness.

The major mechanism for housing low-income groups – overlapping with provision for BME communities – is subsidised provision by the state or social housing, supplemented by rental allowances. Edgar (2004) notes that housing policies for minority ethnic communities have tended mainly to concentrate on ensuring their access to the social rented sector, through providing good practice guidance and monitoring the policies and procedures of social landlords. A similar trend may be observed in research that documented disadvantage in access and allocation of social housing and the need for greater awareness of institutional racism (see *Box 5.1*; see also Netto et al, 2001a; Rutter and Latorre, 2009). However, reduced investment in social housing over several years, exacerbated by recent cuts, has resulted in the growing importance of the private rented sector. Unfortunately, this has not been matched by research attention, particularly on the position of BME communities (Netto et al, 2001a).

An understanding of direct and indirect racial discrimination (as discussed earlier in Chapters 2 and 4) is important for understanding changes in housing policy and practice, and their impacts on BME communities. It is also important to understand what is meant by institutional discrimination.

Box 5.1: The law and racial discrimination

The Race Relations Act 1976 made it unlawful for local authorities to discriminate either directly or indirectly on racial grounds in the provision of goods, facilities and services. This was extended and reinforced by the amendments to the Race Relations Act 2000 and Equality Act 2010. The main provisions of the Equality Act outlaw discrimination in all public authority functions. It also obliges public bodies to promote equality. Public bodies subject to the general duty include central government, local housing authorities and all organisations they contract with, including Registered Social Landlords (RSLs). The Equality Act also covers provision of employment, facilities and goods in the private sector (with some exceptions).

Direct discrimination occurs when a person is treated less favourably on racial grounds than another and may result in deficits such as missed job opportunities or access to services, such as housing. In the housing field, the allocation policies of social housing organisations have been a major focus of attention as a means of addressing direct discrimination. In England, this has been particularly encouraged through the growth of black-led housing associations.

> Indirect racial discrimination is defined as the imposition of conditions or requirements that, while not apparently discriminatory in themselves, have the effect of lowering the proportion of people from certain ethnic groups able to access services or qualify for jobs. Such discrimination may be reflected in the provision of housing that does not meet specific needs. An example of such discrimination is the lack of availability of larger-sized accommodation in the social rented sector. This is significant given the larger family sizes (and households) in certain population groups.

The BME communities covered in this chapter are diverse, including long-established communities in the UK, as well as recent arrivals. The latter include new economic migrants from the eight EU accession (A8) countries, asylum-seekers and refugees. It is also worth acknowledging that significant differences exist in the housing needs, experiences and participation of BME communities, on the bases of class, age, gender, disability, religion, sexual orientation and generation.

Trends in minority ethnic settlement and patterns of disadvantage

As discussed earlier (see Chapter 3), migrants from South Asia and the West Indies came to the UK from the late 1950s onwards to work in industries facing difficulties in recruiting labour from the local population. These groups settled in different parts of the country, depending on employment opportunities. Phillips and Harrison (2010, p 223) note that in the earliest stages of post-war settlement, in the 1950s and 1960s, these migrants were forced by 'poverty, lack of knowledge of housing and blatant racist discrimination' into renting or buying poor-quality housing at the bottom end of the private market. The study notes that development programmes in the early days of post-war slum clearance did not directly target the geographical areas in which black or Asian people were concentrated.

Many of the areas in which BME communities are still concentrated are characterised by high unemployment, low pay and poor services, including housing (Harrison with Davis, 2001; Edgar, 2004). As many studies have demonstrated, patterns of ethnic segregation or concentration are not in themselves problematic, potentially providing valuable opportunities for mutual support (Simpson, 2004; Finney and Simpson, 2009). It is potential restrictions in housing and environmental quality and job choice that are of concern (Harrison with Davis, 2001) or the coexistence of concentrations of minority ethnic households with the concentration of disadvantage (Lakey, 1997). Here it is important to note the role of strategies adopted by individuals within these communities in contributing to changing spatial patterns. For instance, Simpson (2004) argues that demographic evidence shows that Asian people are dispersing, supporting qualitative evidence of a desire to live in mixed neighbourhoods and growing social mobility (Phillips, 2002). This mobility, however, is limited to those with adequate means to move. Thus, people of Indian origin, for example, are much more likely to be able to move up the housing ladder than their Pakistani or Bangladeshi counterparts.

In the 1960s, direct and indirect racial discrimination continued to hinder access to good-quality housing and influence patterns of settlement. Direct discrimination included allocation policies disadvantaging individuals from certain ethnic groups by only allowing them access to poor-quality social rented housing. Other forms of direct discrimination could be seen in the racialised practices of estate agents, 'steering' individuals into certain areas (Phillips, 2002). Yet other forms of direct discrimination may be seen in the practices of financial institutions, which impose less favourable mortgage arrangements on BME communities than the majority population (Third et al, 1997). Indirect racial discrimination may be seen in the lack of larger-sized social rented accommodation, which disadvantages communities whose household sizes are typically larger than in the majority population, notably, Pakistani and Bangladeshi communities (Markkanen, 2009; Jones, 2010).

Phillips and Harrison (2010) note that, from 1997 onwards, New Labour's goal of tackling social exclusion included a well-defined geographical focus based on the premise that deprived neighbourhoods could be 'turned around' with wide-ranging government action addressing child care, drugs, crime, unemployment and public health issues. The study observes that in areas significantly occupied by minority ethnic populations, 'market renewal strategies' were explicitly linked to community cohesion agendas and a response to 'unrest' in several Northern English cities. These disturbances gave rise to concerns that the largely Muslim Pakistani population living in these areas were living 'parallel lives' from the local white populations, and that there was a need to address ethnic segregation (Cantle, 2001). However, analysts have argued that the underlying factors that contributed to patterns of segregation were not acknowledged. For instance, Phillips and Harrison (2010) note that structural constraints such as Islamophobia (accentuated by aspects of the so-called 'War on Terror'), and the perception on the part of BME communities that racial harassment was more likely in certain geographical areas, was not recognised.

MacEwen et al (1994) observed that the allocation of the quality of stock to BME communities became more important given increasing variation in the age, design, condition and reputation of social housing. They confirmed that the concentration of BME groups in particular areas and dwelling types in council housing was only in part a reflection of choice and that various rules and procedures systematically disadvantaged minority ethnic households. Certainly, analysis of statistical data sets revealed many patterns of housing disadvantage: for example, minority ethnic households were more likely to live in flats and bedsits and less likely to live in houses (Scottish Office, 1991; Ratcliffe, 1997); and more likely to live in densely occupied housing and lack exclusive use of a bath or WC (Scottish Office, 1991; Owen, 1993) and central heating (Scottish Office, 1991). More recent research reveals that the disproportionate numbers of BME communities living in poor-quality and overcrowded housing have persisted (Scottish Executive, 2004; Phillips and Harrison, 2010; Netto et al, 2010) and, with cuts in housing budgets, may indeed be on the increase. In Glasgow, for example, there is a sizeable Roma community living in appalling private rented housing.

However, a fuller explanatory account of these patterns of disadvantage would need to take into account historical patterns of settlement (see Chapter 3), geographical concentrations of deprivation, choices made by individuals, structural factors such as poverty (see Chapter 10), unemployment (see Chapter 9), low or no income, and practices by housing providers, estate agents and financial institutions that impact on house purchases and access to the social and private rented sectors. Having said this, equality legislation has contributed to increased awareness of the potential for discrimination through discretionary allocation processes and the need to counter this through monitoring and reviewing the ethnicity of applicants and lets (Jones, 2009). More specifically, legislation placed a public duty on local authorities and registered social landlords to demonstrate equality. Although practice in this area is uneven, blatant discrimination is less evident.

Trends in tenure patterns among minority ethnic households

As discussed earlier, one of the most important changes in the housing market in the UK is the shift towards owner-occupation. A comparison of statistical data between 1982 and 1994 in England found that rates of owner-occupation for all groups increased, except for the Pakistani population (Lakey, 1997). In an audit of Scotland-based research, Netto et al (2001a) observed the identification of owner-occupation as the preferred option in a number of studies. However, the same studies caution against a simplistic view of owner-occupation as a measure of upward mobility in the labour and housing markets, identifying 'reluctant' homeowners who had been forced to buy their homes due to fear or experience of racial harassment,[2] lack of affordable, suitably sized accommodation for large households, or a strong preference for a local area. Andrew and Pannel (2006, cited in Markkanen, 2009) note that with rising house prices and the tightening of mortgage regulations, population groups that traditionally preferred owner-occupation are likely to find increasing difficulties in buying their own homes. Markkanen (2009) reports that BME groups are already over-represented in shared ownership; this will increase if information about this tenure is made more available.

Several areas of institutional discrimination against minority ethnic applicants have been identified in Scotland-based research, including allocation criteria such as waiting times, points for local connection to the area in which housing is sought, discretionary allocations procedures and a failure to publicise vacancies (Netto et al, 2001a). Encouragingly, more recent research conducted in England indicates only limited evidence that social housing providers may, unintentionally, discriminate against BME communities (Rutter and Latorre, 2009). However, the study found that housing allocation policies lacked transparency and were difficult to understand.

Analysis of 2001 census data confirms the persistent under-representation of BME households in Scotland's social rented sector (Scottish Executive, 2004), while Phillips and Harrison (2010) report that all the main minority ethnic groups are now well-represented in the social rented sector, albeit in some cases concentrated in the worst stock within it. However, employing the categories used in a recent study, differential patterns of housing tenure have been highlighted between the 'UK-born' and the 'foreign-born' population arriving in the UK in the last five years (see *Figure 5.1*). The latter, which the study acknowledges are more commonly referred to as 'members of ethnic minority communities', are overwhelmingly housed in the private rented sector, a trend likely to increase with recent cuts to social housing. Migrants to the UK in the last five years make up less than 2% of the total of those in social housing compared to the 90% of those who live in social housing who are UK-born. Of those migrating to the UK in the last five years, the majority are refugees who have been granted permission to remain. This highlights the need to counter common perceptions propagated by much of the media that migrants displace UK-born citizens, and the need for specific attention to meet the needs of these groups (Robinson, 2006; Netto et al, 2010).

Various approaches can facilitate greater access to the social rented sector including increasing the supply and appropriateness of housing, more effective communication between social housing providers and minority ethnic communities, and active engagement with voluntary organisations

Figure 5.1: *Housing tenure distribution by country of birth, 2007*

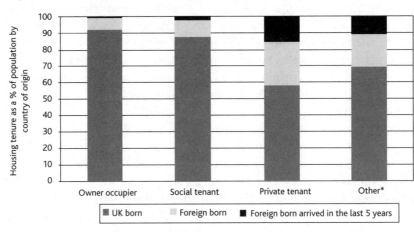

Note: * Includes rent relative of household member or related to work (extracted from Rutter and Latorre, 2009, p 18).

Source: Labour Force Survey and Institute for Public Policy Research calculations.

working with these communities. In addition, greater attention must be paid to the role of the private rented sector in accommodating people on low incomes, including recent migrants. In the next section, we consider lack of access to accommodation, that is, homelessness.

Homelessness in minority ethnic communities

In recent years, policy initiatives directed at addressing homelessness in the UK have been formulated within a proactive, interventionist, preventive strategy (Pawson et al, 2006, 2007). However, despite the high profile accorded to homelessness on the policy agenda, little attention has been paid to revealing the nature and extent of homelessness in BME communities (Netto et al, 2001a; Harrison with Phillips, 2003), especially in Wales and Northern Ireland.

Homelessness statistics indicate that minority ethnic households are three times more likely to be accepted as homeless by local authorities than the general population (Gervais and Rehman, 2005). This represents 21% of households recognised as homeless by local authorities, although accounting for only 8% in the 2001 census (now probably 15% of the UK population) (Gervais and Rehman, 2005). Similarly, analysis of Scottish local authority monitoring data found that the incidence of *recorded* homelessness affecting households from minority ethnic communities was 75% higher than across the population as a whole, with the degree of over-representation varying substantially between BME groups (Netto, 2006). Additionally, the same authors noted 'hidden' homelessness on an appreciable scale, evidenced by overcrowding and over-representation in poor-quality housing.

General accounts of homelessness recognise that explanations extend beyond lack of accommodation to other complex, interrelated factors such as marginalisation, insecurity, lack of choice, vulnerability, isolation and lack of income and employment (Kennet, 1999). In a similar vein, Netto's Scotland-based study (2006) identifies four main factors as contributing to homelessness in BME communities. These include:

1. changes in household formation as a result of having to leave the home of a relative or friend due to overcrowding, relationship breakdown, marital difficulties, intergenerational conflict and domestic abuse;
2. financial difficulties due to low income, unemployment and lack of access to affordable housing;
3. constrained housing options and loss of independent tenancies; and
4. policies and legislation relating to the position of asylum-seekers and refugees, and minority ethnic women escaping domestic violence.

Specific issues relating to the last two factors have been the focus of attention (Gill and Banga, 2008; Jones and Mullins, 2009). Consistent with other research (Gervais and Rehman, 2005), Netto (2006) found that in contrast to homelessness in the majority population, problems associated with substance abuse were not a major contributory factor to homelessness in these communities, and that repeat homelessness was rare.

Worryingly, despite the high incidence of homelessness in BME communities, access to homelessness services by these communities – including the provision of and finding accommodation services, advice-giving on welfare benefits, and facilitating access to employment – is typically problematic (Netto, 2006; Race on the Agenda, 2007). Netto and Gavrielides (2010) argue the case for closer cooperation between mainstream and minority ethnic agencies in addressing the barriers to accessing these services. Areas identified for closer partnership working include increasing awareness of homelessness services in these communities, widening access to early intervention, maintaining ongoing support to vulnerable individuals and informing policy development.

In the next section, we review the role of minority ethnic participation within the social housing sector in England, and specifically the impact of the BME housing policy implemented by the Housing Corporation from 1986 to 2003. We argue that while the Housing Corporation's policy was an innovative programme, its impact has been mixed, with few demonstrable outcomes. Instead, there has been a decline in the significance of 'race' in housing generally and the role of BME-led housing associations specifically. A number of reasons are put forward including changing macro-policy priorities, organisational performance and regulatory focus. This suggests a need for organisations to reconfigure to meet new policy challenges.

The rise of 'race' in the social rented sector

In 1986, 10 years after the Race Relations Act 1976, and five years after serious urban riots (Benyon and Solomos, 1987), the Housing Corporation launched a BME housing policy designed to 'encourage, run and create separate black-run organisations as a channel for providing rented housing' (Harrison, 1995, p 88). The language is stark, contrasting with the current policy approach to equalities in its radicalism. The 1986 BME housing policy was about capacity-building, black leadership and providing alternative sources of housing for minority communities. Implicit in this was the recognition that the so-called mainstream (or white-led) housing associations had not addressed the issue of 'race' equality. Outcomes were dramatic. Direct and targeted investment by the Housing Corporation resulted in the registration of 44 BME housing associations, a modest but important initiative. Symbolically, these community-based organisations were given an opportunity to address housing and related disadvantage in minority communities.

A second five-year plan – *An Independent Future* – (see Housing Corporation, 1998) started in 1992 (Housing Corporation, 1992) and concentrated on making BME housing associations financially viable. One of the consequences of the Housing Act 1988 was enabling housing associations to get investment from the private sector to build and manage housing. This was problematic for BME housing associations. Since they were new organisations, they did not have sufficient time to accumulate the level of reserves needed to subsidise rents (Royce, 1996). Asset value, management capacity and governance were the key indicators taken into account by financiers. BME housing associations were viewed as high risk.

The final Housing Corporation policy – *An Enabling Framework* – from 1998 to 2003 was shaped by the desire to meet minority consumers' needs, irrespective of whether they were tenants of a BME housing association or accommodated in other forms of housing. To this end the focus was on meeting the needs of minority tenants of all housing associations:

> towards ensuring that the expectations of black and minority
> ethnic communities are achieved, whether through the provision
> of adequate social housing by the full-range of landlords (only

some of which will be black-led) or through enabling members of the community to effectively participate in the delivery of services, through equality in the workplace, in management and in board membership. (Whitehead et al, 1998, p 5)

Improving governance and business performance rather than either consolidation or empowerment became key watchwords.

Three main factors explain the declining focus on 'race'. First, BME associations were small organisations and at risk from changes in policy and the economic climate. The perception of high rents ensured the Housing Corporation regulatory spotlight was firmly placed on this sub-sector (Whitehead et al, 1998). Second, development costs became complex and expensive requiring investment in human capital, partnership agreements and legal scrutiny. Third, equality legislation, combined with inspection by the Housing Corporation (latterly Homes and Communities Agency) and the Audit Commission led to improved performance on these issues by the social housing sector as a whole. A debate developed on the added value given by BME housing associations (CIH, 2004). The wider challenges of 'race', communities and residence continue to be discussed by policy and academic communities (see Beider, 2009), but difficulties faced by the BME sub-sector were, ironically, exacerbated by the fact that the few BME housing associations becoming relatively successful were then absorbed into larger mainstream housing associations, losing their cutting edge and specific BME focus.

Declining interest in 'race' and housing: the problem with regulation and representation

There are a number of problems with housing regulation and race that follow from the policy discussion earlier. First, regulators have moved to accommodate 'race' within the much wider prism of equality and or diversity. This parallels the direction of travel from 'race relations' to 'community cohesion', and from the Race Relations Act 1976 to the Equality Act 2010. It could be argued that the movement towards accommodating 'race' within the much wider lens of equalities was a signal that addressing racism is no longer important as a policy priority. We are seeing a similar trend in the housing sector with more resources and priority being afforded to non-'race' equality areas by both the Housing Corporation and Audit Commission. For example, the Housing Corporation (2004b) published a new *Good Practice Note* on equalities and diversity stressing the importance of housing associations dealing with wider issues other than 'race', such as disability and sexuality. This followed an internal publication significantly embracing the wider equality agenda in which 'race' is not mentioned specifically but seen within the context of other levels of disadvantage. A decade after the Macpherson Report (Macpherson, 1999), it could be argued that the policy and regulatory regimes are challenging housing organisations less on 'race' equality and racism and more on community cohesion (Home Office, 2001a, 2001b), a policy approach shifting attention away from racism in many welfare areas (Worley, 2005).

The inference is that 'race' equality should not be seen as an end in itself, but merely as part of the wider landscape that helps address the problems identified by 'community cohesion'. Macpherson wanted to address institutional racism and promote 'race' equality, while community cohesion discusses common norms and shared spaces (see Beider, forthcoming). Housing regulation has become all-embracing and less nuanced at a time when UK society is becoming more diverse and fragmented (see Chapter 3). The need is for specific regulatory interventions on minority housing issues, yet relatively little has been said about the needs and aspirations of the newest migrants, arguably having the greatest housing needs. Recent migration from Eastern Europe, Africa and the Middle East has changed the landscape for housing, 'race' and representation policy in England. Many 'new' BME communities – for example, from Somalia, Afghanistan and Iraq – have very little in common with 'old' BME communities from the Caribbean, India and Pakistan (Goodson and Beider, 2005).

There are a number of problems that need to be considered in adapting the framework for 'race' and representation to respond to these societal changes. First, representation should take account of new barriers to involvement, including language, expectations and awareness of institutions among newcomer communities. New groups may be excluded from being represented within housing institutions because of basic language barriers; housing bodies are unable to keep pace with change in this regard.

Second, the impact of change on 'old minorities', generated by jostling for power and more general community politics, should be explicitly acknowledged. The perception that hard-won influence and resources will be diverted to 'new minorities' requires a careful response. Research has shown that some 'old', established communities are resistant to 'new' communities (such as refugees and asylum-seekers) accessing political networks and representation on local area committees (Beider, 2005). In some instances, this could be viewed as 'recycled racism'. Old minorities are couching new minorities as a problem in terms of the link with neighbourhood decline, and also placing pressures on public resources, for example, by requiring larger family housing. This was very much the way that racism was espoused by the white UK population towards migrants from the Caribbean and Indian subcontinent during the 1950s and 1960s.

It could be argued that new groups are now, in turn, perceived as the undeserving poor. Housing regulation and policy discussion is reluctant to acknowledge or understand these complex power-related conflicts. The focus on representation at one end and building cohesive communities at the other misses important drivers for community change.

Third, the expectations placed on 'BME delegates' in representative models of involvement require reassessment. A single representative cannot represent fragmented and complex communities from minority groups. Yet there is an implicit assumption within the housing regulatory literature that housing organisations should have a representative management committee and senior staff (Housing Corporation, 2002, 2004a). This could lead to tokenism of the worst type, where housing associations simply use their networks to identify an appropriate minority person and tick the box marked 'diverse representation'. Moreover, empowering individuals rather than addressing racism and social justice leads to debates peppered with the terms 'leaders' and 'community leaders', referring to people typically identified and selected by institutions to speak on behalf of communities. This is problematic as a means of fully engaging with communities. It is doubtful whether 'leaders' really represent the diverse groups that compose any community of interest (Mullins et al, 2004) since they may be out of touch with young people or women for example. Indeed, it has been argued that this was one of the roots of the so-called Bradford 'riots' of 2005, older men being co-opted by government to speak on the communities' behalf, a position rejected by younger people (Jan-Khan, 2003). More fundamentally, the discussion about community leaders is racialised, since there is seldom any discussion about 'community leaders' applying to discussion in white communities (also see Atkin et al, 2008).

At the same time as these changes in policy and society, the social housing sector has also been transforming through processes of rationalisation, merger and group structure. There is a strong trend towards streamlining, reducing the size and number of committees, and limiting formal local accountability arrangements. It is widely recognised that traditional forms of representation and governance are no longer fit for purpose (Future Shape of the Sector Commission, 2006). The move towards rationalisation has meant that many smaller associations are joining larger groups. This is especially evident within the specialist BME housing association sector, with very few continuing to exist as independent organisations. Instead, they are becoming part of larger housing associations resulting in concerns about the representation and engagement of minority groups; formal independence has been traded for the promise of wider influence, but the impact on accountability to BME communities is unresolved. Recently, the largest BME housing association collapsed because of governance and financial problems, shaking confidence in this sub-sector.

Rationalisation may mark the end of the BME housing sector, but the decline has been in place for a considerable period. Despite concerns about the performance of some black-led housing associations, there is clear evidence that specialist support led to the emergence of new and important organisations meeting the needs of BME communities and helping the social housing sector as a whole to improve performance (CIH, 2004). Moreover, the knowledge and skills provided by BME housing professionals permeated the wider housing sector, leading to greater racial and cultural awareness and opportunities for leadership of mainstream housing associations. This level of support will not be afforded to new groups when there is evidence to suggest that housing needs are not being met by housing associations, an issue that will have increasing salience as the 'cuts' and housing benefit policies of the Coalition government begin to impact. Problems in awareness, understanding and engagement of new communities may not be easily resolved by housing associations (Markkanen, 2009). We finally consider policy initiatives and developments that offer some potential for improving the housing circumstances of BME communities.

Implications for housing strategies, policy and service delivery

Effective responses to minority ethnic communities need to be embedded within an overall policy context that eliminates unlawful discrimination and promotes racial equality and good 'race' relations within the current community cohesion agenda. The *Code of Practice for Rented Housing* (CRE, 1991) produced by the Commission for Racial Equality remains a useful source of reference. In England, Harrison with Phillips (2003) noted many signs of progress in measures taken to improve the housing circumstances of BME communities. These include: an explicit commitment to racial equality by the UK government; guidance on the development of local authority strategies through consultation with BME organisations; more encouragement to take tougher action against racial harassment; and the role of the National Housing Inspection system in monitoring performance and change. More generally, regulatory bodies need to consider how the regulatory framework can be used to ensure compliance with the Equality Act 2010, which is likely to provide further opportunities to increase understanding of equality law by bringing together different forms of anti-discriminatory legislation and making it easier to understand, despite the smaller emphasis on 'race' as a free-standing dimension. Cuts to social housing mean that increased attention should be paid to the position of BME communities in the private rented sector, an area currently under-researched, but which is likely to grow in importance. We next consider some key areas and potential developments that will improve the housing circumstances of BME communities.

Fair and transparent allocation of housing and the need for ongoing support

Fair and transparent allocation policies play an important role in ensuring equal access to housing for all sections of the population. Netto (2006) calls for allocation policies to give more weight to hidden homelessness in minority ethnic communities and to recognise fear of racial harassment as a major deterrent to living in certain areas, thus narrowing housing options. In a study on refugee pathways to housing, settlement and support in Glasgow, Netto and Fraser (2007) acknowledge challenges faced by housing providers in allocating housing to refugees in perceived safe areas given the limited stock available in the city, but argue that more can be done to tackle anti-social behaviour (including racial harassment). To ensure BME communities are not discriminated against, Blackaby and Chahal (2001, p 90) suggest that a number of areas in the allocations process should be ethnically monitored, including: the proportions of ethnic groups that are offered and let dwellings; comparisons of waiting times between different groups; and whether there are differences between ethnic groups in terms of why offers are refused, including refusals on the grounds of fear of racial harassment.

Choice-based lettings (CBL) approaches in which social landlords advertise homes for let and applicants take the initiative in bidding for vacancies, offer greater transparency than discretionary procedures. Such approaches have the potential for BME individuals to achieve better outcomes than traditional allocation policies since they place house-seekers rather than housing officers in the driving seat, reducing the possibility that an applicant may be made an 'inappropriate offer' (eg in an area that may be perceived to be unsafe for individuals from BME communities). The results of evaluative studies of CBL systems have been mixed in revealing increased interest from BME communities than previously, but not a consistent improvement in the share of lets to BME communities (Pawson et al, 2006; Law, 2007). However, such schemes are not likely to be equally accessible to all sections of the population, possibly hindering the ability of those lacking access to computing facilities or not fluent in English to make bids within the time frame allowed. The effectiveness of such schemes in ensuring more equitable outcomes for BME communities (as well as other vulnerable groups) therefore relies on the incorporation of specific support services to ensure their accessibility.

Monitoring of homelessness services

There is a clear need for regulatory bodies such as the Homelessness Directorate, established in 2002 specifically to deal with homelessness (see www.gemsoutreach.co.uk/IHF/GHD.htm), to set clear expectations on the importance of monitoring service provision. To ensure that an equitable service is provided to homeless applicants from BME communities, Blackaby and Chahal (2001, p 69) suggest monitoring these aspects of service provision (see *Box 5.2*).

> **Box 5.2:** Services to homeless people: what should be monitored?
>
> 1. Breakdown of the ethnic origin of people seeking advice and information, compared with a breakdown of the ethnic origin of households in the local area.
> 2. Comparing the ethnic origins of people applying as homeless, accepted as homeless and accommodated in various types of housing (such as hostels, bed and breakfasts) and permanent accommodation.
> 3. Cross-tabulating the various ethnic groups with the length of time homeless people spend in temporary accommodation.

Future of black-led housing organisations

In the previous section, we reviewed the rise and decline of the black-led housing sector in parallel to macro-policy interventions. These have crystallised around the role of the Housing Corporation's BME housing policies from 1986 to 2003, the publication and positive impact of the Macpherson Report in 1999 and finally the emergence of community cohesion policy following the 'riots' in 2001. As discussed, community cohesion has contributed to a period of stagnation and decline for the black-led housing sector. A rigid determination to focus on similarities between communities, an emphasis on common norms and shared public spaces, inevitably raised concerns about the value of housing associations that not only described themselves as black, but were rooted in the anti-racist struggles of the past. At a stroke, black-led housing organisations became out of step with mainstream policy and began to look dated. Macro-policy has played an important role in the development and decline of the black-led housing sector.

However, it has also been argued that the decline of the black-led housing sector cannot be simply blamed on the problematic nature of community cohesion policy. Recent flaws in governance have been documented by research and in the housing media. A successful future for black-led housing associations could lie in returning to their origin and early growth; that is, as community-based organisations that advocated for greater investment in a range of public service areas. In this way, black-led housing associations could use their considerable experience of organisational change, accessing private finance and leadership skills to influence public policy change. Given the shift in the direction of policy and politics signalled by the new Coalition government, emphasising localism, entrepreneurialism and working on housing as well as other policy domains may lead to new and sustainable types of black-led housing associations emerging.

Questions for discussion

- What are the main patterns of housing disadvantage experienced by BME communities?
- To what extent have legislative and policy initiatives contributed to the improvement of the housing circumstances of BME communities?
- What are the main causes of homelessness in BME communities? How can homelessness in these communities be reduced or prevented?
- What are the factors that have contributed to the rise and fall of black-led housing associations?

Electronic resources

- Equality and Human Rights Commission, Equality Act 2010 Guidance. Available at: www.equalityhumanrights.com/legislative-framework/equality-bill/equality-act-2010-guidance/
- ODPM (2005) 'Tackling Homelessness amongst Ethnic Minority Households'. Available at: www.gosw.gov.uk/497666/docs/164320/emifprojdoc (accessed 22 October 2007).
- Pawson, H., Netto, G. and Jones, C. (2007c) *Homelessness Prevention: A Good Practice Guide*, London: Department of Communities and Local Governance. Available at: www.communities.gov.uk/publications/housing/homelessnessprevention
- Race on the Agenda (2007) *What a Good Homeless Service Would Look Like for BAME Homeless Individuals: Toolkit*, available at www.rota.org.uk/pages/supplement.aspx

Notes

[1] However, note that overcrowding has been recognised as a major and increasing problem in recent years, with minority ethnic communities being twice as likely as white communities to experience overcrowding (Jones, 2010).

[2] Minority ethnic communities' fear or actual experience of racial harassment is well-documented (Chahal, 2007; Law, 2007).

Understanding the influence of ethnicity on health

Saffron Karlsen, Laia Becares and Marilyn Roth

Overview

There is substantial evidence identifying how certain aspects of health and well-being vary by ethnic group. Marked ethnic inequalities have been reported in different measures of health and mortality (Salway et al, 2010). By highlighting examples of ethnic inequalities in health and explaining the drivers of these inequities, this chapter aims to provide a greater understanding of the interrelationships between aspects of minority ethnic status, structural factors and health.

This chapter will:

- present evidence on the patterning of health across different ethnic groups;
- outline different approaches to analysing the relationships between ethnicity and health;
- establish how different analytical approaches can shape our understanding of ethnic inequalities in health; and
- explain how approaches must allow for the ways in which social structures influence health experiences.

Key concepts

ethnic density, exclusion and disadvantage, genetic and biological predisposition, methodological approaches, personal and institutional cultures, racist victimisation, residential concentration, social and group identification

Introduction

The evidence regarding the health disadvantage experienced by many, although not all, people from black and minority ethnic (BME) groups in the UK is compelling (eg Nazroo, 1997a, 1997b, 2001; Erens et al, 2001, Sproston and Mindell, 2006). Similar evidence is available throughout Europe and elsewhere, including in the US (eg Williams, 2001), Latin America (Pan-American Health Organization, 2001), South Africa (Sidiropoulos et al, 1997), Australia (McLennan and Madden, 1999) and New Zealand (Harris et al, 2006). This disadvantage persists for adults and children (Kelly, 2007; Panico and Kelly, 2007; Panico et al, 2007), and across several indicators of morbidity and mortality (Salway et al, 2010).

Table 6.1 presents evidence for ethnic inequalities in a range of health indicators using data from the Health Survey for England (HSE) 2004. HSE 2004 remains the most recent, nationally representative survey of the health of different BME populations in England. The figures shown compare the risk of different aspects of poor health for people from BME groups relative to that of the general population (whose risk is set at 1). Those groups that have a risk greater than 1 have a risk of poor health greater than that of the general population, while those with risks below 1 have a risk of poor health lower than that of the general population.

There are some similarities in the relative risks for certain health outcomes across different minority ethnic groups. For example, men in several minority groups have a significantly lower risk of being obese than men in the general population. Indian, Pakistani and Bangladeshi men and women and Black Caribbean women have between 2.5 and 5.5 times the risk of diabetes of their counterparts in the general population. There are also health indicators where some ethnic groups appear to be at particular risk. Pakistani and Bangladeshi people generally appear to be at greater risk of poor health than the general population, although the size of this risk (and the extent to which it is significantly different from that of the general population) varies by health outcome.

Yet while the differences existing in the health experiences of people with certain ethnic backgrounds are now well-established, gaps remain. Empirical evidence with which to establish the presence of ethnic variations in life expectancy and in cause and other specific aspects of mortality remain limited (Salway et al, 2010). There are also groups that remain generally under-represented in statistics, including new migrant groups, Gypsies, Roma and Travellers, and asylum-seekers and refugees, although there is evidence that these groups experience extreme health disadvantage compared with other groups (Parry et al, 2007; Aspinall and Watters, 2010).[1]

Table 6.1: *Age-standardised[a] risk ratios for specific health outcomes, by minority ethnic group and gender*

	Bad/very bad self-reported health	Limiting long-standing illness	GHQ12 score 4 or more	Any CVD	Diabetes	BMI over 30 (obese)	Raised waist–hip ratio	Hypertension
				Relative risks (standard errors)[b]				
Men								
General population[c]	1.00 (6%)	1.00 (23%)	1.00 (11%)	1.00 (14%)	1.00 (4%)	1.00 (23%)	1.00 (33%)	1.00 (32%)
Black Caribbean	1.37 (0.37)	1.00 (0.14)	1.21 (0.22)	0.73 (0.17)	2.05 (0.54)	1.03 (0.15)	**0.73 (0.13)**	1.37 (0.19)
Black African	0.81 (0.25)	**0.63 (0.12)**	0.88 (0.17)	0.25 (0.10)	1.98 (0.60)	0.79 (0.14)	0.77 (0.18)	1.21 (0.22)
Indian	1.45 (0.27)	1.12 (0.12)	**1.32 (0.19)**	0.91 (0.15)	2.86 (0.43)	0.60 (0.08)	1.15 (0.11)	1.15 (0.13)
Pakistani	**2.33 (0.42)**	1.17 (0.14)	**1.56 (0.28)**	1.28 (0.24)	2.72 (0.54)	0.76 (0.12)	1.46 (0.13)	0.98 (0.19)
Bangladeshi	**3.77 (0.55)**	**1.52 (0.15)**	**1.83 (0.35)**	0.16 (0.69)	3.87 (0.78)	0.22 (0.05)	1.34 (0.16)	0.63 (0.14)
Chinese	0.75 (0.20)	**0.57 (0.10)**	0.76 (0.15)	**0.58 (0.14)**	1.29 (0.36)	0.26 (0.06)	**0.66 (0.13)**	0.78 (0.13)
Irish	1.41 (0.33)	1.11 (0.13)	1.08 (0.21)	1.16 (0.22)	0.67 (0.22)	1.07 (0.15)	0.98 (0.12)	1.13 (0.18)
Women								
General population[c]	1.00 (7%)	1.00 (27%)	1.00 (15%)	1.00 (13%)	1.00 (3%)	1.00 (23%)	1.00 (30%)	1.00 (29%)
Black Caribbean	**1.90 (0.31)**	1.20 (0.11)	1.27 (0.17)	0.89 (0.13)	3.03 (0.49)	1.43 (0.13)	1.42 (0.14)	1.58 (0.19)
Black African	1.68 (0.36)	0.83 (0.11)	1.19 (0.19)	0.83 (0.24)	1.80 (0.61)	2.00 (0.17)	1.64 (0.23)	1.71 (0.37)
Indian	1.39 (0.24)	0.86 (0.09)	0.99 (0.13)	**0.72 (0.12)**	2.46 (0.46)	0.89 (0.08)	1.15 (0.11)	0.91 (0.12)
Pakistani	3.54 (0.49)	**1.60 (0.14)**	**1.73 (0.24)**	0.93 (0.16)	5.32 (0.87)	1.48 (0.14)	**1.77 (0.16)**	1.01 (0.18)
Bangladeshi	**4.02 (0.57)**	**1.22 (0.11)**	1.37 (0.23)	0.83 (0.18)	3.20 (0.77)	0.89 (0.12)	**2.29 (0.17)**	1.43 (0.22)
Chinese	**0.55 (0.20)**	**0.46 (0.08)**	0.83 (0.15)	**0.56 (0.15)**	1.72 (0.48)	0.32 (0.07)	1.00 (0.16)	1.12 (0.20)
Irish	0.74 (0.19)	**0.80 (0.09)**	0.95 (0.13)	0.83 (0.14)	0.84 (0.24)	0.88 (0.10)	**1.27 (0.13)**	0.95 (0.14)

Notes: [a] Age standardisation was conducted separately for men and women, expressing male data to the overall male population and female data to the overall female population. No age standardisation has been introduced to remove the effects of the different age distributions of men and women and this should be borne in mind when comparing data for men and women.
[b] The figures in bold show differences that are statistically significant.
[c] Standardised risk ratio and observed prevalence displayed for the general population.

Source: Health Survey for England (HSE) 2004, general population figures from HSE 2003.

For the rest of this chapter, we present an overview of different 'drivers' (explanatory factors) proposed to explain these ethnic health inequalities to explore how this research can inform our understanding of how and why these patterns emerge.

Understanding the drivers of ethnic inequalities in health and disease

> ... it is important to consider the centrality of racism to any attempt to explain ethnic inequalities in health. Not only are personal experiences of racism and harassment likely to influence health, but racism as a social force will play a central role in structuring the social and economic disadvantage faced by minority ethnic groups ... a racism that has its roots in colonial history. (Nazroo, 2003, p 282)

Theoretical explanations used to justify particular approaches to the investigation of ethnic health inequalities have tended to focus on genetic/biological or cultural/behavioural differences between groups or on the social processes that produce and perpetuate the social disadvantage experienced disproportionately by people with minority ethnic backgrounds and the consequences these have for their health. Here, we consider racism as having a central role in the development of ethnic inequalities in health, which influences health directly and also encourages the perpetuation of social disadvantage (and, in turn, producing health disadvantage). However, we also argue that while approaches exploring genetic/biological, cultural/behavioural and social/structural factors have traditionally been considered as competing (Nazroo, 1998), there are ways in which they reflect similar processes of social exclusion and mistreatment. We discuss how different approaches to understanding ethnic health inequalities can each be considered indicative of the ways in which social/structural disadvantage influences the lives of many people from BME groups in the UK. We will also show how our insight into the drivers of ethnic inequalities in health is affected by the approach taken to investigate them.

We will begin by examining the evidence provided by work to expose the importance of social/structural factors in the development of ethnic inequalities in health. This work explores the health implications of the socio-economic disadvantage and victimisation that is experienced disproportionately by people with minority ethnic backgrounds in the UK and elsewhere. We will then discuss how other influences on ethnic health inequalities can enhance understanding of the impact of structural disadvantage on the lives of people with minority ethnic backgrounds. Finally, we will explore the additional insight offered by more creative theoretical approaches to the investigation of the relationships between ethnicity and health.

Structural components of ethnic differences in health: socio-economic disadvantage

The Marmot Review (2010) – following other research evidence exposing the 'social gradient in health' (see eg Townsend and Davidson, 1982; Marmot et al, 1984; Davey Smith et al, 1990; Wilkinson and Pickett, 2009) – reported that people living in the poorest neighbourhoods will die on average seven years earlier than those living in the richest, and that more of the shorter lives of poorer people will be spent in poor health and with disabilities. Given the concentration of many people with minority ethnic backgrounds in socio-economic disadvantage (detailed in Chapters 5, 9 and 10), it is perhaps not surprising that this has been found to be an important driver of ethnic health inequalities among both adults (Williams, 1999; Nazroo, 2003) and children (Kelly et al, 2006, 2008; Panico et al, 2007). Yet, the impact of socio-economic position on the relationship between ethnicity and health is frequently ignored. Such analytical approaches treat these structural forces more as distractions than as issues worthy of explicit investigation (Nazroo, 2003). Often this is done implicitly, as when statistical models exploring the relationship between ethnicity and health are 'adjusted' for the effects of socio-economic status in the expectation that this will uncover the important 'ethnic' effect. Unfortunately, such approaches rarely contain either the theoretical or empirical work needed to demonstrate what the remaining 'ethnic' effect in a model might be (Nazroo, 1998).

The identification of a residual 'ethnic effect' (following this socio-economic adjustment) is often sufficient to reassure researchers as to the analytical (and theoretical) validity of their approaches. Unfortunately, the problems related to the measures of socio-economic status used for these 'adjustments' suggest that they are not (Kaufman et al, 1997, 1998). The use of a single measure to adjust for socio-economic differences between majority and minority groups assumes a level of homogeneity across them that can be used as the basis of this adjustment: in essence that being part of a particular socio-economic category has the same socio-economic implications regardless of ethnicity. However, people with minority ethnic backgrounds will often be more disadvantaged than white people, even within the same socio-economic bands (Nazroo, 2001). For example, within each occupational band, people from minority ethnic groups are on less prestigious occupational grades with lower incomes, poorer job security, less social working hours and more stressful working conditions. Unemployed people in BME groups have on average been unemployed for longer than their white counterparts and a higher proportion of households in Pakistani and Bangladeshi groups are lacking one or more basic household amenities compared with those in other ethnic groups, regardless of their housing tenure. Indeed, Pakistani and Bangladeshi people have been found to have around half the income of white people, with Pakistani and Bangladeshi people in the (apparently) most affluent classes having average weekly incomes similar to that of white people in the least affluent classes (Nazroo, 1998, 2001). Using measures based on occupational grade, economic activity or housing tenure to adjust for socio-economic variation across ethnic groups may therefore give an appearance of having adjusted for, and thereby removed, any socio-economic differences while much of it remains (Kaufmann et al, 1997, 1998).

Perhaps not surprisingly, the use of more sensitive measures of social position suggest a much greater role for socio-economic status in the generation of ethnic inequalities in health (Nazroo, 1998, 2001; Krieger, 2000). For example, Nazroo (2001) demonstrated how ethnic differences in diagnosed angina and heart disease, which persisted with adjustment for occupational class, were explained in models using a composite 'standard of living' measure developed using information on household overcrowding, whether a household was lacking sole access to one or more amenities (bath/shower, bathroom, inside toilet, kitchen, hot water from a tap, central heating), and certain consumer durables. Indicators that can more adequately account for the socio-economic inequalities between different ethnic groups can therefore provide a very different impression of those approaches that might prove most effective for reducing health variations between them.

The socio-economic disadvantage experienced by people with minority ethnic backgrounds has a significant impact on their health experience and this cannot be ignored. It reflects particular histories of migration, an associated lack of social and cultural capital to seek jobs in the labour market (see Chapters 3 and 4), and experiences of exclusion and victimisation. The residential concentration of people from minority ethnic groups in neighbourhoods with greater socio-economic disadvantage has also been described as a mechanism by which racism operates to restrict the lives of people with minority ethnic backgrounds; a social manifestation of both individual prejudices and institutional discrimination (Acevedo, 2000).

More recently, empirical evidence has examined more directly other ways in which racist victimisation can influence the health experiences of people with different ethnic backgrounds. It is to this work that we now turn.

Structural components of ethnic differences in health: racist victimisation

Empirical evidence for the significant relationships between different markers of racist victimisation and health have been found in the UK, US and elsewhere (Harris et al, 2006; Paradies, 2006; Mohseni and Lindström, 2008). It has been found to affect health directly, through the negative physical and psychological consequences of interpersonal racist verbal or physical violence (Karlsen and Nazroo, 2002a; Karlsen et al, 2005), and indirectly, in the way that institutional racism leads to the identification of minority ethnic groups as biologically and culturally different, and the exclusion and social and economic disadvantage that minority ethnic people experience as a result (Miles, 1989). 'Racism is [then] the primary reason that blacks are disproportionately concentrated in the poorest sectors of the working class and face restricted class mobility' (Krieger et al, 1993, p 97). These various manifestations of racist harassment and discrimination have been shown to have independent effects on the health of its victims. *Figure 6.1* shows how the odds of fair or poor self-rated health increase with exposure to different forms of racist victimisation, including: racially motivated verbal abuse or physical assault; a perception of institutional racism (measured according to whether or not the respondent feels the majority of British employers are discriminatory); socio–economic disadvantage (used as a marker of the impact of institutional racism); and reporting a sense of fear regarding being racially attacked.

Long-term exposure to inferior treatment and a devalued status has been found to damage self-esteem, invalidate self-worth and block aspirations (Parker, 1997; Krieger, 2000). It may shape the content and frequency of stressful life events, and may limit the range of feasible responses to them, as well as the social support available. Associations have been reported between experiences of general (interpersonal) racism and increased smoking, binge drinking and being overweight or obese (Shariff-Marco et al, 2010). Experienced racism in healthcare and other statutory services has been associated with delayed screening for prostate cancer (Shariff-Marco et al, 2010), poor self-rated health, poor physical functioning, mental health problems, smoking and symptoms of cardiovascular disease (Harris et al, 2006).

Establishing the role of racist victimisation in the generation of ethnic inequalities in health is (also) hindered by problems of measurement. These have been discussed in depth elsewhere (Karlsen and Nazroo, 2002a, 2006). In short, the recognition of reportable incidents of racist victimisation is often not straightforward and it has been argued that some coping mechanisms actually discourage the acknowledgement of experiences of

Figure 6.1: *Impact of different forms of victimisation on health*

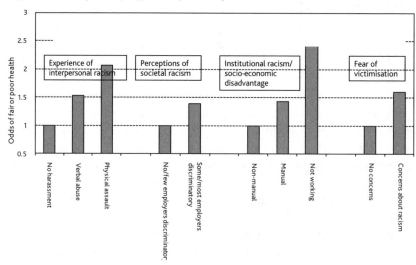

Source: Adapted from Karlsen and Nazroo (2002a, 2002b, 2004).

victimisation (Ruggiero and Taylor, 1995). Although racist victimisation is considered both to generate and also to perpetuate the socio-economic disadvantage experienced disproportionately by many people with minority ethnic backgrounds, direct evidence of such victimisation is difficult to establish.

Again, the relationships between such structural inequality and health are not straightforward. The poverty associated with many areas with greater levels of BME concentration has a negative impact on health. Yet areas with higher concentrations of minority ethnic residents, or particular ethnic density, have also been shown to have protective effects on their residents' physical and mental health (Halpern and Nazroo, 2000; Bécares et al, 2009a, 2009b; Das-Munshi et al, 2010). The 'ethnic density effect' suggests that the enhanced mutual social support and stronger sense of community and belongingness offered by living in close proximity to others with the same ethnic background can buffer, or protect against, the direct and indirect health consequences of experienced racist victimisation (Halpern and Nazroo, 2000; Bécares et al, 2009a) as well as the stigma associated with lower socio-economic status (Pickett and Wilkinson, 2008). *Figure 6.2*, for example, shows the likelihood of reporting poor health for minority ethnic people who have experienced interpersonal racism, relative to those who have not, at varying levels of ethnic density. A (non-significant) buffering or protective effect of ethnic density can be observed for Bangladeshi, Indian and Pakistani people, for whom the detrimental association between experienced discrimination and poor health is smaller at higher levels of ethnic density (Bécares et al, 2009a).

Figure 6.2: *Association between racism and poor self-rated health at varying levels of own-ethnic density among people who have experienced racism, relative to those who have not*

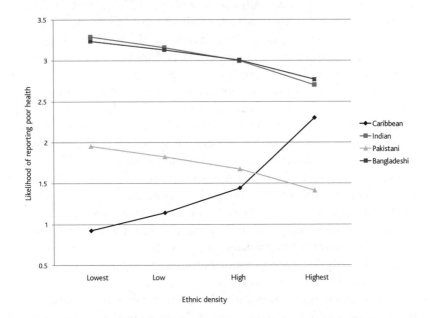

Note: Adjusted for age, sex, individual socio-economic status and area deprivation.
Source: Adapted from Bécares et al (2009a).

There is strong empirical evidence to support the critical role of social/structural factors in the development of ethnic health inequalities, despite the limitations inherent in the methodological approaches often taken to investigate them. We now describe how a recognition of the biological and behavioural influences on ethnic health inequalities – evidence of which has traditionally been considered to disprove the significance of social/structural factors – is affected by the methods adopted to investigate them, and how they mask structural factors that might be at play.

Genetic/biological components of ethnic inequalities in health and disease

Ethnic groups are social constructs, which vary across time and place and are generally poor proxies for genetic markers. Consequently, there is great variation in the extent to which certain genetic traits are concentrated among particular ethnic groups, and how these might impact on their health experience. Despite this, research investigating the drivers of ethnic health inequalities tends to emphasise genetic/biological explanations, at the expense of those describing more structural forces. This genetic/biological focus is encouraged by particular approaches adopted to classify individuals into ethnic categories, and the lack of theoretical consideration given to the 'evidence' regarding the resultant relationships between ethnicity and health (Ellison and Rees Jones, 2002).

'Ethnic' classifications used in many surveys draw on phenotypic characteristics, which have genetic underpinnings (such as skin colour), or geographic/environmental ancestry, which has been shown to influence genetic profile. Drawing group distinctions according to the presence of potential genetic risk factors inevitably leads to a concentration of particular diseases, such as certain types of skin cancer and sickle-cell traits, among individuals in particular ethnic groups. It may be entirely appropriate to use such an approach to assert that particular ethnic groups have geographic or biological ancestries producing a genetic susceptibility to *certain* health conditions. However, this evidence is an insufficient basis from which to assume that ethnic health variations more generally are purely genetic/biological in origin.

Genetic/biological factors can offer insight into ethnic variations in health. But there is a complex interplay between genetic, environmental and socio-economic characteristics to be taken into account before the extent of genetic/biological influences can be definitively established. An adequate understanding of these interrelationships remains distant.

Cultural components of ethnic inequalities in health and disease

In addition to concerns regarding biological differences between ethnic groups, research and policy initiatives frequently draw attention to the health implications of people's 'traditional' lifestyles (Brock et al, 2009). There are many aspects of such 'traditional' lifestyles that may protect health, such as opportunities for improved access to social support, socio-communal engagement or economic and other resources that they may provide (Kelleher, 1996; Halpern and Nazroo, 2000; Roth and Kobayashi, 2008).

However, historically, research approaches have focussed on 'traditional' cultures as the *cause* of poor health outcomes (discussed in Chapter 2).

Importantly, empirical evidence suggests that there is great variation in the extent to which individuals adopt particular health-related behaviours, *within* as well as *between* ethnic groups. **Table 6.2** presents evidence for ethnic inequalities in a range of health-related behaviours. These figures show that our picture of the health consequences of minority ethnic status varies dramatically according to the indicator used, even among groups whose health outcomes (described in **Table 6.1**) appear generally relatively poor. So, ethnic variations in levels of alcohol, fruit and vegetable consumption, and mean fat intake suggest that (non-white) minority ethnic status should, other things being equal, imply good health compared with other groups. However, ethnic variations in the use of salt during cooking, cigarette smoking and physical activity present evidence of minority ethnic 'lifestyles' (for some ethnic and gender groups) that may be more costly for health. While there is evidence that the health implications of some behaviours (such as tobacco chewing) are underestimated among some groups (Roth et al, 2009), these differences are too small to explain health inequalities of the scale described earlier.

This evidence suggests that differences in the lifestyles of different ethnic groups cannot in themselves explain the health inequalities between them. The health implications of these lifestyles are not sufficiently consistent – nor poor – to imply the almost ubiquitous minority ethnic health disadvantage outlined earlier. We would argue, again, that the relationships between ethnicity and health-related behaviours need to be understood in light of the evidence exposing the impact of socio-economic disadvantage and racist victimisation on health and health risk-taking, as described earlier.

The findings presented in **Figure 6.3** suggest that the significantly higher current smoking rates of Bangladeshi compared with white British men included in the Health Surveys for England for 2006, 2007 or 2008 were explained by socio-economic variations between the groups. The smoking rates of Pakistani men were significantly lower than those of white British men after adjusting for socio-economic differences between the groups.

'Cultural factors' can also be considered to affect people's interactions with health and other statutory services: both in terms of how people from minority ethnic groups engage with services and how services respond to their needs. Assessing whether ethnic variations exist in the uptake of statutory services is extremely problematic given differences in how 'needs' might be perceived and issues with ethnic monitoring in general. Despite these problems, there is an increasing body of research identifying important ethnic differences in health service use. Nazroo et al (2009) found that people from some minority ethnic groups were more likely

Table 6.2: Age-standardised risk ratios[a] for health behaviours, by minority ethnic group and gender

	Current cigarette smoker	Drank alcohol three or more days a week in the past year	Did at least 30 minutes moderate physical activity on at least five days a week	Ate at least five portions of fruit and vegetables a day[b]	Mean fat intake score	Adds salt during cooking
	Relative risks (standard errors)[b]					
Men						
General population[c]	1.00 (24%)	1.00 (41%)	1.00 (37%)	1.00 (23%)	1.00 (24.3)	1.00 (56%)
Black Caribbean	1.02 (0.12)	0.75 (0.08)	1.03 (0.09)	1.40 (0.16)	0.85 (0.04)	1.38 (0.07)
Black African	0.80 (0.11)	0.47 (0.08)	0.84 (0.09)	1.40 (0.16)	0.82 (0.03)	1.38 (0.08)
Indian	0.78 (0.09)	0.44 (0.05)	0.75 (0.06)	1.64 (0.15)	0.76 (0.02)	1.69 (0.04)
Pakistani	1.08 (0.11)	0.05 (0.02)	0.64 (0.07)	1.47 (0.14)	0.84 (0.04)	1.69 (0.04)
Bangladeshi	1.43 (0.11)	0.01 (0.01)	0.58 (0.07)	1.48 (0.20)	0.89 (0.04)	1.73 (0.04)
Chinese	0.81 (0.13)	0.49 (0.07)	0.74 (0.07)	1.66 (0.16)	0.80 (0.03)	1.42 (0.07)
Irish	1.30 (0.13)	1.23 (0.10)	1.05 (0.08)	1.14 (0.13)	0.98 (0.04)	0.83 (0.07)
Women						
General population[c]	1.00 (23%)	1.00 (26%)	1.00 (25%)	1.00 (27%)	1.00 (21.2)	1.00 (53%)
Black Caribbean	1.08 (0.11)	0.42 (0.06)	1.17 (0.10)	1.16 (0.09)	0.84 (0.04)	1.33 (0.07)
Black African	0.34 (0.07)	0.28 (0.08)	1.03 (0.10)	1.23 (0.11)	0.92 (0.04)	1.60 (0.08)
Indian	0.23 (0.04)	0.21 (0.04)	0.81 (0.07)	1.37 (0.11)	0.81 (0.02)	1.78 (0.05)
Pakistani	0.19 (0.04)	0.01 (0.01)	0.46 (0.06)	1.19 (0.11)	0.91 (0.04)	1.70 (0.06)
Bangladeshi	0.11 (0.04)	0.00 (0.00)	0.32 (0.06)	1.00 (0.13)	0.84 (0.04)	1.79 (0.05)
Chinese	0.32 (0.07)	0.37 (0.08)	0.59 (0.07)	1.65 (0.13)	0.90 (0.06)	1.49 (0.08)
Irish	1.11 (0.11)	1.06 (0.11)	1.08 (0.11)	1.24 (0.12)	1.00 (0.02)	0.87 (0.08)

Notes: [a] See *Table 6.1* for an explanation on how age-standardisation was carried out in HSE 2004.
[b] The figures in bold show differences that are statistically significant.
[c] Standardised risk ratio and observed prevalence displayed for the general population.
Source: Health Survey for England 2004, general population figures from HSE 2003.

than white majority groups to have visited their GP in the last two weeks. However, people in all minority ethnic groups, including Irish and Chinese people, were less likely to visit a dentist for check-ups and Indian, Pakistani, Bangladeshi and Chinese people had significantly lower levels of hospital utilisation. Gypsies and Travellers, asylum-seekers and refugees have also been found to have poor access to GPs and other primary and secondary care services (Parry et al, 2007; Aspinall and Watters, 2010).

Figure 6.3: *Smoking rates among South Asian compared with white British men, before and after adjusting for household social class*

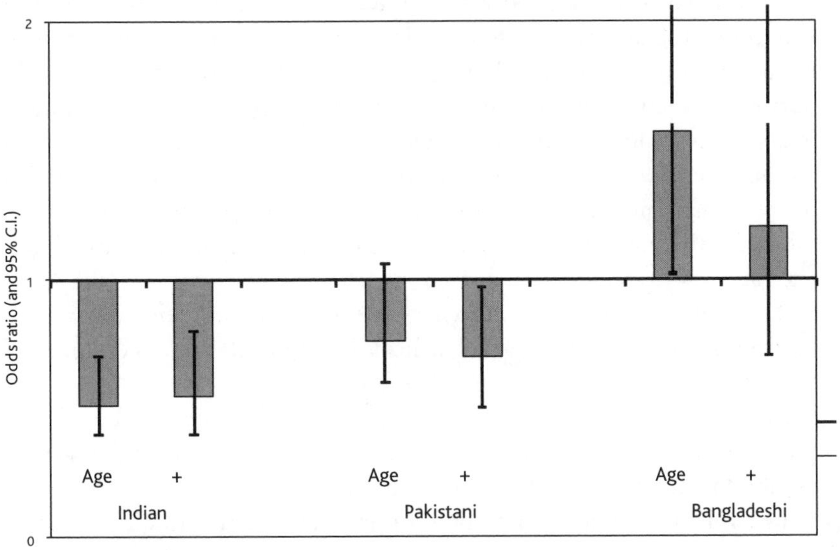

Source: Adapted from Karlsen et al (2011).

Ethnic differences have been found in access to secondary services, particularly for cardiovascular disease (Sekhri et al, 2008; Bethell et al, 2009) and maternity care, which are implicated in the stark ethnic inequalities in maternal mortality rates (Lewis, 2007). There are also particular concerns relating to the experiences of people from different black groups, as well as Gypsies, Travellers, asylum-seekers and refugees, engaging with mental health services. Recent evidence shows that over 54% of black people in inpatient mental health units have been compulsorily detained under the Mental Health Act, compared with 32% generally (NHS Information Office, 2009). Importantly, the community-based evidence which exists does not identify differences that would justify these ethnic variations in inpatient stays (Nazroo and King, 2002). Further, African-Caribbean people have been shown to be more likely to receive medication as the primary source of treatment for mental health problems and are less likely to receive psychotherapy, or talking therapies, than those in other ethnic groups (Bullen and Reeves, 2003; McKenzie et al, 2001).

A recurring theme in research studies relates to the sense among minority ethnic service users of being unwelcome and isolated and of providers being dismissive and disrespectful (Bharj and Salway, 2008; Worth et al, 2009). Figures produced by the Care Quality Commission in 2008/09, for example, suggest that people of Asian/Asian British ethnicity are 50% and Chinese people are 70% less likely than white British people to report that they were always treated with dignity and respect by their GP. Service engagement is directly affected by prior experiences with those services. People who (or know people like them who) have been treated poorly during interactions with health and other services will be discouraged from further engagement; and where they occur, any such interactions will induce additional stress. Consequently, opportunities to access health benefits associated with screening or timely engagement with services following the onset of symptoms may be lost, with implications for health and life.

Salway et al (2010) outline three interrelated ways in which delivery of health services can undermine the health and healthcare experiences of BME people:

- failure to understand and accommodate specific cultural preferences;
- failure to establish effective communication; and
- discriminatory attitudes and behaviours that directly compromise care and cause significant distress among patients and their carers.

While effective communication is clearly problematic for those with limited English ability, it is also hampered by real and perceived cultural barriers, lack of professional confidence, lack of patient empowerment and rushed consultations (Mir, 2008). Providers have been found to hold negative stereotypes and preconceptions about the characteristics and preferences of particular ethnic groups, which in some cases have led to the withholding of particular treatments, potentially directly contributing to health inequalities between ethnic groups (Chowbey et al, 2008; Mir and Sheikh, 2010).

Traditional understandings of health and illness impact on how some people choose to manage and treat their health problems (Mackenzie et al, 2003). There is evidence, for example, that people from some BME groups, such as Chinese people, are more likely to self-medicate and use complementary and alternative medicines than white British people. This trend must be considered in the context of the healthcare system and the degree to which cultural preferences are understood, respected and accommodated (Fink, 2002). Lack of access to information and a lack of familiarity with health systems can also affect people's ability to engage with and exercise choice with regards to their healthcare, particularly (but not only) new migrants and those with poor English language skills. These issues are exacerbated by culturally incompetent services and practitioners. Rather than the 'cultural' drivers of ethnic differences in health emphasising the idiosyncrasies of particular ethnic groups, then, much of the available evidence speaks of the ways in which the *institutional cultures* of statutory services perpetuate the structural disadvantages that BME people experience, acting to limit their access to resources that may improve their health status.

New approaches to understanding ethnic inequalities in health

Here, we have described in detail three broad approaches relating to social/ structural, genetic/biological and cultural/behavioural influences on ethnic inequalities in health. We have focused, particularly, on what each brings to our understanding of the drivers of these inequalities and how the approaches used to investigate them have informed our perception of their nature and causal mechanisms. We end with a discussion of several recent developments in the investigation of ethnic health inequalities that may offer additional insight into the relationships underlying them as well as examples for potential avenues for fruitful future research. These explore the role of religion, migration and processes of social identification for the development of health inequalities. Each of these approaches can be considered to adopt a more creative approach towards the investigation of which aspects of 'ethnicity' might be important for health.

Like ethnicity, religion operates as an important source of personal identity, group cohesion and social and political mobilisation for many ('majority' and 'minority') people. Religion can potentially provide health benefits (Kinnvall, 2002; Ecklund, 2005) and operates both as a focus for victimisation (Poynting and Mason, 2007; Lloyd, 2009) and a resource against social and economic exclusion. Consequently, investigation of religious, or ethnic/religious, inequalities in health may offer valuable opportunities to develop a better appreciation of the drivers of ethnic inequalities in health. *Figure 6.4* plots the age- and gender-adjusted odds ratios and 95% confidence intervals for the risk of self-assessed fair or poor health among South Asian respondents with different ethnic and religious backgrounds compared with white British respondents, using combined data from the 1999 and 2004 Health Surveys for England (Karlsen and Nazroo, 2010). The stark differences in risk between the different Indian (Hindu, Sikh and Muslim) groups offers important additional complexity to the traditional picture of Indian health advantage (relative to Pakistani/Bangladeshi groups and others) presented in models that group individuals by broad ethnic background and provides valuable insight for our understanding of the drivers of ethnic inequalities in health (including, again, the importance of more structural influences).

Figure 6.4: Ethnic/religious differences in self-assessed fair or poor health

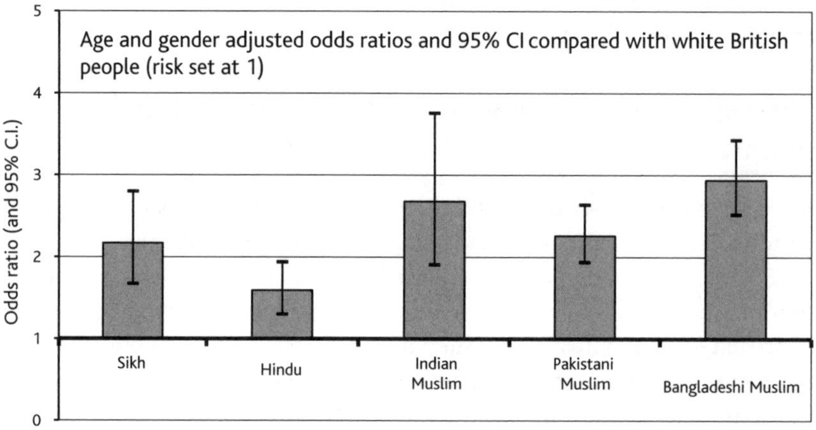

Source: Adapted from Karlsen and Nazroo (2010).

Nazroo et al (2007) took as their starting point a need to explain the apparent health advantages of Caribbean-Americans relative to Caribbean people living in the UK (and African-Americans). The findings from their analyses suggest that health differences between the two Caribbean groups are entirely explained by differences in socio-economic and migration status. The authors conclude that the health differences were explained by the migration from the Caribbean to the US, which:

> happened later than that to the UK, into a different race relations context, at a time when, perhaps, migrants were able to take advantage of the civil rights movement in a way that the pre-existing Black population (and the population in the UK) was not. (Nazroo et al, 2007, p 825)

They argue that migration is an important issue that needs to be considered using approaches which can engage with the way social forces define who migrates and their migrant experience, including:

- the social and economic forces that drive migration;
- the selection of the population into migrant and non-migrant groups;
- the social and economic and political contexts into which migrants arrive; and
- how these contexts develop over time and across generations.

Other research valuable for the investigation of ethnic inequalities in health recognises that it is really only through an exploration that allows for the different ways in which ethnicity forms part of people's lives that we can recognise the dynamic and multidimensional nature of ethnicity, thus truly exploring the interrelationships between aspects of minority ethnic status, structural factors and health. The social exclusion associated with racist victimisation has been found to be strongly associated with the ways people think about, and define, themselves and the social groups that they feel able to consider themselves part of (Karlsen, 2006). Such *racialisation* – the way that racist victimisation and exclusion affects our self-perception – along with socio-economic exclusion has been found to play an important role in explaining ethnic inequalities in health (Karlsen and Nazroo, 2002b).

Summary

Developing a better understanding of the relationships between ethnicity and health is an increasingly important focus for ethnically diverse countries like the UK. We have described how ethnic inequalities in health persist across a broad range of health outcomes and the different ways in which ethnic inequalities in health are usually explained. We highlight several ways in which the approach used to *investigate* ethnic inequalities in health influences how these inequalities are *understood*, which, in turn, affects what strategies and policies might be used to address them. Moreover, we have shown how ethnic inequalities in health might be more usefully considered as structurally driven, associated with factors such as socio-economic disadvantage and social exclusion, than as simply generated by genetic or cultural differences between groups. But rather than considering these as distinct influences on the health of people with minority ethnic backgrounds, we need to consider how they interact to shape the health (and other related) experiences in the daily lives of people with different ethnicities.

Questions for discussion

- What are the main drivers of ethnic inequalities in health?
- In what ways may 'culture' be considered to influence ethnic inequalities in health?
- Why have social/structural explanations traditionally been given less research attention?
- Why is it important to understand the importance of ethnicity as identity in the exploration of ethnic health inequalities?

Electronic resources

- www.marmotreview.org/AssetLibrary/pdfs/Reports/FairSocietyHealthyLives.pdf
- www.ic.nhs.uk/webfiles/publications/mental%20health/NHS%20specialist%20mental%20health%20services/MHMDS09/MH_Bulletin_2004_2009.pdf
- www.bmj.com/cgi/content/full/bmj.39534.571042.BEv1

Note

[1] There is very little evidence for the Roma population.

Not invited to the party? Black and minority ethnic adults and the personalisation of social care

Ossie Stuart

Overview

- examines the impact of social exclusion on disabled people from black and minority ethnic (BME) communities, specifically exploring their potential exclusion from social care as a consequence of personalisation;
- assesses Department of Health initiatives on user-led organisation before focusing on the capacity of BME voluntary-sector groups to deliver and support personalised care, especially in a time of economic recession; and
- concludes by exploring the broad relationship between social care policy and social exclusion, while outlining the potential impact of recent policy ideas such as the 'Big Society', on social care.

Key concepts
disability, personalisation, racism, social care, social exclusion

Introduction

Something has changed in social care. People who use social care services – let us call them 'service users' – will no longer have to endure services not designed to meet their needs. Let us not, however, get carried away; the vast majority of service users endure services that do not meet their needs. Nonetheless, over the last decade, it has dawned on policymakers that delivering the services people actually want might result in better outcomes. As the influential Department of Health document 'Putting people first' put it: 'Older people, people with chronic conditions, disabled people and people with mental health problems have the best possible quality of life and the equality of independent living is fundamental to a socially just society' (DH, 2007a, p 2).

This chapter assesses the extent to which BME service users are likely to benefit from the transformation of adult social care. Will they continue to experience services that have long failed to provide equality of outcome (see Hussain et al, 2002; Vernon, 2002)? Or will the current changes improve their experience? Notwithstanding the considerable diversity found among the UK's BME populations (discussed later), this chapter will take a broad approach to ethnic diversity, reflecting the generic experience of disadvantage and discrimination. Because of this, the chapter has some limitations, but in the absence of more detailed evidence, the arguments are robust, offering a starting point in developing more sophisticated arguments reflecting the contested nature of ethnicity (see Chapter 2).

However, one cannot talk about the transformation of social care without understanding where it all originated. The Disability Movement – that is, groups of activists, academics and writers who are themselves disabled – has campaigned since the 1980s for the modernisation of social care to incorporate ideas such as 'independent living', 'user participation' and 'empowerment' (Oliver, 1996), ideas now taken for granted. This demonstrates the lasting power of the social model of disability, which is especially good at reflecting how societal views, values and norms define the experience of disability rather than medical definitions, which tend to emphasise individual functioning. Social disadvantage occurs not because of the consequences of individual impairment, but because of how societies exclude disabled people. Disabled people, therefore, should not be seen as passive, tragic victims, but as individuals who have to actively engage with their disability to overcome disadvantage. The social model of disability acknowledges the debt owed to disabled people's organisations, which have long demanded greater control and autonomy for those using social care services.

Following direct action and lobbying by groups of disabled people and their allies, and the introduction of the Health and Community Care Act 1990, reform of the care system in England has focused on the idea that the needs of the person should be the basis of a tailored, responsive and flexible personal package of care. The care management approach, for example, aimed to develop individual care plans based on detailed assessments by budget-holding care managers (SCIE, 2009). One of the first 'cash for care' schemes introduced in England to facilitate this was the Independent Living Fund (ILF), established in 1988. This evolved into an arrangement to provide cash support to severely disabled people who chose to live at home (Henwood and Hudson, 2007).

Since 1996, people who have been assessed as eligible for social care support have had the option to negotiate with their care manager and take cash to buy the support they choose. This is known as a 'direct payment'. Direct payments have led to an interest in how 'individual budgets' could help promote choice and control for those using adult social care services. While direct payments use money from a local authority social care budget, individual budgets combine resources from different funding streams (SCIE, 2009). Disabled people from Britain's BME communities, however, have not played much of a role in shaping the assumptions informing this transformation, their voice largely being ignored. Consequently, BME service users are at risk of not benefiting from the choice and flexibility that greater participation in social care promises (Stuart, 2005). Before exploring the implications of this in greater detail, it is necessary to describe the key components of this transformation and modernisation.

The policy context

Social care services in England are undergoing a period of rapid change and reorganisation. The increasing policy interest in personalisation, in which users have greater control and choice over the support they receive, is bound up with these changes. Besides the campaigns of disabled people (Glasby and Littlechild, 2002; Pridmore, 2006), findings from a countrywide pilot of individual budgets (Individual Budgets Evaluation Network [IBSEN]) influenced how personalisation was introduced by the government (Glendinning et al, 2008), as did the more general and continuing government emphasis on ideas such as individual responsibility, the merits of competition and a mixed economy of care, and concerns about the growing cost of social care (DH, 2007a). The Coalition government is fully committed to the personalisation of social care as it fits well with its vision of a 'Big Society', a vision concerned with shifting responsibility (and risk) from the state to the individual. Communities and individuals are thus encouraged to become more involved in decisions that shape their lives (Office for Civil Society, 2010).

Supporting independent living and personal assistance remains a key government priority. The White Paper 'Our health, our care, our say: a new direction for community services' (DH, 2006) set out plans to increase provision of personal payments, amalgamating diverse funding streams into more flexible individual budgets. The document *Improving the Life Chances of Disabled People* further set out a vision for future developments: 'By 2025, disabled people in Britain should have full opportunities and choices to improve their quality of life and will be respected and included as equal members of society' (Prime Minister's Strategy Unit, 2005, p i).

This Independent Living Strategy in England is a five-year scheme to increase the degree of choice and control exercised by disabled people over how support is provided:

> Disabled people have told us that one of the barriers to change is lack of understanding about what independent living means. An important part of the Strategy will be action to promote understanding among service deliverers of how to enable people to have choice and control so that independent living and a personalised approach are integral to the way services are planned and delivered. (Office for Disability Issues, 2008, p 5)

Achieving this greater choice and control for service users involves establishing one *individual budget*, which amalgamates current, diverse funding streams associated with:

- local authority social care;
- integrated community equipment services;
- Disabled Facilities Grants;
- Supporting People for housing-related support;
- Access to Work; and
- Independent Living Fund.

Individual budget-holders are encouraged to devise support plans that help meet their personal outcomes. They can purchase support from social services, the private sector, the voluntary sector and community groups, or neighbours, friends and family members. Help with this support planning can come from care managers, social workers, independent brokerage agencies, family or friends (SCIE, 2009). This can be highly effective, as the example in *Box 7.1* illustrates.

Box 7.1: Merged individual budgets

In spring 2010, three families got together in a Gloucester town and merged the individual budgets received by their three sons with learning disabilities. This enabled the three men to move out of residential accommodation and into a purpose-built shared house. It was also possible to fund a team of personal assistants to support them to live in the community. The parents oversaw the management of the individual budgets. These disabled people were able to participate in their local community in ways that would have been impossible in a residential setting.

Figures published for March 2010 by the Association of Directors of Adult Social Services and the Local Government Association show that there are currently about 170,000 individual budget-holders, an increase of 77,000 (83%) on 2009. Of these, 140,000 are receiving ongoing care and support, with the rest receiving one-off services, such as carers' breaks, equipment and adaptations to homes. Local authorities expect there to be 376,000 people receiving ongoing care and support on individual budgets by April 2011 (Association of Directors of Adult Social Services, 2010).

Further reforms of the social care sector are planned. The development of a National Care Service is under consultation with the aim 'to start the process of transforming adult social care into a system capable of delivering support tailored to individuals and local populations' (DH, 2009b, p 3). Proposals include making basic funding available to each person, rather than only funding those who meet increasingly strict local authority eligibility criteria. This would potentially reduce the divide between service users who fund their support themselves and those who receive funding from the social care system.

Marginalising BME users

There is a tendency in the literature to generalise and treat people of colour as if they are all the same, despite there being important differences between, and within, ethnic groups (see Chapter 2). The term 'BME', although convenient for our purposes here, describes a myriad of different peoples who live in the United Kingdom. All, however, are likely to be discriminated against because of their nationality, colour of skin or belief systems.

The developments in social care outlined earlier have taken place with little or no significant involvement of BME service users or those organisations that speak for these communities (SCIE, 2009). Further, the research has often excluded their experience. This indicates a need for specific investigation into how individual budget programmes could work for these groups. There is an assumption that individual budgets will improve choice and control for BME populations (Audit Commission, 2006), but, as SCIE (2009) pointed out, this has yet to be tested.

There is a risk of repeating the errors of the past without the involvement of this significant group of service users. This absence, however, reminds us of the inherent contradiction that continues at the heart of the welfare state (see Chapter 4). Some argue that one of the roles of the welfare state is to reinforce notions of the family, nation and work in ways consistent with 'British culture' (Williams, 1996). It should also come as no surprise that the recession has enabled politicians to question the right of access to welfare benefits. One of the key policy initiatives of the Coalition government has been to attack those who are deemed to be undeserving of welfare benefits. Alongside revisited concerns about the cost of uncontrolled immigration and the supposed failure of multiculturalism, it is easy to see how issues of 'race', class and family coalesce around BME communities in the UK (Williams, 1996). The reconstruction of social care could, therefore, create a crisis for BME communities, with their conditional access to the welfare state being undermined by institutional assumptions that amount to discrimination (CSCI, 2008). These assumptions help account for an invisibility of BME communities in both local and national arenas. This chapter now explores two examples illustrating how the impact of racism means that it is unlikely that personalisation will change BME people's experience of social care.

Universalism, capacity and choice

A key assumption informing personalisation is that BME communities will benefit from these changes (Audit Commission, 2006). As local users of social care, their interests and views would be addressed through local forms of representation or user involvement. However, criticism of this assumption comes from Ben-Tovin et al (1986). Their study of Wolverhampton and Liverpool identified two ideological trends that amounted to racism at the local level. They called the first trend 'universalism'. The authors argued that in the pursuit of a 'fair' and 'equal' provision, local housing officers, teachers, youth leaders and local councillors obscured the particular needs of black people. Instead, service providers argued that it would be counter to ideals of 'fairness' to focus additional resources on BME communities as a way of addressing the significant specific barriers they faced. There are, of course, significant social, cultural and economic differences between the 1980s and 2010. Nevertheless, it can be argued that 'universalism' can be identified in the move to establish user-led organisations as the resource through which users of social care services make informed choices about their care requirements.

The universalism behind personalisation is apparent in the policy statements of both the Labour and Coalition governments. The 2007 'Putting people first' policy statement aimed to replace paternalistic, reactive care of variable quality with systems focused on prevention, early intervention, enablement and high-quality, personally tailored services:

> In the future, we want people to have maximum choice,
> control and power over the support services they receive. To
> ensure this, the intention is to support at least one local User
> Led Organisation and mainstream mechanisms to develop
> networks that ensure people using services and their families
> have a collective voice, influencing policy and provision. (DH,
> 2007a, pp 2–4)

Ironically, the pursuit of community empowerment creates the risk of
underestimating the significant barriers faced by BME communities.
Current changes assume a level playing field when providing care. This
is not the case. Mainstream services are less likely to accommodate the
needs of BME communities, because such needs are either ignored or
misrepresented (see Chapter 2). At the same time, alternative provision
is often unavailable as mainstream third-sector organisations struggle to
engage with ethnic diversity, while the capacity of potential third-sector
providers who are able to meet the needs of BME communities remains a
problem (see also Chapter 4). For example, in 2008, the Sickle Cell Society
raised £300,000, whereas the Cystic Fibrosis Trust raised £11.5 million
(Hobson, 2008).

Irrespective of its inability to accommodate diversity, can we really expect
an under-resourced and overstretched voluntary sector to assume many
of the functions of the welfare state? Ideas about the Big Society need to
be viewed in this context, particularly since a recent Coalition initiative
provides further evidence for this naive acceptance of universalism. 'Building
a stronger civil society' (Office for Civil Society, 2010) is a strategy aimed at
voluntary and community groups, charities and social enterprises. It builds
upon personalisation in as much as it places empowering communities,
opening up public services and promoting social action at the heart of
the strategy (Office for Civil Society, 2010: 3). As with 'Putting people
first', it could be assumed that BME communities would have the same
opportunities to participate as any other groups.

BME service users are thought to seek out support from their own
communities (DH, 2007b). If this were the case, the 'privileging' of 'user-
led organisations' over other local community organisations would mean
support from BME organisations would be less likely in future. User-led
organisations are identified as the primary vehicle through which the
collective voice of service users will be heard (DH, 2007a). This is critically
important as local authority commissioners will be more likely to look
to user-led organisations to help provide key social care services. The
track record of social care agencies in responding to the needs of BME

communities raises doubts about the ability of commissioners to purchase accessible and appropriate culturally competent care.

The capacity of BME community organisations is again pertinent here. Such organisations have never been good at supporting disabled people within their communities (Greater London Action on Disability, 1991). However, just as the Big Society strategy is launched, Race on the Agenda (ROTA), one of Britain's leading social policy think-tanks focusing exclusively on issues that affect BME communities, reported that BME third-sector organisations had experienced considerable funding cuts, impacting significantly on specialist services available in London. There is no reason to suppose this experience is any different to the rest of the UK. In some cases, ROTA reported losses of up to one fifth of the annual income of some BME charities. BME young people, refugees and migrant communities seem especially hard hit by these cuts (Race on the Agenda, 2009).

The failure to recognise the unique barriers faced by BME users of social care services suggests personalisation might struggle to make a difference. There is an institutional failure to even acknowledge, let alone address, the issues BME communities face in ensuring local empowerment and representation. This failure is further evident in the desultory way the Department of Health consulted BME communities about personalisation. Perhaps the best example of this is the Department of Health's commissioned IBSEN research on the impact of individual budget pilot projects that ran from 2005 to 2007 (Glendinning et al, 2008). The significance of this study is best described by the researchers themselves:

> The study is the first robust UK evaluation of the implementation of this form of personalised approaches to social care and its impact on the individuals involved, the workforce and providers, as well as the support and commissioning processes. The aim was to offer a reliable basis for considering the national roll-out of policies built on principles of personalisation and participation. (Glendinning et al, 2008, p 4)

Despite the study's key role in validating personalisation, IBSEN failed to involve many BME service users. The researchers claimed to have had a good representation of key equality characteristics, including age, ethnicity and household composition. They also interviewed 130 people offered an individual budget. Despite this, they had to acknowledge that few BME service users were interviewed (Glendinning et al, 2008, p 14). The Department of Health's consultation and testing of the policy of personalisation, therefore, went ahead without the meaningful involvement of service users from BME communities. To make matters worse, the necessary legal impact assessment carried out to evaluate the introduction of personalisation for BME populations cited IBSEN's material as its core evidence base. No one would suggest that IBSEN's researchers or Department of Health officers set out to exclude BME communities. Yet, the subsequent inaction has increased the likelihood that personalisation will not mitigate the well-known and long-standing discriminatory outcomes for BME service users (Butt, 2005). Ironically, the barriers faced by BME communities in accessing social care have long been a feature of Department of Health-sponsored research.

One of the few pieces of research exploring the views of BME users looked at direct payments (IFF Research, 2008). Its findings reinforce the view that BME service users' access to social care differs significantly from that of other service users. The study found that more 'black' (66%) and 'Asian' (58%) people employed friends or relatives as personal assistants than 'white' people (39%). The report also indicated important areas for improvement in the administration of direct payments. In particular, 'Asian' employers were much more likely to state that paperwork pertaining to direct payments should be reduced (69%, compared to 29% of all employers); that the local authority should provide 'applicant checking' services (48%, compared to 21% overall); and that there should be more services directed through outreach workers (39%, compared to 15% overall).

The local: community involvement

Alongside universalism, Ben-Tovim et al (1986) also identified another ideology that had a direct effect on discriminatory practice during the 1980s. They described this as 'labourism'. This referred to the maintenance, by mainly white working-class males, of the supremacy of class struggle over any other forms of struggle, such as 'race' or gender. These forms of struggle came to be seen as dividing the working class. It is not my intention to look at the implications of social class for personalisation. Instead, I want to substitute what I will call a disability focus for 'labourism'. By disability focus, I mean the maintenance of the rights of disabled people over any other forms of struggle, such as 'race', which were similarly seen as having the potential to divide the disability movement. This is not to suggest that the Disabled People's Movement is intentionally racist. Disabled people have long been concerned about the lack of engagement with BME disabled people and community groups (Barnes et al, 1999).

My contention here is that the 'user-led' strategy came about as a result of an alliance between disabled people's organisations and the Department of Health. This explains how user-led organisation became a key part in the personalisation of social care. As we have seen, one of the consequences of this might be to further marginalise BME service users (SCIE, 2010c). Gender is another issue, and Morris (1991) has pointed to the dangers of patriarchal assumptions permeating the social model of disability. Morris argues that the social model assumes a 'typical' disabled person is a young man in a wheelchair who is fit, never ill and whose only need is a physically accessible environment. Women's experience is therefore marginalised. Morris's insights are critical when discussing the experience of BME disabled people and personalisation. Ethnocentric and patriarchal assumptions underpinning the social model have meant that it is not possible to talk about the ways BME communities imagine and construct disability (Stuart, 1996). Worse, it assumes that these experiences are less important than the 'real-world' issues of barriers and disability oppression. The consequence of this ethnocentrism within the disability epistemology is that ethnicity is seen, at best, as a diversion from the real, lived experience of disabled people. This assumption helps to explain the disability focus within the user-led organisation project.

The rise of the user-led organisation

User-led organisations represent one of the key Department of Health initiatives aimed at increasing participation and representation among service users, older people and family carers. The intention is that there should be 'support for at least one local user-led organisation and mainstream mechanisms to develop networks, which ensure people using services and their families have a collective voice, influencing policy and provision' (Prime Minister's Strategy Unit, 2005, p 91).

The user-led organisation model has been adapted from the experience of existing service user organisations and, in particular, from Centres for Independent Living. All have their history firmly rooted in that of the Disabled People's Movement (Barnes and Mercer, 2006). Since the 1980s, disabled people challenged the way services were delivered, organising new forms of self-directed provision. This put the policy and practice of independent living firmly on the public agenda. Organisations such as Centres for Independent Living (now also known as Centres for Inclusive Living) emerged as a new form of provision, run and controlled by disabled people (DH, 2007b).

Such developments, however, have again never meaningfully involved BME disabled people or BME community organisations (Hussain et al, 2002; Vernon, 2002). It was assumed that BME disabled people would define themselves as largely disabled people only or use BME and community organisations when appropriate (DH, 2007b). Neither BME disabled people nor their community organisations had much influence on the Disabled People's Movement during the 1980s and 1990s. Pan-impairment organisations often struggle effectively to include those from minority groups. This includes other disabled people such as the deaf community, people with learning difficulties, people from the lesbian, gay, bisexual and transsexual community, and mental health system users; and other groups who may be disabled and/or use independent living services, such as older people, those from BME communities and family carers (DH, 2007b, p 81).

When the Prime Minister's Strategy Unit first proposed user-led organisations as the key vehicle for achieving personalisation, it was the experience of the Disabled People's Movement it turned to. Their influence can be seen in the 2008 publication *Independent Living*, a cross-government strategy about independent living for disabled people (Office for Disability Issues, 2008). While it does mention BME communities on several occasions, the strategy acknowledges that disabled people within these communities have yet to benefit from any aspect of independent living in terms of choice and control over their lives. In addition, it presents disabled people from BME communities as a single homogeneous and undifferentiated group alongside similar undifferentiated groups such as older people and younger disabled people (Office for Disability Issues, 2008). Despite fine words, the government's approach is in danger of being seen as tokenistic. It also provides a clear example of universalism, in which difference is ignored. User-led organisations, as we have seen, struggle to represent the experience of BME communities.

A user-led organisation is one that is run and controlled by people who use support services, including disabled people, mental health service users, people with learning difficulties, older people and their families (DH, 2007c). This has important implications for the future. These user-led organisations will run or support key local services. This is believed to enhance choice and control and ensure services can meet users' requirements. User-led organisations are also expected to represent the views of users. The Department of Health produced 21 design criteria describing what a user-led organisation should look like and what services it should provide (DH, 2007c). One of the key criteria is that it must have a minimum of 75% of the voting members on the management board drawn from the organisation's constituency. This is to ensure control of a user led organisation by the people it represents (DH, 2007c).

The Department of Health found that the Disabled People's Movement had very strong feelings about this 75% rule. The Movement has always taken a robust position on representation. A survey conducted by the National Centre for Independent Living in 2006 revealed that 50% of the 34 Centres for Independent Living within the National Centre for Independent Living network required their boards to comprise 100% disabled people, with 21% requiring 50% or 51%, and 1% requiring 7% (DH, 2007c). The Disabled People's Movement insists that only '"disabled people" should run and control User-Led Organisations' (Morris, 2006). This has created confusion. The Department of Health guidance on creating user-led organisations does use the term disabled people, but at the same time suggests, vaguely, that a user-led organisation should be controlled by that organisation's constituency, some of which would not be disabled (DH, 2007c). 'Service user' has become the most frequently used term to describe a user-led organisation's membership (SCIE, 2010a). This term is not universally welcomed or accepted (Heffernan, 2006). Shaping Our Lives (Bromfield and Beresford, 2006), a national organisation promoting user involvement in decision-making processes, emphasises the importance of seeing 'service user' as an active and positive term, albeit one that should always be based on self-identification.

The history of the user-led organisation is really that of the Disabled People's Movement. Disabled people originally created user-led organisations to be run and controlled by their membership. The Department of Health has largely adopted this form of representation uncritically and ignored its potential for 'race' discrimination. This increases the risk that local user-led organisations will simply become another local organisation that fails to involve BME communities (SCIE, 2010b). The consequences of this are potentially enormous if the government continues to withdraw from its responsibility for state provision and realises its expectations that individuals and volunteerism will fill the gap (Office for Civil Society, 2010). Those advocating the 'Big Society' have made it clear that the voluntary sector must absorb a significant part of the consequences of the proposed social care cuts (Office for Civil Society, 2010). This might have dire consequences for BME community organisations. Already weakened by the recession, and with a history of under-resourcing and capacity (see Atkin and Rollings, 1993), these organisations usually find fund-raising difficult even in better economic circumstances (Chouhan and Lusane, 2004; Race on the Agenda, 2009). The Department of Health's decision to privilege user-led organisations might threaten the existence of some long-established BME organisations, as commissioners are forced to rationalise the services they buy from the voluntary sector.

The dominance of the disability agenda and its disability focus has meant that BME communities have never had the opportunity to shape the debate on the future of a personalised social care. The reasons for this are both historic and the result of institutional racism. As we have seen, BME disabled people are marginalised within the Disabled People's Movement

(Greater London Action on Disability, 1991) and continue to be on the periphery of social care debates (Butt, 2005; Patel, 2005; Stuart, 2005). This is the context in which personalisation will be introduced. The Centre for Integrated Living project, for example, has continually excluded the experience of BME disabled people (Evans and Banton, 2001; Stuart, 2006; Woodin, 2006; DH, 2007a). Far from creating a level playing field, personalisation throws up further potential barriers for BME users (IFF Research, 2008).

The role of the social care professional

Hall argues that it is neither useful nor insightful to adopt a solely materialist approach to explaining racism. Historical specificity is essential in understanding the various sites and arenas where racism and resistance are played out. This allows us to look at the likely response to the consequences of a discriminatory personalised social care sector (Hall, 1997; see also Chapter 2). One such area is the key role social workers will play in the personalised social care system. The reimagining of their role presents a clear opportunity to ensure BME communities are able to benefit to some degree from personalised social care.

Despite being a key source for social care information, the social care professional, usually a social worker and care manager, has tended to view personalisation negatively and with a degree of hostility (Ferguson, 2007). From a professional point of view, bewildering changes have taken place without their involvement. Consequently, they feel that they have had no opportunity to influence what personalisation should look like (Glendinning et al, 2008). Instead, guidance, edicts and directives have been largely imposed on the profession. If they protested, social workers risked being cast as defenders of an obsolete, overly paternal service, where 'one size fits all'.

Iain Ferguson, publishing in the *British Journal of Social Work*, perhaps best captured this mood (Ferguson, 2007). He argued that the popularity of personalisation is due primarily to its congruence with key themes of New Labour thought, such as individualisation and the transfer of risk from the state to the individual. He suggests that the philosophy of personalisation is not one that social workers should accept uncritically given the introduction of markets in social work and social care; the growing neglect of poverty and inequality; its flawed conception of the people who use social work services; its potentially stigmatising view of welfare dependency; and its potential for promoting, rather than challenging, the de-professionalisation of social work. The idea of the Big Society does borrow a number of these concepts, although, if anything, there tends to be an even greater emphasis on the role of individual responsibility. Through responsible and active citizenship, the Big Society is intended to initiate a renaissance in volunteering and philanthropy (Office for Civil Society, 2010).

Though many social workers would find such ideas challenging, their relationship with BME service users has been far from supportive (see Chapters 2 and 4). For example, the experience of many BME communities and mental health care has been one of over-representation in the punitive services (see Chapter 11). Late intervention and stereotypical assumptions frequently characterise care (Rai-Atkins et al, 2002; Wallcraft et al, 2003; Social Exclusion Unit, 2004; Trivedi, 2008), which fails to address the issues service users find important (Burman et al, 2002; Burr, 2002). Will social work repeat these mistakes as personalisation is rolled out? Scepticism about the value of personalisation held by some social workers might not bode well for BME service users and their families. However, there are indications that personalisation is beginning to help social workers find a new role, helping them remove the barriers to social care faced by BME service users.

Social workers will still act as gatekeepers in a personalised social care service, for example, being responsible for 'Fair Access to Care' and support planning for the allocation of an individual budget (Glendinning et al, 2008). More significantly, the level of confidence social workers have in personalisation will determine the degree to which they support and 'sign off on' the innovative and potentially risky solutions their clients wish to adopt. This applies to the level of information provided as well. For BME service users, social workers will remain the main source of information about what an individual budget is and how it can be used. The better the quality of this information, the greater the likelihood that service users might opt for solutions that are non-traditional or unique to them. In other words, social workers are central to the success of personalisation. This is how the IBSEN researchers put it:

> Other factors identified by local authority staff (social work staff) interviewed in the evaluation as facilitating change are not unique to the introduction of personalisation. Like other change management processes, key success factors included active support from the most senior managers and decision makers in the organisation, together with an implementation team that was enthusiastic, able to problem-solve and to bring in other people – IT staff, finance officers, expertise from voluntary and independent sector organisations – as and when required. (Glendinning et al, 2008, p 248)

The realisation within the social work profession was that among those who would probably benefit the most by holding an individual budget, BME service users are the most likely to be dependent on the quality of information and advice they receive. It also means that social workers can help users from these communities create solutions that better fit with their circumstances. In doing so, social workers have found that they can address issues and offer more diversity through personalisation in ways that block contracts with large providers could never resolve. The example in *Box 7.2* explores the potential for this.

Box 7.2: Social work and personalisation

The role of social work in facilitating personalisation is explored in a study of Tameside Metropolitan Borough Council, Windsor and Maidenhead Borough Council, and Wolverhampton City Council by the former Care Services Improvement Partnership (CSIP). Each had a low uptake of direct payments among BME service users (Edwards, 2007), explained by a lack of confidence in the direct payments scheme among local social workers. In Wolverhampton, for example, the project reported that:

> Over a period of four years there has been a growing confidence in the use of direct payments in Wolverhampton. There has been a move away from paternalistic views of the authority knowing best how to meet people's care needs, to one where service users are encouraged to arrange care for themselves. There has been an accompanying recognition that trying to minimise risk may have restricted social care opportunities. Service users are now able to make informed choices about risk themselves. (Edwards, 2007)

In effect, the success of personalisation for the varied BME communities depended upon social workers' commitment to it. What is more important, it requires social workers to accept that BME clients face unique barriers and that they should avoid universalist solutions such as relying upon user-led organisations. By doing so, BME service users will be able to exercise meaningful and informed choices and assess the risks for themselves. The CSIP report demonstrated how this is possible (see *Box 7.3*).

Box 7.3: The success of direct payment

By March 2007, there were 142 users of direct payments (DP) in Tameside. Nearly 20% of these users are from black and minority ethnic (BME) communities. This is an impressive figure, as only 5.2% of the borough's population are from BME communities. This comparative figure makes Tameside the most successful local authority in England in BME take-up of direct payments. This rate has been achieved by regular contact with local community groups, luncheon clubs, and temples and churches. A recently appointed specialist DP worker for BME communities who is fluent in 4 South Asian languages is increasing uptake even further. (Edwards, 2007)

Many social workers are beginning to see opportunities offered by direct payments or individual budgets. Social work has the potential to reinvent itself as a key enabler in the delivery of personalised solutions for BME communities. These changes, however, are largely piecemeal. While some social workers have been able to leverage personalisation to improve practice for BME users, a lack of joined-up policy means others are unlikely to hear about it.

Summary

We began by describing the proposed changes to social care. Called 'Personalisation', its aim is to move away from services controlled by the provider, to services designed and controlled by service users. This transition to a more individualised service provision is assumed particularly to suit BME service users. Yet the consequences of institutional racism mean that their voice is often excluded from personalisation debates. The decision to use user-led organisations as a vehicle for engagement reflects this problem. Historically, user-led organisations run by disabled people's organisations have struggled to reflect the experience of BME service users, largely explained by the primacy of the disability discourse over any other (Woodin, 2006). Evidence highlights the weakness of this approach (Vernon, 2002; Stuart, 2005; Butt, 2005; SCIE, 2010b). Further, the more specialist BME third sector is poorly placed to play a useful role and capacity remains a serious problem. The transformation of social work, however, does offer some hope. The experience of direct payments tells us that, despite initial low uptake among BME service users, well-motivated social workers can make an important difference. It would be reasonable to assume that the same could be applied to individual budgets.

Nonetheless, persistent and long-standing tensions raise concerns that personalisation could fail BME service users. First and foremost, the universalist assumptions of policy planners must be altered to facilitate a greater understanding of the specific barriers faced by BME users. As some pioneering social workers have shown, personalisation will work for BME users if the indirect discrimination they face accessing social care services is acknowledged and addressed. Second, it is important to challenge the ethnocentric approach implicit in discussion about disability and personalisation. This means ideas and concepts might unwittingly be imposed on people for whom they have little or no meaning. Disabled people's organisations have long insisted on the primacy of disability as the defining experience of oppression. Alliances between user-led and BME third-sector organisations could make for more inclusive user representation. Third, for the third sector to play a greater role in the delivery of local services, including personalised social care, it must be acknowledged that BME third-sector organisations face specific challenges and that capacity building is necessary.

Questions for discussion

- To what extent has personalisation in social care struggled to benefit the lives of disabled people from BME communities? How would you explain this?
- How useful is the idea of user-led organisations?
- Why have disabled people's organisations struggled to meet the needs of ethnically diverse communities?
- Discuss more broadly the strengths and weaknesses of the social model of disability in understanding social exclusion.

Further reading

Atkin, K. and Ahmad, W. (1996) *Race and Community Care*, Milton Keynes: Open University Press.

Barnes, C. and Mercer, G. (2006) *Independent Futures: Creating User-Led Disability Services in a Disabling Society*, Bristol: BASW/The Policy Press.

Glasby, J. and Littlechild, R. (2002) *Social Work and Direct Payments*, Bristol: The Policy Press.

Morris, J. (1991) *Pride against Prejudice: Transforming Attitudes to Disability*, London: The Women's Press.

Vernon, A. (2002) *User-Defined Outcomes of Community Care for Asian Disabled People*, Bristol: The Policy Press.

Williams, F. (1989) *Social Policy: A Critical Introduction – Issues of Race, Gender and Class*, Cambridge: Polity Press.

Woodin, S. (2006) *Mapping User-Led Organisations, User-Led Services and Centres for Independent, Integrated, Inclusive Living: A Literature Review Prepared for the Department of Health*, Leeds: University of Leeds.

Electronic resources

- National Centre for Independent Living (NCIL). Available at: www.ncil.org.uk/categoryid21.html
- Social Care Institute for Excellence: A commissioner's guide to developing and sustaining user-led organisations. Available at: www.scie.org.uk/publications/guides/guide36/index.asp
- The Disability Archive UK – the aim of the Disability Archive UK is to provide disabled people, students and scholars with an interest in this and related fields with access to the writings of those disability activists, writers and allies whose work may no longer be easily accessible in the public domain. Available at: www.leeds.ac.uk/disability-studies/archiveuk/
- Putting People First: Transforming Adult Social Care website – the online hub of information, news, events and resources for the Putting People First initiative. Available at: www.puttingpeoplefirst.org.uk/

'Race', education and children's policy

Patrice Lawrence

Overview

This chapter identifies and explores the disparity in educational outcomes and socio-economic circumstances between children of different ethnic backgrounds, and assesses the impact of mainstream children's policy in addressing these inequalities. In particular it:

- reviews the obstacles to developing a successful policy framework for children and young people across all ethnic groups;
- explores the difficulties of understanding what 'ethnicity' means for children and young people in the UK;
- considers reasons for the continuing disparities in education and socio-economic outcomes between different ethnic groups; and
- examines the controversial, but persuasive, critical race theory perspective on the failure of mainstream policy to address racial disadvantage.

Key concepts
children, critical 'race' theory, education, identity, outcomes

Introduction

In 2008, Action for Children (2008) published a report arguing for a new politics for children. It estimated that in the UK, over the previous 21 years, there had been 'over 400 different initiatives, strategies, funding streams, legislative acts and structural changes to services affecting children and young people ... equivalent to over 20 different changes faced by children's services for every year since 1987' (Action for Children, 2008, p 4). This included:

> 40 Green and White Papers published over the last 21 years. Of the 28 White Papers published, 19 were issued by the English Government; five were issued by the Scottish Government; one each by the Welsh and Northern Irish Governments; and finally two White Papers covered the whole of the UK. (Action for Children, 2008, p 4)

To this can be added six changes of the government department responsible for education in England, numerous changes of Secretary of State and the political churn of local and general elections. The 2010 general election culminated in a Conservative and Liberal Democratic Coalition government tackling a £6 billion economic deficit. Yet more change is under way.

Ethnicity and identity

The diversity of the national, ethnic, linguistic and faith backgrounds of UK families undermines neat categorisation as more people straddle multiple demographic 'boxes' or foreground aspects of their identity, such as faith, above national or ethnic heritage (Open Society Institute, 2005).

The troublesome nature of ethnic identification is further complicated by significant numbers of children growing up in families of mixed ethnicity and faith. In 2001, nearly a quarter of a million people recorded their ethnicity as 'mixed', around half of those being under age 16 (Bradford, 2006). Platt's (2008) analysis of the Labour Force Survey for Britain found a significant number of mixed ethnicity and mixed faith households.

It is also useful to consider white ethnicities. The ethnic categories used on most monitoring forms in England offer little information about whiteness and non-British white people. Yet the 2001 census revealed around a quarter of a million people born in European Union member countries (Kyambi, 2005). Following the European Union expansion in May 2004, more than half a million Polish people registered on the Worker's Registration Scheme – many more may have arrived in the UK without registering (Ryan, 2007).[1] Just under a third of the 37,500 people who migrated to Northern Ireland in that year were from the eight new EU members from Eastern Europe (Matheson, 2009).

The history of violent sectarianism in Northern Ireland has contributed to a definition of ethnicity shaped by faith. Paul Connolly's research has explored the early age at which children define themselves as Protestant or Catholic, arguing for the notion of the 'ethnic habitus', the community-embedded ways of thinking, signs, symbols and relationships that children understand to reflect an ethnic group (Connolly, 2009). Connolly defines Protestant and Catholic communities as separate ethnic groups – going beyond skin colour and family nationality that is so often a signifier of ethnicity in England. In Northern Ireland, a child from a 'mixed' relationship is usually a child with one Catholic parent and one of a different, usually Protestant, background.

Gypsies, Roma and Irish Travellers (GRT) are also white ethnic groups that may disappear within statistics. The overt discrimination and racism they face has rarely abated in spite of their legal status as 'racial groups' under racial equality legislation. In January 2005, the MP for Bracknell described in Parliament an illegal encampment of Gypsies in the following terms:

> Ordinary, innocent people – hard-working, normal, straightforward people who live around Bracknell – want to get on with their lives in peace, but they want protection under the law when they are invaded by this scum. They are scum, and I use the word advisedly. People who do what these people have done do not deserve the same human rights as my decent constituents going about their everyday lives.

One could not imagine an MP referring publicly to a different minoritised ethnic group in such offensive terms.

In 2007, retired head teacher Sir Keith Ajegbo chaired the Diversity and Citizenship Curriculum Review for England. He stressed the importance of engaging with 'indigenous white pupils', particularly working–class pupils feeling 'beleaguered and marginalised', exiled from their own culture and history (DfES, 2007, p 33). Alternatively, research with young people in predominantly white areas, concluded that identities are fluid and never complete – 'race' may ultimately 'become a redundant category on which to build an identity' (Asare, 2009, p18).

The ethnic diversity of geographic areas varies across the UK (see Chapter 3), but the majority of children of minority ethnic heritage are likely to be living in urban areas (Dex and Hawkes, 2004). Of the UK minority ethnic population, 45% live in Greater London. It is predicted that 100% of the population increase in London between 2006 and 2020 will be from people of minority ethnic heritage, with the white population declining by 0.1% in the same period (Bains, 2008). There are smaller, but increasing, BME populations in other UK countries, often still concentrated in urban areas such as Belfast, Cardiff and Glasgow.

However, the annual census of pupils in schools shows that there are children of minority ethnic backgrounds in many rural areas, the population growing more rapidly than in urban areas. Population projections for the next 20 years have predicted variable growth in different ethnic groups, more than doubling minority ethnic populations and changing their geographical distribution (Wohland et al, 2010).

Placing people in 'ethnic' boxes for monitoring can appear outdated and simplistic. However, without data, we cannot measure the effectiveness of policy for different groups. For example, in an attempt to assess the impact of Sure Start early years programmes on BME children and families, Craig and colleagues found 'many organisations do not monitor their data effectively in terms of ethnicity despite the fact that, at least for public bodies, ethnic monitoring is one of the critical tools underpinning the legal requirements of the RRAA [Race Relations (Amendment)Act] 2000' (Craig et al, 2007a, p 7). They noted that some Sure Start local programmes, and the national evaluation team, employed unusably broad categories such as 'black' and 'Asian'. (A report on the victimisation of children for the Home Office [Millard and Flatley, 2010] uses the even less satisfactory 'white' and 'non-white', telling us nothing about the victims other than their skin colour.)

Persistent inequalities

White British children make up 80% of the total birth to 15 population in the UK (Matheson, 2009), and around 20% of the White British population. Black, Asian and mixed heritage children form a greater proportion of their ethnic groups – children of 'Mixed' ethnicity constituting half of the total 'Mixed' ethnic group.

Analysis across broad ethnic categories reveals the extent of inequality between children of minority ethnic heritage and their White British peers. This starts from before birth. Minority ethnic mothers, particularly those in poorer areas, are less likely to attend antenatal care and twice as unlikely to attend antenatal classes as white mothers (Kelly, 2004). Infant mortality – children dying within a year of birth – in Caribbean and Pakistani families is more than double that for White British children (ONS, 2008). For GRT families, infant mortality may be up to three times higher than for the rest of the population and there is reportedly a higher rate of miscarriage, stillbirth and preventable maternal death (Cemlyn et al, 2009).

Poor childhood development and experiences can lead to poor future outcomes and intergenerational cycles of poverty and deprivation (HM Treasury, 2008). Many children of minority ethnic heritage will grow up

Figure 8.1: *Percentage of children aged 15 and under of each ethnic group compared to the total population of the ethnic group (rounded up to the nearest whole number)*

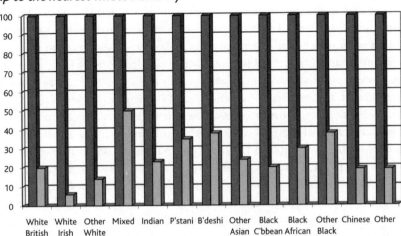

Source: Adapted from 'Age distribution: by ethnic group and sex, April 2001', census, April 2001, Office for National Statistics and General Register Office for Scotland.

in poverty, poorer than white children and adults in the children's ethnic group (Platt, 2007b; see also Chapter 10) and are consequently vulnerable to poorer life outcomes.

Initial findings from the Millennium Cohort Study (a longitudinal study of 15,590 families with children born across the UK in 2000–02, with an oversampling of BME families) noted 'marked' differences in cognitive and development behaviour across children in different ethnic and socio-economic groups at the age of three (Hansen, 2007). English-speaking Pakistani and Bangladeshi children appeared to show a 'severe delay' in vocabulary assessments and, along with Black Caribbean and Black African children, were more likely to be 'delayed' in readiness for school. Children with 'highly educated' parents and those from 'higher-income' families scored highest in the School Readiness assessment. However, caution is advised in interpreting the findings as the authors note that the tests did not take into account the main language spoken at home (what the authors describe as 'cultural factors'), the time the parents have been in the UK or the conditions under which assessments were carried out (Hansen, 2007).

In England, concerns about disparities in early development are also raised by the Early Years Foundation Stage Profile (EYFSP) assessments of pre-school children's ability to reach certain levels in their 'personal, social and emotional development' and 'communication, language and literacy' areas of learning. According to the targets, children of GRT, Pakistani,

Bangladeshi, Black African and Caribbean backgrounds are not reaching good levels of development. Again, poverty is cited as a key factor (DCSF, 2008a, 2008b).

The disparities persist throughout school in England. Chinese, Indian and children of mixed Asian and white heritage continue to outperform children of other ethnic groups at Key Stage 1[2] assessments in reading, writing, mathematics and science, while children of GRT heritage are assessed as significantly underperforming (DCSF, 2009b). This pattern is repeated at Key Stage 4 GCSE level (16 years old).

Nearly 80% of Chinese girls achieve five A★ to C grades including maths and English compared to less than one in ten of the small number of GRT children entered for the examinations (DCSF, 2010). In fact, in 2009, only 119 pupils recorded as 'Traveller of Irish heritage' and 486 pupils recorded as 'Gypsy/Romany' took GCSE examinations, of which just over 9% gained five or more A★–C grades. (The 'ethnic' evaluation of the national Sure Start programme showed that GRT families were particularly ill-served, with less than ten local projects out of more than 700 reviewed claiming to work with them [Craig et al, 2007a].) For further statistics on GCSE attainment by ethnicity see www.education.gov.uk/rsgateway/DB/SFR/s000977/index.shtml

The attainment pattern is similar for post-16 further education. In 2008, Chinese and Mixed White and Asian students achieved considerably above average in 'A' level and equivalent qualifications; Bangladeshi students, 'pupils within the Black category', Pakistani students and students within the Mixed White and Caribbean categories scored below the national average. There was also a significant gap between pupils eligible for free school meals and those who were not (DCSF, 2010).

Children from BME groups are disproportionately likely to be identified as having special educational needs (Lindsay et al, 2006). Lindsay's review found GRT pupils over-represented in many categories of special educational needs; Black Caribbean and Mixed White and Black Caribbean pupils over-represented in the Behavioural, Emotional and Social Difficulties (BESD) category; and Pakistani pupils between two and two and half times more likely to be identified as having serious learning difficulties and sensory impairments.

Seeking evidence of change

In the UK, there are many services delivered by the public, private and voluntary sectors to support families to overcome disadvantage. Some of these are universal – open to all families – and free. Every family with a child under five is currently entitled to a named health visitor to support the child's development. Children under 18, pregnant women and women with a child under 12 months have free dental treatment from the National Health Service and all three and four year olds in England have a right to 12.5 hours of free early education for 38 weeks a year.

Some services are targeted at families identified as disadvantaged: for example, free school meals, breakfast clubs and Sure Start (now often Children's Centres). Numerous policies, initiatives and resources have focused on equalising educational achievement. From 1998 to 2010, the National Strategies professional development programme provided free training and resources to school leaders and early years practitioners across England to raise levels of achievement for specific groups including black children, GRT children and children speaking English as an additional language (National Strategies, 2007, 2009, 2010). The National Strategies also led on supporting the implementation of the Early Years Foundation Stage (EYFS), a curriculum for all settings providing education and care for children under eight. The EYFS has an explicit focus on equality and supporting the uniqueness and value of every child. In 2003, *Aiming High* was launched by the Department for Education and Skills to improve attainment in secondary schools, again targeting minority ethnic groups of Caribbean heritage, asylum-seeking, refugee and GRT pupils (DfES, 2003, 2004).

In spite of these initiatives and the duties placed on public bodies by the Race Relations (Amendment) Act 2000 and the more recent Equality Act 2010, persistent disparities remain. Over two thirds of schools surveyed by the Commission for Racial Equality did not have a plan to show how they intended to redress racial inequality (Scheider-Ross, 2003).

In 2005, the Home Office pulled together the different English government departments' strategies and consulted with the Welsh and Scottish administrations to improve equality of opportunity across different ethnic groups and reported:

> Many (minority ethnic people) still suffer particularly poor outcomes in education, employment, health and other life chances, for a complex mixture of reasons, including racial discrimination, lack of opportunities, inadequate thought in how public services address the needs of different communities, the neighbourhoods they live in, longstanding lack of skills and cultural factors. (Home Office, 2005a, p 8)

In a cross-departmental strategy for racial equality, the then Home Secretary pledged to improve equality in educational outcomes, expand access to high-quality early years services and promote tailored health services to meet the needs of different ethnic and cultural communities.

Barriers to progress

In 2003, an opportunity came to rethink the delivery of services to all children in England. The *Every Child Matters Change for Children* agenda was triggered by the brutal death of an eight-year-old African child on 25 February 2000. Victoria Climbié died from multiple injuries following months of abuse by her great-aunt and her great-aunt's boyfriend – both were convicted of murder and sentenced to life imprisonment in 2001. The extent of Victoria's maltreatment was appalling, but more disturbing was that it was not noticed by statutory services. The subsequent public inquiry, led by Lord Laming, an ex-social worker, pinpointed at least 12 opportunities for services to have intervened, but 'the extent of the failure to protect Victoria was lamentable' (Laming, 2003, p 1).

Lord Laming's report on the inadequacy of the system designed to protect children influenced *Every Child Matters*, the Green Paper that set out wide-sweeping proposals to ensure that 'every child has a chance to fulfil their potential' (Home Office, 2003, p 6). Five desired outcomes for all children and young people – being healthy, staying safe, enjoying and achieving, making a positive contribution, and economic well-being – were given legal force by the Children Act 2004. Children's services were subsequently inspected on those outcomes. The Act also legislated for the formation of children's trusts, embedding a duty for services at front-line delivery, commissioning and strategic levels within local authorities to cooperate for the best interests of all children (DfES, 2004).

Yet evidence suggests that children's policy has benefited some children more than others. Prevatt Goldstein (2006) considers this in a study of the barriers to translating 'race'-related research into policy. Why, she asks, in spite of the outcomes of the Stephen Lawrence Inquiry and the issues about 'race' raised by Lord Laming, did the *Every Child Matters* policy agenda fall silent on racial equality? Prevatt Goldstein points out that the opening statement to the Climbié Inquiry dismissed any suggestion of overt racism directed at Victoria, but focused, along with the media, on 'the role of black workers and of cultural assumptions in terms of "race" rather than racism, and perhaps, instead of racism' (2006, p 27). She recalls the disproportionate focus on the black social worker and black manager in both the Inquiry and media attention, arguing that these two members of staff, who worked for only one of the nine ineffective agencies involved with Victoria, received a level of attention about their ethnicity that the black relative who twice reported the abuse and the black doctor who first diagnosed it did not.

She argues that a simplistic view of what racism is and is not prevented a more sophisticated deconstruction of how racism plays out in the everyday lives of black professionals, families and children. She wonders if 'the proclamation of no overt racism' being evident in the treatment of Victoria distracted from 'racism towards asylum-seekers and to the fact that [racism] may have been internalised by Black as well as White practitioners' (Prevatt Goldstein, 2006, p 27). Had they overlooked the 'interlinking of oppressions', 'colour-based racism, racism against asylum seekers, negative stereotypes about homeless families and of non-English speakers'? And why was there no deep interrogation of the assumption that black workers are experts on black culture? The Inquiry failed to examine 'the more subtle and hidden operations of power that have the effect of disadvantaging one or more ethnic groups' (Gillborn, 2008, p 27).

Acknowledgement of the specific experiences of different ethnic groups and the impact of assumptions, prejudice and racism was absent from *Every Child Matters* policy. The Common Core of Skills and Knowledge for the Children's Workforce in England (DCSF, 2005), developed following *Every Child Matters*, omits racism and ethnicity. It also excludes 'race' equality legislation on its list of relevant legislation, even though public bodies that train and employ the majority of the children's workforce are legally required to comply with the public-sector 'race' equality duties.

Lord Laming (2009) later compiled a progress report on safeguarding children in England following the murder of a White British child, Peter Connelly ('Baby P') in Haringey. Laming's remit was:

> to evaluate the good practice that has been developed since the publication of the report of the Independent Statutory Inquiry following the death of Victoria Climbié, to identify the barriers that are now preventing good practice becoming standard practice, and recommend actions to be taken to make systematic improvements in safeguarding children across the country. (Laming, 2009, p 3)

In this report, there is no specific mention of competency in working with children and young families across many ethnic backgrounds, nor delivering effective services to a culturally diverse society. The opportunity to explore how statutory services can benefit BME children and young people was not taken up. The debate was, however, taken up by Craig and colleagues, assessing the impact of Sure Start on BME families and children in England, as part of a national evaluation programme (Craig et al, 2007a). Inspired by the US Head Start programme, Sure Start was established in 1997 as a flagship New Labour policy, recognising the vital role of high-quality childcare, health and early education services in diminishing the impact of disadvantage and deprivation. The expectation was for community-driven and professionally coordinated services developed with and for local families. The expansion of Sure Start Children's Centres gained prominence in the government's strategy to promote equality of opportunity between different ethnic groups (Home Office, 2005a). Guidance stated a clear expectation that local programmes should gather demographic information on catchment area and ethnic mix; consult with and address the needs of families from minoritised groups or cultures; plan for an atmosphere that encourages social cohesion; identify minority ethnic people to join Sure Start partnerships; and show how services are designed to meet the needs of BME communities (Sure Start, 1999).

The guidance is clear. The extent of its use is not – the scarcity of detailed information about how local programmes worked with different ethnic groups made it impossible to tell (Lloyd and Rafferty, 2006; Craig et al, 2007b). Craig et al's analysis of data gained from national evaluation reports, surveys and guidance concluded that there was generally an 'ad hoc' approach to integrating ethnicity into local programmes. They identified good practice, but this tended to be the exception, and Sure Start's own guidance on developing services with and for minority ethnic communities was frequently ignored. Craig et al suggest that this lack of a consistent and strategic approach to ethnicity has led to 'a missed opportunity' to improve the lives of black and other minority ethnic children and families; all the more disappointing when the huge investment into this single social policy intervention is considered.

The limitations of mainstream children's policy to address equality has long been responded to by minority ethnic communities themselves. Organisations led by and for specific minoritised communities often emerged from the failure of statutory services to integrate diversity (Reid, 2004). An example is the emergence of complementary (or supplementary) schools offering weekend and evening tuition to reverse the unsatisfactory school experience of many BME children. They have made positive and some impressive differences to educational outcomes (Maylor et al, 2010). Yet, unreliable funding and a lack of wider policy influence have limited the impact of community sector involvement (Reid, 2004; Craig et al, 2011a).

'Getting it'

Mainstream children's policy often appears reluctant to explicitly name and challenge racism. Lane, writing about the development of anti-racist early years services, argues that:

> Understanding the true nature of racism is fundamental to understanding how it influences early years practices and procedures. Without such an understanding and, hopefully, a resultant commitment, any work done to counter racism will be unlikely to be successful. It is not about blaming anyone but just about 'getting it'. (Lane, 2008, p 31)

'Getting it', Lane asserts, requires a willingness to understand the many components of racism, a list including racial prejudice, discrimination, harassment, hatred, violence, assumptions, stereotyping, cultural racism, xenoracism and institutional racism.

Lane takes her idea of 'getting it' from a government paper outlining key issues on the disproportionate exclusion of black pupils from school. The authors candidly review the situation:

> Despite overwhelming evidence of unequal outcomes, the response of many organisations when asked about 'race' equality is: 'we treat everybody the same'. Whether they are motivated by indifference, complacency or a mistaken belief that recognising ethnic difference is inconsistent with affording equal value to all people, such 'colour-blind' approaches act as a major barrier to progress in promoting substantive (as opposed to just formal) 'race' equality. (DfES, 2006b, p 29)

The Whitehall government pledged to undertake a multi-pronged campaign reversing the pattern of black children's exclusions. Yet, three years later, Caribbean heritage pupils still remained three times more likely than the overall school population to be excluded (Cooper, 2002; Department for Education, 2010).

What is stopping permanent change?

'Getting it' requires honest and informed discussion, underpinned by understanding of the complex causes and manifestations of racial inequality. Just a glance at online message boards following any 'race'-related news story demonstrates the strong stomach and thick skin required to enter the debate. The media itself is rarely helpful. In an article about the press depiction of Gypsies and Travellers, Rachel Morris (2000, p 213) writes:

> Racist invective by the press infects society in a widespread way; a way in which an unintentionally racist remark by one individual to another cannot. They confirm existing prejudices and create new ones, much as parents do in transferring unexamined aversions to their children.

The depiction of Gypsies, Roma and Travellers is indeed often unpleasant, exemplifying a wider media trait of simplifying, sensationalising and sometimes inaccurately reporting. This reporting is not limited to overtly sensational tabloid papers. In November 2008, *The Guardian* newspaper, traditionally associated with middle-class liberals, was among many reporting that Oxford City Council had 'banned' Christmas as a gesture towards people of other faiths. A subsequent statement by Oxford City Council revealed this to be untrue, but not before the article had stirred up the usual Internet indignation about perceived 'political correctness'.[3]

There are numerous examples of the media's failure to engage in sophisticated debate about racial equality, particularly when linked to children. Lane's carefully researched 350-page work on anti-racism in the early years (Lane, 2008) was distilled into national newspapers' emotive headlines such as that of the *Daily Mail* of November 2008 where it made claims of 'toddlers' being branded racist if they do not like 'spicy food', triggering a stream of highly racist and misogynist emails to the publisher and author. A report on decision-making in the 'care careers' of black and other minority ethnic children emphasised the *lack* of apparent bias or mishandling of their 'care careers' compared to white children (Selwyn et al, 2008). Yet the *Daily Mail* (again) in 2009 blasted social workers as 'family wreckers' where '"race" rules ... rob foster children of a caring home'.

It is hardly surprising that many practitioners and policymakers are overly cautious in discussing racial identity, equality and children's services. Yet, in Northern Ireland, progress is being made. Academics, practitioners and funders recognise the importance of the early years in developing children's attitudes towards difference by implementing an evidence-based training programme and media initiative to counter sectarianism, race and disability discrimination (Connolly, 2009).

Critical race theory

> Imagine a world where a group of people is continually placed at the bottom of the social pile; in schools, in the labour

> market, in housing. Imagine that this group is blamed for its own misfortune: its members are seen as lazy, their families 'dysfunctional'; they're just not smart enough. But what would happen if groups started to pass more tests more frequently than the dominant group? (Gillborn, 2008, p 90)

Critical 'race' theorists argue that equality will not come without a fundamental review of the power dynamics between racialised communities, making the radical assertion that it is not in the interest of dominant white society for that power to shift (Gillborn, 2008). Critical race theory (CRT) is still developing. Founded in the United States towards the end of the 20th century, it argues that racism is not an aberration – the random racist individual – but deeply commonplace and ingrained within society. White supremacy is repositioned from a small, extremist movement to 'the operation of forces that saturate the everyday mundane actions and policies that shape the world in the interest of White people' (Gillborn, 2008, p 35). Unsurprisingly, CRT remains deeply controversial, criticised for seeming to attack liberalism and positive action, for ignoring the impact of social class, and for homogenising and simplifying the lives and intentions of white people. However, proponents like the British educationalist David Gillborn create persuasive arguments in favour of CRT as a tool to analyse persistent inequality.

Gillborn argues that the way statistics are presented, the space and credence given to white points of view over those of minoritised people, and high-profile political rhetoric all sustain a status quo that privileges the white majority. Within a CRT framework, Gillborn reviews the 'evidence' on the underachievement of black pupils, and critiques the steps that have been taken to redress it. He cites the example of his and Heidi Mirza's findings (Gillborn and Mirza, 2000) that black children were some of the highest achievers on starting formal education. He argues that, as this became widely cited, the system of assessment changed and black children plummeted from the highest achievers to the lowest: 'And so the old story of Black educational success at age five has been entirely rewritten. The new assessment has established Black failure as, once again, the norm' (Gillborn, 2008, p 108). Since Gillborn wrote his book, research has indicated that 11-year-old black pupils are 'routinely' marked down by teachers in their assessments, the result of 'unconscious stereotyping' (Burgess and Greaves, 2009).

Gillborn offers two strong examples of how statistics are used to buttress specific ways of thinking that are counter to minoritised pupils' interests. First, there is what he refers to as 'Gap Talk', the frequent assertion that black pupils' GCSE attainment is improving so much that the 'gap' between the higher- and lower-performing groups is closing. Yet, by reviewing official data and the percentage point improvement of black pupils in relation to the improvement of all ethnic groups, Gillborn argues that the most optimistic estimation for the gap to be closed is in 2054. This view is confirmed by the most recent analysis of GCSE performances by ethnic group, which shows some groups doing better than the UK-wide average (eg Chinese students at +11%, Sri Lankan at +8% and Indian at +7%), but some doing considerably worse (Bangladeshi at −9%, Pakistani at −11% and Jamaican at −15%) (Rutter, 2011).

Second, Gillborn explores how the emphasis on white working-class boys has gained public and political momentum, undermining discussion on black pupils' achievement.[4] Statistics certainly point to the fact that White British children on free school meals (FSM) have significantly lower GCSE attainment than their non-FSM peers. In 2009, just over half of White British boys not receiving FSM attained a minimum of five A★ to C GCSE passes including English and Maths compared to 19% of those known to be eligible for FSM. However, only 22% of Caribbean boys on FSM achieved the 'good' GCSE passes compared to 36% of those not eligible. Less affluent Caribbean boys were higher by just three and a half percentage points than their White British peers, with a gulf of nearly 20 percentage points between white boys and Caribbean boys not on FSM. In addition, Caribbean boys are more than three times more likely to be eligible for FSM than their white peers, and so far more likely to be in the lower-performing group. Yet, increasing numbers of news stories that suggest that educational 'improvement' for minority ethnic children has come at the expense of poorer White British children go unchallenged.[5] The fact that no boys recorded as Irish Traveller at all gained 'good' GCSEs is ignored.

Summary

Britain is a country of increasing ethnic diversity and, in the next 20 years, parts that have been predominantly White British will start to look and sound different as new communities move in. Defining 'ethnicity' will become more complicated as we develop new identities from different heritages. There is an argument that the idea of 'race' will become redundant.

However, data show that there are profound inequalities between ethnic groups as they are currently defined. It is difficult to believe that these inequalities will simply disappear. As things stand, it is almost possible to predict which children are more likely to experience better life outcomes in educational achievement, social economic status, health and well-being on the basis of their ethnicity. Children from all ethnic groups can do well, but some children face greater obstacles, starting from before they are born.

Evidence suggests that the resources and initiatives targeted at BME communities, as well as those focusing on redressing poverty, have not made significant improvements to the lives of many black and minority ethnic children – in many cases, these children appear to be absent from policy planning and implementation altogether. That is in spite of data showing clear evidence of need.

CRT offers a persuasive explanation for the persistent disadvantage, but its conclusions are likely to prove too provocative for many policymakers. The Coalition government has pledged to 'promote improved community relations and opportunities for Black, Asian and Minority Ethnic (BAME) communities', maintain the commitment to end child poverty by 2010 and review the delivery of early years and education services (Cabinet Office, 2010a). The Equality Act 2010 has been implemented, albeit in a weakened form, and the delivery of education is being reviewed. Meanwhile, public spending has been severely cut. The impact on children across different ethnic groups has yet to be seen.

There is not space here to discuss the question of BME groups' access to higher education in detail, but it is clear that the disadvantage experienced by these children in schools persists into higher education (Modood et al, 1997; Law, 2005; Platt, 2007a; see also the website of the Higher Education Statistics Agency at: www.hesa.ac.uk). Figures compiled by David Lammy MP using the Freedom of Information (FoI) Act show that 21 Oxford and Cambridge colleges admitted no black students on undergraduate courses in 2009. Merton College, Oxford, has not admitted a single black student in the last five years. The FoI data also show that of more than 1,500 academic and laboratory staff at Cambridge, none are black, although 34 are of British Asian background. The figures also show that large parts of the country never send students to the most prestigious universities. No one from Knowsley, Sandwell and Merthyr Tydfil has gone to Cambridge in seven years. Pupils from Richmond upon Thames have received almost the same number of offers from Oxford as the whole of Scotland. A spokesman for Cambridge University said that 15% of students accepted in 2009 were from minority ethnic backgrounds, but gave no further analysis (*The Guardian*, 7 December 2010, pp 1–2; *The Times*, 7 December 2010, p 13). This disadvantage continues throughout the higher education experience. Despite their relatively high representation as university students, black women are poorly represented in academia (Mirza, 2009) and overall only 0.13% of British professors are black (*The Guardian*, 28 May 2011, p 6).

Questions for discussion

- Why is it difficult to assess the impact of policy on children across different ethnic groups?
- Why do you think 'race' was highlighted in Lord Laming's inquiry into the death of Victoria Climbié, but not in Lord Laming's report following the death of 'Baby P'?
- Why do you think children from some minority ethnic groups are the highest educational achievers?
- How do the media influence discussions on 'race'?

Electronic resources

- A database of resources about the media and how it reports about diverse communities is available at: http://media-diversity.org/en/
- Equality and Human Rights Commission research reports area available at: www.equalityhumanrights.com/publications/our-research/research-reports/
- Research and statistics about education are available at: www.education.gov.uk/rsgateway/
- Articles, films and research about children and race equality area available at: www.ncb.org.uk/ecu_network/bvn/nbvn_home/resources.aspx
- Information on the Early Years Foundation Stage (though currently under review) is available at: http://nationalstrategies.standards.dcsf.gov.uk/earlyyears
- Sure Start and black and minority ethnic population statistics are available at: hwww.ness.bbk.ac.uk/implementation/documents/33.pdf

Notes

[1] There are now thought to be around 600,000 people of Polish origin in the UK, making it the second largest minority in the UK.

[2] Key Stage 1 is the first two years of compulsory schooling between five and seven years of age in England and Wales.

[3] See www.guardian.co.uk/uk/2008/nov/02/christmas-political-correctness-oxford-christian for *The Guardian* coverage and www.oxfordmail.co.uk/news/3815682.Mayor_will_switch_on_Christmas_lights/ for the subsequent response.

[4] In a response to *The Guardian* newspaper report about teachers routinely marking down black pupils, the then Secretary of State refers solely to white working-class children: www.guardian.co.uk/education/2010/apr/04/sats-marking-race-stereotypes

[5] See for instance the *Evening Standard* article 'White working-class boys consigned to scrapheap by Labour and liberal establishment'. Available at: www.thisislondon.co.uk/news/article-23458588-white-working-class-boys-consigned-to-educational-scrapheap-by-labour-and-liberal-establishment.do

Minority ethnic groups in the labour market

Baljinder Virk

Overview

This chapter provides information on various labour-market indicators with respect to minority ethnic groups. It presents up-to-date data on economic activity, employment and unemployment rates, types of employment, and earnings. It also examines explanations for the disadvantages experienced by these groups.

Key concepts
disadvantage and discrimination, economic activity, employment, labour markets, unemployment

Introduction

This chapter contextualises the position of black and minority ethnic (BME) groups in the labour market. It considers the four dimensions of labour-market disadvantage suggested by Thurrow (1969) (lower earnings, higher unemployment, reduced access to educational and training opportunities, and occupational crowding in less desirable jobs). It considers other aspects of the labour market, including economic activity, employment rates and industries, which collectively portray the relative position of BME groups compared with the majority, White British, population. Using data from the Annual Population Survey,[1] the chapter highlights diversity among different groups, and by age and gender. It then reviews the literature on explanations for disadvantage. In particular, it uses Berthoud's (2000a) six explanatory factors as well as some other additional factors affecting labour-market demand and supply of minority ethnic populations. The evidence used here draws on historical references to provide context, with up-to-date evidence where available, to see what improvements, if any, have been made in recent years.

The minority ethnic population in Great Britain

The minority ethnic population in Great Britain has grown since the Second World War, driven by three factors: immigration in response to a demand for labour; refugees seeking asylum; and the natural rate of growth. Migrants from the 'New Commonwealth' countries (former UK colonies) were recruited to fill labour shortages in foundries in the Midlands, textile mills in the North, transport industries (notably in London) and throughout the National Health Service, generally occupying low-paid jobs. The bulk of immigration from the Caribbean took place during 1955–64, from India and Pakistan during 1965–74 and from Bangladesh during 1980–84 (Peach, 1996). African Asians arrived as refugees from Uganda and Kenya in the early 1970s. More recent refugee communities have settled in Britain as a result of war or persecution in their own country (Parekh, 2000a).[2]

The number of people who belong to a minority ethnic group has grown since the 1991 census and now almost 50% of all minority ethnic people were born in Great Britain. BME groups have a much younger age structure than the white population and some minority groups contain more people per household than the average. Bangladeshi households are the largest with a household average of 4.5 people, followed by Pakistanis with 4.1 people (ONS, 2006). As a result, BME groups should represent an expanding proportion of the labour market in the future.

As other chapters have demonstrated, ethnic classification is far from straightforward. The broad ethnic groupings in national data categories mask significant diversity, for example, the 'White Other' category contains those who might describe themselves primarily as Turkish and, within that group, there are at least three distinct subgroupings – mainland Turkish, Turkish Kurds and Cypriot Turks – who have very different labour-market experiences and outcomes (Ennelli et al, 2005). Each ONS ethnic grouping includes people born in the specified region and those born in Great Britain who are second or third generation. Those classified as being from a minority ethnic group, born and educated in Great Britain, are likely to have a different experience of the labour market to recent migrants in the same ethnic classification. Ethnic groupings can also mask social class differences. Research on employment and the labour market is only slowly accommodating such differences, although it is rare for routinely collected data to reflect such subtleties and allow a nuanced understanding of labour–market experiences.

Economic activity and employment rates

In Great Britain in 2008, 24.6 million minority ethnic people were estimated to be of working age, representing 9.7% of the total working-age population (Annual Population Survey, 2008, available at www.nomisweb. co.uk/articles/382.aspx). There are marked variations in economic activity and employment patterns of differing ethnic groups. The economically active population includes people who are employed, self-employed, participating in government employment and training programmes, doing unpaid family work, and those who are unemployed according to the International Labour Organisation's (ILO's) definition.

In 2008, the highest economic activity rate (EAR) for Other White and Other Black males (both 87%) was marginally higher than White British males (84%) (see *Table 9.1*). Indian, Black Caribbean and Other Asian males also had a relatively high EAR at 80% or higher. The lowest EAR was for Chinese males (69%), in part due to the high proportion of full-time students in this group (ONS, 2006).

All the females had a lower EAR than males in the same group, although the Other Mixed and White and Black African males and females had the

Table 9.1: Economic activity rate by ethnicity and gender, 2008 (%)

Ethnic group	Male (%) 16–64	Female (%) 16–59
White British	84	76
Other White	87	74
White and Black Caribbean	72	59
White and Black African	72	69
White and Asian	72	66
Other Mixed	73	71
Indian	83	67
Pakistani	76	30
Bangladeshi	79	37
Other Asian	80	61
Black Caribbean	82	75
Black African	76	59
Other Black	87	71
Chinese	69	64
Other	76	56

Source: Annual Population Survey (2008).

smallest gap (2% and 3%, respectively). Bangladeshi and Pakistani males and females had the highest differences between the rates (42% and 46%, respectively), with females in this group showing the lowest economic activity rates (37% and 30%, respectively). There is also much more variation in the economic activity rates among females than males, ranging from 30% to 76%. Overall, minority ethnic women are less likely to be economically active than White British females.

The EAR is useful because it gives the proportion of people potentially engaged in the labour market, excluding those who are inactive or unemployed due to health or disability. The employment rate, on the other hand, gives the actual figure for people in paid employment with those self-employed. Employment rates follow a similar pattern to the EAR, altered slightly by the different rates of unemployment faced by each minority ethnic group. The highest employment rate was for Other White males followed by White British males (see *Table 9.2*). Of the minority ethnic groups, Indian males had the highest employment rate, followed by Other Asian males. The lowest employment rates for males are experienced by Chinese, Black African and Pakistani groups.

The female employment rate was also highest for Other White and White British females. Bangladeshi and Pakistani females experience the lowest employment rate of all women, which is comparable to their EAR.

Table 9.2: Employment rate by ethnicity and gender, 2008 (%)

Ethnic group	Male (%) 16–64	Female (%) 16–59
White British	79	72
Other White	82	71
White and Black Caribbean	56	53
White and Black African	57	60
White and Asian	66	58
Other Mixed	68	64
Indian	78	61
Pakistani	66	26
Bangladeshi	69	27
Other Asian	73	57
Black Caribbean	69	66
Black African	65	53
Other Black	66	61
Chinese	65	59
Other	68	51

Source: Annual Population Survey (2008).

Types of employment

Industry

The representation of BME groups in industries and sectors is unevenly distributed. In comparison to White British employees, BME groups are under-represented in both primary and secondary sectors, and over-represented in tertiary or service sectors. Certain BME groups are concentrated in particular industries (see *Tables 9.3* and *9.4*). One half of all Bangladeshi men and over one third of Chinese and Other Asian (37% and 35%, respectively) are employed in distribution, hotels and restaurants compared with one in six (17%) of White British men. Over one quarter of Black African, Other Black, Chinese, Other Mixed and White and Asian men are employed in banking, finance and insurance.

Overall, females are largely employed in public administration, education and health and in the distribution, hotels and restaurants industries. Some BME groups are more concentrated in these sectors than White British females. For example over one half of Black Caribbean and Black African females are employed in administration, education and health and in the distribution sector compared with 44% of White British females (see *Table 9.4*). Similarly, for Chinese women, the distribution, hotels and restaurant industry group represents 35% of their total employment compared with 21% of White British females.

Occupation

The industrial distribution of employment powerfully influences the occupational distribution of work. Once again, there is a marked gender specialisation of work imposed on the contrasting specialisation in employment by ethnic group (Owen et al, 2000, p 78).

One in five White British, Indian and Other Asian men are managers and senior officials. The groups least likely to be managers and senior officials are Other Black, White and Black African, and Black African (see *Table 9.5*). While some Black African, Chinese, Indian and White and Asian males are even more likely than White British males to be employed in professional occupations, other minority ethnic males are equally more likely to be employed in elementary occupations compared to White British males, suggesting a wide variation in experience within any particular ethnic grouping.

Table 9.3: Industry of male employment by ethnicity, 2008 (%)

Male	British	Other White	White and Black Caribbean	White and Black African	White and Asian	Other Mixed	Indian	Pakistani	Bangladeshi	Other Asian	Black Caribbean	Black African	Other Black	Chinese	Other
A–B: Agriculture & fishing	2	2	*	*	*	2	*	*	*	*	*	*	*	*	*
C, E: Energy & water	2	*	*	*	2	*	1	1	*	1	1	2	*	1	1
D: Manufacturing	17	17	9	19	8	9	13	12	8	11	11	7	5	7	12
F: Construction	14	15	11	8	6	4	5	3	1	1	11	3	8	4	7
G–H: Distribution, hotels & restaurants	17	19	28	22	19	27	24	29	50	35	15	15	24	37	26
I: Transport & communication	9	8	8	14	6	5	12	26	12	14	12	13	22	5	10
J–K: Banking, finance & insurance etc	17	20	19	18	26	26	25	16	14	15	21	26	28	28	23
L–N: Public administration, education & health	16	13	18	6	20	18	16	11	13	19	19	27	14	13	16
O–Q: Other services	6	6	7	13	12	9	3	3	2	4	9	7	*	5	6
Workplace outside UK	0.02	*	*	*	*	*	*	*	*	*	*	*	*	*	*
	100	100	100	100	100	100	100	100	100	100	100	100	100	100	100

Note: * Sample sizes are too small to provide reliable estimates.

Source: Annual Population Survey (2008).

Table 9.4: *Industry of female employment by ethnicity, 2008 (%)*

Female	British	Other White	White and Black Caribbean	White and Black African	White and Asian	Other Mixed	Indian	Pakistani	Bangladeshi	Other Asian	Black Caribbean	Black African	Other Black	Chinese	Other
A–B: Agriculture & fishing	1	1	*	*	*	*	*	*	*	*	*	*	*	*	*
C, E: Energy & water	1		*	*	*	*	1	*	*	1	1	1	*	*	1
D: Manufacturing	7	11	4	*	10	5	7	9	6	8	5	4	3	5	6
F: Construction	2	2	*	*	*	*	1	*	*	0	1	1	*	*	1
G–H: Distribution, hotels & restaurants	21	20	28	30	20	22	21	28	25	25	16	17	25	35	23
I: Transport & communication	4	4	4	*	4	4	6	4	*	3	4	4	*	3	5
J–K: Banking, finance & insurance etc	15	20	13	19	16	26	19	15	21	13	13	15	24	19	17
L–N: Public administration, education & health	44	34	41	44	37	37	42	42	44	46	56	54	40	32	39
O–Q: Other services	7	8	10	7	13	7	3	2	4	5	5	4	8	5	8
Workplace outside UK	0	*	*	*	*	*	*	*	*	*	*	*	*	*	*
	100	100	100	100	100	100	100	100	100	100	100	100	100	100	100

Note: *Sample sizes are too small to provide reliable estimates.

Source: Annual Population Survey (2008).

Chinese females are more likely to be employed as managers and senior officials and in professional occupations than White British females. This is also true for White and Asian females. However, Indian women are less likely to be employed as managers and senior officials than White British females and when compared with males of their respective groups. Minority ethnic females are more likely than White British females to be employed in sales and customer service occupations.

Employment sector

In 2007, 8.3% of civil service employees were from a BME group. While they are well-represented in junior grades, at 9% of administrative and executive officer grades, they are significantly under-represented in senior grades, making up only 4% of senior civil servants (ONS, 2008a).

The Race Relations (Amendment) Act 2000 only applied to public or publicly funded bodies and there is a consequent lack of data on minority ethnic groups employed in the private sector (Craig et al, 2009b). Specific research on the number of minorities in professional and managerial positions in FTSE 100 companies found that only 40% of companies surveyed responded and, out of those, only 27 of the companies could provide a breakdown of the ethnicity of their employees. Of those that provided data, only 5.4% of employees were from minority ethnic groups, and 3.2% of junior and middle managers and only 1% of senior managers were from these groups. Only three of 129 executive directors were from BME groups. Of the junior and middle managers, the Indian and the Chinese groups were the only BME groups broadly in line with their representation in the wider employee population; amongst senior managers, Indians were the highest (Sanglin-Grant and Schneider, 2000).

Unemployment

Unemployment is a key indicator of labour-market disadvantage. As mentioned earlier, the White British working population has one of the highest employment and the lowest unemployment rates; conversely, minority ethnic people have lower employment and higher unemployment rates.

Table 9.6 shows that the combined unemployment rate for White British males and females was 5.2% in 2008. Analysis by gender shows male unemployment to be lowest for Chinese males, followed by Other White and then White British. It is highest for Other Black, White and Black Caribbean, and White and Black African males. Female unemployment

***Table 9.5:** Major occupation group by ethnicity and gender, 2008 (%)*

Males

	British	Other White	White & Black Caribbean	White & Black African	White and Asian	Other Mixed	Indian	Pakistani	Bangladeshi	Other Asian	Black Caribbean	Black African	Other Black	Chinese	Other
1 Managers and senior officials	20	17	13	8	18	20	20	15	14	20	13	9	7	19	16
2 Professional occupations	13	14	9	6	22	13	25	11	9	12	11	20	13	27	14
3 Associate professional and technical	14	12	13	16	19	23	11	7	7	11	14	10	9	11	15
4 Administrative and secretarial	4	3	5	*	3	7	6	4	7	6	6	8	12	6	4
5 Skilled trades occupations	19	20	12	24	10	11	9	8	16	10	18	4	13	20	11
6 Personal service occupations	2	2	7	*	7	*	2	1	1	5	5	9	9	2	3
7 Sales and customer service occupations	4	3	13	12	7	12	7	11	14	9	8	7	8	4	5
8 Process, plant and machine operatives	11	12	6	9	3	*	9	27	12	12	12	8	9	5	11
9 Elementary occupations	11	16	22	25	10	14	11	14	19	15	14	25	20	7	20
	100	100	100	100	100	100	100	100	100	100	100	100	100	100	100

Females

	British	Other White	White & Black Caribbean	White & Black African	White and Asian	Other Mixed	Indian	Pakistani	Bangladeshi	Other Asian	Black Caribbean	Black African	Other Black	Chinese	Other
1 Managers and senior officials	12	11	3	8	17	11	8	9	9	8	8	4	9	15	8
2 Professional occupations	12	14	6	13	13	15	19	14	10	12	12	11	19	19	12
3 Associate professional and technical	16	15	13	26	14	19	18	12	9	20	17	22	22	23	17
4 Administrative and secretarial	20	16	21	11	18	21	18	16	26	14	21	11	6	9	16
5 Skilled trades occupations	2	2	*	*	*	*	1	*	*	1	2	2	*	4	2
6 Personal service occupations	15	12	22	5	13	12	11	15	17	15	22	24	19	5	18
7 Sales and customer service occupations	11	8	24	12	14	12	13	22	18	12	9	11	17	9	12
8 Process, plant and machine operatives	2	4	*	*	*	*	3	*	*	4	1	1	*	1	2
9 Elementary occupations	10	17	12	23	10	10	9	11	11	15	8	13	9	16	13
	100	100	100	100	100	100	100	100	100	100	100	100	100	100	100

Note: * Sample sizes are too small to provide reliable estimates.
Source: Annual Population Survey (2008).

is lowest for White British women (4.6%) and highest for Bangladeshi women (23.2%).

Table 9.6: Unemployment by ethnicity and gender, 2008 (%)

Ethnic group	Unemployment rate (all) (%)	Men (%)	Women (%)
White British	5.2	5.6	4.6
Other White	5.3	5.2	5.3
White and Black Caribbean	16.5	21.8	10.8
White and Black African	15.3	20.9	10.0
White and Asian	9.0	9.2	8.7
Other Mixed	10.3	7.3	13.2
Indian	6.8	6.1	7.9
Pakistani	13.8	12.7	16.7
Bangladeshi	16.2	12.9	23.2
Other Asian	7.8	8.1	7.4
Black Caribbean	14.0	15.7	12.6
Black African	13.4	14.7	11.9
Other Black	21.2	24.3	17.8
Chinese	6.6	5.1	8
Other	11.2	11.0	11.5

Source: Annual Population Survey (2008): Great Britain, all aged 16 and over.

Table 9.7: Unemployment rate of young people by ethnicity, 2008 (%)

Ethnic group aged 16–24	Men (%)	Women (%)
White British	16.1	14.1
Other White	11.4	10.9
White and Black Caribbean	40.0	29.2
White and Black African	32.3	22.4
White and Asian	20.3	13.0
Other Mixed	11.0	12.3
Indian	19.2	18.7
Pakistani	31.4	27.9
Bangladeshi	24.7	29.8
Other Asian	24.8	20.7
Black Caribbean	37.4	35.9
Black African	33.6	31.4
Other Black	55.6	45.4
Chinese	13.2	17.4
Other	26.2	26.0

Source: Annual Population Survey (2008): Great Britain, aged 16–24.

Youth unemployment is high for all groups, including White British; however, for some BME groups this is particularly high (see **Table 9.7**), for example, over half of Other Black 16- to 24-year-olds are unemployed.

Earnings

Most minority ethnic males earn less than White British males. **Figure 9.1** shows the average gross hourly pay for males and females by ethnic group. Pakistani males earn the least of the males: £3.63 per hour (gross) less than White British males; however, Chinese males earn marginally more by £0.90 per hour (gross). Indian males and Other White and Other Asian males also earn more than British males, but at lower rates.

Figure 9.1: Average hourly pay by ethnicity, 2008

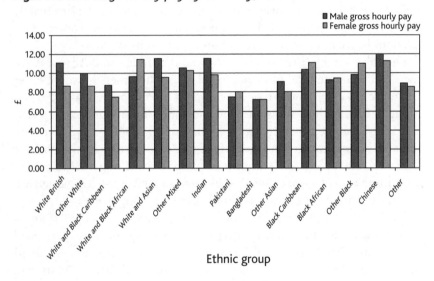

Source: Annual Population Survey (2008).

There is less variation among female pay. While over half of the female minority ethnic groups earn more than White British females, these figures may be misleading as a greater proportion of minority ethnic females work full time compared to White British females (Trade Union Congress, 2002).

Employment disadvantage experienced by minority ethnic groups

Considering the position of BME groups in the labour market over time (using the series of four Policy Studies Institute surveys and those of its predecessors), demonstrates the failure of policy from the 1960s to the 1990s in addressing the labour-market performance of ethnic minorities.

The first survey (Daniel, 1968) showed that migrants were concentrated in manual jobs, in limited industries and in jobs below their levels of qualification. Discrimination was prevalent and focused primarily on skin colour, with darker groups penalised as employers explicitly refused to employ 'coloureds'. In general, Caribbean and Asian people were only employed where there was a shortage of white workers.

The second survey (Smith, 1977) showed very few BME employees in professional and managerial jobs. Although many had penetrated into better, skilled manual jobs, minority ethnic employees were disproportionately concentrated in semi-skilled and unskilled manual work. Despite race relations legislation, similar levels of discrimination continued.

The third survey (Brown, 1984) showed that Indian and African Asian men had the same level of unemployment as white men; however, other BME groups experienced twice the level of unemployment as the white group. Although there was some evidence for optimism for African Asians and young people (irrespective of ethnic group), BME groups were still found to be concentrated in a limited number of industries and occupations. While there were also some improvements in terms of wages, BME groups were more likely to work shifts, less likely to supervise and still earned less (except Black Caribbean women) than the white population.

The fourth (and, to date, last) national survey (Modood et al, 1997) shows growing diversity. In summary: Pakistanis and Bangladeshis experienced serious disadvantage; Caribbeans and Indians often experienced disadvantage, but to a lesser extent; and Chinese and African Asians had reached broad parity with the white population. However, one element common to all minority ethnic males was under-representation as managers and employers in large establishments.

Factors explaining labour-market disadvantage among minority ethnic groups

Traditionally, two general explanations were put forward for the disadvantage experienced by minority ethnic groups in the labour market: migration and discrimination (see later). However, these factors cannot account for all the differences between the groups (Berthoud, 1999), and further explanations have emerged to explain such disadvantage.

Berthoud (2000a) uses a six-factor framework to analyse the position of young Caribbean men in the labour market relative to other groups. This will be used here to consider the labour-market disadvantages experienced by other minority ethnic groups. The six factors are: migration; expectations and stereotypes; discrimination; family structures; alienation; and the structure of the economy. It is important to remember that no single factor can explain minority ethnic disadvantage, that the interplay of factors is complex and that many individuals experience multiple disadvantage, groups such as recent EU and African migrants, and the UK Roma, being good examples of this. Berthoud stresses that some issues may be more relevant than others when considering different minority groups. He also points out that some factors influence labour-market supply, whereas others may influence labour demand, an important consideration for potential policy solutions. The following discussion considers each factor in turn, drawing on available empirical evidence to explain its potential impact on employment.

Migration

People who have recently arrived in Great Britain may be disadvantaged in the labour market compared to longer-term residents. This may be due to various factors including: lower or unrecognised educational qualifications; weaker social capital (networks of contacts); and, by implication, fewer sources of reference to help them gain employment. Newer arrivals may also be unfamiliar with application procedures and interview techniques (Daniel, 1968). Language skills are also important, and poor skills can reduce the range of job opportunities available. While most young ethnic minorities are fluent in English, language problems are prevalent for certain Asian groups in older age cohorts, most of whom are likely to have been born abroad (Modood et al, 1997). Over three quarters of Bangladeshi women aged over 25 and over 40% of Bangladeshi and Pakistani first-generation men do not speak fluent English, impacting on labour-market engagement. For women, this is used to explain their economic inactivity, whereas for men it explains high unemployment (Leslie and Lindley, 2001). Lack of English fluency has also been found to have a negative effect on earnings (Battu and Sloane, 2002; Dustmann and Fabbri, 2003). It would be expected that these issues become less relevant the longer the individual has been in the host country, and tend to be eliminated for second and third generations (Hatton and Wheatley-Price, 1998).[3] However, Heath et al (2000) found 'ethnic penalties' to be of similar magnitude among both second and first generations.

Expectations and stereotypes

Expectations and stereotypes have been found to affect labour-market success. Teachers' expectations are important and can impact on the academic success of pupils. In particular, Caribbean boys are expected to underachieve at school, both by themselves and their teachers, reducing their chances of success (Gillborn, 1990; Sewell, 1997; see also Chapter 8). This has a knock-on effect for those entering the labour market in terms of prospects and lower expectations of employers. In turn, this relative failure of young Caribbean men in the labour market may also contribute to lowering teachers' expectations in schools once again, resulting in a vicious circle. Stereotypes can also lead to the channelling of BME groups into specific occupations, for example, by those who help in making career choices (Cross et al, 1990).

Expectations within minority ethnic households can also influence the labour supply. For some women, employment choices have been found to be influenced by a number of factors, including cultural expectations, family and community pressures; this was found to be the case, for example, for Pakistani and Bangladeshi females in Oldham (Dale et al, no date). Studies of groups who have come from areas where racism is prevalent have also found that workers (eg UK Roma migrating from Slovakia) have low expectations of the labour market.

Discrimination

Wrench and Modood (2000) list research evidence suggesting the operation of discrimination in the UK labour market, including: statistical evidence in the form of census and large-scale surveys such as the Labour Force Survey (LFS); 'discrimination testing', that is, special experiments using actors or fictitious applications; interviews with gatekeepers, for example, the staff of employment agencies; interviews and surveys studying the experience of minorities in the labour market or the workplace; the actions of aggrieved employers; investigations conducted by the then Commission for Racial Equality (CRE);[4] and incidents coming to light at employment tribunals.

Data presented earlier demonstrate the disadvantaged position of ethnic minorities. Similar inequalities were found in analyses of previous LFSs (Jones, 1993; Sly, 1995; Sly et al, 1999), as well as the 1991 Census (Owen, 1992–95; Karn, 1997) and Policy Studies Institute surveys discussed earlier. It would not, however, be correct to say that differences between minority ethnic employment and the general population are all due to discrimination. We need more research establishing when ethnicity makes a difference and when it does not. Analysis of the LFS found a significant unexplained discriminatory element to exist for most BME groups (Lindley, 2005).[5]

Although statistical sources are useful, they are not proof that discrimination is the sole or major explanation for disparities in labour-market participation. Other such methods, relying on smaller sample sizes, have been used, such as discrimination testing. This method uses two or more testers, one belonging to the majority group and the others to minority groups. The testers are matched with the same credentials and apply for the same job. Over a period of repeated testing, if the majority group candidate is systematically selected over the minority ethnic candidate, then this points to discrimination operating. A study of this type was commissioned by the CRE in Nottingham, where discrimination against 'black' and Asian people occurred in nearly half of the jobs tested (Hubbuck and Carter, 1980). The CRE commissioned a repeat study in Nottingham 14 years later to see if there were any improvements; unfortunately, this study found job prospects were bleak for all applicants due to a decade of mass unemployment, but nonetheless BME groups were less likely than white people to get jobs following interview, even when other factors such as class, education and location were controlled (Simpson and Stevenson, 1994). A more recent exercise of matched applications found net discrimination in favour of white names over minority ethnic applications to be 29% (DWP, 2009).

Discrimination testing focused on certain professions has also been undertaken. A study based on the medical profession found that NHS hospitals were twice as likely to select candidates with Anglo-Saxon names for interview over those with Asian names (Esmail and Everington, 1993). A similar study in 1992 (Noon, 1993) examined evidence of racial discrimination among 100 of the UK's largest companies (see *Case Study 9.1*).

Case Study 9.1: Discrimination in the job application process

The Noon (1993) study sent two fictitious speculative application letters to companies. These were substantively the same, other than one was from 'Sanjay Patel' and the other from 'John Evans'. Each applicant was a final MBA student seeking information on employment opportunities within management. The research found that the applicants were equally likely to receive a reply, but better-quality replies (helpful and encouraging) were sent to 'John Evans'. A significant gap was also found between policy and practice. Companies with equal opportunity statements were more likely to treat the applicants equally; however, where discrimination occurred, it was in favour of the white candidate.

The study was repeated six years later (Hoque and Noon, 1999) and found no evidence of unequal treatment. However, the 'disappearance' of discrimination resulted from different companies moving into the top 100, rather than companies in the 1992 study improving their practices. The 1998 study found that having an equal opportunity statement made no difference to the treatment of the applicants. In fact, companies with such statements were more likely to discriminate against the minority ethnic applicant. Another finding was that candidates with Hindu names fared better in the labour market than candidates associated with Sikh or Muslim religions.

The experience of minority ethnic groups provides further corroboration of discrimination. The fourth national survey (Modood et al, 1997) reported that 78% of economically active minority ethnic respondents thought that employers refused people jobs for racial or religious reasons. There was a slight difference in the opinions of the different ethnic groups with the highest figure recorded among those of Caribbean origin, of which 95% believed that such discrimination existed. Surprisingly, apart from the Caribbean group, more white people (90% of the economically active) than other groups thought that employers would refuse someone a job for reasons of race or religion.

However, BME groups were more likely to believe that discrimination was widespread, with 18% believing that 'most' employers discriminate, compared to only 5% of white people. Of Bangladeshis surveyed, 51% thought that employers would discriminate and almost one third responded 'can't say'. This analysis is based on responses of the economically active and may also reflect their low participation rate in the labour market (Modood et al, 1997). Evidence from BME groups themselves of discrimination may be criticised as subjective, although it has been found that ethnic minorities underestimated the discrimination to which they were exposed (Smith, 1977). Moreover, discrimination can be in the form of indirect discrimination (see Chapter 2), which may be harder to detect and prove.

The number of court cases due to discrimination might be an indicator of the extent of the problem (see Chapter 12). Race relations legislation has made racial discrimination illegal (see Chapter 4) and allows aggrieved employees to take discriminatory employers to court. However, employment tribunals on the basis of racial discrimination made up only 1.5% of the total hearings of employment tribunal claims in 2009/10, with only 3% of claims being successful, and most being settled by means of conciliation, withdrawn or dismissed at the hearing (Ministry of Justice and Tribunals Service, 2010). That said, there is a year-on-year increase in employment tribunals based on discrimination on the grounds of religion or belief, although overall they are numerically few and still tiny fractions of such cases: there were no claims in 2002/03, 307 in 2004/05 (Keter and Beale, 2005) and 1,000 in 2009/10 (Ministry of Justice and Tribunals Service, 2010). Also it appears now that 'hidden discrimination' (Trade Union Congress, 2003) is being identified and institutional (indirect) racism in public services is prevalent in the UK (Macpherson, 1999).

Family structures

Family structure impacts upon some BME groups more forcefully than on others (Berthoud, 2000b). In particular, over half (56%) of 'black' or Black British dependent children lived with a lone parent in 2009 compared to only almost one quarter of White British children (23%) (ONS, 2010). Being brought up without a significant male role model might influence a young person's labour-market engagement, for example, unemployment levels for single Black Caribbean males have been twice that of those who are married or live with a partner (Modood et al, 1997). Also, in the case of Pakistani and Bangladeshi females, low activity levels are particularly characteristic of Asian Muslims and are affected by the economic position of their husbands; the wives/partners of unemployed men have lower activity rates than the wives of men with jobs (Modood et al, 1997).

Family structures may also be a factor for the high level of self-employment among certain minority ethnic groups (Basu, 1998) as the extended family may provide free labour or financial assistance. As mentioned earlier in the chapter, some BME groups have larger families than White British families, and childcare and family responsibilities, combined with disproportionately poor access to childcare, affect their supply of labour (Daycare Trust, 2000).

Alienation

Those experiencing perceived, or real, exclusion from employment or other institutions, or witnessing others in their community experiencing such exclusion, may develop a sense of alienation. Young Black Caribbean men may develop a sense of alienation as a consequence of their exclusion from employment (Wrench et al, 1997). Black Caribbean boys may develop a sense of resentment as a result of the stereotypes held of them by teachers, which is in turn perceived by the teachers as a potential threat, reinforcing the image (Gillborn, 1990; Sewell, 1997). As a result of being denied opportunities in the labour market, some may decide to adopt an alternative lifestyle. Many of these issues carry parallels with unemployment and disaffection among young White British men with poor academic achievements; class is obviously, then, a prominent factor. However, it is suggested that the disadvantages of young Black Caribbean men:

> may be seen as a general problem of exclusion and alienation during a period of widening, economic inequality. On the other hand, important elements of the problems facing young Caribbean men are specifically racial and their response may also be based, in part, on a sense of ethnic identity and rejection. (Berthoud, 1999, p 4)

A study of young Bangladeshi men in inner-city London also found them to be alienated from the majority White British as well as other BME groups; this was so whether they were UK-born or Bangladeshi-born (Salway, 2008).

The structure of the economy

There is a lower demand for manual labour for those with limited qualifications and skills due to deindustrialisation and the shift from a manufacturing base since the main migrations of the 1950s–70s occurred (DfEE, 2001). Further, BME groups tend to be highly concentrated in the inner city (Jones, 1993; Modood et al, 1997) where job opportunities are more restricted. That said, BME groups overall are now relatively less concentrated in declining industries than their white counterparts. However, some minority groups may be affected more than others: Indian men and women in particular are well-represented in manufacturing, a sector which suffered a 31,000 loss in jobs between 1995 and 2000 (Cabinet Office, 2000). Industry restructuring has also impacted on certain industries in particular geographical locations – for example, the decline of the textile industry had a specific, negative effect on Pakistanis and Bangladeshis in Northern England (Karn, 1997). Furthermore, there is also a spatial mismatch in that BME groups are not concentrated in areas where jobs have grown (Turok and Edge, 1999).

Minority ethnic groups tend to be affected by the business cycle more than their white counterparts (Jones, 1993; Lindley, 2005). This may be due to the occupations and industries in which they are employed being more sensitive to upturns and downturns in the economy. Berthoud's analysis of LFS data (1999) found that unemployment among Black Caribbeans and Black Africans was largely attributable to their sensitivity to variations in the economic environment.

Other factors affecting demand

It was shown earlier that employment rates for BME groups are lower than those of their white counterparts, reflecting in part the lack of labour-market demand for them. This can be shaped by different factors. One of the dampeners of demand is the lack of companies providing employment opportunities in areas where BME groups live. Lower levels of business activity have been found in areas where such groups are concentrated, and the companies that do exist tend to be smaller than in white-dominant areas, reducing employment opportunities (Cabinet Office, 2000). In fact, the final report of the Cabinet Office study (Cabinet Office, 2003) highlights geography as one of the key determinants of minority ethnic employment rates. Its analysis of LFS data shows that minority ethnic employment rates are highest in Outer London and lowest in West Yorkshire and Greater Manchester.

Demand-side factors affecting BME groups include industrial restructuring (or deindustrialisation), geographical deprivation, discrimination, expectations and stereotypes of employers, and poor levels of public infrastructure. All must be taken into account when trying to explain ethnic diversity within labour-market participation. Local context, for example, might assume particular importance.

Other factors affecting supply

One explanation for minority ethnic labour-market disadvantage focuses on human capital. This may be a factor for some groups, for example, Black Caribbean and Pakistani/Bangladeshi students show the lowest levels of achievement at GCSE level. However, it cannot explain the disadvantage experienced by high-achieving groups as GCSE attainment is highest among Indian and Chinese students, particularly girls who outperform White British students.

Broadly speaking, one would assume that investment in education will lead to higher wages and better job prospects; however, over 30% of Indians, African Asians and Chinese exhibit levels of over-education for their jobs, compared to 20% of their white counterparts (Battu and Sloane, 2002). The same research found 36% of Bangladeshi workers to have fewer qualifications than were required for their job; in other words, they were under-educated. For the overqualified, Berthoud (2000a) found that the returns to education in terms of earnings were less for BME groups than they were for the white population; while a degree reaped an extra £80 per week for the white population, it only increased an Indian's weekly wage by £71 per week, the highest returns for a degree among all minority groups; the lowest returns for a degree were for the African group at a mere £27 per week, while Caribbean and Pakistani/Bangladeshi graduates increased their earning power by £64 and £61 per week, respectively. The most recent research in this area has found that for any given level of qualification, White British men and women are more likely to be employed than minority ethnic groups (Machin et al, 2009).

The supply of minority ethnic labour can also be restricted by poor public transport in areas where many live (Social Exclusion Unit, 2000). A survey of minority ethnic unemployed claimants found that they were less likely than their white counterparts to have access to privately owned transport. Of all minority ethnic claimants, 37% had no form of transport compared with 26% of white claimants. This difference was greater for those over the age of 45, where 45% of minority ethnic claimants had no privately owned transport compared with 23% of white claimants (Shropshire et al, 1999).

More recently, religion and culture have also been presented as significant supply factors (Weller et al, 2001; Ahmad et al, 2003; National Employment Panel, 2010). Lindley's (2002) analysis of the fourth national survey found religion, as well as ethnicity, to be significant, that Hindu Indians appear to fare better in the labour market than Sikh Indians, and that, relative to other 'non-white religions', Muslims experience some unexplained employment penalty. Recent data showed Muslims to have the highest unemployment; in 2008, unemployment for Muslim men was 10%, compared with 4% for Christian men (Annual Population Survey, 2008). The explanation for this probably reflects a complex interplay between socio-economic position and ethnic origin, some of which reflects local contexts, in addition to changing assumptions about how a person's ethnic origin assumes social meaning (see Chapter 2). We know little, for example, at present about how Islamophobia might impact on a person's labour-market participation.

The review presented here is not exhaustive, and many other factors affect the supply of labour such as social class (Heath and McMahon, 1997) and housing tenure (see Chapter 5). Some barriers may not be exclusively related to ethnicity, but may be highly correlated, such as, for some groups, having a criminal record (see Chapter 12) and ill-health (see Chapter 6) (for a more comprehensive literature review, see Cabinet Office, 2000). In summary, though, the supply of ethnic minorities in the labour market can be determined by factors including racial discrimination, human capital, religion and cultural factors, family structures, alienation, discouragement, and social class, among many others.

Conclusion

Despite minority ethnic groups having resided in large numbers in Great Britain for more than half a century and in many cases now having been 'British'-born and educated, they still face disadvantage – sometimes acute – in the labour market. In general, BME groups are more likely to be unemployed and be in low-skill occupations and industries than the White British population. However, there is huge diversity among different minority ethnic groups, which is further complicated by gender and age. Potential differences within groups remain under-researched and need to be a greater feature of further work in this area.

Thurrow's (1969) dimensions of disadvantage are still prevalent in today's labour market. Although some minority groups have progressed, others suffer severe disadvantage. By all indicators considered here, Pakistani and Bangladeshi groups fare worst, and this applies to both genders; other groups about whom we know virtually nothing – particularly recent migrants such as UK Roma and groups subject to the greatest racism, such as Gypsies and Travellers – are also likely to fare worst. Chinese and African Asian groups hold a position of broad parity with the White British population, whereas Indians who came directly from the subcontinent and Black Caribbean groups, who have been in Great Britain the longest, still experience some disadvantages. The evidence presented in this chapter also shows that Black Caribbean women fare much better than Black Caribbean men.

Various factors have been put forward to explain some of these differences. These include migration, alienation, expectations and stereotyping, family structure, the structure of the economy, and discrimination, as well as other factors affecting the demand and supply of minority ethnic labour. There is also evidence that discrimination has most certainly gone beyond skin colour and is also prevalent in terms of culture and religion. Additionally, while discrimination may now be less overt, there is evidence of 'hidden' discrimination and institutional racism.

Although this chapter positions minority groups in the labour market and provides some explanations, it does not look at the impact of policy measures on them. Despite various employment initiatives and legislation, significant disparities persist. Teasing out the complexity of this, while reflecting contested and changing definitions of culture and ethnicity, will be the challenge facing future research into this area. Differences within ethnic groupings are likely to be as important as difference between groupings.

Questions for discussion

- Why in your opinion is the labour-market position for each minority group different?
- What strategies or policy measures could be introduced to eradicate such differences?
- To what extent do you think social class plays a role?
- Reflect on how potential differences within specific ethnic groupings might mediate labour-market participation.

Further reading

Various Cabinet Office reports are worth consulting, especially the detailed reports noted in the reference lists.

Electronic resources

- The Census contains no employment question. The best data source is thus the Annual Population Survey available from the Office for National Statistics or the quarterly Labour Force Survey available at: www.statistics.gov.uk/ssd/surveys/labour_force_survey.asp
- The National Employment Panel is an employer-led body advising government on labour-market policies. It was closed in 2008, but its past reports are available at: www.dwp.gov.uk/publications
- The National Equality report, *An Anatomy of Economic Inequality*, from a Commission chaired by John Hills, brings together a range of evidence including labour-market data: it is available at: www.equalities.gov.uk

Notes

[1] The Annual Population Survey (APS) is basically the same as the Labour Force Survey (LFS), but the LFS is run in quarters. The APS has a bigger sample and, therefore, is usually seen as more accurate. However, according to the Office for National Statistics (ONS) estimates are based on small sample sizes and are, therefore, subject to a margin of uncertainty.

[2] Due to space constraints, this chapter does not consider more recent migrant workers. There is a growing body of research relating to them, for example, Lewis et al (2009) for a regional perspective and Ruhs and Anderson (2010) for a national perspective. The chapter also does not consider Gypsies, Roma and Travellers because there is virtually no useful national data, a point also emphasised in the report of the National Equality Panel (NEP, 2010b).

[3] Many migrant workers in Great Britain on a temporary basis also suffer significantly from poor English skills.

[4] The CRE is now the Equality and Human Rights Commission (EHRC).

[5] The LFS, though quarterly, is of little help in relation to smaller minority populations as its overall sample is fairly small (roughly 60,000 addresses), which cannot capture their experience.

Poverty and income maintenance

Ian Law

Overview

This chapter examines the relationship between poverty and ethnicity, and assesses the impact of a range of policy interventions on black and minority ethnic (BME) groups. It will:

- examine poverty and social exclusion among Gypsies and Travellers;
- examine evidence on child and adult poverty within and across ethnic groups;
- evaluate explanations for ethnic differences in patterns of poverty;
- assess the impact of the economic recession on BME groups;
- examine the links between immigration policy, social assistance and destitution;
- assess the extent to which some BME groups are greater users of social security or certain types of social security; and
- evaluate the impact of recent policy interventions including 'welfare-to-work' policies, the minimum wage and 'race' relations legislation.

Key concepts
benefits, Gypsies, income, poverty, wealth, welfare

Introduction

A complex range of factors have produced consistently higher levels of poverty among BME groups. Across and within BME groups there are widely differing patterns and levels of poverty. This chapter seeks to examine the relationship between poverty and ethnicity, and evaluates explanations for this complicated pattern of racial and ethnic outcomes. Gypsies, Roma and Travellers (GRT)[1] are frequently excluded from these debates despite having significantly poorer outcomes than many other BME groups. We begin, therefore, by looking in-depth at poverty and social exclusion among this group. The section on poverty concludes with a consideration of the impact of the economic recession and welfare cuts on these groups. The next section of this chapter looks at the provision of social security and begins with an assessment of the links with immigration policy, and the ongoing creation of destitution among some groups of asylum-seekers. Then, the pattern of take-up of social security by ethnic minorities is examined. Finally, a selected set of policy interventions is evaluated. This chapter further develops the analysis of racism, ethnicity, migration and social security in Law (2009). It is worth noting that we know relatively little yet about the relationship between poverty and ethnicity within the devolved administrations (see eg Netto et al, 2010).

Poverty

Low incomes and social exclusion (other forms of severe and chronic disadvantage) together constitute the notion of poverty used in this chapter (for further conceptual discussion, see Poverty Site, 2010). Contemporary debates on the nature and extent of poverty among UK minority ethnic communities tend to focus on those groups where there is adequate empirical data from censuses and surveys. This chapter looks closely at recent evidence on ethnicity and poverty using this material (Platt, 2009; Moosa and Woodroffe, 2010; NEP, 2010b).[2] But, if some groups are not enumerated or are 'hidden' within other existing categories, they will be ignored in both academic and policy debates. For this reason, this section begins by examining poverty and marginalisation among GRT groups, whose material conditions are frequently ignored in accounts of ethnicity and poverty. Then child and adult poverty within and across ethnic groups, who are enumerated, is examined together with other evidence on economic inequalities. Racial and ethnic inequalities in patterns of poverty remain a constant and dynamic feature of British society.

Gypsies, Roma and Travellers

The failure to enumerate Gypsies and Travellers in previous censuses in 1991 and 2001, unlike other significant BME groups, is one key cause of the failure of progressive policy and practice interventions in ethnic relations to tackle the discrimination, exclusion and inequalities affecting these groups. A predominant focus on non–white groups in national policy development has also created new forms of exclusion as the specific situation and needs of other groups are largely ignored. The omission of GRT groups from the concept of exclusion, from census data collection and related ethnic monitoring of public services and policy debate and action indicates that their marginalisation from dominant power relations has led to worsening outcomes in education and other key spheres of life. The 2011 census will for the first time include 'Gypsy or Irish Traveller' and Roma categories, which may enable authorities responsible for providing benefits, accommodation, education and health services to ensure that the needs of the GRT communities are accurately assessed and resources properly targeted.

Gypsies moved into the UK from Europe from the 16th century onwards, with a significant community being established around London by the 18th century. The origins and differentiation of groups within this category are complex and may include the formation of groups with both indigenous and non–UK roots. Migration to the UK has been mainly driven by expulsion and repression in mainland Europe together with rejection of sedentary lifestyles and feudal bonds and, more recently, as a result of structured racism. They have often been subject to oppressive vagrancy legislation. There has been a history of conflict between this group and the state, particularly in relation to the enforcement of housing, urban planning and land control laws, affecting family travel and mobility (Morris and Clements, 1999). Welfare outcomes are particularly poor for this group (Cemlyn and Clark, 2005); for example, they have higher levels of infant mortality and lower life expectancy (due to difficulties in accessing health services) than most other groups (Morris and Clements, 2001). Life expectancy for men and women is 10 years lower than the national average and Gypsy and Irish Traveller mothers are 20 times more likely than mothers in the rest of the population to have experienced the death of a child (Van Cleemput et al, 2004).

GRT groups currently fare very badly in many dimensions of equality including longevity, health, education, political participation, influence and voice, identity, expression and self-respect, and legal security. Particular conflicts have arisen over housing and sites, media coverage, and wider hostility, where openly anti-gypsy prejudice is often expressed, far beyond that directed towards other minorities. The criminalisation of these groups has been accompanied by many high-profile conflicts including where they have been criminalised for being homeless (since those living on unauthorised encampments are very often legally homeless), criminalised for pursuing a nomadic way of life and suffer collective punishment for the crimes of specific individuals, whereby whole settlements are evicted because of the behaviour of some members (TLRP, 2007). Many Gypsy and Traveller families have been forced off land they owned, finding it increasingly difficult to find stopping places across the UK and bringing them into greater conflict with other people and local institutions. A reduction in local authority sites and growth in the GRT population means that now over 30% of this group live on unauthorised sites. Having nowhere to stop, they are sometimes forced to occupy public places; this has hugely detrimental impacts on health, mortality, education and labour-market position (TLRP, 2008).

Examination of the patterns of social exclusion facing this group confirms that there is a severe lack of adequate data on this group in relation to labour-market position and poverty. Successive governments and research studies have failed both to identify the nature and extent of the economic context for this group, and to go on to address these issues in the context of national and subnational anti-poverty and social inclusion strategies (Cemlyn and Clark, 2005). However, the Social Exclusion Unit (2000), the Institute for Public Policy Research (Crawley, 2004) and the work of the now defunct Commission for Racial Equality (CRE, 2006) have begun to highlight this group in terms of racism and ethnic inequality. Cemlyn and Clark confirm that many Gypsy and Traveller children are 'poor in multiple and different ways'. Many are financially poor and there are many dimensions to this 'poverty'. Also, despite the paucity of robust data on the income of Gypsy and Traveller families, both anecdotal information and other studies show that some families have few financial resources. Gypsy and Traveller culture has been identified as strongly family-oriented and child–centred and these family and extended family networks are seen as primarily providing support in difficult times. Gypsy and Traveller economies often involve family-based self-employed activities, which are flexible, adaptable and opportunistic in relation to gaps and opportunities in mainstream economic markets. This includes declining traditional work in areas such as farm work and scrapping, and other newer economic activity in market trading and construction. Moreover, there has been a decline in previous economic outlets for Gypsies and Travellers, particularly in crowded urban environments (Power, 2004). Roma migrating since the A8/A2[3] EU accessions have found themselves vulnerable to economic and housing exploitation by gangmasters.

Local authority restrictions on working activities on official sites, such as pursuing trading activities or operating businesses, have undermined aspects of the Traveller economy (Kiddle, 1999). Many find that simply being a Gypsy or Traveller, and lacking basic literacy skills, prevents them from accessing mainstream wage labour jobs or training. Because of this, access to social security benefits is important for some families. However, research has shown levels of discrimination in accessing benefits for those who are frequently nomadic, with some evidence of specific surveillance directed towards Gypsies and Travellers on the assumption that they commit benefit fraud, with the result that families can be denied benefit where there is little, if any, evidence of actual fraud (Cemlyn and Clark, 2005, p 153). A review of evidence (Cemlyn et al, 2009) confirms these patterns, identifying continuing high rates of mortality, suicide and substance abuse, worse health outcomes, declining educational outcomes and extremely low participation in secondary education, low employment rates, and high poverty rates.

In many local authority areas, despite conflict with residents and media hostility, efforts have been made to improve communication, social inclusion and provision of services to both settled and non-settled Gypsy and Traveller families. A recent evaluation of multi-agency partnership working to achieve these objectives in Scotland concluded that many families had been helped towards the services they needed and were able to describe how this had helped health and well-being. But, as yet, these developments have not achieved generalised impacts across the Gypsy/Traveller community as a whole (Macneil et al, 2005). Here, additional resourcing was seen as constituting positive discrimination and this was supported by many agencies, given the clear failures of non-specific mainstream service delivery. The UK experience can provide a range of examples of innovative practice across different local authority areas as new ways are found to improve patterns of provision, but substantial inequalities remain and future prospects look grim. The Coalition government has already sparked protest (IRR, 2010) from campaigners and academics over cuts and cancellations to progressive policies incentivising local authorities to develop Gypsy and Traveller sites in the Housing and Communities Agency (HCA) budget.

The Conservative Planning Green Paper in 2010 (available at www.conservatives.com/News/News_stories/2010/02/~/media/Files/Green%20Papers/planning-green-paper.ashx) also threatened to scrap Planning and Housing Circulars, which had started to give Gypsies, Travellers and Showmen a 'level playing field' in planning disputes with local authorities and planning inspectors. Also the Conservative Party, according to Communities and Local Government Secretary Eric Pickles, will revive elements of the Criminal Justice and Public Order Act 1994 to turn trespass from a civil into a criminal offence. This means that Travellers refusing to move from land not privately owned by them could be arrested by police or forcibly evicted. Gypsy and Traveller Accommodation Needs Assessments have identified targets for sites for Gypsies and Travellers and yards for Showmen and progress was starting to be made. Matthew Brindley, spokesman for the Irish Traveller Movement, was reported as saying that:

> Over a decade's campaigning work has been destroyed overnight by this coalition ... if the communities don't have stable accommodation, that impacts on the health and education of our children, and the health and employment of our adults. Accommodation is the overriding factor. It is a catalyst to all the other severe problems faced by this incredibly vulnerable community. (Hill, 2010)

Deteriorating welfare outcomes for this group parallel Roma experiences in Central and Eastern Europe where, for example, desegregation measures in education have failed to improve access to education (Law and Swann, 2011).

Comparing child and adult poverty

Children from those BME groups enumerated more adequately in censuses and surveys are clearly over-represented among poor children. Ethnic minorities make up 12% of the population and 15% of all children, but 25% of children who are in poverty (author's own analysis of Households Below Average Income figures 2003/04–2005/06; see also Platt, 2009), increasing to 750,000 children in 2010 (Sharma, 2007).

It is clear from **Table 10.1** that all BME groups have higher rates of child poverty than the White British group, and that Bangladeshi and Pakistani

Table 10.1: Children's poverty rates: rolling averages (before housing costs), Great Britain

	2001/02–2003/04	2002/03–2004/05	2003/04–2005/06	2004/05–2006/07
White British	20	20	19	20
Indian	28	28	30	27
Pakistani	59	56	53	53
Bangladeshi	72	66	65	58
Black Caribbean	31	27	30	26
Black African	38	38	37	35

Note: The poverty threshold is defined as 60% of median equivalent income before housing costs. Bases: 2001/02–2003/04: 26,208; 2002/03–2003/04: 26,897; 2003/04–2005/06: 26,291; 2004/05–2006/07: 25,249, as presented in Platt (2009, p 25).

Source: Households Below Average Income data 2001/02, 2002/03, 2003/04, 2004/05, 2005/06 and 2006/07, weighted.

children (primarily Muslims) experience the highest levels of poverty. Within BME groups, Black Caribbean children have the lowest levels of child poverty. Between 2001 and 2007, racial and ethnic differentials have reduced, as there has been a decline in child poverty among ethnic minorities but not among White British children, with Bangladeshis experiencing the greatest fall in poverty rates. Overall, this data confirms three key points: first, the significant level of diversity across ethnic groups; second, the persistence of greater poverty among BME groups; and, third, some impact of poverty reduction measures on those BME groups with the highest risks of poverty.

Are there differences in child poverty rates and adult poverty rates within ethnic groups? Platt's analysis showed that generally child poverty rates were higher than adult rates across all ethnic groups, with for example 54% of working-age Bangladeshi adults in poverty (before housing costs) compared with 64% of children from that group, and 13% of White British working-age adults in poverty compared with 19% of children (2009, pp 26–7). The general pattern of ethnic differentials in poverty rates was also consistent, whether the focus was on children, adults or all individuals.

Explaining ethnic differences in poverty

Why are there differences in poverty rates across ethnic groups and how should we set about explaining these patterns? It would be most useful to start by examining those measurable factors that are linked to differences in poverty risks, such as employment status, migration history and family structure. Reasons for arrival and its timing have implications for employment and employment history, with earlier migrants being concentrated in manufacturing, and in areas and industries, for example the textile industry, which subsequently suffered from processes of deindustrialisation. Later migrants were concentrated less in Northern industrial towns and more in the Midlands and, particularly, London. Forced settlement in poorer areas can also result in more limited educational opportunities, restricting options for future, non-migrant, generations. Employment in vulnerable sectors, alongside discrimination, concentration in poorer areas that offer fewer opportunities and, for some groups, notably Pakistanis, Bangladeshis and Black Caribbeans, greater difficulty in obtaining high levels of qualifications, have resulted in both high unemployment for many minority groups, especially Caribbeans, Pakistanis and, particularly, Bangladeshis, and much higher rates of self-employment among certain groups, in particular, Indians, Chinese and Pakistanis (Pritchard and Dorling, 2006). The role of ethnicity in determining differential labour-market outcomes for BME groups has been described as an 'ethnic penalty' (Heath and McMahon,

1997). Recent research on persistent employment disadvantage (Tyers et al, 2006) confirms that the huge employment penalty faced by Pakistani and Bangladeshi women has not changed much in 30 years. As most of these women are Muslims, it appears that religion is more important than ethnic group as a predictor of female employment penalties. Among all social groups it is only disabled people who are as unlikely to move into employment as Muslim women. Overall, the ethnic employment gap will remain significant for at least another century (Philips, 2007). BME groups are disproportionately represented amongst the Department for Work and Pension's (DWP's) 'most disadvantaged customer group', facing multiple complex barriers to work, including employer attitudes, area-based factors, human capital and 'negotiating identities' in relation to family life, religious and cultural values, and work (Hasluck and Green, 2007). The cumulative impact of these factors means that ethnic differentials in poverty are due both to measurable and unmeasurable factors. When all measurable factors are taken into account 'unexplained differences in poverty risk between otherwise similar families or children from different ethnic groups' (Platt, 2009, pp 57–8) may exist – an *ethnic poverty penalty*.

The presence of an ethnic penalty is itself an invitation for further investigation and explanation, also indicating that there is a reason for targeting policy remedies towards particular groups (eg to increase pay or benefit take-up), as well as using policy monitoring of the overall poverty of different ethnic groups to evaluate the effectiveness of mainstream measures. Differences summarised by the ethnic penalty might include differences in: pay that the children's parents and family receive for their work; benefits they are eligible for or take up; additional sources of income available to the family; and the ways in which these intersect in potentially complex ways (Platt, 2009, p 57). Ethnic minorities are at higher risk of poverty because of their concentration among those key 'at risk' groups including lone-parent families, workless households and large families, but there are other factors at work here too. Other factors contributing to differences in poverty across ethnic groups include 'rates of employment, hours of work and pay, non-take-up of benefits and credits, numbers of adults in employment relative to dependants within the household, and lack of additional "buffers" such as savings, sources of credit or alternative incomes' (Platt, 2009, p 6). Two recent studies have also examined stark ethnic differences in poverty rates and their causes, concluding that they are determined by a variety of factors including persistent discrimination, patterns of educational qualification, labour-market outcomes, housing locations, disabilities and ill-health (Clark and Drinkwater, 2007; Palmer and Kenway, 2007).

The National Equality Panel report (NEP, 2010a, 2010b) summarised current evidence on some of these key factors in its analysis of contemporary economic inequality, confirming that 'There remain deep-seated and systematic differences in economic outcomes between social groups across all of the dimensions we have examined – including between different ethnic groups' (NEP, 2010a, p 1).

Median total household wealth varies considerably by ethnicity, from only £15,000 for Bangladeshi households to around £75,000 for Black Caribbean, £97,000 for Pakistani and £200,000 or more for Indian and White British households. Those from Bangladeshi and Pakistani households have a median equivalent net income of only £238 per week, compared to the national median of £393 (NEP, 2010b, p 233). In education, some BME groups improve their test scores from below the national average as they move through compulsory schooling, but at 16, Pakistani, Black African and Black Caribbean boys' attainment in England is still well below the national average. Children recorded as having Traveller, Roma or Gypsy backgrounds have a pattern of educational attainment that declines during the school years, resulting in much worse results than any other group, with ethnic differentials steadily widening. This group, together with black and Pakistani/Bangladeshi students, are also less likely to go to more prestigious universities or to get higher-class degrees (NEP, 2010a, p 16). Despite Chinese, Indian and Black Africans having higher education qualifications than the White British population, nearly all minority groups are less likely to be in paid employment than White British men and women, and, for some groups, differences in unemployment rates are as great for the 'second generation' as for those born outside the UK. Pakistani and Bangladeshi Muslim men and Black African Christian men have an 'ethnic pay penalty', not explained by factors such as age, occupational classification, family circumstances and qualifications, earning 13–21% less than White British Christian men (Longhi and Platt, 2008). Even one of the groups with the most successful educational outcomes, the Chinese, faced an 'ethnic pay penalty' of 11% (NEP, 2010b, p 228). Evidence on current levels of racial discrimination in the labour market shows that this persists at a consistently high level of 35% in the private sector but drops to 4% in the public sector (Wood et al, 2009). Levels of discrimination were similar across all ethnic groups studied, applying equally to both men and women.

Economic crisis, welfare cuts and future prospects

BME groups currently experience disadvantage in a variety of areas, including employment, education, housing, health, crime and political participation (Mawhinney, 2010). The relative vulnerability of ethnic minorities in various market contexts means that the current economic recession and associated cuts in welfare are having and will have a greater negative impact on these groups. Almost half (48%) of young black people are unemployed compared with the rate of unemployment among white men (21%), with mixed ethnic groups having the greatest overall increase rising from 21% in March 2008 to 35% in November 2009 (IPPR, 2010). Lower employment means more poverty. Ethnic minority women experience higher rates of poverty than white women and a recent report argues that the economic recession presents two major risks (Moosa and Woodroffe, 2010, p 5). First, that ethnic minority women will be locked into their destitution for the foreseeable future, and, second, that anti-poverty approaches marginalise the needs of ethnic minority women through failing to recognise and address those needs. Such women are being pathologised and ignored. A focus on poverty at the household level also fails to capture what is happening to individuals within intra-household relations and particularly women (Moosa and Woodroffe, 2010, p 43).

The increased threat of financial exclusion facing ethnic minorities has also been recently highlighted by the Runnymede Trust (Mawhinney, 2010). Key findings here include lower levels of savings, lower take-up of contents, health, buildings and life insurance, and poorer pensions among ethnic minorities, together with higher levels of debt and forms of direct and indirect racial discrimination in accessing credit both for ethnic minority small businesses and individuals.

In the five years to 2003/04, both in-work and out-of-work child poverty fell for the only time in the last 30 years (Macinnes et al, 2009, p 9). This fall also included a reduction in racial and ethnic inequalities. Even before the economic crisis in 2008/09, child poverty was increasing with the overall picture steadily becoming worse in the last five years, and likely to increase further. Current statements and policy indications from the Coalition government indicate that this will be the case. The June 2010 Budget, with a regressive VAT rise and the freezing of levels of child benefit for three years, will have a disproportionately greater impact on ethnic minorities. Immediately after the 2010 election, a review of the national context of poverty and welfare was issued by the government (Cabinet Office, 2010b). This confirms the worsening context with income inequality at its highest level since 1961, increases in severe poverty since 2004/05 and continuing differentials in terms of ethnicity.

Welfare

Migration, welfare and destitution

British state policy towards migrants and minorities demonstrates a 'long pedigree of racism' (Craig, 2007). Regulation to exclude 'aliens', denizens (permanent settlers without British nationality) and particular racialised categories of British citizens from access to welfare benefits is evident in immigration legislation and wider social policy reforms from the Victorian period onwards. Poor Law rules, pensions law, aliens legislation as well as National Insurance criteria incorporated such practices (Williams, 1989). The racialisation of the British welfare state drew on eugenic notions of the quality of the race and nation to maintain imperialism, and to manage both the 'burden' of the black, Asian, Irish and Jewish poor and the perceived threat of such groups to the jobs and wages of those in the 'new' mass trades unions. Post-war welfare reforms and immigration legislation have continued to institutionalise racially exclusionary rules that determine eligibility to welfare benefits; these include residence tests, rules on 'recourse to public funds' and sponsorship conditions. New Labour continued and amplified previous Conservative policy in relation to welfare, immigration and asylum (Morris, 2007; Somerville, 2007), reducing the benefit rights of asylum-seekers, tightening job search requirements and introducing availability tests and migration controls, except for particularly skilled migrants. The Immigration Act 1999 established the National Asylum Support Service (NASS), separate from Department of Social Security provision, to arrange accommodation and provide vouchers at 70% of income support rates for adults (100% for child dependants). Following a campaign led by the Transport and General Workers' Union, cash replaced vouchers in 2002, but the provision of funds for basic support remains with NASS and distinct from social security, although tied into income support rates. Also for those on Section 4 'Hard Case' support (failed asylum-seekers who temporarily cannot be returned to their country of origin) vouchers continue to be used (Somerville, 2007). A concerted set of measures, systematically reducing support for asylum-seekers, has been implemented, including withdrawing support to 'late' applicants, unsuccessful applicants and some families. Increasing exclusion of this group from work and public services including social housing, non-emergency healthcare and secondary healthcare for failed asylum-seekers led to widespread destitution as identified by the UK Parliamentary Joint Committee on Human Rights (2007). This has most recently been identified for those processed through the New Asylum Model (Lewis, 2007). A recent study by the Refugee Council focused on asylum-seekers in receipt of 'Section 4' support, surveying organisations across England and interviewing asylum-seekers. It concluded:

> people are unable to shop around for cheaper and more appropriate food or other essential goods, are unable to buy sufficient food and toiletries to meet their needs, cannot keep in contact with friends, families and legal representatives, and are unable to pay for travel to essential appointments. It is clear that using vouchers as a means of support and subsistence is causing unnecessary hardship and having a detrimental effect on many asylum-seekers' physical and mental well-being.... Some asylum-seekers are being forced to survive on vouchers for many years. (Cited in NEP, 2010b, p 249)

Outside the UK, in an examination of the social rights of immigrants in the USA, Germany and Sweden, Sainsbury (2006) demonstrates the value of analysis that connects welfare regimes with immigration policy regimes and different forms and categories of immigration. She found that non-citizens received better entitlements in comprehensive welfare states like Germany and Sweden than in the 'incomplete' welfare state of the USA, and that differences for female migrants were evident with lower levels of benefit in Germany than Sweden. So, different immigration regimes produce differing policy logics of exclusion and inclusion in welfare provision. These logics rest upon ethical, moral and philosophical principles that frequently conflict with human rights principles, children's rights and other policy goals such as reducing child poverty and ensuring freedom of movement within the EU. New moves to reinstate passport controls in the EU reflect rising hostility to migrants and mobilisation of this hostility through the success and influence of racial nationalism and associated political parties, as in Denmark.

Ethnic minorities and benefits

All BME groups show a greater use of means-tested benefits than the white population, making relatively lower use of non-income-related benefits, despite the receipt of child benefit being substantially higher among minority groups, especially among Pakistanis and Bangladeshis. Greater dependence on means-tested elements is due to:

- *Greater poverty* – a wide-ranging review of ethnicity and poverty in the UK, drawing on research evidence from 350 studies carried out from 1991 onwards, shows that over half of Pakistani, Bangladeshi and Black

African children in Britain are growing up in poverty (Platt, 2007b). Stark ethnic differences in poverty rates are determined by various factors including persistent discrimination, patterns of educational qualification, labour-market outcomes, housing locations, disabilities and ill-health (Palmer and Kenway, 2007; Platt, 2009).

- *Excess unemployment* – which leads to higher claiming of income support and income-based job-seeker's allowance. This is evidenced among all minority groups, but particularly among Pakistanis, Bangladeshis and Black Caribbeans (DSS, 2001; NEP, 2010a).
- *Different patterns of family structure* – for example, Bangladeshis, and to a lesser extent Pakistanis, have large families compared to the national average. Large families are more likely to be in poverty and harder to support on the relatively low earnings that apply to the sectors in which these families are most likely to be concentrated (Berthoud, 2000b; Platt, 2009).
- *Long-term poverty* – among pensioners or the unemployed. Some minority groups are less likely to have accrued assets and are thus more likely to need to claim income support or the minimum income guarantee. Throughout their lives, some minority groups would appear to acquire fewer assets or savings, giving them less of a cushion during periods of unemployment and translating into greater hardship in old age. Nearly 60% of Pakistanis and Bangladeshis had no savings compared with 28% of the population as a whole while over 80% had savings below £1,500 (ONS, 2001).

On the other hand, BME groups have a lower reliance on contributory benefits, but a greater use of the categorical child benefit. The reasons for this include:

- *Different age profiles* – all minority groups have a younger population profile than the population as a whole, which accounts in part for higher rates of child benefit receipt among minority groups. The median age among these groups is 10 years below that of the whole population (26 compared with 36).
- *Differential fertility* – Pakistanis and Bangladeshis also have higher female fertility, with families started at a younger age (Peach, 1996).
- *Unemployment* – for some BME groups this is both more prevalent and more likely to be long term, particularly for Caribbeans (NEP, 2010a). Thus, entitlement to contributions-based jobseeker's allowance is less likely.
- *Insufficient residence to build up contributions records* – for those who migrated in adulthood, the opportunity to build up a contributions record sufficient

to claim the basic state pension may not have been available, while for those who migrated recently, such as refugees, a contributions record may not have been acquired.

- *Interrupted contributions records* – for those with attachments to the country of origin, contributions records may have been interrupted due to extended visits to those countries.

The impact of recent policy interventions

'Welfare-to-work' policies, which aim to move people into work, begin to address some of the issues of those who have had limited options of employment. These could be expected to have a greater impact on members of certain minority groups, given higher unemployment rates amongst Caribbean males, Pakistanis and Bangladeshis, and, to a lesser extent, Indians. Black Caribbean lone mothers might also be anticipated to benefit from options offered through welfare-to-work given their existing greater propensity to take employment. The New Deals are notable in having been subject to ethnic monitoring of both participation and outcomes. Despite non-comprehensive coverage of ethnicity, indications are, however, that different groups experience different pathways through and out of provision (DWP, 2002a; Hasluck and Green, 2007). According to figures to the end of 2001, Indians are over-represented in moves into employment and Bangladeshis are most likely to take up the voluntary-sector option, with Black Africans more likely to take up further education and training. Thus, as *Jobs for All* (DfEE, 1999) indicates, there may be particular issues in the operation and effectiveness of welfare-to-work for different ethnic groups. Additionally, there is evidence that access to the New Deals is limited by the greater tendency to enable BME groups to remain on income support rather than income-based job-seeker's allowance. While this may protect BME group members to a certain extent from the coercive aspects of welfare-to-work, it may also reduce opportunities.

For those in work, the national minimum wage provides some protection against low wages, but BME workers are more likely to be unaware of and not receive the minimum wage (Low Pay Commission, 2007). Tax credits may improve work incentives for groups, such as Bangladeshis and Pakistanis, who tend to have larger families and low wages, and higher rates of disability. Current evidence suggests that black and especially Pakistani and Bangladeshi families are over-represented in the Working Families' Tax Credit caseload (PIU, 2002, p 139). On the other hand, increases to income support child payments have improved out-of-work benefit rates, particularly for larger families and families with young children. While positive for the overall welfare of those on benefit, these latter changes may also tend to reinforce some of the existing patterns in claiming.

The Race Relations (Amendment) Act 2000 requires public authorities to produce 'race' equality strategies. The DWP's 'race' equality strategy document *Equality, Opportunity and Independence for All* (2002b) committed the department to assessing possible differential impacts of its services and policies, prioritising monitoring and evaluation in relation to the possible scale of the impact. It also committed the DWP to effective ethnic monitoring in all areas of delivery and among its employees, and to evaluations of future policy impact, on which it has failed to deliver. The Commission for Racial Equality's final report in 2007 (CRE, 2007a) (before its amalgamation into the Equality and Human Rights Commission) identified poor progress across all Whitehall departments in the implementation of 'race' equality strategies. The continuing failure to demonstrate compliance with 'race' equality requirements in the administration of benefits has recently been confirmed by Aspinall and Mitton (2007) with particular reference to local authority provision of housing and council tax benefits. However, it is not simply the case that individual agencies reforming their practices will transform the delivery of social security to BME groups; rather, that has to be part of a process that looks more fundamentally at the context of and restrictions on people's lives (eg as the Social Exclusion Unit [2000] did), and also considers the way policy regulations themselves are created and maintained. Recent debate has highlighted the problem of hyper- or super-diversity, where professionals and managers face substantial dilemmas in responding to the needs of culturally complex societies (Vertovec, 2006; Mir, 2007). The dangers of simplistic approaches to these questions are exemplified in discussion of 'ethnic managerialism' in the Benefits Agency (Law, 1997), where failure to adequately identify customer needs leads to poor service, and most recently in relation to ethnic minority women (Moosa and Woodroffe, 2010). The national evaluation of Sure Start, a cross-departmental initiative aiming to enhance the life chances of children less than four years old growing up in disadvantaged neighbourhoods, identified the failure to address ethnicity, which, in the programme, was 'fragmented, partial or lacking altogether' (Craig et al, 2007a, p ii). Here outcomes for BME groups could not even be identified because of a failure to undertake detailed ethnic monitoring. This has been a notable failure of DWP activity for decades. In the most recent review of the experiences of ethnic minority claimants, in this case, those claiming disability benefits, significant problems are again identified (Jones and Tracy, 2010). These groups of claimants reported lower levels of satisfaction with this service, were generally less aware and knowledgeable about the benefits available to them, and took a longer time to find out about the help available. Weaker knowledge and understanding of the benefits system among ethnic minorities, and particularly among more recently arrived migrants, had a range of negative impacts on claimants' experiences and a range of barriers to claiming remained in place (Jones and Tracy, 2010, pp 9–10).

Summary

In examining the relationship between poverty and ethnicity, it is clear that there is both a significant level of diversity across ethnic groups and the persistence of greater poverty among BME groups. There has also been some impact of poverty reduction measures on those minority groups with the highest risks of poverty. Current indications are that the worsening economic context and associated welfare cuts will impact heavily on BME groups. In the UK, income inequality is at its highest level since 1961, there have been increases in severe poverty since 2004/05 and continuing differentials in terms of ethnicity. Gypsies and Travellers continue to be in the worst situation of any minority group. Racialisation of migration and welfare has led to poor welfare outcomes for migrants and minorities in the UK. Past immigration policy has structured the settlement patterns and current opportunities of many minority groups and thus their relative dependence on social security, and there have been explicit links between immigration rules and social security entitlements. Although there is significant diversity of circumstances and experiences among and within different BME groups, there is often a high risk of unemployment, poverty, reliance on means-tested benefits and under-claiming. Persistent disadvantage and complex barriers to both work and benefits are experienced by minority groups. The creation of destitution among some asylum-seekers, the rise in unemployment differentials and the failure by the DWP to implement statutory 'race' equality strategies (DWP, 2003) are all further signs indicating poor prospects for the future.

Questions for discussion

- Why do Gypsies and Travellers tend to be ignored in debates over poverty and ethnicity?
- Why do patterns of social security receipt vary between ethnic groups?
- How have 'welfare-to-work' policies and the introduction of the minimum wage impacted on BME groups?
- To what extent has race relations legislation led to improvements in the delivery of social security to BME groups?

Notes

[1] Roma here does not allude to UK Roma migrating since 1993 from mainland Europe.

[2] The Joseph Rowntree Foundation is currently funding a programme that may provide further insights.

[3] A8 and A2 refer to the eight and two Eastern and Central European countries that acceded to the EU in 2004 and 2007, respectively.

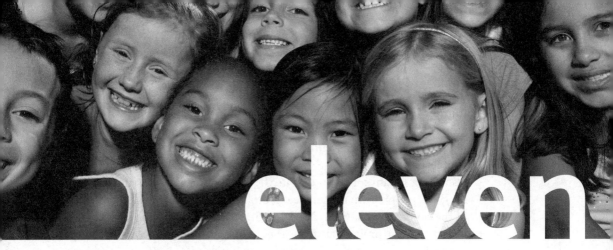

Theorising 'race', ethnicity and mental health

Frank Keating

Overview

The disparities in mental health and mental health service provision for black and minority ethnic[1] (BME) communities in the UK are well-documented, but have not been adequately understood or theorised. This chapter will:

- review how ethnicity and mental (ill-)health have been theorised;
- examine policy and practice responses in the UK, including ethnic-specific service provision in mainstream services;
- explore the advantages and disadvantages of current provision; and
- pay specific attention to diversity within and across groups, particularly women, refugees and asylum-seekers.

Key concepts
culture, gender, madness, mental health, service delivery

Introduction

Meeting the mental health needs of people from BME communities is an area for public concern. A substantial body of research shows that these groups are disproportionately represented in mental health statistics. On the one hand, there is evidence of over-representation in relation to diagnoses such as schizophrenia, while, on the other, there is under-representation in relation to diagnoses such as affective disorder. The Care

Quality Commission, the health watchdog in England, annually conducts a one-day census of mental health inpatient wards in England. Its 2011 report (Care Quality Commission, 2011) paints a bleak picture for BME people, in particular those of African and Caribbean background. This disturbing situation persists despite the fact that needs, issues and concerns for BME people with mental health problems have been pushed to the fore of the policy agenda (DH, 2003, 2005). However, achieving good mental health care for individuals from these communities is one of the biggest challenges for mental health services in England and Wales (Healthcare Commission, 2005) because disparities in rates of mental illness, treatment, care and outcomes remain. Explanations for this seemingly intractable situation are varied.

Theorising mental illness

The mental health arena transcends disciplinary boundaries, including psychiatry, nursing, psychology and social work. This offers significant challenges in defining what mental illness means. Definitions of mental (ill-) health are influenced by cultural, social and political forces. Unfortunately, biomedical explanations, deriving from psychiatry, have dominated the discourse and the search for more social and sociological explanations has been hampered. The underlying assumption of the more medically oriented approach is that psychiatric symptoms are universal and uniformly manifested.

There are competing perspectives on what constitutes mental illness. Bracken and Thomas (2005) argue that our knowledge of mental illness and distress is incomplete and new ways of thinking about them are continually emerging. Coppock and Hopton (2000) suggest that there is ample evidence to show that mental illness is not merely a biological issue, but is also affected by social and political circumstances. Moreover, subjective perceptions, cultural frameworks and recognition of mental illness as invisible make it less tractable than physical illness. Regardless of the perspective or approach taken to understand mental illness, it is clear that when a person is assigned a label of mental illness, they take on an identity that is stigmatised and valued negatively (Fernando, 2006; Glasgow Anti-Stigma Partnership, 2007). Mental illness can be deeply dehumanising and alienating. It is generally regarded with anxiety and fear, leading to rejection and exclusion. People with mental health problems continue to be among the most disadvantaged and socially excluded groups in society (Social Exclusion Unit, 2004).

The World Health Organisation views mental health as: 'a state of well-being in which the individual realises his or her own abilities, can cope with the normal stresses of life, can work productively and fruitfully, and is able to make a contribution to his or her community' (World Health Organisation, 2010). This definition assumes that there is a universal dimension to an understanding of mental health, ignoring that these understandings are relative and contextual (Fernando, 2003). Moreover, there is little known about whether BME communities share or subscribe to this understanding of mental health. Defining mental illness is ultimately a political, social and cultural issue and more work is needed to explore their views and perspectives on mental (ill-)health and how this may affect their willingness to seek help when needed.

Ethnicity and mental health

One enters a contested area of knowledge when concepts such as 'race', ethnicity and mental illness are linked. Most authors propose that a key to understanding issues of 'race', culture and ethnicity is to be clear about how these are defined. I would argue differently. Following the lead of Cooper et al (2005; see also Chapter 2), 'race' and 'ethnicity' should be viewed as social constructions, with different individual and societal meanings depending on the context in which they are applied. Important to consider are the meanings attached to 'race' and its sub-components of 'ethnicity', culture and racism. These concepts carry what Knowles (1999, p 125) terms 'the edifice of negative social meanings'. One cannot, therefore, assume that all people from BME groups will assign similar meaning and value to being cast in the role of 'other' and by implication in an inferior position. They may not therefore identify themselves as being part of an institutionally racist situation. Ethnicity also constitutes only one, albeit important, dimension of the identities of BME people, but it intersects with other social divisions such as age, ability, class, gender and sexuality.

Dressler (1993) argues that epidemiology has failed to formulate useful theories of ethnicity that can be used to evaluate ethnic group differences in mental health. He offers a review of models traditionally used and suggests a model to usefully explain the disparities in mental health for minority groups (see *Box 11.1*). He posits that an understanding of the inequalities and disparities in health – and, I would assert, equally in mental health – can provide insights into the social processes that underpin these inequalities (see Chapter 6). More importantly, such an understanding can form a useful basis for strategies to address or even overcome inequalities in mental health.

Box 11.1: Explanations for health inequalities

Dressler (1993), writing about health inequalities in the US, reviewed three models that have been used to explain ethnic differences in health and offers a fourth that can be utilised to achieve a fuller understanding of these. These models are relevant to a UK context as they reflect how inequalities in mental health have been theorised in the UK.

Racial-genetic model

This model is premised on the hypothesis that phenotypic and genetic features, such as skin colour, predispose certain groups (ie minorities) to ill-health. Despite the fact that such views have been refuted, there is a body of research that still attempts to use ethnicity as a signifier for mental illness (Singh, 2005).

Health-behaviour lifestyle model

A basic premise of this model is that differences between ethnic groups are a function of unhealthy behaviours such as smoking, alcohol and drug misuse. In the UK, this hypothesis has been used to link schizophrenia with excess use of cannabis, thus the term 'cannabis psychosis' has been introduced and offered as an explanation for the elevated rates of schizophrenia for certain groups such as African Caribbeans. However, there is inconclusive evidence of the association between excess use of cannabis and psychosis, so this model does not provide adequate explanations for inequalities in mental health.

A socio-economic model

This model posits that the differences in mental health between certain groups can be ascribed to factors such as poverty, education, employment and so on. Such an explanation may be of partial use, especially given that BME groups in the UK fare worse across all social indicators such as education, employment, housing and so on. Cooper et al (2008) have shown that socio-economic status alone does not account for these differences. However, this model does not take into account differential access to these resources and therefore cannot fully explain the inequalities that these groups experience in mental health.

A social-structural model

Building on the socio-economic model, this hypothesis states that the structural position of BME groups in society and the continued discrimination against them in a racialised society contribute significantly to the inequalities that they experience in mental health. In the UK, this has been explored and confirmed by, for example, Karlsen and Nazroo (2002a), McKenzie et al (2008) and Sharpley et al (2001). More specifically, Cooper et al (2008) found that perceived disadvantage mediated the relationship between ethnicity and psychosis.

Source: Adapted from Dressler (1993).

Key thinkers in this area have sought biological explanations for disparities in diagnosis of mental (ill-)health; others have looked for more social explanations (Morgan et al, 2004; McKenzie, 2006), while still others offer racism as a causal factor (Fernando, 2003; McKenzie, 2006). However, none of these hypotheses fully explain why the mental health situation for black people has persisted over the last 30 years. For example, the hypothesis which suggests that racism based on skin colour is a causal factor does not explain the mental health disparities for Irish communities in England (Pilgrim, 2005). Life stressors have also been suggested as a causal factor, but Gilvarry et al (1999) found no differences in life stressors between 'white' and 'black' ethnic groups, but did find that black people will attribute adverse life events to racism. Karlsen (2007b) also illustrated how adverse life events can have a damaging effect on the mental health of black people. The implications of this are that people from minority groups may therefore be disinclined to use services that they perceive as prejudiced against them.

Discrimination, disadvantage and mental health

Karlsen (2007a) illustrated the connections between racial discrimination and poor health, concluding that people from BME groups experience poorer health due to negative attitudes towards them (see Chapter 6). They also often find themselves in situations considered as risk factors for mental illness. These include exclusion from school (84% of children excluded from schools are boys from Caribbean backgrounds); social deprivation as a result of unemployment; prevalence of crime and drug cultures; and over-representation in prison populations (White, 2006). For BME groups, these experiences are all underpinned or informed by their experiences of racism, which may influence their help-seeking behaviour. The reasons for not seeking help may be due to fear of the possible consequences, such as loss of status, control, independence and autonomy (White, 2006). The problems are compounded for minority groups based on their perceptions of mental health services and a belief that these services will discriminate against them (Keating and Robertson, 2004). More importantly, there exists a real and potent fear that engagement with mental health services will lead to their death (Keating and Robertson, 2004). Fountain and

Hicks (2010) found that fears of engagement also related to the social repercussions that may arise as a result of accessing mental health services. I therefore argue that prior to improving aspects of mental health service delivery, such as access to care, appropriate treatment and so on, we need a critical understanding of the connections between culture, ethnicity, 'race', racism and mental illness.

Another issue to consider is the impact of racial disadvantage and discrimination on individuals, their families and communities. Patel and Fatimilehin (1999) suggest that the impact of racism is psychological, social and material. The effects of these are likely to be detrimental to mental health, for some minimal, but for others of great significance to their emotional well-being (Karlsen, 2007a). The impact of racism has to be analysed in the context of histories of migration, alienation, subordination and the way in which these groups have been and continue to be stigmatised in society.

Karlsen et al (2005) suggested that an understanding of the relationship between these concepts may help us grasp the disparities for BME groups in mental health services. Nazroo (2003) suggests that social and economic inequalities are the chief explanations for inequalities in health and mental health and finds that experiences of racial harassment and discrimination have been consistently linked to poorer self-reported health and outcomes.

'Blackness' and 'madness' – the negative spiral

Keating et al (2002) demonstrate that stereotypical views of black people, racism, cultural ignorance, stigma and the anxiety associated with mental illness often combine to undermine the way in which mental health services assess and respond to the needs of BME communities. Other authors have directed attention to the disproportionate rate of hospital admissions, adverse pathways to care, such as the involvement of the police, and overuse of the Mental Health Act for some groups (Morgan et al, 2004; Moffat et al, 2006). So for African and Caribbean men, being seen as 'big, black, bad, dangerous and mad' can lead to conceptions that they are less deserving of treatment that would lead them to pathways of recovery.

Minority groups with mental health problems face at least four forces that underpin their experiences:

(1) how BME people are treated in society;
(2) how people with mental health problems are perceived in society;
(3) the power of institutions to control and coerce people with mental health problems; and

(4) the perceptions of BME people that mental health services are discriminatory and dangerous.

Their experiences in society have an impact on their mental and emotional well-being. These experiences, in turn, influence how they experience and perceive mental health services. Their (historical and contemporary) marginal position in society affects how they are treated in mental health services – and these various experiences interact to produce what Trivedi (2002) terms 'a spiral of oppression'. Black people do not trust mental health services and those who work within them fear them, which means there is lack of engagement on both sides. The spiral is presented in ***Figure 11.1*** and the challenge for mental health professionals is therefore to break this spiral (see, eg, Norfolk, Suffolk and Cambridgeshire Strategic Health Authority, 2003).

Establishing mental health status in minority ethnic groups

Assessing the true extent of mental illness in BME communities is difficult and complex. There is conflicting and contradictory evidence on who is affected by mental illness in these communities. The first systematic attempt at gathering information on the mental health status of BME groups in hospital settings in England and Wales was derived from the 'Count Me In' census in 2006 (Healthcare Commission, 2007). This has lately been extended to include community mental health settings.

The rates that have been presented show significant differences for certain minority groups. Differences between groups are natural and should be expected, but when these differences are due to social factors and the allocation of or access to resources they should be construed as disparities or inequalities (Schwartz and Meyer, 2010).

There are commonalities across groups, but there is also diversity within and across groups. A common finding is that the risk of psychosis is elevated in nearly all BME groups compared with the White British group (Kirkbride et al, 2008).

In addition, the following common experiences across BME groups have been documented in relation to disparities in mental health diagnosis, access to services and outcomes. These groups commonly experience:

- stigma, stereotypical views and racism and negative social repercussions, which ultimately mean that these groups are reluctant to seek help;
- cultural barriers including language, particularly for some Black Africans and older generations of South Asian and Chinese people;

- culturally inappropriate or insensitive services;
- services that are unable to engage with contextual factors; and
- social risk factors such as unemployment, poverty and educational attainment (Bhui et al, 2003; DH, 2007d; Fountain and Hicks, 2010).

Figure 11.1: *The spiral of oppression*

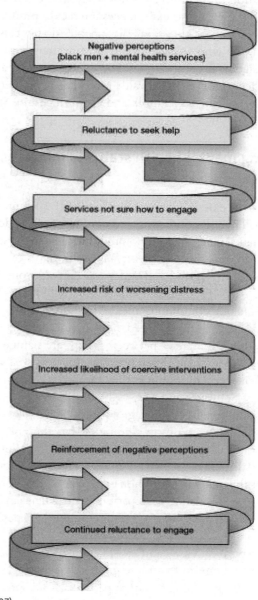

Source: Keating (2007)

Experiences that are particular to certain minority ethnic groups are summarised as follows:

- South Asian groups commonly experience:
  - loneliness and isolation, particularly for Bangladeshi groups;
  - higher rates of alcohol misuse for men, particularly for Pakistani and Muslim men who drink;
  - low rates of access to healthcare such as primary care services;
  - higher rates of suicide and self-harm for women; and
  - lack of knowledge about services, particularly for older people (DH, 2007a; McKenzie et al, 2008; Hurcombe et al, 2010).

- African and Caribbean groups commonly experience:
  - elevated rates of schizophrenia;
  - aversive pathways to care;
  - greater involvement of the police in admission to mental health care;
  - controlling and harsher treatments;
  - high rates of suicide for young men with a diagnosis of schizophrenia; and
  - low access to psychological support (Sharpley et al, 2001; Bhui et al, 2003; Hunt et al, 2003; DH, 2007a; Fountain and Hicks, 2010).

There are groups for which relatively little is known in relation to mental health. For example, the mental health needs of the Chinese community are under-researched with difficulties with language and socio-economic status defined as significant risk factors for mental (ill-)health (Au and Tang, 2009). A mixed-methods study exploring the mental health needs of the Chinese community in Birmingham (Huang and Spurgeon, 2006) found a high level of psychiatric morbidity compared to the general population. Particular groups affected were older people, students and migrant workers. The evidence shows that Chinese people in the UK continue to use traditional medicines for mental health problems and it is important for mainstream services to find ways of working that can incorporate and accommodate such practices into providing appropriate mental health care for these communities (Tighe and Tran, 2010). However, a scoping exercise in Scotland focusing on perceptions of mental well-being in Chinese and Pakistani communities drew 51% of its English-written literature from China (Newbigging et al, 2008; see also NHS Health Scotland, 2008). Researchers may thus need to look outside Europe more often for their sources.

Issues for particular groups

Women

Significant levels of need have been identified for BME women. Figures suggest that more women than men will experience some form of mental health problem (Bird, 1999; Wilson, 2001; McManus et al, 2009). The National Psychiatric Morbidity Survey (McManus et al, 2009), for example, reported that the rates for common mental disorder among women were higher for Asian women. Edge (2010) also points out that there is evidence that women from BME groups, in particular African Caribbean groups, are at increased risk for mental health problems in the perinatal period. However, Kotecha (2009, p 71) argues that 'a potent mix of gender blindness and negative views of minority cultures further contributes to BME women's mental health needs being neglected across the spectrum of research, policy development, service provision and practice.' For example, a policy document relating to women's mental health (DH, 2002) paid scant attention to the issues for women from BME groups. A review of this policy in 2010 (NMHDU, 2010) reports that there are still significant gaps in personalised services for women from these groups. It found that a number of community engagement projects have been developed through the Delivering Race Equality Programme (DH, 2005), but these are largely in the voluntary sector and there is still a need to ensure equal access to mental health care for the diverse needs of women (Fountain and Hicks, 2010; NMHDU, 2010).

McKenzie et al (2008) found that the rates of suicide for older Asian women were double that of the general population. Earlier evidence showed higher rates for young Asian women (Raleigh et al, 1990), but McKenzie et al found that the rate for younger Asian women was only marginally raised. They conclude that there are a number of factors that may explain the fall in rates for younger Asian women, such as demographic change and the way stress is managed in these communities, but this needs further research attention. They recommend that further research is needed to explain the increased rates for older Asian women and that this group should be a target for a prevention strategy.

Refugee and asylum-seeker women require specific attention. Gill and Banga (2008) suggest that these women are less likely to access services due to lack of awareness of options available. Domestic violence and abuse have also been identified as significant risk factors for mental distress due to barriers to reporting abuse and protecting 'family honour'.

It has been suggested that a range of accessible services are needed to support women, specifically those with children, women at risk of suicide and refugees and asylum-seekers (Wilson, 2001; Gill and Banga, 2009; Kotecha, 2009; Edge, 2010). Services should respond to a diverse range of needs, and gender and ethnicity should be key variables in measuring service access and outcomes for BME women.

Refugees and asylum-seekers

Refugees and asylum-seekers are among the most vulnerable and isolated groups in the UK (Patel, 2009). Refugees experience stress, acculturation, losses and life events that are mediators for mental disorder. However, 'the refugee experience' is not a natural dimension of the human experience and should therefore not automatically be associated with mental ill-health. However, these experiences can lead to higher levels of distress. Similar to other migrant groups and more settled communities, there are problems with access to mental health services for refugees and asylum-seekers. This is often compounded by their eligibility or entitlement to services or the fact that their distress resulting from traumatic experiences is pathologised by mental health professionals. Identifying mental illness within refugee groups is problematic due to language, the cultural explanatory models for mental illness, their economic and political contexts, and public perceptions of their status (Watters and Ingleby, 2004; Patel, 2009). Professionals need to be aware of the health and social care needs of refugees and asylum-seekers, and alert to risks of suicide (Bhui et al, 2006). Gaining access to sustainable housing (Jones and Mullins, 2009) and sustainable employment can have a positive impact on the emotional well-being of refugees and asylum-seekers. Mental health promotion strategies should aim to reduce isolation and promote opportunities for employment and education, underpinned by a partnership approach to overcome the discrimination and isolation of these communities (Burnett and Peel, 2001; Burnett, 2009).

Gypsies and travellers

Gypsies and Travellers have a long-standing presence in the UK, yet they are treated with hostility and misunderstanding (Cemlyn, 2008). As discussed in Chapter 10 they experience significant levels of disadvantage, reflected in their access to health and mental health services. Matthews (2008) found scant reference to the health needs of these groups in the policy arena. Cultural beliefs associated with mental health also affect their willingness to seek help for mental health problems. This is often compounded by a lack of sensitivity and understanding on the part of health professionals (Parry et al, 2007). It has been suggested that a piecemeal approach to service provision for Gypsies and Travellers contributes to the high levels of social exclusion they experience in health and social care services (Cemlyn, 2008). Improving the cultural competence of professionals and outreach services and partnership working with Gypsies and Travellers can go some way to combat the discrimination and exclusion they face (Parry et al, 2007; Cemlyn, 2008).

Experiencing mental health services

Psychiatry is the only branch of medicine that can legitimately forcibly treat, restrain and control individuals. These functions of providing care, control and accommodation are delivered through a network of mental health services such as community mental health teams and early interventions teams (Rogers and Pilgrim, 2001). Mental health professionals have the power to name and rename emotional distress. Pilgrim (2005) argues that racial biases mean that these groups are disproportionately dealt with by specialist mental health services, and as these services are characterised by coercive practices, this constitutes structural disadvantage. Contributing to the disadvantages that BME groups experience in mental health services is the 'risk agenda' dominating mental health policy over the recent past.

Minority groups' experiences of mental health services are characterised by access to services they do not want and lack of receipt of services they need (Keating et al, 2002). There is evidence of complex pathways into mental health care often involving the police and the criminal justice system (Moffat et al, 2006). The England and Wales 'Count Me In' census of 2009 demonstrated that referral rates from general practitioners and community mental health teams were lower than average among some minority groups. Overall, admission rates were higher for minority ethnic groups at 23% of the total inpatient population, although they only constitute 8% of the general population. Rates of detention under the Mental Health Act 1983 were between 19% and 38% higher than average. These rates were particularly elevated for black groups and higher than average for Pakistani groups. Higher rates of control and restraint applied mainly to black groups, but also to White Irish and White Other groups. Certain groups – in particular Indian, Bangladeshi, Black Caribbean and Other Black groups – were more likely to be subject to Community Treatment Orders (Care Quality Commission, 2011).

It is clear that individuals from these minority groups do not receive equal care. This situation seems unchanging as is illustrated by a study exploring the experiences of mental health service users of African and Caribbean communities in Birmingham (Rabiee and Smith, 2007). This found that service users have negative perceptions of mainstream mental health services. The service user survey as part of the BME 'Count Me In' census of 2005 in England and Wales (Mental Health Act Commission, 2006) reported that black service users were most disadvantaged in inpatient services, reported higher levels of dissatisfaction with their care and were more likely to experience harsher treatments such as control and restraint.

Experience in the black-led voluntary sector

There is evidence that the black-led voluntary sector (BVS) offers appropriate and relevant support to minority groups (Keating et al, 2002; Fountain and Hicks, 2010; Knifton et al, 2010). They work from conceptual frameworks of mental distress that embrace the whole person instead of narrowly defined categories of mental illness (Saheliya, 2008; Fernando and Keating, 2009a; Mohammed, 2010). Services in this sector are valued because they make critical observations about psychiatry and its limitations, but they also include an understanding of the political reality of the experiences of minority ethnic groups (Moffat et al, 2006; Mohammed, 2010; see also Fernando and Keating, 2009b). However, these services face problems of short-term contracts, inadequate funding and limited opportunities for developing robust infrastructures. The intelligence (knowledge and skills) potentially gleaned from services in this sector has not been incorporated into mainstream service delivery, nor has there been an extensive evaluation of their contribution to reducing inequality.

A policy response

There has been a significant lack of policy response to reduce racial disparities in mental health at both national and local levels. A tragic, but significant, marker for BME communities has been the death of David (Rocky) Bennett while being restrained by nursing staff on a medium secure ward. After a long struggle by his family to achieve justice, an inquiry concluded that mental health services are institutionally racist. The government subsequently published an action plan for Delivering Race Equality (DRE) in England and Wales (DH, 2005), the first national plan to address inequalities in mental health for BME groups. This plan had three building blocks: to develop more and appropriate and responsive services; better-quality information; and increased community engagement. Laudable as these intentions were, they contained weaknesses. DRE focused on organisational change, but failed to appreciate the heterogeneity in communities and the complex identities and practices they contained (Bhui, 2002). It also failed to appreciate that the inequalities in mental health for black people that exist cannot be separated from the general inequalities these communities experience in society. Moreover, the problem seems to have been framed in the context of culture; therefore, the focus was on developing a culturally competent workforce. Fernando (2003) argues that a focus on culture can in itself be racist and has to be examined in this context. Cultural competence has arguably led to a narrow focus on aspects such as dietary requirements, religious and spiritual practices, and appropriate environments. These factors are important, but often mean that more serious issues of institutional processes and practices that discriminate against BME communities are overlooked and left intact (see Gunaratnam, 2008a).

The DRE programme did offer opportunities to redress the situation through its programme of community engagement, whereby it funded 80 community projects to assess the needs of BME communities and established Community Development Worker (CDW) posts in Mental Health Trusts (DH, 2009a). These projects seemed to have a narrow focus on needs assessment despite the needs of these communities already being documented in research – what we need instead are strategies for meeting these needs. Walker and Craig (2009) evaluated the role of DRE mental health CDWs and found that they were mainly involved in community engagement, scoping and mapping activities, and mental health awareness; very few had direct involvement in service delivery or development. They concluded that CDWs are in a position to facilitate engagement with BME communities, but must be located in strategic partnership structures to support 'race' equality. In reality, most were in marginal positions, remote from policymaking centres, poorly paid and supported, with limited budgetary scope, and unable to make effective use of their findings. Fountain and Hicks (2010), in their evaluation of the community engagement dimension of DRE, found that some of the benefits identified were: greater awareness of community needs; better access to services; and improved links between communities, providers and commissioners. The final reports of the DRE programme acknowledge that the 'roots of the inequalities for BME communities lie in social, not biological, factors so the responsibility for remedial action extends to all the agencies that influence public mental health and well-being' (NMHDU, 2010, p 2; see also Wilson, 2010).

Responding positively

This section will provide pointers to ways in which disparities in mental health for BME groups can be addressed.

Suggestion 1: 'Talking "race", talking mental illness'

Practitioners need to make connections between a person's lived experience, behaviour and distress. In research on *Breaking the Circles of Fear*, Keating et al (2002) found that mental health professionals were fearful of talking about issues of 'race' and culture, fearing being cast as racist or 'getting it wrong'. Inevitably, by *not* talking about these issues, they get it wrong. I suggest that a starting point is to engage in a dialogue about 'race' and mental illness. Engaging with and reflecting on the inequality, discrimination and oppression that arise from social divisions in society is deeply challenging. It is an invitation to examine who we are: our experiences of advantages and disadvantages, power and powerlessness, inclusion and exclusion (Williams and Keating, 2005).

Suggestion 2: 'Creating safe spaces of entry'

The pathways into services for some BME groups have been described as problematic (Keating et al, 2002; Care Quality Commission, 2011). BME people are more likely to come into contact with services via the police or criminal justice system or on the instigation of family members. Given the fraught nature of relationships between BME communities, the police and other institutions of social control, and the deep mistrust they have of them, it is important to find alternative ways of engaging these groups with mental health services, but more importantly to help them deal with the stresses of racism and everyday life more effectively. BME groups need safe points of 'entry' into talking about their emotional distress. Individuals from minority groups need to be encouraged to talk about their concerns, in non-stigmatising and safe environments. Safe spaces can only be created when mental health services change their negative perceptions of these communities, work to establish positive relationships with them and offer services addressing their lived experiences.

Suggestion 3: 'People need care that helps them to find their way back to meaningful existence, meaningful relationships, meaningful connections, restored identity'

When BME people come into contact with mental health services they are offered standard medicalised responses to their situation and needs (Fountain and Hicks, 2010). Service users report that mental health workers view them only in terms of their diagnosis and tend to deal with 'their illness' in isolation from other aspects of their lives (Keating et al, 2002). This narrow focus on biological factors means that other contributing factors to their distress or impacting on their treatment often go undetected, untreated and unresolved. This leads service users to conclude that services are inhumane, treating them without respect and dignity. We need social care and welfare services to provide responses that speak to people's life circumstances, including that of racism, inequality and discrimination. This means incorporating their experiences and viewpoints in an assessment of their situation, making sense of the everyday activities of life. Practitioners are required to document the concrete details of people's lives. A significant aspect of understanding lived experience is to identify sources of oppression and tease out the overlaps and intersections between 'race', ethnicity, culture, age, class, gender, religion, disability and sexuality. Work in Scotland that has involved partnerships with BME voluntary organisations and engaging BME service users in definitions of mental well-being are examples (Newbigging et al, 2008; Saheliya, 2008; Knifton et al, 2010).

Summary

Eradicating disparities in mental health treatment and outcomes for BME people requires changes in how these communities are viewed. Making services more humane at the interpersonal level is deeply important. Everyone values positive relationships: they are key to good emotional and social functioning. People who have been excluded, marginalised and have suffered emotional distress are in greater need of positive relationships. Mental health services should build positive working relationships with BME individuals and engage with the ideals they have of themselves. The over-representation and negative experiences of black men in mental health services call for a multidisciplinary and multi-agency approach, involving service providers such as the criminal justice system, the educational system and others outside the field of mental health. There should be a greater focus on prevention and early intervention and an active programme of mental health promotion aimed at minority groups. There is a small, but growing, black service user movement and their efforts should be supported. Improving mental and emotional well-being for BME communities should be anchored in history, broader societal conditions and their lived experiences, including experiences of racism, but also how they have survived in the face of adversity. We need services that address cultural diversity and eradicate inequality, and professional cultures that enable practitioners to reflect on these issues in the quest to promote and provide mental health services that are just, fair and equal.

In exploring the relationship between mental (ill-)health, ethnicity and racism, it is clear that we encounter complex issues affecting access to mental health care and the appropriateness of services to BME communities. There have been measures at national and local levels to address the disparities that BME groups face. Progress in engaging communities has been limited (Fountain and Hicks, 2010). Addressing racism and racial inequalities in mental health seems to be the most effective route to improving the mental health and well-being of these communities.

Questions for discussion

- Why do BME communities experience difficulties in accessing appropriate mental health care?
- Explore ways in which mental health care for BME groups can be improved.
- A number of theoretical positions and examples of how they play out in practice are mentioned. Discuss the pros and cons of each, and note the evidence used to support your discussion.
- Why have specific minority groups made greater use of mental health services?

Electronic resources

All of the following resources should be of interest to those wishing to explore these issues.

- www.healthscotland.com
- http://refugeeintegration.homeoffice.gov.uk/Health/index.asp
- www.raceequalityfoundation.org.uk/
- www.rota.org.uk
- www.raceforhealth.org
- www.blackmentalhealth.org.uk
- www.bmementalhealth.org.uk
- www.afiyatrust.org.uk
- www.ethnichealth.org.uk
- www.sahelya.org.uk

Note
[1] This chapter predominantly draws on research and practice evidence with African and Caribbean men in England. It acknowledges diversity in mental health services but notes the limited research with wider groups, and in other UK countries. Generalisations are therefore limited, although experiences of racism and discrimination are common and well documented in other chapters of this book.

Young people and criminal justice

Bankole Cole

Overview

This chapter:

- provides an appraisal of the political response to youth offending and welfare in Britain over the past 30 years;
- examines the extent to which provisions are made for young people of different ethnicities and genders; and
- deliberates over the extent to which ethnicity should be a key factor in the provision of welfare needs for youths caught up in the criminal justice system (CJS).

Key concepts
crime, criminal justice, data, offending, police, youth

Introduction

In most societies, young people are often referred to as the future generation. Behind this image is the notion that the state and society ought to care for its young people, providing them with what it believes is required for them to grow into useful adults. Although the age groups that constitute 'youth' vary between different countries, what is common is that they usually include children and adolescents – the most vulnerable, dependent age groups. In 2007, young people represented a fifth of the EU population (European Commission, 2009). The aim of this chapter is to discuss the part that 'ethnicity' has played in the provision of state welfare support to young people who have broken the law or are at risk of offending, including those who are victims or at risk of being victims of crime. Here, 'youth'/young people is used to refer both to juveniles (10–17 years old) and young adults up to the age of 25, although more is said about the former than the latter. This is due to the fact that the Youth Justice System deals with 10–17 year olds and most government documents on youth welfare also target this age group.

Ethnicities, youth and crime

British official ('Section 95') statistics on 'race' and the criminal justice system show that there is a disparity in offending between youths of different ethnicities. British black and minority ethnic (BME) youths are over-represented in official crime figures, although findings from Youth Offender Surveys (self-report studies) have shown that British white youths are more likely to admit to having committed more crimes than their non-white counterparts (Home Office, 2005b, 2006). Official statistics also show that BME youths are disproportionately represented at every stage of the youth and adult CJS from stop-and-search through to sentence (Ministry of Justice, 2010a). Whereas there are no reliable official statistics on the offending rates of non-British youths living in the country as asylum-seekers or refugees, the association of these groups with crime has been the subject of much contemporary media and public attention (see Malloch and Stanley, 2005; Rudiger, 2007; Cooper, 2009). The issue is compounded by the fact that 'detention' and 'imprisonment' are often used interchangeably when referring to asylum-seekers, whereas the former may not refer to confinement as a result of the commission of a criminal offence, but is often the consequence of the (often unwitting) violation of immigration regulations (Banks, 2008; also, for similar treatment of asylum-seekers in other European countries, see Lynch and Simon, 1999). However, a report published by Scotland Yard maintained that there has been an increase in the numbers of young asylum-seekers and refugees with significant post-traumatic stress conditions, believed to have resulted from having witnessed significant violent situations prior to their arrival in the UK, and consequently becoming engaged in gang activities in London. There was concern expressed that these foreign youths were having a disproportionately negative impact on their peer groups (MPS, 2007). David Green, director of the CIVITAS think tank argued:

> We are importing 15, 16, 17 and 18-year-olds brought up in countries with an anarchistic warlord culture, in which carrying

knives and guns is routine. That is no exaggeration. We are asking for trouble if we do not confront this issue. (*Mail Online*, 2007; also, on Polish gangs in Scotland, see Scottish Government Social Research, 2010a).

The terrorist attacks on the London transport system in 2005, carried out by British Muslim youths of minority origins, have led to a 'moral panic' (Islamophobia) about British youths of Islamic faith being potential terrorists (on Islamophobia and Muslim youths in France, see Jackson, 2010). Thus, anti-terrorism control and prevention policies and tactics, 'the Prevent Strategy' (HM Government, 2008c), have targeted Islamic (mainly Pakistani) youths and their communities as potential 'breeding grounds' for so-called 'home-grown' terrorism. Ethnicity is acknowledged in popular and official perceptions and accounts of criminals. Available crime data and research have also shown that youth crime victimisation differs with ethnicity. For example, BME youths are disproportionately represented among victims of racially motivated anti-social behaviour and crimes, while the perpetrators of these offences are disproportionately white youths (Janssen, 2006; Craig et al, 2009a; also, for reports on youth racism in Scotland, see Scottish Executive, 2005; *Times Online*, 2009).

Of particular concern is that young people are increasingly becoming victims of their own offending. Figures on weapon-related crimes show that the majority of offenders and victims of these crimes are youths (HC, 2007; also, on youth gangs in Scotland, see Scottish Government Social Research, 2010b). It is also believed that the age at which youths are becoming involved in crime is getting younger, and disparities between the rates for different sexes are also becoming smaller (Feilzer and Hood, 2004; YJB, 2009). It is reasonable, therefore, to assert that differential rates of offending by youths of different ethnicities should call for different explanations and, if so, measures to address youth offending and victimisation should have some regard for the question of ethnicity.

The context

Britain has witnessed centuries of entry across its boundaries of peoples of different ethnicities, both whites and non-whites, who have settled in the country and had families. It is believed that non-whites have lived in Britain for more than 1,000 years. However, it was only after the end of the First World War, when soldiers from the colonies who fought for Britain were settled in the 'mother country', that the existence of non-whites in Britain started to become an issue of substantial public debate. Larger numbers of immigrants from the colonies (now British Commonwealth) were invited by the British government after the Second World War to occupy low-paid jobs that had become vacant as a result of the wars (see Bowling and Phillips, 2002; see also Chapter 3). The majority of these post-war 'immigrants' settled in the poorest and most deprived neighbourhoods of big cities, the result of prejudice and discrimination from their hosts and also because these offered the cheapest housing. As most of the 'immigrants' were employed in the lowest-paid jobs, social mobility was limited. The result was that many remained permanently living in these areas, and more so as white neighbours moved out into more affluent areas (see Cook and Hudson, 1993; see also Chapter 5). Thus, the descendants of these immigrants, now British citizens, have grown up in some of Britain's most deprived inner-city areas. Like their parents and grandparents, they have a history of experiencing racial prejudice and discrimination from fellow white youths and neighbours (Solomos, 2003).

Recent immigration, particularly since the expansion of the European Union, has led to migration of European 'white ethnicities' into Britain, mainly as migrant labour. In addition, other ethnicities, both whites and non-whites, have entered Britain from different parts of the world on humanitarian grounds, as asylum-seekers and refugees, and many coming with their families, including children. The majority of asylum-seekers and refugees in Britain also live in some of the most deprived parts of the country (given that they were offered housing that was vacant because no one else would live in it). Like the British non-whites, they also experience racial prejudice from local white populations (see Hemmerman et al, 2007). The arrival of peoples of different ethnicities over the last 60 years makes Britain one of the most ethnically diverse countries in Europe.

Youth offending is linked to living in deprived neighbourhoods, where the highest proportions of recorded adult crimes take place (see Government Office for London, 2007; Bangs et al, 2008). Other factors linked to offending, such as low educational achievement and drugs misuse, are also partly consequences of living in deprived neighbourhoods (see Scarman, 1981; Bradshaw et al, 2004). As Britain's minority ethnic youths are more likely than their white counterparts to experience life in deprived, mainly inner-city areas, their disproportionate involvement in crime is thus also partly explained. In addition, research evidence has shown that BME youths encounter racial discrimination in employment, education and housing, resulting in them being even more socially excluded than their white counterparts (Cole and Wardak, 2006; see also Chapters 5, 8 and 9, this volume). Similar conditions are experienced by BME youths in many European countries (see Kalunta-Crumpton, 2010). Living in deprived areas, with little or no support networks or educational and employment opportunities, places many refugee and asylum-seeker youths in similarly vulnerable positions (see Cooper, 2009). The delay in the processing of applications for support, insecurity of residence and restrictions to benefits and work has often driven these refugee youths and their parents into poverty (see Solomon, 2006, cited in Cooper, 2009). It is also reasonable to argue, therefore, that differential exposure to exclusion and the experience of discrimination in access to state welfare (albeit by BME youths) are the two most important factors that explain differential offending by youths of different ethnicities in Britain. To be fair to youths of all ethnicities, policies to address youth offending and victimisation must acknowledge this fact.

Prior to 1992, before the first national statistics on 'race' and the CJS were published, knowledge about the criminality of different ethnicities came from police data. In 1975, the Metropolitan Police (Met) produced the first ethnically coded statistics for street robbery in the capital, figures based on dubious classifications of 'race'. For example, the 'mixed race' ethnic category was not included in the ethnic classifications used. This meant that persons of mixed white and black parentage were generally classified as 'black' (see Fitzgerald and Sibbitt, 1997). In spite of this ethnic miscategorisation, the Met announced that young black youths in London were disproportionately involved in street robbery (mugging) and that the victims were mainly whites. Based on this data, the Met and other police forces in Britain began a campaign of surveillance and quasi-militaristic policing of Britain's inner cities, where the majority of black youths live, in the quest to clamp down on muggers (see Lea and Young, 1993). Police tactics included indiscriminate use of the stop-and-search vagrancy law of 1824 to stop, question and search mainly minority youths on suspicion of being muggers (Hall et al, 1978). This police action exacerbated the already-strained relationship between the police and inner-city black youths, built up as a result of previous encounters in the 1950s/60s (Gaskell and Smith, 1985; Gaskell, 1986; Solomos, 1988; Loader, 1996; Bowling and Phillips, 2002). This was a key factor leading to the inner-city disorders (riots) of the 1980s in which minority youths, especially those of black ethnic origins, were disproportionately involved (Hall et al, 1978; Keith, 1993; Lea and Young, 1993). The 1980s' disturbances were a landmark in British history in the sense that they alerted the government to take seriously the concerns and needs of the emerging BME youth population in the inner cities.

The legacy of Scarman

In April 1981, Lord Scarman was appointed to inquire into the reasons behind the disorders that took place in Brixton (London). What is remarkable about the Scarman Report (Scarman, 1981) is the fact that his analysis of the disturbances went beyond the clashes with the police on the streets of Brixton into the aspects of social policy and welfare issues that underlay them. Thus, the report provided an analysis of the social and economic conditions in Brixton on the eve of the disturbances, compared with those in the other inner-city areas where similar disturbances had occurred. Scarman concluded that while differences undoubtedly existed between these areas, the similarities were more striking. He described these similarities as: 'A high ethnic minority population, high unemployment, a declining economic base, a decaying physical environment, bad housing, lack of amenities, social problems including family breakdown, a high rate of crime and heavy policing' (Scarman, 1981, p 12).

Scarman explained how the disproportionate experience of deprivation and poverty of BME (mainly Black Caribbean) youths compared with their white counterparts elsewhere and the clash with the police are inextricably linked: first, in terms of how, by living much of their lives on the streets, black youths were more likely than other youths to be brought more frequently into contact with the police, more so as they were also more likely to be involved in street crimes (Scarman, 1981, p 11); and, second, how 'unimaginative and inflexible policing can make the tensions which deprivation engenders greatly worse' (Scarman, 1981, p 100). Thus, Scarman emphasised the need to tackle the welfare needs of the minority youths who lived in these communities if the perceived crime problem were fully to be addressed. As he put it:

> While good policing can help diminish tension and avoid disorder, it cannot remove the causes of social stress where these are ... deeply embedded in fundamental economic and social conditions. Any attempts to resolve the circumstances from which the disorders ... sprang cannot ... be limited to recommendations about policing but must embrace the wider social context in which policing is carried out. (Scarman, 1981, p 100)

Accordingly, Scarman highlighted what he regarded as the welfare problems that are linked to offending by BME youths living in the inner cities. These factors have since become key points in subsequent policy debates about BME youth offending in Britain. They include:

- Disproportionate experience of social deprivation or social exclusion.
- Inadequate welfare support; for example, in housing, resulting in homelessness, sleeping rough or squatting in the streets.
- Enforced idleness because of economic insecurity or unemployment.

- Underachievement in school resulting from truancy or school exclusion and the irrelevance of school curricula to the needs of black youths.
- Family breakdown: the lack of a role model resulting from a disproportionate number of single-parent families among the black population (the problem of absent fathers) as well as disproportionate numbers of black children in local authority care (the 'absentee father' was presented as a family feature [stereotype] peculiar to Black Caribbean families).
- Lack of recreational facilities to counteract boredom and idleness (Scarman, 1981, pp 4–16).

Scarman stressed the point that white youths also suffer from these problems, but that BME youths do so much more. More importantly, he discussed the part that racial discrimination had played in limiting access to state welfare for BME youths – a factor exacerbating their social exclusion. In addition, Scarman demonstrated that racial discrimination was also intrinsic in the actions of the police that led to the disturbances. However, he dismissed the view that the British police were institutionally racist. Instead, he believed that the racism that existed inside some of Britain's police forces was caused by a handful of 'rotten apples' among the police officers (Scarman, 1981, pp 64–74). Whereas this position has been rejected by subsequent evidence (Macpherson, 1999), the Scarman Report set a precedent by highlighting the importance of police racism in the discussion of BME youth offending.

Finally, Scarman talked about conflicting policies between local and central governments being 'a source of confusion and reduced drive' (Scarman, 1981, p 101). Whereas there was evidence that some efforts were being made to address racial disadvantage, Scarman maintained that there was a lack of a sufficiently well-coordinated programme for combating the problem. He was also dismayed that the private sector was not fully involved in the process. As he put it 'the private sector is not an alternative to adequate public sector involvement: both are needed' (Scarman, 1981, p 102). Scarman insisted that unless a clear lead was given by government in this area 'there can be no hope of an effective response' (Scarman, 1981, p 108). However, he expressed concern that 'a policy of direct co-ordinated attack on racial disadvantage inevitably means that the ethnic minorities will enjoy for a time a positive discrimination in their favour' (Scarman, 1981, p 135). He feared that this could provide a legitimate and understandable backlash from the majority British white population. Accordingly, he concluded that 'special programmes for ethnic minority groups should only be instituted where the need for them is clearly made out' (Scarman, 1981, p 109).

The Scarman Report could be interpreted to infer different meanings. It could be read to imply a call for social inclusion or demand for social citizenship rights by those British youths of minority origins who had become marginalised or alienated through a combination of racial discrimination and economic decline (see Lea, 2003). It could also be read as an appeal for social justice for the minority youths living predominantly in Britain's inner cities; the need to address their disadvantage or neglect in the provision of public and welfare services; as well as their racist treatment by the police. The report also covered broad issues around urban regeneration, 'race' relations, policing and equal opportunities (see Scarman, 1981, pp 100–12). A crucial defect in the report, however, was the overemphasis placed on youths of African Caribbean origins. However well-intended, the report merely shifted attention to the problems of black youths at the expense of those of youths of other ethnicities. Until recently, when Asian youths entered the scene through the platform of the clampdown on 'home-grown terrorism', much of the debates about BME youths and the British CJS were focused exclusively on Black Caribbean youths – an emphasis not matched by welfare support to address their needs. In contrast, white youths are rarely mentioned but, arguably, not forgotten in welfare provisions available to address youth problems.

Criminal justice or welfare

Whereas Scarman stressed the need to prioritise the welfare needs of black youths living in impoverished inner-city areas in order to address their offending, the Conservative governments of the 1980s/90s gave more priority to the policing recommendations in the report than the welfare ones. New laws on police powers and public order were passed in 1984 and 1986, respectively; and steps were taken to implement the 'community policing' recommendations of the report to ensure that the police engaged more positively with minority communities and are generally more accountable.

The Conservative Party approach to youth justice is rooted in the neo-conservative theory of crime and is often said to be based on the 'justice' as opposed to the 'welfare' model of youth justice (see Muncie, 2009, ch 8). A combination of both perspectives means that the Conservatives see crime as the result of individual deliberate actions: 'a matter of choice – a course of action freely chosen by pathological individuals with no self-control who [threaten] the very moral fabric of society' (Muncie, 2009, p 140).

As regards youths who commit crimes, therefore, the Conservatives believe that the main causes are: lack of self-control or indiscipline, weakened social bonds, association with delinquent peers, parental irresponsibility, the lack of a secure family upbringing or parental discipline, family breakdown (absent fathers), underachievement in school mainly as a result of truanting, idleness or being work-shy, and moral decline, epitomised, for example, by drugs misuse (Muncie, 2009). Thus, youth crime is placed within the larger context of societal decline – the result of the 'ill effects of modernisation and affluence, which have led to the erosion of traditional values based around morality and duty to the family and wider community' (Gunter, 2010, p x).

The moral panic about rising youth offending in the 1980s/90s provided Conservative governments with a justification for adopting a punitive stance towards youths breaking the law. A new Criminal Justice Act was passed in 1991, based on the principle of 'just deserts', with a strong focus on individual and parental responsibility. The law introduced a variety of sanctions that could be used for children and young persons who commit crimes, as well as for parents. This punitive stand on youth offending was matched, however, by the Conservative government's poor record on youth welfare. Their stringent approach to the provision of state welfare meant that the youths were systematically marginalised and neglected. For example, youths not in full-time education were, in 1991, denied social security benefits (Craig, 1991). In addition, the reduction in the numbers of affordable accommodation, the result of market-driven housing policies, led to increased youth homelessness (see Hutson and Liddiard, 1994). Furthermore, Conservative youth employment and training initiatives to 'help' youths gain employment left many young people in precarious situations of economic uncertainty and disaffection, including high unemployment, with minority youths generally, and girls in particular, most affected (see Griffin, 1985; Cockburn, 1987; Wallace, 1987).

Additionally, the Conservatives started a process of managerialising youth justice, whereby the driving forces for the youth justice system were 'effectiveness', 'centralisation of authority', 'inter-agency cooperation and partnership', 'value for money' and 'efficiency'. Most important is the Conservatives' pride in themselves as being a political party that promotes fairness, equality, cohesion and inclusion, but not diversity. In 2006, David Cameron (then leader of the opposition) had the following to say on multiculturalism:

> People from ethnic minorities are today less likely than ever before to encounter old-fashioned racism but, instead, they've become enmeshed in multicultural policies that racialise them anew. The principle of equality – that all people should be treated the same regardless of background, colour or creed – has become replaced with the principle of diversity, where all

cultural identities must be given separate public recognition. However well-intentioned, the effect is that people end up being treated differently which merely fuels discontent. It also promotes tribalism between different religious and ethnic groups. Ethnic and faith communities compete for public resources and recognition instead of uniting on the basis of shared interests. Multicultural policies provide a powerful incentive to proclaim one's victim status. This leads to a grievance culture – a zero sum game that views every concession to one group as a slight to others. (Cameron, 2006)

Recently, Cameron has announced that 'multiculturalism is dead', although he had little to say on the subject of racism. Thus, one can reasonably assume that ethnicity was not a key factor in these Conservative governments' approaches on youth justice and welfare. A close scrutiny of their policies indicates a preference for differences according to social class, whereby youths who live in deprived communities were seen as experiencing similar criminogenic problems, having collective needs, therefore, irrespective of their ethnicities. The consequence of the developments in the 1980s and 1990s was the gradual, but distinctive, move of youth justice away from welfare into criminal justice. Youths who commit crimes were to be seen as a problem for the CJS, not for the 'welfare state'. The Conservative era also marked the beginning of an 'inclusive' approach to youth justice; one that does not prioritise ethnicity. The idea that youths who commit crimes have 'common' characteristics and it is these that ought to be tackled started to dominate popular and political discourses. As mentioned earlier, these characteristics are believed to be self-imposed; therefore, discipline (punishment), not welfare, is the answer. Not giving due recognition to ethnic 'diversity' meant that a 'one-size-fits-all' approach was adopted in youth justice issues during the 1980s and early 1990s under Conservative regimes.

New Labour – old ideas

The 1997 'New' Labour government was greatly influenced by the left-realist criminological theory of crime (see Matthews and Young, 1992; Young, 1997). This view of crime states that whereas the root causes of crime lie in 'relative' deprivation and social exclusion or marginalisation, the explanation for social action and reaction should be the same and people should be seen as being responsible for their actions (cf. Carlen, 1992). A left-realist approach to youth crime, therefore, would tackle youth social and economic exclusion head-on, but, at the same time, mete out appropriate punishments to those who break the law. This position was captured in the New Labour slogan of 'tough on crime and tough on the causes of crime'; but, according to Young (2002), New Labour, in fact, adopted a 'weak' definition of exclusion, seen as self-imposed by a lazy and idle underclass – a value shared with previous Conservative governments.

Muncie (2009) argued that the New Labour era was a culmination of different youth justice discourses ranging from the liberal justice position of viewing youths as rational actors, to neoliberal and neo-conservative positions seeing youths as irresponsible, dangerous and immoral. These views have produced youth policies consisting of a package of intrusive 'prevention' strategies to curb offending and reoffending and compel discipline. These policies have been supported by punitive approaches ranging from measures to clamp down on youth anti-social behaviour right through to more legal provisions to ensure that youths, on the one hand, face up to their offending behaviour while parents, on the other, take responsibility for their children's criminal or deviant behaviour. Muncie concluded that, under New Labour, 'there appears an almost universal political consensus that the root cause of youth crime lies in a breakdown of morality associated with dysfunctional families and a feckless underclass' (2009, p 146). New Labour youth policies were laid down in a series of policy documents published in 1997 (for key examples, see *Box 12.1*).

Box 12.1: New Labour on youth crime and justice

Allowing young people to drift into a life of crime undermines their welfare and denies them the opportunity to develop into fully contributing members of society. To prevent offending and re-offending by young people, we must stop making excuses for youth crime. Children above the age of criminal responsibility are generally mature enough to be accountable for their actions and the law should recognise this. (*No More Excuses* – Home Office, 1997a, Introduction)

Those children who show signs of criminal behaviour at an early age ... often come from communities and families which are unstable, chaotic and suffer from a number of problems. Their parents are likely to have a criminal record, to neglect their children, or to exercise low levels of supervision and harsh and erratic discipline, and themselves to come from similar families. Children who offend are also more likely than others to fail at school, to play truant persistently, to behave disruptively or be permanently excluded from school.... Those who spend their leisure time in unstructured and unsupervised activity on the streets are more at risk of offending. There is also evidence that those whose friends engage in delinquent activity

> are more likely to do so themselves than those whose friends do not. The Government believes that it is essential to intervene with children at risk of becoming offenders as early as possible. It is also essential to develop strategies for intervention on the basis of sound knowledge about what works.... The Government [also] believes that parents who need help receive it, and that those parents who are unwilling to take their responsibilities seriously are required to face up to them. (*Preventing Children Offending* – Home Office, 2007b, chs 2, 5)

> Young people who commit crime must face up to the consequences of their actions for themselves and for others and take responsibility for their actions. The parents of young offenders must also recognise their responsibility for the actions of their children.... Punishment is important as a means of expressing society's condemnation of unlawful behaviour and as a deterrent. Punishment should be proportionate to the offence but progressively tougher if young people continue to offend ... punishment for young offenders should be complemented by intervention to change their behaviour and prevent them offending again. (*Tackling Youth Crime* – Home Office, 1997c, Introduction)

As a result of these policy ideas, laws were enacted between 1997 and 2008 that brought youth offending on a par with that of adults, in terms of their subjection to the criminal law and the CJS (see Cavadino and Dignan, 2007). For example, the Crime and Disorder Act 1998, abolished the age-old legal tradition of *doli incapax* (someone who cannot legally be held responsible for their actions) for 10–13 year olds and introduced, instead, a range of 'early intervention' child orders for children under the age of 10 years 'to catch them before they start'. New Labour also pursued the managerialisation process started by the Conservatives, but on an even greater scale. The 1998 Act created the Youth Justice Board for England and Wales, a new executive Non-Departmental Public Body (NDPB) responsible for the supervision, monitoring and assessment of all aspects of the youth justice system. Multi-agency Youth Offending Teams (YOTs) were created to manage the delivery of local youth justice services. Various partnership arrangements were also established with the voluntary and private sectors to execute the government's youth crime control initiatives.

The focus of New Labour's youth justice programme was allegedly 'prevention'. On this platform was built a range of initiatives involving schools, private, voluntary and faith groups (the third sector), communities, and government departments (see Home Office, 2009; Neuberger, 2009). Some of these initiatives included joint projects in the areas of family support and youth mentoring services, mental health, drugs, housing, and the provision of positive activities in deprived communities for disadvantaged youths at risk of offending as well as those identified as having complex support needs (see HM Government, 2007, 2008a, 2009). In many cases, the government simply built upon the preventive work that voluntary-sector groups were already doing with youths in these communities, including black communities.

Particular emphasis was put on working with faith groups to help reach youths in communities perceived to be 'hard to reach' (see Cabinet Office, 2006, 2007; NOMS and the YJB, 2007; DCLG, 2008; Ministry of Justice, 2008; Ministry of Justice and NOMS, 2008). Faith groups have been used to help raise awareness of government youth initiatives, for example, in Muslim communities, thereby increasing programme and project take-up rates in these communities. Faith groups have also been involved in the setting up of gang exit and safe haven programmes to support youths wanting to leave gangs, and those becoming involved with gangs because they saw it as a way to stay safe (HM Government, 2007, 2008a, 2009).

Policy documents detailed the government's plans to address youth offending and other youth issues, including *Every Child Matters* (Home Office, 2003), *Youth Matters: Next Steps* (DfES, 2006a), *Aiming High for Young People* (a ten-year strategy for positive activities) (DCSF, 2007a), *The Children's Plan* (DCSF, 2007b), *Youth Crime Action Plan* (HM Government, 2008b), *Youth Task Force Action Plan* (DCSF, 2008a) and *Targeted Youth Support: Next Steps* (DCSF, 2009a). In these documents, the New Labour government asserted its commitment to the welfare of children and young people, and reiterated its devotion to multi-agency working and the prioritising of 'local needs' in the delivery of youth services.

However, like previous Conservative governments, the extent to which different ethnicities were prioritised in the delivery of youth services to address youth offending remained unclear. The majority of government documents on youths that referred to ethnicity mainly talked about black youths. For example, in March 2006, the Labour Party commissioned a House of Commons Home Affairs Committee (hereinafter referred to as the Committee) to inquire into the persistent problem of the over-representation of black youths in the CJS. In May 2007, the Committee published its report, consisting of 67 main recommendations (HC, 2007).

In many ways, the Committee report was simply a replay of the Scarman Report published 25 years earlier. Like Scarman, the Committee identified the causes of black youths offending as emanating mainly from their disproportionate subjection to social exclusion; educational underachievement compounded by high levels of school exclusion and a high unemployment rate; a lack of positive role models for young black people (especially boys) as a result of the predominance of single-parent families (absent fathers) within black communities; mental health problems; lack of housing or homelessness; drugs misuse; having no safe places to play in the community; and the negative effect of popular music and culture on black youths (HC, 2007, ch 2). The Committee was particularly concerned about the disproportionate involvement of black youths in criminal youth affiliations or 'gangs', especially the fact that many youths, both male and female, were joining gangs as a 'protective measure' in order to prevent themselves from being the victims of other 'gangs' (Home Office, 2002; HC, 2007, pp 21–4). Finally, like Scarman, the Committee maintained that whereas discrimination within the CJS might be a contributory factor, it was so 'only in some instances' (HC, 2007, p 45).

The Committee has been criticised for focusing mainly on black youths and ignoring youths of other ethnicities (Bowling and Phillips, 2006). However, in responses to the Committee report (HM Government, 2007, 2008a, 2009), the New Labour government made efforts to show that, unless otherwise specified, the majority of ongoing initiatives were meant for youths of all ethnicities. The common denominators were: youths living in 'challenging' or deprived environments, offending or at risk of offending. Several pages in the government's three responses were devoted to detailing the large amounts of money that the government had spent or intended to spend to support youth crime prevention, diversion and control schemes as well as to support youth victims of crime. Some of the initiatives mentioned in the responses included efforts that had been or were being made to:

- ensure that parenting support services are accessible, appropriate and relevant to BME families' needs;
- expand existing mentoring schemes in schools and communities, and introduce further mentoring by peers and ex-offenders for young adults in prisons;
- reduce the school exclusion rate of black youths;
- ensure all schools fully meet their responsibilities under the Race Relations (Amendment) Act 2000 to eliminate unlawful discrimination and promote equality of opportunity and good relations between persons of all ethnic groups;
- ensure that proper educational provision is made for young people who are excluded from school;
- ensure that the school curricula are relevant to the needs of black youths as well as empower them;
- make schools safer by expanding the Safer Schools partnerships scheme and increasing after-school police patrols in known high-crime areas;

- ensure that available drug treatment facilities for youths are accessible to and are meeting the needs of youths of all ethnicities;
- increase awareness of, and access to, safe spaces in areas of high deprivation in which young people can meet informally and gain access to information about organised (positive) activities, help and advice;
- tackle gang membership more seriously by setting up more youth gang exit programmes, paying more attention to the provision of 'safe-houses', providing mentoring and positive activities in the communities for youths caught up in youth affiliations but not yet involved in crime, arresting gang members, and providing more support at schools to help youths say 'no' to gang membership;
- tackle gun and knife crimes by giving continuing financial support to existing national initiatives such as the Tackling Gangs Action Programme (TGAP) and Tackling Knives Action Programme(TKAP) and similar local police initiatives (MPS, 1998; GMP, 2004, 2008) and encouraging the development of similar initiatives elsewhere.
- use the media to raise awareness amongst youths about the dangers of becoming involved in violent crimes (Don't Trigger, 2007; It Doesn't Have to Happen, 2008);
- engage youths at risk of offending in positive activities that would involve them in expressing their creativity positively in music, creative arts and other cultural activities and sports; to empower young people; raise their self-esteem, confidence and aspirations; endow them with skills and knowledge required for the workforce; and ultimately divert them away from offending (see Ozbox, 2005; Kickz, 2006; Music Manifesto, 2006; DCSF, 2008b; Find Your Talent, 2009–11; Positive Futures, 2011);
- ensure that support provided by the YOTs meets the needs of young black people;
- tailor support and services that youths receive within the CJS to individual needs, not age, ensuring continuity of support when an offender moves from the youth justice system into an adult one (Calverley et al, 2004);
- improve youths' trust and confidence in the use of police 'stop-and-search' powers and encourage youths from minority backgrounds to choose the police as a future career option;
- engage with young people, for example, through local youth forums set up by the police and local Crime and Disorder Reduction Partnerships (CDRPs) in which young people can come together to talk about their concerns;
- support youths who are victims of crime to make sure that they do not turn to crime in response to being a victim; and

- help young offenders leaving custody reintegrate into the labour market and get accommodation on release (for full details, see HM Government, 2007, 2008a, 2009).

On first reading, this long list of initiatives has a 'welfare' edge to it. A closer look, however, reveals the darker side of 'welfare': discipline, remoralisation, responsibility, engagement and 'equal' opportunities. Known key welfare issues connected with youth offending, such as homelessness and unemployment, were hardly mentioned in any of these reports. For a political party that claimed to uphold the policy principle of 'what works', it was surprising that New Labour chose to ignore research findings showing that 'multi-agency' partnership working does not necessarily deliver a better or more efficient system and may actually present barriers to tackling youth crime (see Cook, 2006).

Most importantly, for a political party that introduced the 16+1 ethnic code classifications and pledged to support diversity, it was surprising that no mention was made of whether the welfare needs of these various ethnic groups differed or whether the system could deliver to all ethnic categories. Efforts to address ethnic differences in these provisions have been tokenistic, left mainly to the 'third sector'.

Gender, youth and justice

Studies conducted on gender and the CJS have shown that the reasons why young women enter the CJS are slightly different from those of young men (Smith and McAra, 2004; Gelsthorpe, 2006; Gelsthorpe and Sharpe, 2006). However, partly as a result of the small number of women in the CJS, there has been a tendency to treat all young women and their offending in a similar way (YJB, 2009). Gender was not specifically mentioned in most of the initiatives described in the HM Government (2007, 2008a, 2009) responses, the exception being the 'positive activities' where the information indicated that they were available to both young women and men (eg Ozbox, 2005; Kickz, 2006). Although arguments in favour of 'gender-responsive strategies' and initiatives for women are developing (see Shaw and Hannah-Moffat, 2000, 2004; Hedderman, 2004), the bulk of the arguments that have been put forward so far have been for adult women. Unlike for adults, it is often assumed that the risk factors for young women's offending are the same as or similar to those identified for boys, namely, peer pressure, boredom, education, family issues and alcohol. However, experience has shown that young women (girls) in the youth justice system do not respond in the same way to treatment as their male counterparts (YJB, 2009). This is an area where further research is needed.

With regard to ethnicity, there is no concrete evidence yet on whether the offending behaviour of young women of different ethnicities differs; after all, it was only in 2010 that the first set of racially coded statistics on females arrested by the police was published (Ministry of Justice, 2010b). However, this process has at least started.

Conclusion

It is doubtful whether governments can accommodate the criminal justice needs of youths of all ethnicities. A politically convenient approach appears to be to substitute 'social class' for 'race' or ethnicity. Although this is an inadequate approach, it is one that, as the present book demonstrates (see Chapter 2), recognises the importance of social circumstances that cut across ethnic boundaries. Dell and Boe (2000) have argued that to prioritise 'race' or ethnicity in addressing offending behaviour would be to assume that offending behaviour arises more from racial experience than from shared common life histories. According to them:

> Individuals differ due to their racialized experiences but they also resemble one another due to common life experiences. The overall implication is that caution must be exercised in focussing … exclusively on race. The lack of attention to similarity across racial categories may result in overlooking or minimizing elements of individual shared life histories that may contribute to understanding and identifying criminogenic factors (risk and needs). (Dell and Boe, 2000, p iv)

The need to prioritise 'shared experiences' over 'race' is shared by those who have recently claimed that the 'race' or ethnicity dimension is overplayed and that in today's multicultural and modern Britain, we should 'celebrate' shared experiences rather than emphasise difference (see eg Mizra, 2010). Cole (2008), however, argues that racialised experiences should not be undermined. Scarman has shown that disadvantage in education, housing and employment, which minority youths disproportionately suffer, is a key factor in understanding their criminality. There is no clear evidence that this situation has changed significantly today. While it may be true that 'the younger you are, the less prejudiced' (Phillips, 2009), the reverse is not the case; that is, that the younger you are, the less society and the CJS is prejudiced against you. British youths are aware that their disadvantaged position in society has not diminished but increased. The recent increase in university tuition fees is a case in point. Minority ethnic youths are aware that criminal labels attached to them are also increasing.

Research in England and Wales has shown that the most frequent form of explanation offered to account for offending by black and Asian offenders is racism in school, society and within the criminal justice system (Denney, 1992; Calverley et al, 2004). Cole (2008) has argued that the risk of reoffending is high where offenders are confronted by racism after the completion of a sentence; therefore, the need to tackle racism in the criminal justice and welfare systems is paramount. 'Celebrating' difference is not divisive. In fact, it is a fundamental requirement of true democracy.

Summary

- British official crime and CJS statistics have revealed that there are differences in offending by and victimisation of youths of different ethnicities.
- The Scarman report into the 1980s' riots in some English inner cities set a precedent by prioritising welfare over criminal justice (policing) as the way of addressing the offending behaviour of (predominantly black) youths who live in the inner cities.
- Subsequent political responses to youth offending and welfare appeared to have ignored 'ethnic' differences and focused on tackling known criminogenic needs, irrespective of ethnicity.
- Neglect of other ethnicities is seen in the fact that recent official reports on youths focused only on black youths. However, the Labour Party's responses made reference to all ethnicities in its analysis of ongoing initiatives to deal with youth offending.
- Multi-agency partnerships between government agencies and the third sector appear to be the most favoured approach to addressing youth welfare issues. At a glance, this gives an impression of the empowerment of non-government agencies and communities in youth issues. The reality, however, is that government control continued 'at a distance' through its monopoly of youth justice policies.
- So far, there is still low priority given to female youths.
- At the present time, the youth justice and welfare systems are yet to provide adequately for youths of all ethnicities, but the question remains as to whether ethnicity or 'shared experiences' should be the guiding principle.

Questions for discussion

- What are the reasons for the disproportionate representation of BME youths in the criminal justice system? How do you think that these causes can be addressed through a reform of the state welfare system?

- Would the approach to welfare provisions for youths at risk of offending have been different had Lord Scarman's recommendations on welfare been fully implemented?
- What should be the priority in welfare provision for youths at risk of offending and those who offend: ethnicity or 'shared experiences'?
- How should gender be approached in welfare provision for youths of all ethnicities involved in the criminal justice system?

Further reading

Bhui, S. (ed) (2009) *Race and Criminal Justice*, London: Sage.

Ministry of Justice (2010b) *Statistics on Women and the Criminal Justice System*, London: HMSO.

Endnote

Karl Atkin, Sangeeta Chattoo, Gary Craig and Ronny Flynn

In February 2011, British Prime Minister Cameron announced the 'failure of multiculturalism' and the need to facilitate a collective national identity. Criticising what he saw as the passive tolerance of different cultural values, identified as potentially undermining the collectively agreed, normative assumptions associated with 'Britishness', Cameron argued for an 'active liberalism'. There are of course problems in defining what, at best, can only be an imagined (and contested) national identity underpinned by the state-sponsored policy of community cohesion, superseding multiculturalism from 2003 onwards (see Chapter 4). Nevertheless, the speech reflects an ongoing struggle to come to terms with cultural and religious difference in a super-diverse nation state. It is arguable whether the notion of Britishness, as representing a coherent set of values, is something to which all members of the British population would subscribe, or, even if they did, if it would mark it out as distinctive from other national identities.

Primarily, the context of Cameron's speech was extremism. This has come to dominate current policy discourses on ethnicity and 'race', reminding us how our understanding of ethnicity and 'race' continues to be extremely sensitive to political context. For many, linking members of all or any minorities in general with terrorism — and using this association as the basis of policy — was a disgraceful elision. Cameron's concerns, however, reflect an even more fundamental tension and one that was, perhaps surprisingly, one focus of this book. Our interpretation of the problem (and solution) is very different to Cameron's. Nonetheless, we accept the need critically to reflect on the past, learning from previous mistakes, in a way that encourages active citizenship and celebrates the dynamic, vibrant and diverse nature of civil society. A more responsive social policy, both in terms of practical endeavour and theoretical reconciliation, should be at the forefront of such debates, particularly since themes such as citizenship, collective engagement, the provision of welfare, social inclusion and the elimination of social inequalities have been central to the development of the discipline. This makes social policy's relative silence on ethnic diversity all the more puzzling.

One major theme, reflected in all the chapters here, is the continued marginalisation, exclusion and disadvantage of most minority ethnic groups, and women in particular, despite 50 years of policy initiatives. Such marginalisation is often the result of political inaction. Where legislation is introduced, it is frequently undermined by a failure to act. This includes a failure to monitor ethnicity in service delivery as much as a failure on the part of research and policy plans to ensure that ethnicity is incorporated as an intrinsic dimension in the collection and use of evidence. Even where evidence points clearly to the need for restorative action – as, for example, in the case of the close association between ethnicity and poverty – responses tend to be broad-brush rather than being effectively targeted at those most disadvantaged. The evidence presented here fundamentally challenges these notions, highlighting deep structural inequalities that prevent minority ethnic groups from achieving their own full potential as citizens.

While thinking about citizenship in a postmodern, globalised and fluid world of transnational or diasporic identities, we need to understand the concept as one that challenges traditional boundaries of nationhood and state. A man born in Bangladesh, living in Keighley, might, depending on context, view himself as a Bangladeshi, a Yorkshireman, an Englishman or a UK or European citizen, for example. At the same time, we acknowledge that multiculturalism as a political project has yet to find an ideal solution to reconciling notions of difference and diversity within a framework of fundamental human rights that can be considered universal. For example, gender or intergenerational relationships within some minority groups will appear to be oppressive to others who take a particular secular-liberal or feminist viewpoint. At the same time, the issues of racialisation and essentialisation of these religious or cultural groups, as well as socio-economic inequalities and forms of discrimination in the labour market, highlight the double standards within the liberal democratic tradition of Western European politics (see Werbner and Modood, 1997). The inclusion of Muslims and the recognition of religious identities in public spaces within a secular state – symbolised in the different responses to the controversy over wearing the headscarf in Britain and France – remains an important challenge for the liberal and egalitarian agenda of multiculturalism as an ongoing project of political justice (Modood et al, 2006).

This book provides, we believe, a far-reaching (if necessarily incomplete) overview of the likely challenges facing those committed to ensuring that social policy can meaningfully engage with ethnicity and 'race'. There are core themes running across the three major sections of the book. First, conceptual clarity is an important starting point in making sense of and accepting the complexities associated with defining 'race', ethnicity and different forms of racism, exclusion and discrimination, resulting in the socio-economic and political marginalisation of particular minority groups. This includes questioning definitions of the 'other' and how we perceive cultural difference, while simultaneously developing policies that acknowledge the need to challenge discrimination, lack of appropriate access and inequities in service provision at various levels. Ethnicity as a conceptual framework for locating identities is sensitive to context, time and place. However, adopting such a social-constructivist view needs to be embraced in a way that avoids fragmentation and relativism, recognising its consequences. A disciplined commitment to encouraging better policy and practice cannot afford to overlook its intended outcomes.

Second, in taking a long historical view of the various sectors of welfare, this book reminds us, yet again, that there is much to learn from the past. As is clear from the analytical chapter (Chapter 2), long-standing problems of discrimination and inequity, though now relatively clearly identified, often remain unresolved or are reinvented periodically. Essentialism, long discredited in most academic circles, is beginning to re-emerge, at the same time as research, policy and practice slowly respond to the multicultural nature of British society. In many ways, our understanding of ethnicity has become increasingly sophisticated and the well-understood processes of disadvantage and discrimination, alongside a new-found interest in cultural identity, sometimes deludes us into thinking that there is indeed little now to be done. Our growing awareness, however, has not always equated with more responsive welfare provision and, indeed, there is a widespread fear that the modest gains of the past few years are being rolled back; witness, for example, elements within public bodies such as the police and employers (taking their cue from government) arguing that 'race' relations legislation is becoming a burden, little more than red tape, rather than an expression of social justice.

Debates about the complex nature of ethnic identity seem to be ignored, as mainstream research, unfamiliar with such debates, applies idiosyncratic and poorly contextualised ideas of ethnicity. Consequently, racism remains prevalent in services that ought to be concerned with equal opportunity and providing adequate welfare for all, regardless of skin colour or ethnic origin. This impedes access to services for BME people and undermines their claims to full citizenship. Where change has come, it is often as a result of the actions of minorities themselves (see Chapters 4 and 12). The northern 'disturbances' of the early 2000s – in conjunction with the incremental gains made through legislation and policy – might have had a similar effect in terms of thinking about structural disadvantage. Unfortunately, in the aftermath of the 9/11 and 7/7 bombings and growing Islamophobia, the stark socio-economic disadvantage experienced by a majority of Muslims became overshadowed.

Indeed, popular discriminatory rhetoric against Muslims – promoted energetically by the red-top media – now increasingly blames them for their marginalisation and requires them to assimilate and promote a national identity. Community cohesion, discussed in Chapter 4, is in reality a return to the language of assimilation rather than a move forward to a culture of respect for diversity and difference. The new focus on cohesion is quite clearly a way of reframing the 'race' equality discourse to deflect attention away from the growth of racism in British society. Surprisingly, many of those active in policy and research appear to accept this reframing without challenging its underlying assumptions. As academics and researchers, we strongly endorse approaches akin to 'critical race theory' (described in Chapter 8) as a means to understanding why we are now witnessing the dismantling of many progressive policy initiatives – such as the black housing sector – which were beginning to tackle racism more directly.

Hence, as others remind us, focusing on the needs of minority ethnic populations is not the same as responding to those needs (see Chapter 2). Despite a willingness on the part of liberal welfare states to tackle discrimination, public organisations not only struggle to reconcile key ideas – such as institutional racism and community cohesion – within a policy framework, but often lack a political strategy or commitment to initiate change or confront negative developments such as the growth of racist behaviour or the rise of far-right political groups. On the one hand, the idea of super-diversity is finding both academic and policy acceptance, as both the multifaceted nature of identity politics and discrimination find discursive expression within public debates. On the other, our ideas about discrimination and disadvantage do not easily map on to previously familiar lines associated with ethnicity (and 'race'), gender, social class, disability, sexuality, faith and age. Nonetheless, accommodating diversity within more general meta-narratives associated with social justice and social inclusion remains, we would suggest, a continued and ever-important goal for social policy. The recent change in legislation towards a single equalities framework captured in the Single Equalities Act 2010 symbolises this cross-cutting of themes, although its impact on tackling racism in its various guises remains to be seen, particularly since its provisions have been weakened by the Coalition government. As is clear from this volume, racism remains a deeply serious political issue affecting the life chances of millions of British citizens, rather than, as continues to be the case, a slightly troubling but marginal issue that most politicians and policymakers simply wish away.

Despite David Cameron's unease with the idea, others – including Parekh and Modood – forcefully argue that the multicultural nature of the UK cannot be denied; and that the political project of multiculturalism, rather than being dead, has hardly been started. This brings us face to face with the promise and limitations of multiculturalism as a political theory or perspective (rather than a specific policy as understood by Cameron). Parekh defines a multicultural perspective as comprising three interrelated principles: that human beings are culturally embedded; the inevitability and desirability of cultural diversity and inter-cultural dialogue; and plurality within each culture (2000a, p 338). Here we have a notion of different cultural, religious and other social groups being in dialogue with each other, rather than living in segregated ghettos, also recognising and respecting difference. The sense of belonging and togetherness is derived from membership of a common political community with mutual interests and rights as citizens, and sharing fundamental moral principles upholding social justice and democracy (Parekh, 2000a, p 341). Diversity, therefore, does not necessarily mean fragmentation, but rather an interconnected society, which can accommodate difference in different forms. This challenge is ever-present as new minorities arrive within the UK and settle there, a process characterised more at present by recycled forms of racism than by acceptance of greater diversity and difference.

The changing nature of the union will offer further challenges. Many in Scotland strive for independence and it is beginning to enact policies diverging from those found in England; Wales may follow suit. Debates about ethnicity might, therefore, begin to have a different feel, especially within the context of national identity. Long-standing tensions in Northern Ireland reflect the importance of faith as a marker of disadvantage and discrimination; ethnicity may also grow in significance. We would argue that the core themes identified in this book have relevance throughout the UK, although many current debates have a very English 'slant' – a deficit further compounded by the lack of reliable evidence in other parts of the union (Netto et al, 2010).

In writing and editing this book, we aimed to challenge concepts, processes and social policies sustaining the economic, political and cultural marginalisation of people with minority ethnic origins. By providing a historical view of welfare provision and policies related to 'race' and ethnicity over time, we highlighted conceptual shifts, leading to positive and, at times, retrograde policy moves. Some chapters representing particular welfare sectors might, however, read more like a description of how far the achievements of these historical shifts have fallen short of the goals of equal opportunity and anti-racism, highlighting gaps between policy and practice. To that extent, the, at times, uneven nature of this collection represents the internal developments within a particular sector, its own history and culture of representation and critique. Reading across these chapters allows the reader to see how far we have come in some sectors and how far we lag behind in others, perhaps making use of the gains in one area to accelerate progress elsewhere. Since the terms of a particular discourse constitute a field and its subject (Foucault, 1983), it is hard to provide a self-critique from within. We are aware, for example, that even though we tried to challenge the ascription of ethnicity to only people of minority ethnic groups, most of the chapters in the book do not deal with white majority or even minority ethnic groups. This, in turn, reflects a lack of contributors or research from Wales and Northern Ireland, an absence far from that we desired. We hope the volume as a whole inspires new ways of approaching welfare and social policy, destabilising old power dynamics between the majority and the minority or 'host' and 'immigrant' groups, in anticipation of a society that is equal, inclusive, fair and just for all.

References

ABSWAP (Association of Black Social Workers and Allied Professions) (1983) *Black Children in Care: Evidence to the House of Commons Social Services Committee*, London: ABSWAP.

Acevedo, G.D. (2000) 'Residential segregation and the epidemiology of infectious diseases', *Social Science & Medicine*, vol 51, pp 1143–61.

Action for Children (2008) 'As long as it takes: a new politics for children'. Available at: www.actionforchildren.org.uk/media/144001/alait.pdf

Adamson, S., Craig, G. and Wilkinson, M. (2008) *Migrant Workers in the Humber Sub-region*, Hull: Humber Improvement Programme.

Ahmad, F., Modood, T. and Lissenburgh, S. (2003) *South Asian Women and Employment in Britain: the Interaction of Gender and Ethnicity*, London: Policy Studies Institute.

Ahmad, W.I.U. (ed) (1994) *'Race' and Health in Contemporary Britain*, Buckingham: Open University Press.

Ahmad, W.I.U. and Bradby, H. (2007) 'Locating ethnicity and health: exploring concepts and contexts', *Sociology of Health and Illness*, vol 29, no 6, pp 793–811.

Ahmad, W.I.U. and Husband, C. (1993) 'Religious identity, citizenship and welfare', *American Journal of Islamic Social Science*, vol 10, no 2, pp 217–33.

Ali, N. (2003) 'Diaspora and nation: displacement and the politics of Kashmiri identity in Britain', *Contemporary South Asia*, vol 12, no 4, pp 471–80.

Anderson, B. (1991) *Imagined Communities*, London: Verso.

Andrew, M. and Pannell, B. (2006) 'Housing choices by the young', *CML Housing Finance* 7, pp 1–12.

Anionwu, E. and Atkin, K. (2001) *The Politics of Sickle Cell and Thalassaemia*, Buckingham: Open University Press.

Ansari, H. (2004) *Muslims in Britain*, London: Hurst and Co.

Anthias, F. (1992) *Ethnicity, Class, Gender and Migration: Greek Cypriots in Britain*, Avebury: Aldershot.

Anthias, F. and Yuval-Davis, N. (1983) 'Contextualising feminism: gender, ethnic and class divisions', *Feminist Review*, no 15, pp 62–75.

Anthias, F. and Yuval-Davis, N. (1992) *Racialised Boundaries: Race, Nation, Gender, Colour and Class and the Anti-Racist Struggle*, London/New York: Routledge.

Asare, Y. (2009) *'Them and Us': Race Equality Interventions in Predominantly White Schools*, London: The Runnymede Trust.

Aspinall, P. and Mitton, L. (2007) 'Are English local authorities' practices on housing and council tax benefit administration meeting race equality requirements?', *Critical Social Policy*, vol 27, pp 381–414.

Aspinall, P.J. and Watters, C. (2010) *Refugees and Asylum Seekers: a Review from an Equality and Human Rights Perspective*, Research report 52, Manchester: Equality and Human Rights Commission.

Association of Directors of Adult Social Services (2010) 'Progress in the delivery of Personal Budgets 2010'. Available at: www.adass.org.uk/index. php?option=com_content&view=article&id=328

Athwal, H., Bourne, J. and Wood, R. (2010) *Racial Violence: the Buried Issue*, London: Institute of Race Relations.

Atkin, K. (2009) 'Making sense of ethnic diversity, difference and disadvantage within the context of multicultural societies', in L. Culley, N. Hudson and F. Van Rooij (eds) *Marginalised Reproduction: Ethnicity, Infertility and Reproductive Technologies*, London: Earthscan, pp 49–63.

Atkin, K. and Ahmad, W. (eds) (1996) *Race and Community Care*, Milton Keynes: Open University Press.

Atkin, K. and Ahmad, W.I.U. (2000) 'Living with a sickle cell disorder: how young people negotiate their care and treatment', in W.I.U. Ahmad (ed) *Ethnicity, Disability and Chronic Illness*, Buckingham: Open University Press, pp 45–66.

Atkin, K. and Anionwu, E. (2010) *The Social Consequences of Sickle Cell and Thalassaemia: Improving the Quality of Support*, Better Health Briefing Paper 17, London: Race Equality Foundation, pp 1–7.

Atkin, K. and Chattoo, S. (2006) 'Approaches to conducting qualitative research in ethnically diverse populations', in J. Nazroo (ed) *Methodological Issues in Research Relating to Black and Minority Ethnic Groups: Publishing the Evidence*, London: Taylor Francis, pp 95–115.

Atkin, K. and Chattoo, S. (2007) 'The dilemmas of providing welfare in an ethnically diverse state: seeking reconciliation in the role of a "reflexive practitioner"', *Policy & Politics*, vol 35, no 3, pp 379–95.

Atkin, K. and Rollings, J. (1993) 'Community care and voluntary provision: a review of the literature', *New Community*, vol 19, no 4, pp 659–67.

Atkin, K., Ahmed, S., Green, J. and Hewison, J. (2008) 'Decision making and ante-natal screening for sickle cell and thalassaemia disorders: to what extent do faith and religious identity mediate choice?', *Current Sociology*, vol 56, no 1, pp 77–98.

Au, S. and Tang, R. (2009) 'Mental health services for Chinese people', in S. Fernando and F. Keating (eds) *Mental Health in a Multi-Ethnic Society: a Multidisciplinary Handbook*, London: Routledge, pp 235–58.

Audit Commission (2006) *Choosing Well: Analysing the Costs and Benefits of Choice in Local Public Services*, London: Audit Commission.

Bains, B. (2008) *GLA 2007 Round Ethnic Group Projections*, London: Greater London Authority.

Ballard, R. (1989) 'Social work with black people: what's the difference?', in C. Rojek, G. Peacock and S. Collins (eds) *The Haunt of Misery: Critical Essays in Caring and Helping*, London: Tavistock, pp 123–47.

Bangs, M., Roe, S. and Higgins, N. (2008) 'Geographic patterns of crime' in C. Kershaw, S. Nicholas and A. Walker (eds) *Crime in England and Wales 2007/08*, Home Office Statistical Bulletin 07/08, London: HMSO.

Banks, J. (2008) 'The criminalisation of asylum seekers and asylum policy', *Prison Service Journal*, no 175, pp 43–9.

Banton, M. (1987) *Racial Theories*, Cambridge: Cambridge University Press.

Banton, M. (2000) 'Ethnic conflict', *Sociology*, vol 34, pp 481–98.

Barnes, C. and Mercer, G. (2006) *Independent Futures: Creating User-Led Disability Services in a Disabling Society*, Bristol: BASW/The Policy Press.

Barnes, C., Mercer, G. and Shakespeare, T. (1999) *Exploring Disability: a Sociological Introduction*, London: Polity Press.

Barth, F. (ed) (1969) *Ethnic Groups and Boundaries: The Social Organisation of Culture Difference*, London: Allen and Unwin.

Basu, A. (1998) 'The role of institutional support in Asian entrepreneurial expansion in Britain', *Journal of Small Business and Enterprise Development*, vol 5, no 4 (December), pp 317–26.

Battu, H. and Sloane, P.J. (2002) 'To what extent are ethnic minorities in Britain over-educated?', *International Journal of Manpower*, vol 23, no 3, pp 192–203.

Batty, D. (2003) 'Britain's looming GP crisis'. Available at: http://www.buzzle.com/editorials/8-26-2003-44687.asp (accessed 29 December 2010).

Bauman, Z. (1992) *Intimations of Postmodernity*, London: Routledge.

Baumann, G. (1997) 'Dominant and demotic discourses of culture: their relevance to multi-ethnic alliances', in P. Werbner and T. Modood (eds) *Debating Cultural Hybridity: Multi-Cultural Identities and the Politics of Anti-Racism*, London: Zed Books, pp 209–25.

BBC (2002) 'A short history of immigration'. Available at: http://news. bbc.co.uk/hi/english/static/in_depth/uk/2002/race/short_history_of_ immigration.stm#1914 (accessed 29 December 2010).

BBC News (1999) 'Asian children suffer vitamin deficiency', 1 January. Available at: http://news.bbc.co.uk/1/hi/health/245537.stm (accessed 29 December 2010).

BBC News (2007) 'Nicol Stephen condemns dawn raids'. Available at: http://news.bbc.co.uk/2/hi/uk_news/scotland/6320959.stm

BBC Wales (no date) 'Dr Gwynfor Evans'. Available at: www.bbc.co.uk/ wales/southeast/halloffame/public_life/gwynfor_evans.shtml

Beaumont, P. (2010) 'Kosovo breakaway from Serbia was legal, world court rules', *The Guardian*. Available at: www.guardian.co.uk/world/2010/ jul/22/kosovo-breakaway-serbia-legal-world-court (accessed 11 January 2011).

Bécares, L., Nazroo, J. and Stafford, M. (2009a) 'The buffering effects of ethnic density on experienced racism and health', *Health & Place*, vol 15, pp 670–8.

Bécares, L., Nazroo, J. and Stafford, M. (2009b) 'The ethnic density effect on alcohol use among minority ethnic people in the UK', *Journal of Epidemiology and Community*, doi:10.1136/jech.2009.087114.

Beckett, A. (2009) *When the Lights Went out: Britain in the Seventies*, London: Faber and Faber.

Beider, H. (2005) 'Housing, social capital and integration', Paper presented to ENHR, Reykjavik, 29 June–3 July 2005.

Beider, H. (2009) 'Guest introduction: rethinking race and housing', *Housing Studies*, vol 24, no 4, pp 405–15.

Beider, H. (forthcoming) *Housing, Race and Community Cohesion*, Oxford: Wiley-Blackwell.

Ben-Tovin, G., Gabriel, J., Law, I. and Stredder, K. (1986) *The Local Politics of Race*, London: Macmillan.

Benyon, J. and Solomos, J. (eds) (1987) *The Roots of Urban Unrest*, Oxford: Pergamon Press.

Berthoud, R. (1999) *Young Caribbean Men and the Labour Market: a Comparison with Other Ethnic Groups*, York: York Publishing Services Ltd.

Berthoud, R. (2000a) 'Ethnic employment penalties in Britain', *Journal of Ethnic and Migration Studies*, vol 26, no 3, pp 389–416.

Berthoud, R. (2000b) *Family Formation in Multi-Cultural Britain: Three Patterns of Diversity*, Colchester: University of Essex.

Bethell, H., Lewin, R. and Dalal, H. (2009) 'Cardiac rehabilitation in the United Kingdom', *Heart*, vol 95, no 4, p 271.

Be-Utd (2010) 'John Denham – government is committed to tackling inequality and disadvantage wherever it exists', 10 January. Available at: www.be-utd.org/2010/01/john-denham-government-is-committed-to-tackling-inequality-and-disadvantage-wherever-it-exists/ (accessed 29 December 2010).

Bhabha, H. (1994) *The Location of Culture*, London: Routledge.

Bharj, K. and Salway, S. (2008) *Addressing Ethnic Inequalities in Maternity Service Experiences and Outcomes: Responding to Women's Needs and Preferences*, Better Health Briefing no 11, London: Race Equality Foundation.

Bhavnani, K. and Phoenix, A. (1994) *Shifting Identities Shifting Racisms: A Feminism and Psychology Reader*, London: Sage Publications.

Bhavnani, R., Mirza, H.S. and Meetoo, V. (2005) *Tackling the Roots of Racism, Lessons for Success*, Bristol: The Policy Press.

Bhui, K. (ed) (2002) *Racism and Mental Health: Prejudice and Suffering*, London: Jessica Kingsley.

Bhui, K., Stansfeld, S., Hull, S., Priebe, S., Mole, F. and Feder, G. (2003) 'Ethnic variations in pathways to and use of specialist mental health services in the UK: systematic review', *The British Journal of Psychiatry*, vol 182, pp 105–16.

Bhui, K., McKenzie, K. and Gill, P. (2004) 'Delivering mental health service for a diverse society', *British Medical Journal*, vol 329, pp 363–4.

Bhui, K., Craig, T., Mohamud, S., Warfa, N., Stansfeld, S.A., Thornicroft, G., Curtis, S. and McCrone, P. (2006) 'Mental disorders among Somali refugees: developing culturally appropriate measures and assessing socio-cultural risk factors', *Social Psychiatry and Epidemiology*, vol 41, pp 400–8.

Bird, L. (1999) *The Fundamental Facts*, London: Mental Health Foundation.

Bivins, R. (2007) 'The "English Disease" or "Asian Rickets"? Medical responses to postcolonial immigration', *Bulletin of the History of Medicine*, vol 81, no 3, pp 533–68.

Blackaby, B. and Chahal, K. (2001) *Black and Minority Ethnic Housing Strategies: a Good Practice Guide*, London: Chartered Institute of Housing, Federation of Black Housing Organisations and the Housing Corporation

Blakemore, K. (1990) 'Does age matter? The case of old age in minority ethnic groups', in B. Bytheway et al (eds) *Becoming and Being Old: Sociological Approaches to Later Life*, London: Sage, pp 158–76.

Bogg, E. (1926) *The Charm of the Hambletons*, Thirsk: publisher unknown.

Bowling, B. and Phillips, C. (2002) *Racism, Crime and Justice*, London: Longman.

Bowling, B. and Phillips, C. (2006) *Young Black People and the Criminal Justice System*, submission to the House of Commons Home Affairs Committee Inquiry, October, London: Kings College.

Bracken, P. and Thomas P. (2005) *Postpsychiatry: Mental Health in a Postmodern World*, Oxford: Oxford University Press.

Bradford, B. (2006) 'Who are the "mixed" ethnic group?' Available at: http://www.statistics.gov.uk/articles/nojournal/Mixed_ethnic_groups_pdf.pdf (accessed 11 August 2010).

Bradford and District Infant Mortality Commission (2006) *Final Report*, Bradford: Bradford Vision. Available at www.ebm.bradford.nhs.uk/BDIMC.

Bradshaw, J., Kemp, P., Baldwin, S. and Rowe, A. (2004) *The Drivers of Social Exclusion*, London: Office of the Deputy Prime Minister, ch 8, pp 8–99.

Brah, A. (1996) *Cartographies of Diaspora: Contesting Identities*, London: Routledge.

Branfield, F. and Beresford, P. (2006) *Making User Involvement Work*, York: Joseph Rowntree Foundation.

Brendon, R. (2002) *The Dark Valley: A Panorama of the 1930s*, New York: Vintage Books.

Brock, A.S., Nightingale, C.M., Owen, C.G., Rudnicka, A.R., McNamara, M.C., Prynne, C.J., Stephen, A.M., Cook, D.G. and Whincup, P.H. (2009) 'Nutritional composition of the diets of South Asian, black African Caribbean and white European children in the UK: the child heart and health study in England', *Journal of Epidemiology and Community Health*, vol 63, p 59.

Brown, C. (1984) *Black and White Britain: The Third PSI Survey*, London: Heinemann.

Brown, C. (2006) 'Moving on: reflections on oral history and migrant communities in Britain', *Oral History*, vol 34, no 1, pp 69–80.

Brown, R. (1995) 'Racism and immigration in Britain', *International Socialism Journal*. Available at: http://pubs.socialistreviewindex.org.uk/isj68/brown.htm (accessed 29 December 2010).

Bryan, B., Dadzie, S. and Scafe, S. (1985) *The Heart of the Race: Black Women's Lives in Britain*, London: Virago.

Bullen, N. and Reeves, R. (2003) *Acute Inpatient Survey. National Overview 2001/02*, London: Department of Health.

Burgess, S. and Greaves, E. (2009) *Test Scores, Subjective Assessment and Stereotyping of Ethnic Minorities*, Bristol: University of Bristol.

Burleigh, M. (2005) *Earthly Powers: Religion and Politics in Europe from the French Revolution to the Great War*, London: Harper Collins.

Burman, E., Chantier, K. and Batsieer, J. (2002) 'Service responses to South Asian women who attempt suicide or self-harm: challenges for service commissioning and delivery', *Critical Social Policy*, vol 22, pp 641–68.

Burnett, A. (2009) 'The Sanctuary Practice in Hackney', in S. Fernando and F. Keating (eds) *Mental Health in a Multi-Ethnic Society: a Multidisciplinary Handbook*, London: Routledge, pp 217–25.

Burnett, A. and Peel, M. (2001) 'Health needs of asylum seekers and refugees', *British Medical Journal*, vol 322, pp 544–7.

Burr, J. (2002) 'Cultural stereotypes of women from South Asian communities: mental health care professionals' explanations for patterns of suicide and depression', *Social Science and Medicine*, vol 55, pp 835–45.

Butt, J. (2005) '"Are we there yet?" Identifying the characteristics of social care organisations that successfully promote diversity', in J. Butt, B. Patel and O. Stuart (eds) *Race Equality Discussion Papers, Part of Stakeholder Participation Discussion Papers*, London: Social Care Institute for Excellence, pp 3-29.

Cabinet Office (2000) *Ethnic Minorities and the Labour Market: Interim Analytical Report*, London: Strategy Unit.

Cabinet Office (2003) *Ethnic Minorities and the Labour Market: Final Report*, London: Strategy Unit.

Cabinet Office (2006) *Partnership in Public Services an Action Plan for Third Sector Involvement*, London: HM Treasury/Cabinet Office.

Cabinet Office (2007) *The Future Role of the Third Sector in Social and Economic Regeneration: Final Report*, London: HM Treasury/Cabinet Office.

Cabinet Office (2010a) *The Coalition: Our Programme for Government*. Available at: http://www.cabinetoffice.gov.uk/media/409088/pfg_coalition.pdf (accessed 25 August 2010).

Cabinet Office (2010b) *State of the Nation, Poverty, Worklessness and Welfare Dependency in the UK*, London: Cabinet Office.

Calverley, A., Cole, B., Kaur, G., Lewis, S., Raynor, P., Sadeghi, S., Smith, D., Vanstone, M. and Wardak, A. (2004) *Black and Asian Offenders on Probation*, Home Office Research Study 277, London: Home Office.

Cameron, D. (2006) 'Speech to Ethnic Media Conference', 29 November. Available at: http://www.conservatives.com/News/Speeches/2006/11/David_Cameron_speech_to_Ethnic_Media_Conference.aspx (accessed 17 November 2010).

Cantle, T. (2001) *Community Cohesion: a Report of the Independent Review Team*, London: Home Office.

Carby, H. (1982) 'Schooling in Babylon', in Centre for Contemporary Cultural Studies (ed) *The Empire Strikes Back: Race and Racism in 70s Britain*, London: Hutchinson, in association with the Centre for Contemporary Cultural Studies University of Birmingham, pp 83–111.

Care Quality Commission (2011) *Count Me in 2010: Results of the 2010 National Census of Inpatients and Patients on Supervised Community Treatment in Mental Health and Learning Disability Services in England and Wales*, London: Care Quality Commission.

Carlen, P. (1992) 'Criminal women and criminal justice: the limits to, and potential of, feminist and left realist perspectives', in J. Young and R. Matthews (eds) *Issues in Realist Criminology*, London: Sage, pp 51–69.

Cashmore, E. and Troyna, B. (1990) *Introduction to Race Relations*, Basingstoke: Falmer Press.

Cavadino, M. and Dignan, J. (2007) *The Penal System: An Introduction* (3rd edn), London: Sage.

CCCS (Centre for Contemporary Cultural Studies) (ed) (1982) *The Empire Strikes Back: Race and Racism in 70s Britain*, London: Hutchinson, in association with the CCCS University of Birmingham.

Cemlyn, S. (2008) 'Human rights and Gypsies and Travellers: an exploration of the application of a human rights perspective to social work with minority communities', *British Journal of Social Work*, vol 38, pp 153–73.

Cemlyn, S. and Briskman, L. (2002) 'Social (dys)welfare within a hostile state', *Social Work Education*, vol 21, no 1, pp 49–69.

Cemlyn, S. and Clark, C. (2005) 'The social exclusion of Gypsy and Traveller children', in G. Preston (ed) *At Greatest Risk: The Children Most Likely to Be Poor*, London: CPAG, pp 146–62.

Cemlyn, S., Greenfields, M., Burnett, S., Matthews, Z. and Whitwell, C. (2009) 'Inequalities experienced by Gypsy and Traveller communities: a review'. Available at: http://www.equalityhumanrights.com/publications/our-research/research-reports/research-reports-11-20/ (accessed 16 August 2010).

Chahal, K. (2007) *Racist Harassment and Support Services*, Better Housing Briefing Paper 2, London: Race Equality Foundation.

Chan, C.K., Bowpitt, G., Cole, B., Somerville, P. and Chan, J.Y. (2003) *The UK Chinese People*, Nottingham: Nottingham Trent University.

Chattoo, S. (2008) 'The moral economy of selfhood and caring: negotiating boundaries of personal care as embodied moral practice', *Sociology of Health and Illness*, vol 30, pp 550–64.

Chattoo, S. and Ahmad, W.I.U. (2004) 'The meaning of cancer: illness, biography and social identity', in D. Kelleher and G. Leavey (eds) *Identity and Health*, London: Routledge.

Chattoo, S., Crawshaw, M. and Atkin, K. (2010) *The Experience of Cancer-Related Fertility Impairment among People of South Asian and White Origin: Final Report to CRUK*, York: University of York.

Cheong, P., Edwards, R., Golbourne, H. and Solomos, J. (2007) 'Immigration, social cohesion and social capital', *Critical Social Policy*, vol 27, no 1, pp 27–49.

Chouhan, K. (2009) 'Cohesion creep', Paper presented to 'Rethinking Community Cohesion – Different Perspectives on Segregation and Community Relations' conference, University of Birmingham, 14 October.

Chouhan, K. and Lusane, C. (2004) *Black Voluntary and Community Sector Funding: Its Impact on Civic Engagement and Capacity Building*, York: Joseph Rowntree Foundation.

Chowbey, P., Salway, S., Gerrish, K., Ismail, M. and Moullin, M. (2008) *Responding to Diverse Needs: Eating Disorders in 'BME Communities' in Sheffield*, Sheffield: South Yorkshire Eating Disorders Association.

CIC (Commission on Integration and Cohesion) (2007) *Our Shared Future*. Available at: http://collections.europarchive.org/tna/20080726153624/http://www.integrationandcohesion.org.uk/~/media/assets/www.integrationandcohesion.org.uk/our_shared_future%20pdf.ashx (accessed 29 December 2010).

CIH (Chartered Institute of Housing) (2004) *The Future of BME Housing Associations*, Coventry: CIH.

Clark, C. (2006) *Here to Stay*, Hertford: University of Hertfordshire Press.

Clark, C. (2007) *Iron Kingdom: the Rise and Downfall of Prussia*, London: Penguin.

Clark, K. and Drinkwater, S. (2007) *Ethnic Minorities in the Labour Market: Dynamics and Diversity*, York: Joseph Rowntree Foundation.

Clifford, L. (2010) 'UK visa holders get biggest welcome in Scotland'. Available at: www.globalvisas.com/news/uk_visa_holders_get_biggest_welcome_in_scotland2302.html (accessed 30 May 2011).

CMPO (Centre for Market and Public Organisation) (2010) 'Black pupils are routinely marked down by teachers'. Available at: www.bristol.ac.uk/cmpo/news/2010/463.html

Coard, B. (1971) *How the West Indian Child Is Made Educationally Subnormal in the British School System: the Scandal of the Black Child in Schools in Britain*, London: New Beacon Books.

Cockburn, C. (1987) *Two-Track Training: Sex Inequalities and the YTS*, London: Macmillan.

Cole, B. (2008) 'Working with ethnic diversity', in S. Green, E. Lancaster and S. Feasey (eds) *Addressing Offending Behaviour*, Cullompton: Willan, pp 402–25.

Cole, B. and Wardak, A. (2006) 'Black and Asian men on probation: social exclusion, discrimination and experience of criminal justice', in S. Lewis, P. Raynor, D. Smith and A. Wardak (eds) *Race and Probation*, Cullompton: Willan.

Cole, R. (2010) 'Immigrants to face English language test', 10 June. Available at: http://news.sky.com/skynews/Home/UK-News/Immigrants-Coming-To-Britain-To-Marry-Or-Join-Partners-Will-Have-To-Take-English-Language-Test/Article/201006215646122 (accessed 13 June 2010).

Connolly, P. (2009) *Developing Programmes to Promote Ethnic Diversity in Early Childhood: Lessons from Northern Ireland*, The Hague: Bernard Van Leer Foundation.

Cook, D. (2006) *Criminal and Social Justice*, London: Sage.

Cook, D. and Hudson, B. (1993) *Racism and Criminology*, London: Sage.

Cooper, C. (2002) *Understanding School Exclusion*, Hull: Education Now/ University of Hull.

Cooper, C. (2009) 'Refugees, asylum seekers and criminal justice', in S. Bhui (ed) *Race and Criminal Justice*, London: Sage, pp 137–53.

Cooper, C., Morgan, C., Byrne, M., Dazzan, P., Morgan, G., Hutchinson, G., Doody, G.A., Harrison, G., Leff, J., Ismail, K., Murray, R., Bebbington, P.E. and Fearon, P. (2008) 'Perceptions of disadvantage, ethnicity and psychosis', *The British Journal of Psychiatry*, vol 192, pp 185–90.

Cooper, L., Beach, M.C., Johnson, R.L. and Inui, T.S. (2005) 'Delving below the surface: understanding how race and ethnicity influence relationships in health care', *Journal of General Internal Medicine*, vol 21, pp S21–S27.

Coppock, V. and Hopton, J. (2000) *Critical Perspectives on Mental Health*, London: Routledge.

Craig, G. (2001) *Fit for Nothing*, London: Children's Society.

Craig, G. (2007) 'Cunning, unprincipled, loathsome: the racist tail wags the welfare dog', *Journal of Social Policy*, vol 36, no 4, pp 605–23.

Craig, G. (2011a) 'Forward to the past? Does the Black and Minority Ethnic third sector have a future?', *Voluntary Sector Review*, vol 2, no 3, in press.

Craig, G. (2011b) *The UK Roma*, unpublished report, mimeo, copies available from the author.

Craig, G., Kaur, S., Mumtax, S. and Elliott-White, N. (2000) *Giving Voice*, Huddersfield, Age Concern.

Craig, G., Adamson, S., Ali, N., Ali, S., Atkins, I., Dadze-Arthur, A., Elliott, C. and Murtuja, B. (2007a) *Sure Start and Black and Minority Ethnic Populations*, London: HMSO.

Craig, G., Gaus, A., Wilkinson, M., Skrivankova, K. and McQuade, A. (2007b) *Contemporary Slavery in the UK*, York: Joseph Rowntree Foundation.

Craig, G., Adamson, S., Cole, B., Law, I. and Chan, C.K. (2009a) *Hidden from Public View? Racism against the UK's Chinese Population*, London: DCLG/Min Quan.

Craig, G., Adamson, S., Ali, N. and Demsash, F. (2009b) *Mapping Rapidly Changing Ethnic Minority Populations*, York: Joseph Rowntree Foundation.

Crawley, H. (2004) *Moving Forward: the Provisions of Accommodation for Travellers and Gypsies*, London: IPPR.

CRE (Commission for Racial Equality) (1991) *The Code of Practice for Rented Housing*, London: Commission for Racial Equality.

CRE (2006) *Common Ground – Equality, Good Race Relations and Sites for Gypsies and Irish Travellers*, London: Commission for Racial Equality.

CRE (2007a) *Annual Report and Accounts 2006/07*, London: Commission for Racial Equality.

CRE (2007b) *Shadow Report: United Kingdom's Second Report to the Council of Europe under the Framework Convention for the Protection of National Minorities*, London: Commission for Racial Equality.

CRER (Centre for Research in Ethnic Relations) (1992) *Ethnic Minorities in Great Britain*, Coventry: Centre for Research in Ethnic Relations, University of Warwick.

Cross, M., Wrench, J. and Barnett, S. (1990) *Ethnic Minorities and the Careers Service: an Investigation into Processes of Assessment and Placement*, Department of Employment Research Paper no 73, London: HMSO.

CSCI (Commission for Social Care Inspection (2008) 'Putting people first: equality and diversity matters 2: providing appropriate services for black and minority ethnic people'. Care Quality Commission. Available at: http://www.cqc.org.uk/_db/_documents/QISC_Web%20pdf.pdf (accessed 14 January 2011).

Culley, L. and Hudson, N. (2009) 'Commonalities, differences and possibilities: culture and infertility in British South Asian communities', in L. Culley, N. Hudson and F. van Rooij (eds) *Marginalized Reproduction: Ethnicity, Infertility and New Reproductive Technologies*, London: Earthscan, pp 97–116.

Dabydeen, D., Gilmore, J. and Jones, C. (eds) (2010) *Oxford Companion to Black History*, Oxford: Oxford University Press.

Dale, A., Shaheen, N., Kalra, V. and Fieldhouse, E. (no date) 'The labour market prospects for Pakistani and Bangladeshi women', Working Paper 11. Available at: http://www.leeds.ac.uk/esrcfutureofwork/downloads/workingpaperdownloads/Paper11.pdf (accessed 5 March 2006).

Daniel, W.W. (1968) *Racial Discrimination in England*, Harmondsworth: Penguin.

Darr, A. (2009) 'Cousin marriage, cultural blaming and equity in service delivery', *Diversity in Health and Care*, vol 6, pp 7–9.

Das-Munshi, J., Bécares, L., Dewey, M., Stansfeld, S. and Prince, M. (2010) 'Understanding the effect of ethnic density on mental health: multi-level investigation on survey data from England', *British Medical Journal*, vol 341, c5367.

Davey-Smith, G., Bartley, M. and Blane, D. (1990) 'The Black Report on socioeconomic inequalities in health 10 years on', *British Medical Journal*, vol 301, pp 373–7.

Daycare Trust (2000) *Investing in Success*, London: Daycare Trust.

DCLG (Department for Communities and Local Government) (2008) *Face to Face and Side by Side: a Framework for Partnership in Our Multi Faith Society*, London: CLG Publications.

DCLG (2010) *Tackling Race Inequality: A Statement on Race*, London: Department for Communities and Local Government.

DCSF (Department for Children, Schools and Families) (2005) *Common Core of Skills and Knowledge for the Children's Workforce*, London: DCSF.

DCSF (2007a) *Aiming High for Young People: a Ten Year Strategy for Positive Activities*, London: DCSF.

DCSF (2007b) *The Children's Plan*, London: DCSF.

DCSF (2008a) *Youth Task Force Action Plan*, London: DCSF.

DCSF (2008b) *Building Brighter Futures: Next Steps for the Children's Workforce*, Nottingham: DCSF Publications.

DCSF (2009a) *Targeted Youth Support: Next Steps*, London: HMSO.

DCSF (2009b) *Key Stage 1 Attainment by Pupil Characteristics, England 2008/2009*, London: DCSF.

DCSF (2010) *Key Stage 4 Attainment by Pupil Characteristics, England 2008/09*, London: DCSF.

Dell, C.A. and Boe, R. (2000) *An Examination of Aboriginal and Caucasian Women Offender Risk and Needs Factors*, Ottawa: Research Branch, Correctional Services of Canada.

Denney, D. (1992) *Racism and Anti-Racism in Probation*, London: Routledge.

Department for Education (2010) *Permanent and Fixed Period Exclusions from Schools and Exclusion Appeals in England, 2008/2009*, London: Department of Education.

Dex, S. and Hawkes, D. (2004) 'Household structure and characteristics', in S. Dex and H. Joshi (eds) *Millennium Cohort Study First Survey: A User's Guide to Initial Findings, 22 to 23*, London: Centre for Longitudinal Studies.

DfEE (Department for Education and Employment) (1999) *Jobs for All*, London: DfEE.

DfEE (2001) *Employer Skills Survey*, London: DfEE.

DfES (Department for Education and Skills) (2003) *Aiming High: Improving the Achievement of Minority Ethnic Pupils*, London: DfES.

DfES (2004) 'Aiming high: guidance on supporting the education of asylum seeking and refugee children'. Available at: www.standards.dfes.gov.uk/ethnicminorities/links_and_publications/AH_Gdnc_AS_RFG_Apr04/asylumguidance.pdf

DfES (2006a) *Youth Matters: Next Steps*, London: DfES.

DfES (2006b) *Getting it. Getting it Right*, London: DfES.

DfES (2007) 'Curriculum review – diversity and citizenship'. Available at: http://publications.education.gov.uk/eOrderingDownload/DfES_Diversity_&_Citizenship.pdf (accessed 1 September 2010).

DH (Department of Health) (2002) *Women's Mental Health: Into the Mainstream*, London: Department of Health.

DH (2003) *Delivering Race Equality: A Framework for Action, Mental Health Services Consultation Document*, London: Department of Health.

DH (2005) *Delivering Race Equality in Mental Health Care: An Action Plan for Reform Inside and Outside Services and the Government's Response to the Independent Inquiry into the Death of David Bennett*, London: Department of Health.

DH (2006) 'Our health, our care, our say: a new direction for community services: A brief guide'. Available at: www.dh.gov.uk/en/Publicationsandstatistics/Publications/PublicationsPolicyAndGuidance/DH_4127602 (accessed 15 February 2011).

DH (2007a) 'Putting people first, a shared vision and commitment to the transformation of adult social care'. Available at: www.puttingpeoplefirst.org.uk/ (accessed 27 September 2010).

DH (2007b) 'Mapping the capacity and potential for user-led organisations in England: a summary of the main findings from a national research study commissioned by the Department of Health'. Available at: http://www.dh.gov.uk/en/Publicationsandstatistics/Publications/PublicationsPolicyAndGuidance/DH_078538 (accessed 1 October 2010).

DH (2007c) *User-Led Organisations Project Policy*, prepared by Social Care, Local Government & Care Partnerships Directorate, London: Department of Health.

DH (2007d) *Positive Steps: Supporting Race Equality in Mental Healthcare*, London: Department of Health.

DH (2009a) *Delivering Race Equality in Mental Health Care: a Review*, London: Department of Health.

DH (2009b) 'Transforming adult social care', LAC (DoH) 1, London: Department of Health.

Dobson, R.B. (1995) *Clifford's Tower and the Jewish People of Medieval York*, London: English Heritage.

Dominelli, L. (2004) *Social Work: Theory and Practice for a Changing Profession*, Cambridge: Polity Press.

Don't Trigger (2007) Don't Trigger campaign. Available at: www.dont-trigger.com/ (accessed 22 January 2011).

Dorling, D. (1995) *A New Social Atlas of Britain*, Chichester: Wiley.

Doyal, L., Hunt, G. and Mellor, J. (1980) *Migrant Workers in the NHS*, London: Polytechnic of North London.

Dressler, W.D. (1993) 'Health in the African American community: accounting for health inequalities', *Medical Anthropology Quarterly*, vol 7, no 4, pp 325–45.

DSS (Department of Social Security) (2001) *Family Resources Survey. Great Britain 1999–2000*, Leeds: Corporate Document Services.

Dustmann, C. and Fabbri, F. (2003) 'Language proficiency and labour market performance of immigrants in the UK', *The Economic Journal*, vol 113, no 489, pp 695–71.

Dustmann, C., Frattini, T. and Halls, C. (2009) *Assessing the Fiscal Costs and Benefits of A8 Migration to the UK*, CReAM Discussion Paper 18/09, London: Centre for Research and Analysis of Migration, pp 1–39.

DWP (Department for Work and Pensions) (2002a) 'New deal for young people and long-term unemployed people aged 25+: statistics to December 2001', *Statistics First Release*, February.

DWP (2002b) *Equality, Opportunity and Independence for All*, Race Equality Consultation Document, London: Department for Work and Pensions.

DWP (2003) *Realising Race Equality in the Department for Work and Pensions*, London: Department for Work and Pensions.

DWP (2009) *A Test for Racial Discrimination in Recruitment Practices in British Cities*, Research Report no 207, London: DWP.

Ecklund, E.H. (2005) '"Us" and "them": the role of religion in mediating and challenging the "model minority" and other civic boundaries', *Ethnic and Racial Studies*, vol 28, no 1, pp 132–50.

Edgar, B. (2004) *Policy Measures to Ensure Access to Decent Housing for Migrants and Ethnic Minorities*, Dundee/St Andrews: Joint University Centre for Scottish Research.

Edge, D. (2010) 'Perinatal mental health care for black and minority ethnic (BME) women: a scoping review of provision in England', *Ethnicity and Inequalities in Health and Social Care*, vol 3, no 3, pp 24–32.

Edwards, T. (2007) 'BME communities – increasing the uptake of direct payments. Local authority examples'. Available at: www.thinklocalactpersonal.org.uk/latest/index

EHRC (Equality and Human Rights Commission) (no date) 'Race Equality Duty'. Available at: www.equalityhumanrights.com/public-sector-duties/what-are-the-public-sector-duties/ (accessed 29 June 2010).

Eliaeson, S. (2002) *Max Weber's Methodologies*, Cambridge: Polity Press.

Ellison, G.T.H. and Rees Jones, I. (2002) 'Social identities and the "new genetics": scientific and social consequences', *Critical Public Health*, vol 12, pp 265–82.

Eltis, D. (2000) *The Rise of African Slavery in the Americas*, Hartford, CT: Yale University Press.

Eltis, D. and Richardson, P.D. (2010) *Atlas of the Slave Trade*, Hartford, CT: Yale University Press.

Ennelli, P., Modood, T. and Bradley, H. (2005) *Young Turks and Kurds*, York: Joseph Rowntree Foundation.

Equiano, O. (2007 [1789]) *The Interesting Narrative of the Life of Olaudah Equiano*, Harmondsworth: Penguin.

Erens, B., Primatesta, P. and Prior, G. (2001) *Health Survey for England 1999: the Health of Minority Ethnic Groups*, London: TSO.

Esmail, A. and Everington, S. (1993) 'Racial discrimination against doctors from ethnic minorities', *British Medical Journal*, vol 306, pp 691–2.

Essed, P. (1994) 'Making and breaking ethnic boundaries: women's studies, diversity, and racism', *Women's Studies Quarterly*, vol 22, nos 3/4, pp 232–49.

European Commission (2009) *Youth in Europe: A Statistical Portrait*, Luxembourg: European Union.

Evans, R.J. (2005) *The Third Reich in Power*, London: Allen Lane.

Evans, R. and Banton, M. (2001) *Learning from Experience: Involving Black Disabled People in Shaping Services*, Leamington Spa: Council of Disabled People.

Fanshawe, S. and Sriskanarajah, D. (2010) *You Can't Put Me in a Box: Super-Diversity and the End of Identity Politics in Britain*, London: Institute for Public Policy Research.

Feilzer, M. and Hood, R. (2004) *Differences or Discrimination: Minority Ethnic Young People in the Youth Justice System*, London: Youth Justice Board.

Feminist Review (1984) 'Many voices, one chant: black feminist perspectives', special issue, no 17.

Fenton, S. (2003) *Ethnicity*, Cambridge: Polity Press.

Ferguson, I. (2007) 'Increasing user choice or privatising risk? The antinomies of personalisation', *British Journal of Social Work*, vol 37, no 3, pp 387–403.

Fernando, S. (2003) *Cultural Diversity, Mental Health and Psychiatry: the Struggle Against Racism*, Hove: Brunner-Routledge.

Fernando, S. (2006) 'Stigma, racism and power', *Ethnic Network Journal*, vol 1, no 1, pp 24–8.

Fernando, S. and Keating, F. (2009a) 'The way ahead', in S. Fernando and F. Keating (eds) *Mental Health in a Multi-Ethnic Society: a Multidisciplinary Handbook*, London: Routledge, pp 235–58.

Fernando, S. and Keating, F. (eds) (2009b) *Mental Health in a Multi-Ethnic Society: A Multidisciplinary Handbook*, London: Routledge.

Find Your Talent (2009–11), www.findyourtalent.org/ (accessed 22 January 2011).

Fink, S. (2002) 'International efforts spotlight traditional, complementary, and alternative medicine', *American Journal of Public Health*, vol 92, no 10, pp 1734–9.

Finney, N. and Simpson, L. (2009) *'Sleepwalking to Segregation'? Challenging Myths about Race and Migration*, Bristol: The Policy Press.

Fitzgerald, M. and Sibbitt, R. (1997) *Ethnic Monitoring in Police Forces: a Beginning*, London: Home Office.

Forrest, R. and Kearns, A. (2000) 'Social cohesion, social capital and the neighbourhood', Paper presented to ESRC Cities Programme Neighbourhood Colloquium, Liverpool.

Foucault, M. (1983) *The Order of Things: An Archaeology of the Human Sciences*, London: Routledge.

Foucault, M. (2002) *Archaeology of Knowledge*, London: Routledge.

Fountain, J. and Hicks, J. (2010) *Delivering Race Equality in Mental Health Care: Report on the Findings and Outcomes of the Community Engagement Programme 2005–2008*, Preston: University of Central Lancashire.

Fryer, P. (1984) *Staying Power*, London: Pluto Press.

Future Shape of the Sector Commission (2006) *Working Brief*, London: London and Quadrant.

Gaskell, G. (1986) 'Black youth and the police', *Policing*, vol 2, no 1, pp 26–34.

Gaskell, G. and Smith, P. (1985) 'Young blacks' hostility to the police: an investigation into its causes', *New Community*, vol 12, no 1, pp 66–74.

Gelsthorpe, L. (2006) 'The experiences of female minority ethnic offenders: the other "other"', in S. Lewis, P. Raynor, D. Smith and A. Wardak (eds) *Race and Probation*, Cullompton: Willan.

Gelsthorpe, L. and Sharpe, G. (2006) 'Gender, youth and justice', in B. Goldson and J. Muncie (eds) *Youth Crime and Justice*, London: Sage, pp 47–61.

Gervais, M. and Rehman, H. (2005) *Causes of Homelessness amongst Ethnic Minority Population*, London: CLG.

Gill, A. and Banga, B. (2009) *Black Minority Ethnic and Refugee Women, Domestic Violence and Access to Housing*, Better Housing Briefing Paper 9, London: Race Equality Foundation.

Gillborn, D. (1990) *'Race', Ethnicity and Education*, London: Unwin Hyman.

Gillborn, D. (2008) *Racism and Education – Coincidence or Conspiracy*, Routledge: Abingdon.

Gillborn, D. and Mirza, H. (2000) *Educational Inequality: Mapping Race, Class and Gender*, London: Institute of Education.

Gilroy, P. (1992) *There Ain't No Black in the Union Jack*, London: Routledge.

Gilroy, P. (2007) *Black Britain: a Photographic History*, London: Saqi Books.

Gilvarry, C.M., Walsh, E., Samele, C., Hutchinson, G., Mallet, R., Rabe-Hesket, S., Fahy, T., van Os, J. and Murray, R.M. (1999) 'Life events, ethnicity and perceptions of discrimination in patients with severe mental illness', *Social Psychiatry and Psychiatric Epidemiology*, vol 34, no 11, pp 600–8.

Glasby, J. and Littlechild, R. (2002) *Social Work and Direct Payments*, Bristol: The Policy Press.

Glasgow, D. (1980) *The Black Underclass*. London: Jossey Bass.

Glasgow Anti-Stigma Partnership (2007) 'Mosaics of meaning: full report. Exploring stigma and discrimination towards mental health problems with black and minority ethnic communities in Glasgow'. Available at: www.seemescotland.org (accessed 23 May 2011).

Glendenning, L. (2006) 'Citizenship guide fails its history exam', *The Guardian*. Available at: www.guardian.co.uk/immigration/story/0,,1764292,00.html (accessed 13 June 2010).

Glendinning, C., Challis, D., Fernández, J.L., Jacobs, S., Jones, K., Knapp, M., Manthorpe, J., Moran, N., Netten, A., Stevens, M. and Wilberforce, M. (2008) *Evaluation of the Individual Budgets Pilot Programme, Summary Report*, York: Social Policy Research Unit.

GMP (Greater Manchester Police) (2004) 'Xcalibre'. Available at: www.gmp.police.uk/xcalibre (accessed 23 January 2011).

GMP (2008) 'Operation Cougar'. Available at: www.gmp.police.uk/live/mainsite.nsf/9ff3beb1e031a4258025709e004315a1/8A2EECECD112BCA88025759B00552D16 (accessed 23 January 2011).

Goodson, L. and Beider, H. (2006) *Black and Minority Ethnic Communities in the Eastern Corridor*, Birmingham: Birmingham City Council.

Gouldbourne, H. (1998) *Race Relations in Britain since 1945*, London: Macmillan Press.

Government Equalities Office (2010) 'Equality Act 2010'. Available at: www.equalities.gov.uk/equality_bill.aspx (accessed 29 December 2010).

Government Office for London (2007) *Indices of Deprivation*, London: Corporate Information and Analysis Team, Government Office for London.

Greater London Action on Disability (1991) '"Race and disability": a dialogue for action', Conference report of a two-day event for services users and providers, May. Available at: www.leeds.ac.uk/disability-studies/archiveuk/GLAD/a%20dialogue%20for%20action%20-%20conf%20report.pdf (accessed 14 January 2011).

Griffin, C. (1985) *Typically Girls?*, London: Routledge.

Guardian (2003) 'Born everywhere and raised in Britain', Special Supplement, 18 October.

Gunaratnam, Y. (1997) 'Culture is not enough: a critique of multiculturalism in palliative care', in D. Field, J. Hockey and N. Small (eds) *Death, Gender and Ethnicity*, London: Routledge, pp 166–86.

Gunaratnam, Y. (2008a) 'Care, artistry and what might be', *Ethnicity and Inequalities in Health and Social Care*, vol 1, no 1, pp 9–17.

Gunaratnam, Y. (2008b) 'From competence of vulnerability: care, ethics and elders from racialized minorities', *Mortality*, vol 13, no 1, pp 24–41.

Gunter, A. (2010) *Growing up Bad? Black Youth, 'Road' Culture and Badness in an East London Neighbourhood*, London: The Tufnell Press.

Hall, S. (1992) 'New ethnicities', in J. Donald and A. Rattansi (eds) *Race, Culture and Difference*, London: Sage.

Hall, S. (1996) 'Introduction: who needs identity', in S. Hall and P. du Gay (eds) *Questions of Cultural Identity*, London: Sage, pp 1–7.

Hall, S., Critcher, C., Jefferson, T., Clarke, J. and Roberts, B. (1978) *Policing the Crisis: Mugging, the State and Law and Order*, London: Macmillan Press.

Halpern, D. and Nazroo, J. (2000) 'The ethnic density effect: results from a national community survey of England and Wales', *The International Journal of Social Psychiatry*, vol 46, no 1, pp 34–46.

Hamlin, C. (2009) *Cholera: The Biography*, Oxford: Oxford University Press.

Hansen, K. (2007) *Millennium Cohort Study Second Survey: A User's Guide to Initial Findings*, London: Centre for Longitudinal Studies.

Hansen, R. (1999) 'The Kenyan Asians, British Politics, and the Commonwealth Immigrants Act, 1968', *The Historical Journal*, vol 42, no 3, pp 809–34.

Harris, R., Tobias, M., Jeffreys, M., Waldegrave, K., Karlsen, S. and Nazroo, J. (2006) 'Racism and health: the relationship between experience of racial discrimination and health in New Zealand', *Social Science and Medicine*, vol 63, pp 1428–41.

Harrison, M. (1995) *Housing, 'Race', Social Policy and Empowerment*, Aldershot: Avebury.

Harrison, M., with Davis, C. (2001) *Housing, Social Policy and Difference: Disability, Gender, Ethnicity and Housing*, Bristol: The Policy Press.

Harrison, M., with Phillips, D. (2003) *Housing and Black and Minority Ethnic Communities: Review of the Evidence Base*, London: Office of the Deputy Prime Minister.

Hasluck, C. and Green, A.E. (2007) *What Works for Whom? A Review of Evidence and Meta-Analysis for the Department for Work and Pensions*, Research Report no 407, London: DWP.

Hatton, T.J. and Wheatley-Price, S. (1998) *Migration, Migrants and Policy in the United Kingdom*, Centre for Economic Policy Research Discussion Paper No 1960, London: CEPR.

Hawes, D. and Perez, B. (1995) *The Gypsy and the State: the Ethnic Cleansing of British Society*, Bristol: SAUS Publications.

HC (House of Commons Home Affairs Committee) (2007) *Young Black People and the Criminal Justice System*, Second Report of Session 2006–07, vol 1, House of Commons Home Affairs Committee, London: HMSO.

Healthcare Commission (2005) *Count Me In: Results of a National Census of Inpatients in Mental Health Hospitals and Facilities in England and Wales*, London: Healthcare Commission.

Healthcare Commission (2007) *Count Me In: Results of the 2006 National Census of Inpatients in Mental Health Hospitals and Facilities in England and Wales*, London: Healthcare Commission.

Healthcare Commission (2009) *Tackling the Challenge: Promoting Race Equality in the NHS in England*, London: Healthcare Commission.

Heath, A. and McMahon, D. (1997) 'Education and occupational attainments: the impact of ethnic origins', in V. Karn (ed) *Ethnicity in the 1991 Census. Volume Four: Employment, Education and Housing among the Ethnic Minority Populations of Britain*, London: TSO.

Heath, A., McMahon, D. and Roberts, J. (2000) 'Ethnic differences in the labour market: a comparison of the samples of anonymised records and Labour Force Survey', *Journal of the Royal Statistical Society, Series A – Statistics in Society*, vol 163, no 3, pp 341–61.

Hedderman, C. (2004) 'The "criminogenic" needs of women offenders', in G. McIvor (ed) *Women Who Offend*, London: Jessica Kingsley.

Heffernan, K. (2006) 'Social work, new public management and the language of "service user"', *British Journal of Social Work*, vol 36, no 1, pp 139–47.

Hemmerman, L., Law, I., Simms, J. and Sirriyeh, A. (2007) *Situating Racist Hostility and Understanding the Impact of Racist Victimisation in Leeds*, Leeds: Centre for Ethnicity and Racism Studies.

Henderson, P. and Kaur, R. (1999) *Rural Racism*, London: CDF/SIA.

Henwood, M. and Hudson, B. (2007) 'The Independent Living Funds – what does the future hold?', *Journal of Integrated Care*, vol 15, no 4, pp 36–42.

Herald Scotland (2010) 'Coalition must heed student visa warning'. Available at: www.heraldscotland.com/mobile/comment/herald-view/coalition-must-heed-student-visa-warning-1.1060628 (accessed 30 May 2011).

Hero, D. (1991) *Black British, White British: A History of Race Relations in Britain*, London: Grafton.

Hickman, M., Crowley, H. and Mai, N. (2008) *Immigration and Social Cohesion in the UK*, York: Joseph Rowntree Foundation.

Hill, A. (2010) 'Gypsies prepare to fight government housing policy', *The Guardian*, 8 June. Available at: www.guardian.co.uk/society/2010/jun/08/gypsy-traveller-housing-government-backlash

Hills, J. (2010) *An Anatomy of Economic Inequality in the UK*, London: National Equalities Office.

HM Government (2007) *The Government's Response to the House of Commons Home Affairs Select Committee Report: Young Black People and the Criminal Justice System*, London: TSO.

HM Government (2008a) *Home Affairs Select Committee Inquiry: Young Black People and the Criminal Justice System*, First Annual Report, London: HMSO.

HM Government (2008b) *Youth Crime Action Plan 2008*, London: HMSO.

HM Government (2008c) *The Prevent Strategy*, London: HMSO.

HM Government (2009) *Home Affairs Select Committee Inquiry: Young Black People and the Criminal Justice System*, Second Annual Report, London: TSO.

HM Treasury (2008) *Ending Child Poverty: Everybody's Business*, London: HM Treasury.

Hobson, J. (2008) 'Sickle cell disease is spreading through the UK', *The Times*, 22 September.

Holland, M., Gill, G. and Burrell, S. (2009) *Cholera and Conflict*, Leeds: Medical Museum Press.

Home Office (1997a) 'No more excuses – a new approach to tackling youth crime in England and Wales'. Available at: www.nationalarchives.gov.uk/ERORecords/HO/421/2/cpd/jou/nme.htm (accessed 21 November 2010).

Home Office (1997b) 'Preventing children offending: a consultative document'. Available at: www.nationalarchives.gov.uk/ERORecords/HO/421/2/cpd/jou/prev1.htm (accessed 22 November 2010).

Home Office (1997c) *Tackling Youth Crime*, London: Home Office.

Home Office (2001a) *Building Cohesive Communities*, London: Home Office.

Home Office (2001b) *Community Cohesion: A Report of the Independent Reviewing Team*, London: Home Office.

Home Office (2002) *Shootings, Gangs and Violent Incidents in Manchester*, Crime Reduction Research Series Paper 13, London: HMSO.

Home Office (2003) *Every Child Matters*, London: HMSO.

Home Office (2004) *Strength in Diversity: Towards a Community Cohesion and Race Equality Strategy*, London: Home Office.

Home Office (2005a) *Improving Opportunity, Strengthening Society: The Government's Strategy to Increase Race Equality and Community Cohesion*, London: Home Office.

Home Office (2005b) *Minority Ethnic Groups and Crime: Findings from the Offending, Crime and Justice Survey 2003* (2nd edn), Home Office Online Report 33/05, London: HMSO.

Home Office (2006) *Young People and Crime: Findings from the 2005 Offending, Crime and Justice Survey*, London: HMSO.

Home Office (2009) *Engaging Communities in Criminal Justice*, London: HMSO.

Hopkins, P. (2004) 'Everyday racism in Scotland: a case study of East Pollockshields', *Scottish Affairs*, No 49. Available at: www.scottishaffairs. org/backiss/pdfs/sa49/sa49_Hopkins.pdf

Hoque, K. and Noon, M. (1999) 'Racial discrimination in speculative applications: new optimism six years on?', *Human Resource Management Journal*, vol 9, no 3, pp 71–83.

Housing Corporation (1992) *An Independent Future: Black and Minority Ethnic Housing Association Strategy 1992–1996*, London: Housing Corporation.

Housing Corporation (1998) *Black and Minority Ethnic Housing Policy*, London: Housing Corporation.

Housing Corporation (2002) *Regulatory Code Good Practice Note*, London: Housing Corporation.

Housing Corporation (2004a) *BME Association Rent Restructuring Grant Announced*, London: Housing Corporation.

Housing Corporation (2004b) *Regulatory Code Good Practice Note*, London: Housing Corporation.

Huang, S. and Spurgeon, A. (2006) 'The mental health of Chinese immigrants in Birmingham, UK', *Ethnicity and Health*, vol 11, no 14, pp 365–87.

Hubbuck, J. and Carter, S. (1980) *Half a Chance? A Report on Job Discrimination against Young Blacks in Nottingham*, London: CRE.

Hunt, I.M., Robinson, J., Bickley, H., Meehan, J., Parsons, R., McCann, K., Flynn, S., Burns, J., Shaw, J., Kapur, N. and Appleby, L. (2003) 'Suicides in ethnic minorities within 12 months of contact with mental health services: national clinical survey', *The British Journal of Psychiatry*, vol 183, pp 156–60.

Huntington, S. (1996) *The Clash of Civilisations and the Remaking of World Order*, New York: Simon and Schuster.

Hurcombe, R., Bayley, R. and Goodman, A. (2010) *Ethnicity and Alcohol: A Review of the UK Literature*, York: Joseph Rowntree Foundation.

Hussain, Y., Atkin, K. and Ahmad, W. (2002) *South Asian Disabled Young People and Their Families*, Bristol: The Policy Press.

Hutson, S. and Liddiard, M. (1994) *Youth Homelessness: The Construction of a Social Issue*, London: Macmillan.

ICoCo (Institute of Community Cohesion) (2009) *Prospectus*, Coventry: Institute of Community Cohesion.

IFF Research (2008) *Employment Aspects and Workforce Implications of Direct Payments*, Leeds: Skills for Care.

Information Centre (2008) *National Diabetes Audit: Key Findings about the Quality of Care for Children and Young People with Diabetes in England and Wales*, London: The Information Centre.

Inhorn, M.C. (2006) 'Making Muslim babies: IVF and gamete donation in Sunni versus Shi'a Islam', *Culture, Medicine and Psychiatry*, vol 30, pp 427–50.

IPPR (Institute for Public Policy Research) (2007) *Britain's Immigrants: An Economic Profile*, London: IPPR.

IPPR (2010) *Recession Leaves Half Young Black People Unemployed*, London: IPPR.

IRR (Institute of Race Relations) (2010) 'Defend the remaining travelling Gypsies and Travellers, and Showmen', 3 June. Available at: www.irr.org.uk/2010/june/ha000019.html

It Doesn't Have to Happen (2008), www.bebo.com/itdoesnthavetohappen (accessed 22 January 2011).

Jackson, P.I. (2010) 'Race, crime and criminal justice in France', in A. Kalunta-Crumpton (ed) *Race, Crime and Criminal Justice: International Perspectives*, Basingstoke: Palgrave, pp 51–71.

James, L. (2005) *The Rise and Fall of the British Empire*, London: Abacus.

Jan-Khan, M. (2003) 'The right to riot', *Community Development Journal*, vol 38, pp 32–42.

Jansson, K. (2006) *Black and Minority Ethnic Groups' Experiences and Perceptions of Crime, Racially Motivated Crime and the Police: Findings from the 2004/05 British Crime Survey*, London: Home Office.

Jayaweera, H. and Choudhury, T. (2008) *Immigration, Faith and Cohesion*, York: Joseph Rowntree Foundation.

Johnston, P. (2007) 'Brown's manifesto for Britishness', *The Daily Telegraph*, 13 January. Available at: www.telegraph.co.uk/news/uknews/1539369/Browns-manifesto-for-Britishness.html

Jones, A. (2009) *Monitoring the Ethnicity of Housing Service Users: Forty Years of Progress?*, Better Housing Briefing Paper 15, London: Race Equality Foundation.

Jones, A. (2010) *Black and Minority Ethnic Communities' Experience of Overcrowding*, Better Housing Briefing Paper 16, London: Race Equality Foundation.

Jones, M. and Tracy, I. (2010) *Ethnic Minorities' Experiences of Claiming Disability Benefit*, Research Report no 609, London: Department of Work and Pensions.

Jones, P.A. and Mullins, A. (2009) *Refugee Community Organisations: Working in Partnership to Improve Access to Housing Services*, Better Housing Briefing Paper no 12, London: Race Equality Foundation.

Jones, T. (1993) *Britain's Ethnic Minorities*, London: Policy Studies Institute.

Judd, D. (1996) *Empire: The British Imperial Experience from 1765 to the Present*, London: Harper Collins.

JUST (2009) *Evidence to the Home Office Select Committee on the Preventing Extremism Agenda*, Bradford: JUST West Yorkshire.

Kalunta-Crumpton, A. (ed) (2010) *Race, Crime and Criminal Justice: International Perspectives*, Basingstoke: Palgrave

Karlsen, S. (2006) 'A quantitative and qualitative exploration of the processes associated with ethnic identification', PhD dissertation, Department of Epidemiology and Public Health, University College London.

Karlsen, S. (2007a) *Ethnic Inequalities in Health: The Impact of Racism*, Better Health Briefing Paper no 3, London: Race Equality Foundation.

Karlsen, S. (2007b) '"I felt like I was the same as everybody else but then I was being treated differently": Recognising the impact of others on ethnic identification'. Available at: www.ssrg.org.uk/events/2007.asp (accessed 11 August 2010).

Karlsen, S. and Nazroo, J. (2002a) 'The relationship between racial discrimination, social class and health among minority ethnic groups', *American Journal of Public Health*, vol 92, no 4, pp 624–31.

Karlsen, S. and Nazroo, J.Y. (2002b) 'Agency and structure: the impact of ethnic identity and racism on the health of minority ethnic people', *Sociology of Health and Illness*, vol 24, no 1, pp 1–20.

Karlsen, S. and Nazroo, J.Y. (2004) 'Fear of racism and health', *Journal of Epidemiology and Community Health*, vol 58, no 12, pp 1017–18.

Karlsen, S. and Nazroo, J.Y. (2006) 'Defining and measuring ethnicity and "race": theoretical and conceptual issues for health and social care research', in J.Y. Nazroo (ed) *Health and Social Research in Multi-Ethnic Societies*, Oxford: Routledge.

Karlsen, S. and Nazroo, J.Y. (2010) 'Religious and ethnic differences in health: evidence from the Health Surveys for England 1999 and 2004', *Ethnicity and Health*, vol 15, no 6, pp 549–68.

Karlsen, S., Nazroo, J.Y., McKenzie, K., Bhui, K. and Weich, S. (2005) 'Racism, psychosis and common mental disorder among minority ethnic groups in England', *Psychological Medicine*, vol 35, no 12, pp 1795–1803.

Karlsen, S., Millward, D. and Sandford, A. (2011) 'Investigating ethnic differences in current cigarette smoking over time using the Health Surveys for England', *European Journal of Public Health*, in press.

Karn, V. (ed) (1997) *Ethnicity in the 1991 Census, Volume 4: Employment, Education and Housing among Ethnic Minority Populations in Britain*, London: ONS.

Kaufman, J.S., Cooper, R.S. and McGee, D.L. (1997) 'Socioeconomic status and health in blacks and whites: the problem of residual confounding and the resiliency of race', *Epidemiology*, vol 8, pp 621–8.

Kaufman, J.S., Long, A.E., Liao, Y., Cooper, R.S. and McGee, D.L. (1998) 'The relation between income and mortality in US blacks and whites', *Epidemiology*, vol 9, no 2, pp 147–55.

Keating, F. (2007) *African and Caribbean Men and Mental Health*, Better Health Briefing Paper no 5, London: Race Equality Foundation.

Keating, F. and Robertson, D. (2004) 'Fear, black people and mental illness: a vicious circle?', *Health and Social Care in the Community*, vol 12, no 5, pp 439–47.

Keating, F., Robertson, D., Francis, F. and McCulloch, A. (2002) *Breaking the Circles of Fear: A Review of the Relationship between Mental Health Services and African and Caribbean Communities*, London: The Sainsbury Centre for Mental Health.

Keay, J. (2004) *India: A History*, London: Harper Collins.

Keith, M. (1993) *Race, Riots and Policing: Lore and Disorder in a Multi-racist Society*, London: UCL.

Kelleher, D. (1996) 'A defence of the use of the terms "ethnicity" and "culture"', in D. Kelleher and S. Hillier (eds) *Researching Cultural Differences in Health*, London: Routledge.

Kelly, Y.M. (2004) 'Pregnancy, labour and delivery', *Millennium Cohort Study First Survey: A User's Guide to Initial Findings*, 77, London: Centre for Longitudinal Studies.

Kelly, Y. (2007) 'The health of infants at the beginning of the twenty-first century', in E. Garrett, C. Galley, N. Shelton and R.I. Woods (eds) *Infant Mortality: A Continuing Social Problem*, Aldershot: Ashgate.

Kelly, Y., Sacker, A., Schoon, I. and Nazroo, J. (2006) 'Ethnic differences in achievement of developmental milestones by 9 months of age', *Developmental Medicine and Child Neurology*, vol 48, pp 825–30.

Kelly, Y., Panico, L., Bartley, M. and Marmot, M. (2008) 'Why does birthweight vary among ethnic groups in the UK? Findings from the Millennium Cohort Study', *Journal of Public Health*, vol 31, pp 131–7.

Kennett, P. (1999) 'Homelessness, citizenship and social exclusion', in P. Kennet and A. Marsh (eds) *Homelessness: Exploring the New Terrain*, Bristol: The Policy Press.

Kerr, A. and Cunningham-Burley, S. (2000) 'On ambivalence and risk: reflexive modernity and the new human genetics', *Sociology*, vol 34, no 2, pp 283–304.

Keter, V. and Beale, E. (2005) 'Employment Tribunals (Representation and Assistance in Discrimination Proceedings) Bill'. House of Commons Library. Research Paper 05/59, 26 August. Available at: www.parliament.uk/commons/lib/research/rp2005/rp05-059.pdf (accessed 2 December 2010).

Kickz (2006) Official website of the Premier League, www.premierleague.com/page/Kickz (accessed 23 January 2011).

Kiddle, C. (1999) *Traveller Children: A Voice for Themselves*, London: Jessica Kingsley.

Kim-Godwin, Y.S., Clarke, P.N. and Barton, L. (2001) 'A model for the delivery of culturally competent community care', *Journal of Advanced Nursing*, vol 35, no 6, pp 918–25.

Kinnvall, C. (2002) 'Nationalism, religion and the search for chosen traumas: comparing Sikh and Hindu identity constructions', *Ethnicities*, vol 2, no 1, pp 79–106.

Kirkbride, J.B., Barker, D., Cowden, F., Stamp, R., Yang, M., Jones, P.B. and Coid, J.W. (2008) 'Psychosis, ethnicity and socio-economic status', *The British Journal of Psychiatry*, vol 193, pp 18–24.

Knifton, L., Gervais, M., Newbigging, K., Mirza, N., Quinn, N., Wilson, N. and Hunkins-Hutchinson, E. (2010) 'Community conversation: addressing mental health stigma with ethnic minority communities', *Social Psychiatry and Psychiatric Epidemiology*, vol 45, no 4, pp 497–504.

Knowles, C. (1999) 'Race, identities and lives', *The Sociological Review*, vol 47, no 1, pp 110-35.

Koshy, S. (2008) 'Introduction', in S. Koshy and R. Radhakrishnan (eds) *Transnational South Asians: The Making of a Neo-Diaspora*, India: Oxford University Press, pp 1–44.

Kotecha, N. (2009) 'Black and minority ethnic women', in S. Fernando and F. Keating (eds) *Mental Health in a Multi-Ethnic Society: A Multidisciplinary Handbook*, London: Routledge, pp 58–71.

Kowalczewski, P.S. (1982) 'Race and education: racism, diversity and inequality, implications for multicultural education', *Oxford Review of Education*, vol 8, no 2, pp 145–61.

Krieger, N. (2000) 'Discrimination and health', in L. Berkman and I. Kawachi (eds) *Social Epidemiology*, Oxford: Oxford University Press.

Krieger, N., Rowley, D.L., Herman, A.A., Avery, B. and Philips, M.T. (1993) 'Racism, sexism and social class: implications for studies of health, disease and wellbeing', *American Journal of Preventive Medicine*, vol 9 (supplement 2), pp 82–122.

Kumar, K. (2008) 'Core ethnicities and the problem of multiculturalism: the British case', in J. Eade, M. Barrett, C. Flood and R. Race (eds) *Advancing Multiculturalism, Post 7/7*, Newcastle: Cambridge Scholars Publishing, pp 116–34.

Kuper, A. (2002) 'Incest, cousin marriage and the origin of human sciences in nineteenth century England', *The Past and Present Society*, vol 174, pp 158–83.

Kyambi, S. (2005) *Beyond Black and White*, London: IPPR.

Kymlicka, W. (2001) *Politics in the Vernacular: Nationalism, Multiculturalism and Citizenship*, Oxford: Oxford University Press.

Kynaston, D. (2008) *Austerity Britain, 1945–1951: Tales of a New Jerusalem*, London: Bloomsbury.

Lakey, J. (1997) 'Neighbourhoods and housing', in T. Modood and R. Berthoud, with J. Lakey, J. Nazroo, P. Smith, S. Virdee and S. Beishon (eds) *Ethnic Minorities in Britain: Diversity and Disadvantage*, London: Policy Studies Institute.

Laming, Lord (2003) *Report of an Inquiry into the death of Victoria Climbié*, Cm 5730, London: The Stationery Office.

Laming, Lord (2009) *The Protection of Children in England: A Progress Report*, London: The Stationery Office.

Lane, J. (2008) *Young Children and Racial Justice*, London: National Children's Bureau.

Law, I. (1997) 'Modernity, anti-racism and ethnic managerialism', *Policy Studies*, vol 18, nos 3/4, pp 189–206.

Law, I. (2003) *Race, Ethnicity and Social Policy*, Hemel Hempstead: Prentice Hall.

Law, I. (2005) *Racism, Ethnicity and Social Policy* (2nd edn), Hemel Hempstead: Prentice Hall.

Law, I. (2007) *Housing Choice and Racist Hostility*, Better Housing Briefing Paper no 4, London: Race Equality Foundation.

Law, I. (2009) 'Racism, ethnicity and migration', in J. Millar (ed) *Understanding Social Security*, Bristol: The Policy Press.

Law, I. (2010) 'Migration, ethnicity and racism: frameworks and formations', in I. Law (ed) *Racism and Ethnicity, Global Debates, Dilemmas, Directions*, London: Pearson, pp 121–5.

Law, I. and Swann, S. (2011) *Ethnicity and Education in England and Europe, Gangstas, Geeks and Gorjas*, Aldershot: Ashgate.

Lawrence, E. (1982) 'In the abundance of water the fool is thirsty: sociology and black "pathology"', in CCCS (ed) *The Empire Strikes Back*, London: Hutchinson, pp 95–142.

Lea, J. (2003) 'From Brixton to Bradford: ideology and discourse on race and urban violence in the United Kingdom'. Available at: www.bunker8. pwp.blueyonder.co.uk/misc/riots.htm (accessed 8 November 2010).

Lea, J. and Young, J. (1993) *What is to be Done about Law and Order?* (rev edn), London: Pluto.

Leslie, D. and Lindley, J. (2001) 'The impact of language ability on employment and earnings of Britain's ethnic communities', *Economica*, vol 68, no 272, pp 587–606.

Lester, A. (2009) 'Multiculturalism and free speech', Speech at De Montfort University, 10 June. Available at: www.blackstonechambers.com/news/publications/multiculturalism.html

Levy, A. (2007) *Small Island*, Harmondsworth: Penguin.

Lewis, G. (2007) *The Confidential Enquiry into Maternal and Child Health (CEMACH). Saving Mothers' Lives: Reviewing Maternal Deaths to Make Motherhood Safer – 2003–2005*, London: CEMACH.

Lewis, H. (2007) *Destitution in Leeds*, York: Joseph Rowntree Charitable Trust.

Lewis, H. and Craig, G. (2010) 'Exclusion and assimilation: the lot of Britain's ethnic minorities', Paper presented to symposium on International Multiculturalism, Deakin University, Melbourne, 25–26 November.

Lewis, H., Craig, G., Adamson, S. and Wilkinson, M. (2009) *Refugees, Asylum Seekers and Migrants in Yorkshire and Humber*, Leeds: Yorkshire Futures.

LGA (Local Government Association) (2002) *Guidance on Community Cohesion*, London: Local Government Association.

Lindley, J. (2002) 'Race or religion? The impact of religion on the employment and earnings of Britain's ethnic communities', *Journal of Ethnic and Migration Studies*, vol 28, no 3 (July), pp 427–42.

Lindley, J. (2005) 'Explaining ethnic unemployment and activity rates: evidence from the QLFS in the 1990s and 2000s', *Bulletin of Economic Research*, vol 57, p 2.

Lindsay, G., Pather, S. and Strand, S. (2006) *Special Educational Needs and Ethnicity: Issues of Over- and Under-Representation*, Coventry: University of Warwick/DCSF.

Lloyd, C. (2009) *2007–08 Citizenship Survey: Identity and Values Topic Report*, London: Department for Communities and Local Government.

Lloyd, N. and Rafferty, A. (2006) *Black and Minority Ethnic Families and Sure Start: Findings from Local Evaluation Reports*, London: NESS.

Llwyd, A. (2004) *Cymru Ddu*, Cardiff: Butetown History and Arts Centre.

Lo, M.M. and Stacey, C.L. (2008) 'Beyond cultural competence: Bourdieu, patients and clinical encounters', *Sociology of Health and Illness*, vol 30, no 5, pp 741–55.

Loader, I. (1996) *Youth, Policing and Democracy*, London: Macmillan.

Longhi, S. and Platt, L. (2008) *Pay Gaps across Equalities Areas*, London: Equality and Human Rights Commission.

Low Pay Commission (2007) *National Minimum Wage*, Cm 7056, London: The Stationery Office.

Lupton, R. and Power, A. (2004) *Ethnic Minority Groups in Britain*, CASE–Brookings Census Briefs, London: LSE.

Lynch, J.P. and Simon, R.J. (1999) 'A comparative assessment of criminal involvement among immigrants and natives across seven nations', *International Criminal Justice Review*, vol 9, pp 1–17.

Maan, B. (2004) *The New Scots*, Glasgow: John Donald.

MacEwen, M., Dalton, M. and Murie, A. (1994) *Race and Housing in Scotland: A Literature Review and Bibliography*, Edinburgh: Edinburgh College of Art/Heriot Watt University.

Machin, S., Murphy, R. and Soobedar, Z. (2009) *Differences in the Labour Market Gains from Higher Education Participation*, London: LSE.

Macinnes, T., Kenway, P. and Parekh, A. (2009) *Monitoring Poverty and Social Exclusion*, York: Joseph Rowntree Foundation.

Mackenzie, E., Taylor, L., Bloom, B., Hufford, D. and Johnson, J. (2003) 'Minority ethnic use of complementary and alternative medicine (CAM): a national probability survey of CAM utilizers', *Alternative Therapies in Health and Medicine*, vol 9, no 4, pp 50–6.

Macneil, M., Stradling, R. and Clark, A. (2005) *Promoting the Health and Wellbeing of Gypsy/Travellers in Highland*, Scotland: Highland Council.

Macpherson, W. (1999) *Stephen Lawrence Inquiry: Report of an Inquiry by Sir William Macpherson of Cluny*, Cm 4262-I, London: The Stationery Office.

Mail Online (2007) 'Immigrants from war-torn countries fuelling gang crime', *Mail Online*. Available at: www.dailymail.co.uk/news/article-451995/Immigrants-war-torn-countries-fuelling-gang-crime.html (accessed 8 January 2011).

Malloch, M.S. and Stanley, E. (2005) 'The detention of asylum seekers in the UK: representing risk, managing the dangerous', *Punishment and Society*, vol 7, no 1, pp 53–71.

Mama, A. (1984) 'Black women, the economic crisis and the British state', *Feminist Review*, no 17, pp 21–35.

Markkanen, S. (2009) *Looking to the Future: Changing Black and Minority Ethnic Housing Needs and Aspirations*, Better Housing Briefing Paper no 11, London: Race Equality Foundation.

Marmot, M.G., Shipley, M.J. and Rose, G. (1984) 'Inequalities in death – specific explanations of a general pattern?', *The Lancet*, vol 1, pp 1003–6.

Marmot Review (2010) *Fair Society, Healthy Lives: Strategic Review of Health Inequalities in England Post-2010*. Available at: www.instituteofhealthequity. org/Content/FileManager/pdf/fairsocietyhealthylives.pdf

Martin, R. (2010) 'Forced sterilisation: a western issue too'. *The Guardian*. Available at: www.guardian.co.uk/commentisfree/libertycentral/2010/may/04/forced-sterilisation-women-motherhood (accessed 4 May 2010).

Matheson, J. (2009) 'National statistician's annual article on the population: a demographic review', in ONS (Office for National Statistics), *Population Trends 138*, London: ONS, p 9.

Matras, Y. (no date) 'Romani linguistics and Romani language projects'. Available at: at http://romani.humanities.manchester.ac.uk (accessed 10 April 2008).

Matthews, Z. (2008) *The Health of Gypsies and Travellers in the UK*, Better Health Briefing No 18, London: Race Equality Foundation.

Matthews, R. and Young, J. (eds) (1992) *Issues in Realist Criminology*, London: Sage.

Mawhinney, P. (2010) *Seeking Sound Advice, Financial Inclusion and Ethnicity*, London: Runnymede Trust.

Mayall, D. (1995) *English Gypsies and State Policies*, Hatfield: University of Hertfordshire Press.

Maylor, U., Glass, K., Issa, T., Abol Kuyok, K., Minty, S., Rose, A., Ross, A., Tanner, E., Finch, S., Low, N., Taylor, E., Tipping, S. and Purdon, S. (2010) *Impact of Supplementary Schools on Pupils' Attainment: An Investigation into What Factors Contribute to Educational Improvements*, London: DCSF.

Mazower, M. (1998) *Dark Continent: Europe's Twentieth Century*, London: Penguin.

McCulloch, A. (2007) 'The changing structure of ethnic diversity and segregation in England, 1991–2001', *Environment and Planning A*, vol 39, no 4, pp 909–27.

McGarry, A., Hainsworth, P. and Gilligan, C. (2008) *Elected Representatives/ Political Parties and Minority Ethnic Communities in Northern Ireland*, Belfast: Community Relations Council.

McKenzie, K. (2006) 'Racial discrimination and mental health', *Psychiatry*, vol 5, no 11, pp 383–7.

McKenzie, K., Samele, C., van Horn, E., Tatten, T., van Os, J. and Murray, R.B. (2001) 'Comparison of the outcome of the treatment of psychosis for people of Caribbean origin living in the UK and British whites: report from the UK700 trial', *British Journal of Psychiatry*, vol 178, pp 160–5.

McKenzie, K., Bhui, K., Nanchahal, K. and Blizard, B. (2008) 'Suicide rates in people of South Asian origin in England and Wales: 1993–2003', *The British Journal of Psychiatry*, vol 193, pp 406–9.

McLennan, W. and Madden, R. (1999) *The Health and Welfare of Australia's Aboriginal and Torres Strait Islander Peoples*, Commonwealth of Australia: Australian Bureau of Statistics.

McLoughlin, S. (2009) 'From diasporas to multi-locality: writing British Asian cities'. Available at: www.leeds.ac.uk/brasian/assets/papers/WBAC003.pdf (accessed 29 December 2010).

McManus, S., Meltzer, H., Brugha, T., Bebbington, P. and Jenkins, R. (2009) *Adult Psychiatric Morbidity in England: Results of a Household Survey 2007*, Leeds: NHS Information Centre for Health and Social Care.

Mental Health Act Commission (2006) *Count Me in: The National Mental Health and Ethnicity Census 2005 Service User Survey*, Nottingham: Mental Health Act Commission.

Miles, R. (1989) *Racism*, London: Routledge.

Millard, B. and Flatley, J. (2010) *Experimental Statistics on Victimisation of Children Aged 10 to 15: Findings from the British Crime Survey for the Year Ending December 2009*, Home Office Statistical Bulletin no11/10, London: Home Office.

Ministry of Justice (2008) *Third Sector Strategy: Improving Policies and Securing Better Public Services through Effective Partnerships (2008–2011)*, London: Ministry of Justice.

Ministry of Justice (2010a) *Statistics on Race and the Criminal Justice System*, London: HMSO.

Ministry of Justice (2010b) *Statistics on Women and the Criminal Justice System*, London: HMSO.

Ministry of Justice and NOMS (National Offender Management System) (2008) *Working with the Third Sector to Reduce Re-Offending: Securing Effective Partnerships (2008–2011)*, London: Ministry of Justice.

Ministry of Justice and Tribunals Service (2010) 'Employment tribunal and EAT statistics 2009–2010 (GB)'. Available at: www.justice.gov.uk/tribs-et-eat-annual-stats-april09-march10.pdf (accessed 5 January 2010).

Mir, G. (2007) *Effective Communication with Service Users*, London: Race Equality Foundation.

Mir, G. (2008) 'Effective communication with service users', *Ethnicity and Inequalities in Health and Social Care*, vol 1, no 1, pp 71–8.

Mir, G. and Sheikh, A. (2010) '"Fasting and prayer don't concern the doctors ... they don't even know what it is": communication, decision-making and perceived social relations of Pakistani Muslim patients with long-term illnesses', *Ethnicity & Health*. Available at: www.informaworld.com/smpp/content~db=all~content=a922839101

Mirza, H.S. (2003) '"All the women are white, all the blacks are men – but some of us are brave": mapping the consequences of invisibility for black and minority ethnic women in Britain', in D. Mason (ed) *Explaining Ethnic Differences: Changing Patterns of Disadvantage in Britain*, Bristol: The Policy Press.

Mirza, H. (2009a) 'Plotting a history: black and post-colonial feminisms in "new times"', *Race, Ethnicity and Education*, vol 12, no 1, pp 1–10.

Mirza, H.S. (2009b) *Race, Gender and Educational Desire: Why Black Women Succeed and Fail*, London: Routledge.

Mizra, M. (2010) 'Rethinking race', *Prospect*, October, pp 31–2.

Modood, T. (1997) '"Difference", cultural racism and anti-racism', in P. Werbner and T. Modood (eds) *Debating Cultural Hybridity: Multi-Cultural Identities and Politics of Anti-Racism*, London: Zed Books, pp 154–72.

Modood, T. (2008) 'South Asian Assertiveness in Britain', in S. Koshy and R. Radhakrishnan (eds) *Transnational South Asians: The Making of a Neo-Diaspora*, India: Oxford University Press, pp 124–45.

Modood, T., Berthoud, R., Lakey, J., Nazroo, J., Smith, P., Virdee, S. and Beishon, S. (1997) *Ethnic Minorities in Britain: Diversity and Disadvantage*, London: Policy Studies Institute.

Modood, T., Tryandafyllidou, A. and Zapata-Barrero, R. (2006) *Multiculturalism, Muslims and Citizenship: A European Approach*, London: Routledge.

Moffat, J., Sass, B., McKenzie, K. and Bhui, K. (2006) *Improving Pathways into Mental Health Care for Black and Ethnic Minority Groups: A Systematic Review of the Grey Literature*, London: Queen Mary School of Medicine and Dentistry.

Mohammed, R. (2010) 'From the editor', *Agenda*, vol 34, pp 5–6.

Mohseni, M. and Lindström, M. (2008) 'Ethnic differences in anticipated discrimination, generalised trust in other people and self-rated health: a population-based study in Sweden', *Ethnicity and Health*, vol 13, no 5, pp 417–34.

Moosa, Z. and Woodroffe, J. (2010) *Poverty Pathways: Ethnic Minority Women's Livelihoods*, London: Fawcett.

Morgan, C., Mallett, R., Hutchinson, G. and Leff, J. (2004) 'Negative pathways to psychiatric care and ethnicity: the bridge between social science and psychiatry', *Social Science and Medicine*, vol 58, pp 739–52.

Morris, J. (1991) *Pride against Prejudice: Transforming Attitudes to Disability*, London: The Women's Press.

Morris, J. (2006) *Centres for Independent Living/Local User-Led Organisations: A Discussion Paper*, London: Department of Health.

Morris, L. (2007) 'New Labour's community of rights: welfare, immigration and asylum', *Journal of Social Policy*, vol 36, no 1, pp 39–57.

Morris, R. (2000) 'Gypsies, Travellers and the media: press regulation and racism in the UK'. Available at: www.law.cf.ac.uk/tlru/Tolleys.pdf (accessed 24 August 2010).

Morris, R. and Clements, L. (eds) (1999) *Gaining Ground: Law Reform for Gypsies and Travellers,* Hertford: University of Hertfordshire Press.

Morris, R. and Clements, L. (2001) *Disability, Social Care, Health and Travelling People,* Cardiff: Traveller Law Research Unit.

Moving Here (no date) 'Working lives'. Available at: www.movinghere.org.uk/galleries/histories/asian/working_lives/working_lives.htm (accessed 29 December 2010).

MPS (Metropolitan Police Service) (1998) 'Trident'. Available at: www.met.police.uk/scd/specialist_units/trident.htm (accessed 23 January 2011).

MPS (2007) 'MPS response to guns, gangs and knives in London'. Available at: www.mpa.gov.uk/committees/x-cop/2007/070503/05/ (accessed 8 January 2011).

Muir, H. (2005) 'Files show police hostility to Windrush generation: Racism from the top down in 1950s reports by Met officers'. Available at: www.guardian.co.uk/uk/2005/feb/16/race.world (accessed 29 December 2010).

Mullen, S. (2005) *It Wisnae Us,* Glasgow: GARA.

Mullins, D., Beider, H. and Rowlands, R. (2004) *Empowering Communities, Improving Housing: Involving Black and Minority Ethnic Tenants and Communities,* London: ODPM.

Muncie, J. (2009) *Youth and Crime* (3rd edn), London: Sage.

Music Manifesto (2006) *Making Every Child's Music Matter: Music Manifesto Report No 2. A Consultation for Action,* London: The Music Manifesto.

Nairn, T. (2003) *The Breakup of Britain* (3rd edn), Edinburgh: Big Thinking.

National Employment Panel (2010) *The Structure of Economic Inequality in the UK,* London: National Equalities Office. Available at: http://www.equalities.gov.uk/pdf/NEP%20Report%20bookmarkedfinal.pdf (accessed 5 January 2010).

National Strategies (2007) 'Supporting children learning English as an additional language: guidance for practitioners in the Early Years Foundation Stage'. Was available at: http://nationalstrategies.standards.dcsf.gov.uk/node/84861 (accessed 17 August 2010), now held online by The National Archives.

National Strategies (2009) 'Building futures: developing trust – a focus on provision for children from Gypsy, Roma and Traveller backgrounds in the Early Years Foundation Stage'. Was available at: http://nationalstrategies.standards.dcsf.gov.uk/node/235051 (accessed 17 August 2010), now held online by The National Archives.

National Strategies (2010) 'Building futures: believing in children – a focus on provision for black children in the Early Years Foundation Stage'. Was available at: http://nationalstrategies.standards.dcsf.gov.uk/node/170378 (accessed 17 August 2010), now held online by The National Archives.

Nazroo, J. (1997a) *The Health of Ethnic Minorities*, London: Policy Studies Institute.

Nazroo, J.Y. (1997b) *Ethnicity and Mental Health: Findings from a National Community Survey*, London: Policy Studies Institute.

Nazroo, J.Y. (1998) 'Genetic, cultural or socio-economic vulnerability? Explaining ethnic inequalities in health', *Sociology of Health and Illness*, vol 20, no 5, pp 710–30.

Nazroo, J.Y. (2001) *Ethnicity, Class and Health*, London: Policy Studies Institute.

Nazroo, J.Y. (2003) 'The structuring of ethnic inequalities in health: economic position, racial discrimination and racism', *American Journal of Public Health*, vol 93, no 2, pp 277–84.

Nazroo, J. and King, M. (2002) 'Psychosis – symptoms and estimated rates', in K. Sproston and J. Nazroo (eds) *Minority Ethnic Psychiatric Illness Rates in the Community (EMPIRIC)*, London: The Stationery Office.

Nazroo, J.Y., Jackson, J., Karlsen, S. and Torres, M. (2007) 'The black diaspora and health inequalities in the US and England: does where you go and how you get there make a difference?', *Sociology of Health and Illness*, vol 29, no 6, pp 811–30.

Nazroo, J.Y., Falaschetti, E., Pierce, M. and Primatesta, P. (2009) 'Ethnic inequalities in access to and outcomes of healthcare: analysis of the health survey for England', *Journal of Epidemiology and Community Health*, vol 63, no 12, pp 1022–7.

Neale, M., Craig, G. and Wilkinson, M. (2009) *Marginalised and Excluded? York's Traveller Community*, York: York Travellers Trust.

NEP (National Equality Panel) (2010a) *Summary: An Anatomy of Economic Inequality in the UK*, London: Government Equalities Office/LSE.

NEP (2010b) *An anatomy of economic inequality in the UK*, London: Government Equalities Office/LSE.

Netto, G. (2006) 'Vulnerability to homelessness: use of services and homelessness prevention in black and minority ethnic communities', *Housing Studies*, vol 21, no 4, pp 581–603.

Netto, G. and Fraser, A. (2007) *Refugee Routes to Housing, Support and Settlement in Scotland*, Glasgow: Scottish Refugee Council/AAGHA.

Netto, G. and Gavrielides, T. (2010) *Linking Black and Minority Ethnic Organisations with Mainstream Homeless Service Providers*, Better Housing Briefing 15, London: Race Equality Foundation.

Netto, G., Arshad, R., deLima, P., Almeida, D., Diniz, F., MacEwen, M., Patel, V. and Syed, R. (2001a) *Audit of Research on Minority Ethnic Issues in Scotland from a 'Race' Perspective*, Edinburgh: Scottish Executive.

Netto, G., Gaag, S., Thanki, M., Bondi, L. and Munro, M. (2001b) *A Suitable Space: Improving Counselling Services for Asian People*, Bristol: The Policy Press.

Netto, G., Sosenko, F. and Bramley, G. (2010) *A Review of Poverty and Ethnicity in Scotland*, York: Joseph Rowntree Foundation.

Neuberger, Baroness (2009) *Volunteering across the CJS*, London: Cabinet Office.

Newbigging, K., Bola, M. and Shah, A. (2008) *Scoping Exercise with Black and Minority Ethnic Groups on Perceptions of Mental Wellbeing in Scotland*, Edinburgh: NHS Health Scotland/University of Central Lancashire.

NHS Health Scotland (2008) *Finding Strength from Within: Report on Three Local Projects Looking at Mental Health and Recovery with People from Some of the Black and Minority Ethnic Communities in Edinburgh*, Edinburgh: NHS Scotland.

NHS Information Office (2009) 'Mental health bulletin: third report from Mental Health Minimum Dataset (MHMDS) annual returns, 2004–2009', Health and Social Care Information Centre. Available at: hwww.ic.nhs.uk/webfiles/publications/mental%20health/NHS%20specialist%20mental%20health%20services/MHMDS09/MH_Bulletin_2004_2009.pdf

NMHDU (National Mental Health Development Unit) (2010) *Working towards Women's Well-Being: Unfinished Business*, London: National Mental Health Development Unit.

NOMS (National Offender Management System) and the YJB (Youth Justice Board) (2007) *Believing We Can: Promoting the Contribution Faith-Based Organisations Can Make to Reducing Adult and Youth Re-Offending: A Consultative Document*, London: NOMS and YJB.

Noon, M. (1993) 'Racial discrimination in speculative application: evidence from the UK's top 100 firms', *Human Resource Management Journal*, vol 3, no 4, pp 35–47.

Norfolk, Suffolk and Cambridgeshire Strategic Health Authority (2003) *Independent Inquiry into the Death of David Bennett*, Norfolk: Cambridgeshire Strategic Health Authority.

NYBSB (North Yorkshire BME Strategy Board) (2006) *Ethnic Minorities in Rural Areas: a Thinkpiece for DEFRA*, Easingwold: NYBSB.

Office for Civil Society (2010) 'Building a stronger civil society, a strategy for voluntary and community groups, charities and social enterprises'. Available at: www.cabinetoffice.gov.uk/media/426261/building-stronger-civil-society.pdf (accessed 1 December 2010).

Office for Disability Issues (2008) *Independent Living: A Cross-Government Strategy about Independent Living for Disabled People*, London: Office for Disability Issues. Available at: www.officefordisability.gov.uk/docs/wor/ind/ilr-executive-report.pdf (accessed 15 January 2011).

Oliver, M. (1996) *Understanding Disability: From Theory to Practice*, London: Macmillan.

ONS (Office for National Statistics) (1993) *Ethnicity in the 1991 Census* (3 vols), London: HMSO.

ONS (2001) *Social Trends 31*, London: The Stationery Office.

ONS (2006) 'Focus on ethnicity and religion'. Available at: www.statistics.gov.uk/downloads/theme_compendia/foer2006/Foer_main.pdf (accessed 15 December 2010).

ONS (2008a) 'Civil service employment'. Available at: www.statistics.gov.uk/pdfdir/cs0708.pdf (accessed 15 December 2010).

ONS (2008b) 'Large differences in infant mortality by ethnic group'. Available at: http://www.statistics.gov.uk/pdfdir/imeth0608.pdf (accessed 28 June 2010).

ONS (2008c) 'Annual population survey', London: ONS.

ONS (2009a) 'Focus on ethnicity and identity – age/sex distribution'. Available at: www.statistics.gov.uk/cci/nugget.asp?id=456

ONS (2009b) 'Emigration reaches record high in 2008', Press release, 26 November. Available at: www.statistics.gov.uk/pdfdir/mignr1109.pdf (accessed 29 December 2010).

ONS (2010) 'Social trends, no 40'. Available at: www.statistics.gov.uk/downloads/theme_social/Social-Trends40/ST40_2010_FINAL.pdf (accessed 7 January 2010).

Open Society Institute (2005) 'Muslims in the UK – policies for engaged citizens'. Available at: http://www.fairuk.org/docs/OSI2004%20complete%20report.pdf (accessed 11 August 2010).

Ouseley, H. (2001) *Community Pride Not Prejudice*, Bradford: Bradford Vision.

Owen, D. (1993) 'Ethnic minorities in Great Britain: housing and family characteristics', 1991 Census Statistical Paper 4, Coventry: National Ethnic Minority Data Archive, Centre for Research in Ethnic Relations, University of Warwick.

Owen, D. (1992–95) *1991 Census Statistical Papers 1–9*, Coventry: Centre for Research in Ethnic Relations, University of Warwick/CRE.

Owen, D. (2006) 'Demographic profiles and social cohesion of minority ethnic communities in England and Wales', *Community, Work and Family*, vol 9, no 3, pp 251–72.

Owen, D., Green, G., Pitcher, J. and Maguire, M. (2000) *Ethnic Minority Participation and Achievements in Education, Training and the Labour Market*, Research Report no 225, London: Department for Education and Employment.

Ozbox (2005) Crimestoppers home page. Available at: http://ozbox.org/# (accessed 23 January 2011).

Palmer, G. and Kenway, P. (2007) *Poverty among Ethnic Groups: How and Why Does It Differ?*, York: JRF.

Pan-American Health Organization (2001) *Equity in Health: From an Ethnic Perspective*, Washington, DC: Pan American Health Organization.

Panico, L. and Kelly, Y. (2007) 'Ethnic differences in childhood cognitive development: findings from the Millennium Cohort Study', *Journal of Epidemiology and Community Health*, vol 61(Supplement 1), p A36.

Panico, L., Bartley, M., Marmot, M., Nazroo, J. and Kelly, Y. (2007) 'Ethnic variation in childhood asthma and wheezing illnesses: findings from the Millennium Cohort Study', *International Journal of Epidemiology*, vol 36, no 5, pp 1093–102.

Papadopoulos, I., Tilkim, M. and Lees, S. (2004) 'Promoting cultural competence in health care through a research-based intervention in the UK', *Diversity in Health and Social Care*, vol 1, no 2, pp 107–16.

Papastergiadis, N. (1997) 'Tracing hybridity in theory', in P. Werbner and T. Modood (eds) *Debating Cultural Hybridity: Multi-Cultural Identities and the Politics of Anti-Racism*, London: Zed Books, pp 257–81.

Paradies, Y. (2006) 'A systematic review of empirical research on self-reported racism and health', *International Journal of Epidemiology*, vol 35, no 4, p 888.

Parekh, B. (2000a) *The Future of Multi-Ethnic Britain*, London: The Runnymede Trust.

Parekh, B. (2000b) *Rethinking Multiculturalism*, Harvard: Harvard University Press.

Parker, H. (1997) 'Beyond ethnic categories: why racism should be a variable in health services research', *Journal of Health Services Research Policy*, vol 2, no 4, pp 256–9.

Parliamentary Joint Committee on Human Rights (2007) *The Treatment of Asylum Seekers, 10th Report*, HC 60-I, London: The Stationery Office.

Parmar, P. (1982) 'Gender, race and class: Asian women in resistance', in CCCS (ed) *The Empire Strikes Back*, London: Hutchinson.

Parry, G., Van Cleemput, P., Peters, J., Walters, S., Thomas, K. and Cooper, C. (2007) 'Health status of Gypsies and Travellers in England', *Journal of Epidemiology and Community Health*, vol 61, pp 98–204.

Patel, B. (2005) 'The social care needs of refugees and asylum seekers', in J. Butt, B. Patel and O. Stuart (eds) *Race Equality Discussion Papers, Part of Stakeholder Participation Discussion Papers*, London: Social Care Institute for Excellence, pp 31–51.

Patel, N. (2009) 'Developing psychological services for refugee survivors of torture', in S. Fernando and F. Keating (eds) *Mental Health in a Multi-Ethnic Society: A Multidisciplinary Handbook*, London: Routledge.

Patel, N. and Fatimilehin, I. (1999) 'Racism and mental health', in C. Newness, G. Holmes and C. Dunn (eds) *This is Madness: A Critical Look at Psychiatry and the Future of Mental Health Services*, Ross-on-Wye: PCC Books.

Pati, A. (2003) 'Passage from India'. Available at: www.buzzle.com/editorials/8-26-2003-44687.asp (accessed 29 December 2010).

Patterson, S. (1965) *Dark Strangers*, Harmondsworth: Pelican.

Pawson, H., Donohoe, A., Jones, C., Watkins, D., Fancy, C., Netto, G., Clegg, S. and Thomas, A. (2006) *Monitoring the Longer-Term Impact of Choice-Based Lettings*, London: Department for Communities and Local Government. Available at: www.communities.gov.uk/publications/housing/monitoringlonger

Pawson, H., Netto, G., Jones, C., Wager, F., Fancy, C. and Lomax, D. (2007) *Evaluating Homelessness Prevention*, London: CLG. Available at: www.communities.gov.uk/publications/housing/preventhomelessness

Peach, C. (ed) (1996) *Ethnicity in the 1991 Census* (vol 2), London: HMSO.

Pennie, P. and Best, F. (1990) *How the Black Family is Pathologised by the Social Services Systems*, London: ABSWAP.

Peukert, J.K. (1991) *The Weimar Republic*, London: Penguin.

Phillips, D. (2002) *Movement to Opportunity? South Asian Relocation in Northern Cities*, End of Award Report, Economic and Social Research Council R000238038, Leeds: School of Geography, University of Leeds.

Phillips, D. (2009) 'Parallel lives?', Paper presented to 'Rethinking Community Cohesion – different perspectives on segregation and community relations' conference, University of Birmingham, 14 October.

Phillips, D. and Harrison, M. (2010) 'Constructing an integrated society: historical lessons for tackling black and minority ethnic housing segregation in Britain', *Housing Studies*, vol 25, no 2, pp 221–37.

Phillips, M. and Phillips, T. (1998) *Windrush*, London: Harper Collins.

Phillips, T. (2005) 'After 7/7: sleepwalking to segregation', speech to Manchester Council for Community Relations, 22 September.

Phillips, T. (2007) 'Equality and human rights: siblings or just rivals', *Benefits*, vol 15, no 2, pp 127–38.

Phillips, T. (2009) 'Why Britain is now the least racist country in Europe', *Daily Mail*. Available at: www.dailymail.co.uk/debate/article-1121442/Trevor Phillips-Why-Britain-Least-racist-country-Europe.html

Phoenix, A. (2009) 'De-colonising practices: negotiating narratives from racialised and gendered experiences of education', *Race, Ethnicity and Education*, vol 12, no 1, pp 101–14.

Pickett, K.E. and Wilkinson, R. (2008) 'People like us: ethnic group density effects on health', *Ethnicity and Health*, vol 13, pp 321–34.

Pilgrim, D. (2005) *Key Concepts in Mental Health*, London: Sage.

PIU (Performance and Innovation Unit) (2002) *Ethnic Minorities and the Labour Market: Interim Analytical Report*, London: Cabinet Office.

Platt, L. (2003a) *Ethnicity and Poverty*, York: Joseph Rowntree Foundation.

Platt, L. (2003b) *Parallel Lives?*, London: Child Poverty Action Group.

Platt, L. (2007a) 'Making education count: the effects of ethnicity and qualifications on intergenerational social class mobility', *Sociological Review*, vol 55, no 3, pp 485–508.

Platt, L. (2007b) *Poverty and Ethnicity in the UK*, Bristol: The Policy Press.

Platt, L. (2008) *Ethnicity and Family – Relationships Within and Between Ethnic Groups: An Analysis Using the Labour Force Survey*, London: Institute for Economic and Social Research/University of Essex.

Platt, L. (2009) *Ethnicity and Child Poverty*, Research Report no 576, London: Department for Work and Pensions.

Pollard, N., Latorre, M. and Sriskandarajah, D. (2008) *Floodgates or Turnstiles?*, London: IPPR.

Porter, R. (1989) *Health for Sale*, Manchester: Manchester University Press.

Porter, R. (1991) *English Society in the 18th Century*, London: Penguin.

Porter, R. (1999) *The Greatest Benefit to Mankind: A Medical History of Humanity from Antiquity to Present*, London: Fontana.

Porter, R. (2001) *Enlightenment: Britain and the Creation of the Modern World*, London: Penguin.

Positive Futures (2011) home page, www.posfutures.org.uk (accessed 22 January 2011).

Poverty Site (2010) *Relative Poverty, Absolute Poverty and Social Exclusion*, York: Joseph Rowntree Foundation. Available at: www.poverty.org.uk/summary/social%20exclusion.shtml

Power, C. (2004) *Room to Roam: England's Irish Travellers*, London: Action Group for Irish Youth/Community Fund.

Poynting, S. and Mason, V. (2007) 'The resistible rise of Islamophobia: anti-Muslim racism in the UK and Australia before 11 September 2001', *Journal of Sociology*, vol 43, no 1, pp 61–86.

Prevatt Goldstein, B. (2006) 'A study of the barriers in translating "race" related research into policy', *Research Policy and Planning*, vol 24, no 1, pp 24–38.

Pridmore, A. (2006) 'Disability activism, independent living and direct payments', Paper presented to 'Independent Living and Direct Payments: the National Picture' conference, Weetwood Hall Hotel, Leeds. Available at: www.disability-archive.leeds.ac.uk/ (accessed 27 September 2010).

Prime Minister's Strategy Unit (2005) *Improving the Life Chances of Disabled People: Final Report*, London: Cabinet Office. Available at: http://tna.europarchive.org/20061101075403/http://www.strategy.gov.uk/work_areas/disability/ (accessed 15 February 2011).

Pritchard, J. and Dorling, D. (2006) *Ethnic Minority Populations and the Labour Market: An Analysis of the 1991 and 2001 Census*, Research Summary no 333, London: DWP.

Quirk, J. (2009) *Unfinished Business*, Paris: UNESCO.

Rabiee, F. and Smith, P. (2007) *Being Understood, Being Respected: An Evaluation of the Statutory and Voluntary Mental Health Service Provision for Members of African and African Caribbean Communities in Birmingham*, Birmingham: University of Central England and ACAR.

Race on the Agenda (2007) *The Visible and Hidden Dimensions of BAME Homelessness*, London: ROTA.

Race on the Agenda (2009) *The Economic Downturn and the Black, Asian and Minority Ethnic (BAME) Third Sector*, London: Race on the Agenda. Available at: www.rota.org.uk/Downloads/Recession%20Report%20-%20ROTA%202009%20Ex%20Summary.pdf (accessed 30 September 2010).

Rai-Atkins, A., Ali Jama, A., Wright, N., Scott, V., Perring, C., Craig, G. and Katbamna, S. (2002) *Best Practice in Mental Health: Advocacy for African, Caribbean and South Asian Communities*, Bristol: The Policy Press.

Raleigh, V.S., Bulusu, L. and Balarajan, R. (1990) 'Suicides among immigrants from the Indian subcontinent,' *British Journal of Psychiatry*, vol 156, pp 46–50.

Ratcliffe, P. (1997) '"Race," ethnicity and housing differentials in Britain', in V. Karn (ed) *Ethnicity in the 1991 Census, Volume 4, Employment, Education and Housing among the Ethnic Minority Populations of Britain*, London: The Stationery Office.

Reid, M. (2004) *The Black and Minority Ethnic Voluntary and Community Sector: A Literature Review*, London: Ethnic Minority Foundation.

Remennick, L. (2006) 'The quest for the perfect baby: why do Israeli women seek prenatal genetic testing?', *Sociology of Health and Illness*, vol 28, no 1, pp 21–53.

Rex, J. (1969) 'Race as a social category', *Journal of Biosocial Science*, Supplement 1, pp 145–52.

Robinson, V. (2006) *Mapping the Field: Refugee Housing in Wales*, London: HACT.

Rogers, A. and Pilgrim, D. (2001) '"Pulling down churches": accounting for the new mental health users' movement', *Sociology of Health and Illness*, vol 13, no 2, pp 129–48.

Roth, M.A. and Kobayashi, K.M. (2008) 'The use of complementary and alternative medicine among Chinese Canadians', *Journal of Immigrant and Minority Health*, vol 10, no 6, pp 517–28.

Roth, M.A., Aitsi-Selmi, A., Wardle, H. and Mindell, J. (2009) 'Under-reporting of tobacco use among Bangladeshi women in England', *Journal of Public Health*, vol 31, no 3, p 326.

Rouse, C. (2009) *Uncertain Suffering: Racial Health Disparities and Sickle Cell Disease*, Berkley: University of California Press.

Royce, C. (1996) *Financing Black and Minority Ethnic Housing Associations*, York: Joseph Rowntree Foundation.

Rudiger, A. (2007) *Prisoners of Terrorism? The Impact of Anti-Terrorism Measures on Refugees and Asylum Seekers in Britain*, London: Refugee Council.

Ruggiero, K.M. and Taylor, D.M. (1995) 'Coping with discrimination: how disadvantaged group members perceive the discrimination that confronts them', *Journal of Personality and Social Psychology*, vol 68, no 5, pp 826–38.

Ruhs, M. and Anderson, B. (eds) (2010) *Who Needs Migrant Workers?*, Oxford: Oxford University Press.

Runnymede Trust, commissioned by the Hindu Forum of Great Britain (2009) *Connecting British Hindus: An Inquiry into the Identity and Public Engagement of Hindus in Britain*, London: Hindu Forum of Great Britain/DCLG.

Rutter, J. (2011) 'Migration, migrants and child poverty', *Poverty*, no 138, pp 6–10.

Rutter, J. and Latorre, M. (2009) *Social Housing Allocation and Immigrant Communities*, Manchester: Equalities and Human Rights Commission.

Rutter, J., Cooley, L., Reynolds, S. and Sheldon, R. (2007) *From Refugee to Citizen: 'Standing on My Own Two Feet'*, London: Refugee Support.

Rutter, J., Cooley, L., Jones, N. and Pillai, R. (2008) *Moving up Together*, London: IPPR.

Ryan, L. (2007) 'Recent Polish migrants in London: language, housing and employment'. Available at: http://www.ssrg.org.uk/events/2007.asp (accessed 11 August 2010).

Saheliya (2009) *Outside the Box: Health in Mind*, Edinburgh: Scottish Recovery Network, Lothian.

Said, E. (2003) *Orientalism*, London: Penguin.

Sainsbury, D. (2006) 'Immigrants' social rights in comparative perspective: welfare regimes, forms of immigration and immigration policy regimes', *Journal of European Social Policy*, vol 16, no 3, pp 229–42.

Sales, R. (2007) *Understanding Immigration and Refugee Policy: Contradictions and Continuities*, Bristol: The Policy Press.

Salway, S. (2008) 'Labour market experiences of young UK Bangladeshi men: identity, inclusion and exclusion in inner-city London', *Ethnic and Racial Studies*, vol 31, no 6, pp 1126–52.

Salway, S., Karlsen, S. and Hyde, M. (2010) 'Race and ethnicity', in P. Allmark, S. Salway and H. Piercy (eds) *Life and Health: An Evidence Review and Synthesis for the Equality and Human Rights Commission's Triennial Review 2010*, Sheffield: Sheffield Hallam University.

Sanglin-Grant, S. and Schneider, R. (2000) *Moving on up? Racial Equality and the Corporate Agenda. A Study of FTSE 100 Companies*, London: The Runnymede Trust.

Scarman, The Rt Hon Lord (1981) *The Brixton Disorders 10–12 April 1981*. London: HMSO.

Schama, S. (2005) *Rough Crossings*, London: BBC Publications.

Scheider-Ross, L. (2003) *Towards Racial Equality – an Evaluation of the Public Duty to Promote Racial Equality and Good Racial Relations in England and Wales (2002)*, London: Commission for Racial Equality.

Schwartz, S. and Meyer, H. (2010) 'Mental health disparities research', *Social Science and Medicine*, vol 70, no 8, pp 111-18.

SCIE (Social Care Institute for Excellence) (2009) 'Research briefing 20: the implementation of individual budget schemes in adult social care'. Available at: www.scie.org.uk/publications/briefings/briefing20/index. asp (accessed 30 November 2010).

SCIE (2010a) 'Workforce development SCIE guide 36. A commissioner's guide to developing and sustaining user-led organisations'. Available at: www.scie.org.uk/publications/guides/guide36/files/ULOs.pdf (accessed 15 February 2011).

SCIE (2010b) 'A commissioner's guide to developing and sustaining user-led organisations'. Available at: www.scie.org.uk/publications/guides/ guide36/index.asp (accessed 1 December 2010).

SCIE (2010c) '"The diversity of ULOs" in a commissioner's guide to developing and sustaining user-led organisations'. Available at: www. scie.org.uk/publications/guides/guide36/understanding/diversity.asp (accessed 14 January 2011).

Scottish Executive (2004) *Analysis of 2001 Census Data*, Edinburgh: Scottish Executive.

Scottish Executive (2005) *Measurement of the Extent of Youth Crime in Scotland*, Edinburgh: DTZ Pieda Consulting.

Scottish Government Social Research (2010a) *Troublesome Youth Groups, Gangs and Knife Carrying in Scotland*, Edinburgh: Queens Printers of Scotland.

Scottish Government Social Research (2010b) *Gang Membership and Knife Carrying: Findings from the Edinburgh Study of Youth Transitions and Crime*, Edinburgh: Queens Printers of Scotland.

Scottish Office (1991) *Ethnic Minorities in Scotland*, Edinburgh: Scottish Office.

Sekhri, N., Timmis, A., Chen, R., Junghans,C., Walsh, N., Zaman, J., Eldridge, S., Hemmingway, H. and Feder, G. (2008) 'Inequity of access to investigation and effect on clinical outcomes: prognostic study of coronary angiography for suspected stable angina pectoris', *British Medical Journal*. Available at: www.bmj.com/cgi/content/full/bmj.39534.571042.BEv1

Selwyn J., Harris, P., Quinton, D., Nawaz, S., Wijedasa, D. and Wood, M. (2008) 'Pathways to permanence for black, Asian and mixed ethnicity children: dilemmas, decision-making and outcomes'. Available at: www.bristol.ac.uk/sps/research/projects/completed/2008/rk6417/rk6417finalreport.pdf (accessed 23 August 2010).

Sewell,T. (1997) *Black Masculinities and Schooling*, Stoke-on-Trent:Trentham Books.

Shariff-Marco, S., Klassen, A.C. and Bowie, J.V. (2010) 'Racial/ethnic differences in self-reported racism and its association with cancer-related health behaviours', *American Journal of Public Health*, vol 100, no 2, pp 364–74.

Sharma, N. (2007) *It Doesn't Happen Here: The Reality of Child Poverty in the UK*, Ilford: Barnardos.

Sharpley, M., Hutchinson, G., Murray, R.M. and McKenzie, K. (2001) 'Understanding the excess of psychosis among the African Caribbean population in England: review of current hypotheses', *British Journal of Psychiatry*, vol 178, Supplement 40, ss 60–8.

Shaw, A. (2000) *Kinship and Continuity: Pakistani Families in Britain*, Singapore: Harwood Academic Publishers.

Shaw, A. (2001) 'Kinship, cultural preference and immigration: consanguinous marriage among British Pakistanis', *The Journal of the Royal Anthropological Institute*, vol 7, no 2, pp 315–34.

Shaw, M. and Hannah-Moffat, K. (2000) 'Gender, diversity and risk assessment in Canadian corrections', *Probation Journal*, vol 47, pp 163–72.

Shaw, M. and Hannah-Moffat, K. (2004) 'How cognitive skills forgot about gender and diversity', in G. Mair (ed) *What Matters in Probation*, Cullompton:Willan.

Shropshire, J., Warton, R. and Walker, R. (1999) *Unemployment and Jobseeking: the Experience of Ethnic Minorities*, Research Report RR106, London: Department for Education and Employment.

Sidiropoulos, E., Jeffery, A., Mackay, S., Forgey, H., Chipps, C. and Corrigan, T. (1997) *South Africa Survey 1996/97*, Johannesburg: South African Institute of Race Relations.

Simpson, A. and Stevenson, J. (1994) *Half a Chance, Still?*, Nottingham: Nottingham and District Racial Equality Council.

Simpson, L. (2004) 'Statistics of racial segregation: measures, evidence and policy', *Urban Studies*, vol 41, no 3, pp 661–81.

Singh, P. (2005) *No Home, No Job: Moving on from Transitional Spaces*, London: Off the Streets and onto Work.

Sivanandan, A. (1982) *A Different Hunger: Writings on Black Resistance*, London: Pluto Press.

Sivanandan, A. (1985) 'RAT and the degradation of black struggle', *Race and Class*, vol 26, no 4, pp 1–33.

Skellington, R. and Morris, P. (1996a) 'Minority ethnic groups in the UK: a profile', in R. Skellington and P. Morris (eds) *'Race' in Britain Today* (2nd edn), London: Sage/Open University.

Skellington, R. and Morris, P. (eds) (1996b) *'Race' in Britain Today* (2nd edn), London: Sage/Open University.

Sly, F. (1995) 'Ethnic groups and the labour market: analyses from the spring 1994 Labour Force Survey', *Employment Gazette*, June, pp 251–62.

Sly, F., Thair, T. and Risdon, A. (1999) 'Trends in the labour market participation of ethnic groups', *Labour Market Trends*, December, pp 631–8.

Smith, D.J. (1977) *Racial Disadvantage in Britain: the PEP Report*, Harmondsworth: Penguin.

Smith, D. and McAra, L. (2004) *Gender and Youth Offending*, Edinburgh: The University of Edinburgh.

Smith, S.J. (1989) *The Politics of Race and Residence*, Cambridge: Polity Press.

Social Exclusion Unit (2000) *Minority Ethnic Issues in Social Exclusion and Neighbourhood Renewal*, London: Cabinet Office.

Social Exclusion Unit (2004) *Mental Health and Social Exclusion*, London: ODPM.

Solomon, E. (2006) 'Asylum and criminality', unpublished presentation to ICAR and Children House Asylum and Security Seminar, 27 March.

Solomos, J. (1988) *Black Youth, Racism and the State*, Cambridge: Cambridge University Press.

Solomos, J. (2003) *Race and Racism in Britain* (3rd edn), Basingstoke: Palgrave.

Somerville, W. (2007) *Immigration under New Labour*, Bristol: The Policy Press.

Southall Black Sisters (2008) 'Southall Black Sisters' victory against Ealing Council – judgement from Lord Justice Moses released'. Available at: www.southallblacksisters.org.uk/savesbs.htm (accessed 29 December 2010).

Sproston, K. and Mindell, J. (eds) (2006) *Health Survey for England 2004: The Health of Minority Ethnic Groups*, London: The Information Centre.

Stuart, O. (1996) 'Yes we mean black disabled people too: thoughts on community care and disabled people from black or minority ethnic communities', in K. Atkin and W. Ahmad (eds) *Race and Community Care*, Milton Keynes: Open University Press, pp 89–104.

Stuart, O. (2005) 'How can independent living become a viable option for black or minority ethnic service users and carers?', in J. Butt, B. Patel and O. Stuart (eds) *Race Equality Discussion Papers, Part of Stakeholder Participation Discussion Papers*, London: Social Care Institute for Excellence, pp 53–73.

Stuart, O. (2006) *Will Community-Based Support Services Make Direct Payments a Viable Option for Black or Minority Ethnic Service Users and Carers?*, London: Social Care Institute for Excellence.

Sure Start (1999) *Sure Start for All: Guidance on Involving Minority Ethnic Children and Families*, London: DfEE.

Taylor, C. (1994) *Multiculturalism: Examining the Politics of Recognition*, Princeton: Princeton University Press.

Third, H., Wainwright, S. and Pawson, H. (1997) *Constraint and Choice for Minority Ethnic Home Owners in Scotland*, Edinburgh: Scottish Homes.

Thurrow, L.C. (1969) *Poverty and Discrimination*, Washington, DC: Brookings Institute.

Tighe, M. and Tran, C.T.L. (2010) 'Improving access to traditional Chinese medicine: lessons in pluralism from a UK Chinese national healthy living centre', *Ethnicity and Inequalities in Health and Social Care*, vol 3, no 3, pp 38–43.

Times Online (2009) 'Rise in race crime against non-whites: around half the victims of race crimes in Scotland were of Asian origin and 95 percent of the perpetrators whites', 31 March. Available at: www.timesonline.co.uk/tol/news/uk/scotland/article6011657.ece (accessed 28 January 2011).

TLRP (Travellers Law Reform Project) (2007) 'Response to discrimination law review: a framework for fairness: proposals for a single equality bill for Great Britain – a consultation paper'. Available at: www.travellerslaw.org.uk/pdfs/single_equality_response.pdf

TLRP (2008) 'The Education and Skills Bill and related matters'. Available at: www.travellerslaw.org.uk/pdfs/education_and_skills_bill.pdf

Townsend, P. and Davidson, N. (eds) (1982) *Inequalities in Health: The Black Report*, Harmondsworth: Penguin.

Trades Union Congress (2002) 'Black and underpaid: how black workers lose out on pay', Press release issued 12 April.

Trades Union Congress (2003) 'Labour market programmes', Briefing document issued 31 January. Available at: www.tuc.org.uk/law/tuc-13413-f0.cfm (accessed 6 December 2011).

Travis, A. (2010) 'Time for new approach to race relations, minister urges', *The Guardian*. Available at: www.guardian.co.uk/world/2010/jan/14/john-denham-race-relations (accessed 29 December 2010).

Trivedi, P. (2002) 'Racism, social exclusion and mental health: a black service user's perspective' in K. Bhui (ed) *Racism and Mental Health: Prejudice and Suffering*, London: Jessica Kingsley, pp 71–82.

Trivedi, P. (2008) 'Black service "user involvement" – rhetoric or reality? A black user's experience', in S. Fernando and F. Keating (eds) *Mental Health in a Multi-Ethnic Society*, London: Routledge, pp 136–46.

Troyna, B. (1984) 'The "educational underachievement" of black pupils', *British Journal of Sociology of Education*, vol 5, no 2, pp 153–66.

Turner, A.W. (2008) *Crisis? What Crisis? Britain in the 1970s*, London: Aurum Press.

Turok, I. and Edge, N. (1999) *The Jobs Gap in Britain's Cities*, Bristol: The Policy Press.

Tyers, C., Hurstfield, J., Willison, R. and Page, R. (2006) *Barriers to Employment for Pakistanis and Bangladeshis in Britain*, Research Summary 360, London: Department for Work and Pensions.

Van Cleemput, P., Parry, G., Peters, J., Moore, J., Walters, S., Thomas, K. and Cooper, C. (2004) *The Health Status of Gypsies and Travellers in England*, Sheffield: University of Sheffield.

Vasista, V. (2010) *'Snowy Peaks': Ethnic Diversity at the Top*, London: Runnymede Trust.

Vernon, A. (2002) *User-Defined Outcomes of Community Care for Asian Disabled People*, Bristol: The Policy Press.

Vertovec, S. (2006) *The Emergence of Super-Diversity in Britain*, Compass Working Paper no 25, Oxford: University of Oxford.

Wade, P. (2007) 'Race, ethnicity and nation: perspectives from kinship and genetics', in P. Wade (ed) *Race, Ethnicity and Nation: Perspectives from Kinship and Genetics*, Oxford: Berghan Books, pp 1–32.

Walker, R. and Craig, G. (2009) *Community Development Workers for Black and Minority Ethnic Mental Health: Embedding Sustainable Change*, London: National Mental Health Development Unit.

Wallace, C. (1987) *For Richer, for Poorer: Growing Up In and Out of Work*, London: Tavistock.

Wallcraft, J., Read, J. and Sweeney, A. (2003) *On Our Own Terms: Users and Survivors of Mental Health Services Working Together for Support and Change*, London: Sainsbury Centre for Mental Health.

Walvin, J. (1984) *Passage to Britain*, Harmondsworth: Pelican.

Watters, C. and Ingleby, D. (2004) 'Locations of care: meeting the mental health and social care needs of refugees in Europe', *International Journal of Law and Psychiatry*, vol 27, pp 549–70.

Weekes-Bernard, D. (ed) (2010) *Widening Participation and 'Race' Equality*, London: Runnymede Trust.

Weller, P., Feldman, A. and Purdam, K. (2001) *Religious Discrimination in England and Wales*, Home Office Research Study no 220, London: Home Office.

Werbner, P. (1997) 'Introduction: the dialectics of cultural hybridity', in P. Werbner and T. Modood (eds) *Debating Cultural Hybridity: Multicultural Identities and the Politics of Anti-Racism*, London: Zed Books, pp 1–28.

Werbner, P. and Modood, T. (eds) (1997) *Debating Cultural Hybridity: Multicultural Identities and the Politics of Anti-Racism*, London: Zed Books.

White, A. (2002) *Social Focus in Brief: Ethnicity*, London: Office for National Statistics.

White, A. (2006) 'Men and mental well-being – encouraging gender sensitivity', *The Mental Health Review*, vol 11, no 4, pp 3–6.

Whitehead, C., Marshall, D., Royce, C., Saw, P. and Woodrow, J. (1998) *A Level Playing Field? Rents, Viability and Value in BME Housing Associations*, York: Joseph Rowntree Foundation.

Wilkinson, M. and Craig, G. (2011) 'Wilful negligence' in E. Carmel, A. Cerami and T. Papadopoulos (eds) *Migration and Welfare in the New Europe*, Bristol: The Policy Press, pp 177–96.

Wilkinson, M., Craig, G. and Gaus, A. (2009) *Turning the Tide*, Oxford: Oxfam.

Wilkinson, R. and Pickett, K. (2009) *The Spirit Level: Why More Equal Societies Almost Always Do Better*, London: Allen Lane.

Williams, C. (2005) *A Tolerant Nation*, Cardiff: University of Wales Press.

Williams, D. (1999) 'Race, SES, and health: the added effects of racism and discrimination', *Annals of the New York Academy of Science*, vol 896, pp 173–88.

Williams, D.R. (2001) 'Racial variations in adult health status: patterns, paradoxes and prospects', in N. Smelser, W.J. Wilson and F. Mitchell (eds) *America Becoming: Racial Trends and Their Consequences*, National Research Council Commission on Behavioral and Social Sciences and Education, Washington, DC: National Academy of Sciences Press.

Williams, F. (1989) *Social Policy: A Critical Introduction*, Cambridge: Polity.

Williams, F. (1996) '"Race", welfare and community care: a historical perspective', in W.I.U. Ahmad and K. Atkin (eds) *Race and Community Care*, Buckingham: Open University Press, pp 15–28.

Williams, J. and Keating, F. (2005) 'Social inequalities and mental health', in A. Bell and P. Lindley (eds) *Beyond the Water Towers: The Unfinished Revolution in Mental Health Services 1985–2005*, London: Sainsbury Centre for Mental Health.

Wills, J., Datta, K., Evans, Y., Herbert, J., May, J. and McIlwaine, C. (2010) *Global Cities at Work*, London: Pluto Press.

Wilson, M. (2001) 'Black women and mental health: working towards inclusive services', *Feminist Review*, vol 68, pp 24–51.

Wilson, M. (2010) *Delivering Race Equality Action Plan: a Five Year Review*, London: National Mental Health Development Unit.

Winder, R. (2004) *Bloody Foreigners*, London: Little Brown.

Wohland, P., Rees, P., Norman, P., Boden, P. and Jasinska, M. (2010) 'Ethnic population projections for the UK and local areas, 2001–2051', Working Paper no 10/02, School of Geography, University of Leeds. Available at: www.geog.leeds.ac.uk/index.php?id=712 (accessed 2 February 2011).

Wood, M., Hales, J., Purdon, S., Sejersen, T., Hayllar, O. (2009) *A Test for Racial Discrimination Recruitment Practice in British Cities*, DWP Research Report no 670, Norwich: The Stationery Office.

Woodin, S. (2006) *Mapping User-Led Organisations, User-Led Services and Centres for Independent, Integrated, Inclusive Living: A Literature Review Prepared for the Department of Health*, Leeds: University of Leeds.

World Health Organisation (2010) 'Mental health: strengthening our response', Fact Sheet no 220. Available at: www.who.int/mediacentre/factsheets/fs220/en/ (accessed 3 February 2011).

Worley, C. (2005) '"It's not about race. It's about the community": New Labour and "community cohesion"', *Critical Social Policy*, vol 25, pp 483–96.

Worth, A., Irshad, T., Bhopal, R., Brown, D., Lawton, J., Grant, E., Murray, S., Kendall, M., Adam, J., Gardee, R. and Sheikh, A. (2009) 'Vulnerability and access to care for South Asian Sikh and Muslim patients with life limiting illness in Scotland: prospective longitudinal qualitative study', *British Medical Journal*, vol 338, p b183.

Wrench, J. and Modood, T. (2000) *The Effectiveness of Employment Equality Policies in Relation to Immigrants and Ethnic Minorities in the UK*, Geneva: International Labour Office.

Wrench, J., Hassan, E. and Owen, D. (1997) *Ambition and Marginalisation: a Qualitative Study of Under-Achieving Young Men of Afro-Caribbean Origin*, London: The Stationery Office.

YJB (Youth Justice Board) (2009) *Girls and Offending: Patterns, Perceptions and Interventions*, London: Youth Justice Board.

Young, J. (1997) 'Left realist criminology: radical in its analysis, realist in its policy', in M. Maguire, R. Morgan and R. Reiner (eds) *The Handbook of Criminology* (2nd edn), Oxford: Clarendon Press.

Young, J. (2002) 'Critical criminology in the 21st century: critique, irony and the always unfinished', in K. Carrington and R. Hogg (eds) *Critical Criminology*, Cullompton: Willan.

Yousaf, H. (2010) 'Threads of the Scottish tartan: the SNP's vision for race equality in Scotland', in J. McGrigor, R. Brown, H. Yousaf and J. Lamont (eds) *Achieving Race Equality in Scotland*, London: Runnymede Trust. Available at: www.runnymedetrust.org/uploads/publications/pdfs/AchievingRaceEqualityInScotland-2010.pdf

Yuval-Davis, N. (2006) 'Intersectionality and feminist politics', *European Journal of Women's Studies*, vol 13, no 3, pp 193–209.

Zuberi, T. (2001) *Thicker Than Blood: How Racial Statistics Lie*, Minneapolis: University of Minnesota Press.

Index

Note: The following abbreviations have been used – f = figure; n = note; t = table